Give the homemade love of *Taste of Home!*

These cozy dishes will warm the hearts of your family and friends every time.

67

83

177

Delicious homemade food always brings people together. That is why *Taste of Home* was founded over 25 years ago: to share the culinary creations of home cooks like you, while inspiring others to make their own flavorful fare that their family and friends will ask for time and again.

Flip through *Taste of Home Annual Recipes* and you'll find 463 delectable dishes as well as the heartwarming stories behind each one. Before you know it, you'll soon be discovering your own family's newly cherished favorites.

This edition features an entire year's worth of recipes from the magazine, plus hundreds of tasty bonus dishes never before seen in the publication. Consider these:

- **Breakfast & Brunch**
  Start your mornings right with classic pancakes and waffles, savory surprises and refreshing yogurt bowls.

- **Quick Fixes**
  Even on your busiest days, you can create these yummy meals in a snap.

- **Spa Day at Home**
  Pampering yourself has never been so delicious! Invite your friends over to share delightful drinks, healthful finger foods and beauty products you can make yourself.

Five icons help you make the most of kitchen time:

- = Finished in 30 minutes or less
- = Lower in calories, fat and sodium
- = Made in a slow cooker
- **5i** = Made with 5 or fewer ingredients (excluding water, salt, pepper and canola/olive oil)
- ❄ = Includes freezing/reheating instructions

Savor every moment and meal with *Taste of Home.* We've got you covered with the recipes—now all that's left to do is set the table and make new tasty memories!

PLEASING RECIPES

For new family favorites sure to make mealtime memorable, leaf through *Taste of Home Annual Recipes.* Dig in to Chicken Biscuit Skillet (top) for a quick, convenient main dish that will satisfy everyone at your table. To simmer your way to a light meatless dinner packed with southwest flavor, try Slow-Cooked Stuffed Peppers (center). And for a cute treat that tucks a candy cup inside each easy homemade cookie, indulge in Miniature Peanut Butter Treats (bottom).

Taste of Home

© 2020 RDA Enthusiast Brands, LLC.
1610 N. 2nd St., Suite 102, Milwaukee WI
53212-3906

MONGOLIAN CHICKEN
PAGE 74

Executive Editor: Mark Hagen
Senior Art Director:
Raeann Thompson
Editor: Christine Rukavena
Art Director: Maggie Conners
Graphic Designer: Arielle Jardine
Copy Editor: Dulcie Shoener
Editorial Intern: Daniella Peters
Cover Photographer: Mark Derse
Set Stylist: Melissa Franco
Food Stylist: Josh Rink

Pictured on front cover:
Creamy Cranberry
Cheesecake, p. 204;
Bohemian Collards, p. 234;
Wild Rice-Stuffed Pork Loin,
p. 271; Butternut Squash Mac
& Cheese, p. 231

Pictured on back cover:
Apricot-Apple Cider, p. 226;
Makeover Cheddar Biscuits,
p. 142

**International Standard
Book Number:**
D 978-1-61765-913-3
U 978-1-61765-914-0

**International Standard
Serial Number:**
1094-3463

Component Number:
D 117400070H
U 117400072H

Printed in U.S.A.
13 5 7 9 10 8 6 4 2

Contents

Appetizers & Beverages............**4**

Salads & Dressings **16**

Soups & Sandwiches...............**32**

Quick Fixes.............................**48**

Main Dishes............................**68**

Meal Planner...........................**94**

Side Dishes &
  Condiments.......................**108**

Breads, Rolls & Muffins........**132**

Breakfast & Brunch...............**146**

Cookies, Bars & Candies.....**168**

Cakes & Pies.........................**180**

Just Desserts.........................**192**

Holiday & Seasonal
  Celebrations.......................**208**

Potluck Pleasers...................**256**

Pop-Up Party........................**272**

Spa Day at Home.................**290**

Cook's Quick Reference.....**302**

Indexes..................................**304**

Get Social with Us!

 Like Us:
facebook.com/tasteofhome

 Pin Us:
pinterest.com/taste_of_home

Follow Us:
@tasteofhome

Tweet Us:
twitter.com/tasteofhome

To find a recipe: tasteofhome.com

To submit a recipe: tasteofhome.com/submit

To find out about other *Taste of Home* **products:**
shoptasteofhome.com

Appetizers & Beverages

Everyone loves a good party...and this chapter has the perfect nosh and sip for your next gathering. Find cocktails, mocktails, 10-minute bites and fancy apps here.

BANG BANG SHRIMP CAKE SLIDERS

My family loves these shrimp sliders. The bang bang slaw dressing and shrimp cake patties can be made ahead. When ready to serve, toss the cabbage slaw and sear the shrimp cakes, then assemble and enjoy.
—Kim Banick, Turner, OR

PREP: 30 MIN. + CHILLING
COOK: 10 MIN./BATCH • **MAKES:** 12 SLIDERS

- 1 lb. uncooked shrimp (41-50 per lb.), peeled and deveined
- 1 large egg, lightly beaten
- ½ cup finely chopped sweet red pepper
- 6 green onions, chopped and divided
- 1 Tbsp. minced fresh gingerroot
- ¼ tsp. salt
- 1 cup panko (Japanese) bread crumbs
- ¼ cup mayonnaise
- 1 Tbsp. Sriracha chili sauce
- 1 Tbsp. sweet chili sauce
- 5 cups shredded Chinese or napa cabbage
- 12 mini buns or dinner rolls
- 3 Tbsp. canola oil
  Additional Sriracha chili sauce, optional

1. Place shrimp in a food processor; pulse until chopped. In a large bowl, combine the egg, red pepper, 4 green onions, ginger and salt. Add shrimp and bread crumbs; mix gently. Shape into twelve ½-in.-thick patties. Refrigerate 20 minutes.

2. Meanwhile, in a large bowl, combine mayonnaise and the chili sauces; stir in cabbage and remaining green onions. Place buns on a baking sheet, cut sides up. Broil 3-4 in. from heat until golden brown, 2-3 minutes.

3. In a large skillet, heat oil over medium heat. Add shrimp cakes in batches; cook until golden brown, 4-5 minutes on each side. Serve on toasted buns with slaw; secure with toothpicks. If desired, serve with additional chili sauce.

1 SLIDER: *210 cal., 10g fat (1g sat. fat), 63mg chol., 321mg sod., 20g carb. (3g sugars, 1g fiber), 11g pro.*

SALTED CARAMEL & DARK CHOCOLATE FIGS

Here's a special appetizer that won't last long! Fruit, caramel and rich dark chocolate add a sweet touch to this grown-up dipped fruit.
—Taste of Home *Test Kitchen*

PREP: 30 MIN. + STANDING
MAKES: 1 DOZEN

- 12 large toothpicks
- 12 dried figs
- 4 oz. fresh goat cheese
- 1 tsp. honey
- 1 tsp. balsamic vinegar
- 1 pkg. (11 oz.) Kraft caramel bits
- 2 Tbsp. water
- ⅓ cup finely chopped almonds
- 1½ cups dark chocolate chips, melted
  Coarse sea salt

1. Line a baking sheet with waxed paper and grease the paper; set aside.

2. Insert a toothpick into each fig. Make a ½-in. cut on the side of each fig. Combine the cheese, honey and vinegar in a small bowl. Transfer to a heavy-duty resealable plastic bag; cut a small hole in a corner of bag. Pipe cheese mixture into figs.

3. Melt caramels and water in a microwave; stir until smooth. Dip each fig into caramel; turn to coat. Place on prepared pan; let stand until set.

4. Place almonds in a small shallow bowl. Dip bottom third of each fig into melted chocolate; allow excess to drip off. Dip into almonds and sprinkle with salt. Return to pan; let stand until set.

1 FIG: *308 cal., 15g fat (9g sat. fat), 6mg chol., 124mg sod., 47g carb. (40g sugars, 3g fiber), 4g pro.*

KIM BANICK
TURNER, OR

BANG BANG SHRIMP CAKE SLIDERS

SALTY DOG SANGRIA

ZIPPY CURRY DIP

It's easy to encourage everyone to eat their vegetables when this creamy dip is served alongside. The curry flavor gets stronger the longer the dip stands, so I like to make it in advance.
—Priscilla Steffke, Wausau, WI

TAKES: 10 MIN. • **MAKES:** ABOUT 1 CUP

- ½ cup sour cream
- ½ cup mayonnaise
- 1 Tbsp. sugar
- 1 tsp. prepared horseradish
- 1 tsp. grated onion
- 1 tsp. cider vinegar
- ½ to 1 tsp. curry powder
- ½ tsp. garlic salt
  Assorted fresh vegetables or potato chips

In a small bowl, combine the first eight ingredients. Refrigerate until serving. Serve with vegetables or chips.
2 TBSP.: 137 cal., 14g fat (3g sat. fat), 15mg chol., 198mg sod., 2g carb. (2g sugars, 0 fiber), 1g pro.

SALTY DOG SANGRIA

Mix up grapefruit vodka, ginger ale, grapefruit juice, a little wine and simple syrup and what do you get? A perfectly refreshing and beautiful sipper fit for any holiday or special gathering.
—Becky Hardin, St. Peters, MO

PREP: 30 MIN. + CHILLING • **MAKES:** 16 SERVINGS (¾ CUP EACH)

- 1 cup sugar
- 1 cup water
- 2 bottles (750 ml each) rose wine
- 2 cups ruby red grapefruit juice
- 1 can (12 oz.) ginger ale
- 1 cup ruby red grapefruit-flavored vodka
  Grapefruit slices
  Coarse sea salt and grated grapefruit zest

1. In a small saucepan, bring sugar and water to a boil. Reduce heat; simmer 10 minutes. Cool completely. Transfer to a large pitcher. Stir in the wine, juice, ginger ale, vodka and grapefruit slices. Refrigerate at least 2 hours.
2. Using water, moisten the rims of 16 wine glasses. Mix salt and grapefruit zest on a plate; hold each glass upside down and dip rim into salt mixture. Set aside. Discard remaining salt mixture on plate. Serve sangria in prepared glasses over ice.
¾ CUP: 186 cal., 0 fat (0 sat. fat), 0 chol., 2mg sod., 24g carb. (15g sugars, 0 fiber), 0 pro.

> **TEST KITCHEN TIP**
> Try to find salt that is as coarse as possible for garnishing the rim. Regular table salt can be very salty and overpower the flavor of the sangria.

ZIPPY CURRY DIP

BARBECUED MEATBALLS

POMEGRANATE PISTACHIO CROSTINI

Pomegranate seeds intrigue me, so I sliced French bread, smeared it with cream cheese, and added seeds, pistachios and chocolate.
—Elisabeth Larsen, Pleasant Grove, UT

TAKES: 30 MIN. • **MAKES:** 3 DOZEN

- 36   slices French bread baguette (¼ in. thick)
- 1   Tbsp. butter, melted
- 4   oz. cream cheese, softened
- 2   Tbsp. orange juice
- 1   Tbsp. honey
- 1   cup pomegranate seeds
- ½   cup finely chopped pistachios
- 2   oz. dark chocolate candy bar, grated

1. Preheat oven to 400°. Arrange bread slices on an ungreased baking sheet; brush tops with butter. Bake until lightly toasted, 4-6 minutes. Remove from pan to a wire rack to cool.
2. Beat cream cheese, orange juice and honey until blended; spread over toasts. Top with remaining ingredients.
1 APPETIZER: *44 cal., 3g fat (1g sat. fat), 5mg chol., 46mg sod., 5g carb. (2g sugars, 0 fiber), 1g pro.*

BARBECUED MEATBALLS

Grape jelly and chili sauce are the secrets that make these meatballs so fantastic. If I'm serving them at a party, I make the meatballs and sauce in advance and reheat them right before guests arrive.
—Irma Schnuelle, Manitowoc, WI

PREP: 20 MIN. • **COOK:** 15 MIN. • **MAKES:** ABOUT 3 DOZEN

- ½   cup dry bread crumbs
- ⅓   cup finely chopped onion
- ¼   cup whole milk
- 1   large egg, lightly beaten
- 1   Tbsp. minced fresh parsley
- 1   tsp. salt
- 1   tsp. Worcestershire sauce
- ½   tsp. pepper
- 1   lb. lean ground beef (90% lean)
- ¼   cup canola oil
- 1   bottle (12 oz.) chili sauce
- 1   jar (10 oz.) grape jelly

1. In a large bowl, combine the first 8 ingredients. Crumble beef over mixture and mix well. Shape into 1-in. balls. In a large skillet, brown meatballs in oil on all sides.
2. Remove meatballs and drain. In the same skillet, combine chili sauce and jelly; cook and stir over medium heat until jelly has melted. Return meatballs to pan; heat through.
1 MEATBALL: *71 cal., 3g fat (1g sat. fat), 13mg chol., 215mg sod., 9g carb. (7g sugars, 0 fiber), 3g pro.*

POMEGRANATE PISTACHIO CROSTINI

FRUITY HORSERADISH CREAM CHEESE

Typically called a Jezebel sauce, this sweet, fruity topping has an underlying bite from horseradish. It pairs well with cream cheese and is a standout over grilled pork or chicken.
—Rita Reifenstein, Evans City, PA

TAKES: 10 MIN. • **MAKES:** 1⅓ CUPS

- 1 pkg. (8 oz.) fat-free cream cheese
- ⅓ cup apple jelly, warmed
- 1 Tbsp. prepared horseradish
- 1½ tsp. ground mustard
- ⅓ cup apricot spreadable fruit
  Assorted crackers

Place cream cheese on a serving plate. In a small microwave-safe bowl, heat jelly until warmed. Stir in horseradish and mustard until blended. Stir in spreadable fruit; spoon over cream cheese. Serve with crackers. Refrigerate leftovers.

2 TBSP.: *73 cal., 0 fat (0 sat. fat), 2mg chol., 128mg sod., 14g carb. (11g sugars, 0 fiber), 3g pro.*

CHICKEN SKEWERS WITH COOL AVOCADO SAUCE

I'm always looking for lighter recipes to take on tailgate outings—and this one works fabulously for grilling. Just whip up the marinade, add the chicken and take it along to the pregame festivities.
—Veronica Callaghan, Glastonbury, CT

PREP: 25 MIN. + MARINATING • **GRILL:** 10 MIN.
MAKES: 16 SKEWERS (¾ CUP SAUCE)

- 1 lb. boneless skinless chicken breasts
- ½ cup lime juice
- 1 Tbsp. balsamic vinegar
- 2 tsp. minced chipotle pepper in adobo sauce
- ½ tsp. salt
SAUCE
- 1 medium ripe avocado, peeled and pitted
- ½ cup fat-free sour cream
- 2 Tbsp. minced fresh cilantro
- 2 tsp. lime juice
- 1 tsp. grated lime zest
- ¼ tsp. salt

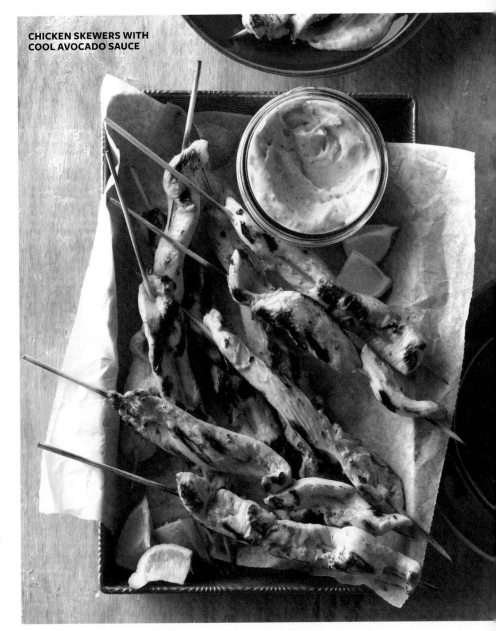

CHICKEN SKEWERS WITH COOL AVOCADO SAUCE

1. Flatten chicken to ¼-in. thickness; cut lengthwise into sixteen 1-in.-wide strips. In a large bowl, combine the lime juice, vinegar, chipotle pepper and salt; add the chicken and turn to coat. Cover and refrigerate for 30 minutes.

2. Meanwhile, for the sauce, place the remaining ingredients in a food processor; cover and process until blended. Transfer to a serving bowl; cover and refrigerate until serving.

3. Drain chicken, discarding marinade from bowl. Thread meat onto 4 metal or soaked wooden skewers. On a lightly oiled rack, grill skewers, covered, over medium heat or broil 4 in. from the heat for 8-12 minutes or until no longer pink, turning frequently. Serve with sauce.

1 SKEWER WITH ABOUT 2 TSP. SAUCE: *59 cal., 3g fat (0 sat. fat), 17mg chol., 74mg sod., 3g carb. (1g sugars, 1g fiber), 6g pro.* **Diabetic exchanges:** *1 lean meat, ½ fat.*

BEEF WELLINGTON FRIED WONTONS

These tasty appetizers scale down classic beef Wellington to an ideal party size. They feel fancy and fun!
—Dianne Phillips, Tallapoosa, GA

PREP: 35 MIN. • **COOK:** 25 MIN.
MAKES: 3½ DOZEN

- ½ lb. lean ground beef (90% lean)
- 1 Tbsp. butter
- 1 Tbsp. olive oil
- 2 garlic cloves, minced
- 1½ tsp. chopped shallot
- 1 cup each chopped fresh shiitake, baby portobello and white mushrooms
- ¼ cup dry red wine
- 1 Tbsp. minced fresh parsley
- ½ tsp. salt
- ¼ tsp. pepper
- 1 pkg. (12 oz.) wonton wrappers
- 1 large egg
- 1 Tbsp. water
  Oil for deep-fat frying

1. In a small skillet, cook beef over medium heat until no longer pink, breaking into crumbles, 4-5 minutes; transfer to a large bowl. In the same skillet, heat butter and olive oil over medium-high heat. Add the garlic and shallot; cook 1 minute longer. Stir in mushrooms and wine. Cook until mushrooms are tender, 8-10 minutes; add to beef. Stir in parsley, salt and pepper.
2. Place about 2 tsp. filling in the center of each wonton wrapper. Combine egg and water. Moisten wonton edges with egg mixture; fold opposite corners over filling and press to seal.
3. In an electric skillet, heat oil to 375°. Fry wontons, a few at a time, until golden brown, 60-90 seconds on each side. Drain on paper towels. Serve warm.
FREEZE OPTION: Place filled wontons on a baking sheet and place in the freezer until they're firm, then transfer to an airtight container and freeze. Thaw overnight in the fridge and cook as directed.
1 WONTON: *47 cal., 2g fat (1g sat. fat), 9mg chol., 82mg sod., 5g carb. (0 sugars, 0 fiber), 2g pro.*

GRILLED BRUSCHETTA

This is my go-to appetizer in the summer when tomatoes and basil are fresh from the garden. The balsamic glaze takes this bruschetta recipe over the top. I like to use a Tuscan herb or basil-infused olive oil for this. But it works well with plain olive oil, too.
—Brittany Allyn, Mesa, AZ

PREP: 30 MIN. • **GRILL:** 5 MIN.
MAKES: 16 SERVINGS

- ½ cup balsamic vinegar
- 1½ cups chopped and seeded plum tomatoes
- 2 Tbsp. finely chopped shallot
- 1 Tbsp. minced fresh basil
- 2 tsp. plus 3 Tbsp. olive oil, divided
- 1 garlic clove, minced
- 16 slices French bread baguette (½ in. thick)
  Sea salt and grated Parmesan cheese

1. In a small saucepan, bring vinegar to a boil; cook until liquid is reduced to 3 Tbsp., 8-10 minutes. Remove from the heat. Meanwhile, combine tomatoes, shallot, basil, 2 tsp. olive oil and garlic. Cover and refrigerate until serving.
2. Brush remaining oil over both sides of baguette slices. Grill, uncovered, over medium heat until golden brown on both sides.
3. Top toasts with tomato mixture. Drizzle with balsamic syrup; sprinkle with sea salt and Parmesan. Serve immediately.
1 APPETIZER: *58 cal., 3g fat (0 sat. fat), 0 chol., 49mg sod., 7g carb. (3g sugars, 0 fiber), 1g pro.* **Diabetic exchanges:** *½ starch, ½ fat.*

BEEF WELLINGTON FRIED WONTONS

BRITTANY ALLYN
MESA, AZ

GRILLED BRUSCHETTA

HONEY-BARBECUE
CHICKEN WINGS

BAKED ONION DIP

Some people like this cheesy dip so much that they can't tear themselves away from the appetizer table to eat their dinner.
—Mona Zignego, Hartford, WI

PREP: 5 MIN. • **BAKE:** 40 MIN. • **MAKES:** 16 SERVINGS (2 CUPS)

1   cup mayonnaise
1   cup chopped sweet onion
1   Tbsp. grated Parmesan cheese
¼   tsp. garlic salt
1   cup shredded Swiss cheese
    Minced fresh parsley, optional
    Assorted crackers

1. In a large bowl, combine mayonnaise, onion, Parmesan cheese and garlic salt; stir in Swiss cheese. Spoon into a 1-qt. baking dish.
2. Bake, uncovered, at 325° until golden brown, about 40 minutes. If desired, sprinkle with parsley. Serve with crackers.
2 TBSP.: *131 cal., 13g fat (3g sat. fat), 11mg chol., 127mg sod., 1g carb. (1g sugars, 0 fiber), 2g pro.*

HONEY-BARBECUE CHICKEN WINGS

The slightly sweet barbecue flavor of the sauce provides mass appeal—and the need to keep eating more wings!
—Taste of Home *Test Kitchen*

PREP: 20 MIN. • **COOK:** 10 MIN./BATCH • **MAKES:** 2 DOZEN

2½   lbs. whole chicken wings
½   cup reduced-sodium soy sauce
½   cup barbecue sauce
½   cup honey
1   cup all-purpose flour
2   tsp. salt
2   tsp. paprika
¼   tsp. pepper
    Oil for deep-fat frying

1. Cut wings into 3 sections; discard wing tip sections. In a small saucepan, combine the soy sauce, barbecue sauce and honey. Bring to a boil; cook until liquid is reduced to about 1 cup.
2. Meanwhile, in a large bowl, combine the flour, salt, paprika and pepper. Add wings, a few at a time, and toss to coat.
3. In an electric skillet or deep fryer, heat oil to 375°. Fry wings, a few at a time, until no longer pink, 3-4 minutes on each side. Drain on paper towels. Transfer wings to a large bowl; add sauce and toss to coat. Serve immediately.
NOTE: Uncooked chicken wing sections (wingettes) may be substituted for whole chicken wings.
1 PIECE: *129 cal., 8g fat (1g sat. fat), 15mg chol., 419mg sod., 8g carb. (7g sugars, 0 fiber), 6g pro.*

BAKED ONION DIP

FROZEN CHERRY MARGARITAS

(SHOWN ON PAGE 4)

When summer rolls around, I start thinking about all the fun drinks I can whip up to stay cool. This frozen cherry margarita is a favorite of mine. It's so delicious, and the deep red color is amazing.
—Crystal Jo Bruns, Iliff, CO

TAKES: 15 MIN. • **MAKES:** 4 SERVINGS

    Lime wedges
    Kosher salt
1 cup cherry juice blend
4 oz. tequila
1 Tbsp. lime juice
1 pkg. (12 oz.) frozen pitted dark sweet cherries
    Honey, optional

1. Using lime wedges, moisten the rims of 4 margarita or cocktail glasses. Set aside lime wedges for garnish. Sprinkle salt on a plate; hold each glass upside down and dip rim into salt. Set aside. Discard remaining salt on plate.

2. In a blender, combine the cherry juice, tequila, lime juice, cherries and, if desired, honey to sweeten to taste; cover and process until blended. Pour into prepared glasses. Garnish with the lime wedges. Serve immediately.

¾ **CUP:** *155 cal., 0 fat (0 sat. fat), 0 chol., 3mg sod., 23g carb. (16g sugars, 1g fiber), 1g pro.*

MUSHROOM & SMOKED GOUDA PUFF

It's so very easy, but it looks and tastes gourmet. Dinner party guests will be impressed with this perfect starter course. Serve with a spicy mustard for dipping if desired.
—Christina Singer, Bellefontaine, OH

PREP: 30 MIN. • **BAKE:** 30 MIN. + STANDING
MAKES: 8 SERVINGS

4½ tsp. butter
½ cup sliced fresh mushrooms
½ cup sliced baby portobello mushrooms
¼ cup chopped fresh shiitake mushrooms
1 shallot, minced
2 tsp. minced fresh thyme
¼ tsp. salt

MUSHROOM & SMOKED GOUDA PUFF

⅛ tsp. pepper
1 sheet frozen puff pastry, thawed
½ cup shredded smoked Gouda cheese
1 large egg
2 Tbsp. water

1. Preheat oven to 350°. In a large skillet, heat butter over medium-high heat. Add mushrooms and shallot; cook and stir until tender, about 5 minutes. Stir in thyme, salt and pepper.

2. Unfold puff pastry. Spread mushroom mixture to within 1 in. of edges. Sprinkle with the cheese. Roll up jelly-roll style; pinch seam and ends to seal. Place on a parchment-lined baking sheet, seam side down. In a small bowl, whisk egg and water; brush over pastry. Cut slits in top.

3. Bake until golden brown, about 30 minutes. Let stand for 10 minutes before cutting.

1 SLICE: *210 cal., 13g fat (5g sat. fat), 37mg chol., 260mg sod., 19g carb. (1g sugars, 2g fiber), 5g pro.*

TEST KITCHEN TIP

Feel free to swap in your favorite mushrooms, or some of the freshest you can find at your local market. You can also experiment with the cheese here—try a sharp cheddar, a creamy provolone or a blend of different cheeses.

STUFFED ASIAGO-BASIL MUSHROOMS

HOT GINGER COFFEE

This warm drink is wonderful after shoveling, skiing or sledding.
—Audrey Thibodeau, Gilbert, AZ

TAKES: 25 MIN. • **MAKES:** 6 SERVINGS

- 6 Tbsp. ground coffee (not instant)
- 1 Tbsp. grated orange zest
- 1 Tbsp. chopped crystallized ginger
- ½ tsp. ground cinnamon
- 6 cups cold water
  Whipped cream, cinnamon sticks and/or additional orange zest, optional

1. Combine the coffee, orange zest, ginger and cinnamon; pour into a coffee filter. Brew according to manufacturer's directions.
2. Pour into mugs; if desired, garnish with whipped cream, cinnamon sticks and orange zest.
NOTE: Look for crystallized or candied ginger in the spice or baking section of your grocery store.
1 CUP: *22 cal., 0 fat (0 sat. fat), 0 chol., 3mg sod., 5g carb. (2g sugars, 0 fiber), 1g pro.*

SMOKY CHICKEN SPREAD

The unique smoky flavor in this spread comes from smoked almonds. It turns your favorite crackers into a hearty snack. Don't expect many leftovers!
—Mary Beth Wagner, Rio, WI

PREP: 15 MIN. + CHILLING
MAKES: 4 CUPS

- ¾ cup mayonnaise
- ¼ cup finely chopped onion
- 1 Tbsp. honey
- ½ tsp. seasoned salt
- ⅛ tsp. pepper
- 3 cups finely chopped cooked chicken
- ½ cup finely chopped celery
- ½ cup coarsely chopped smoked almonds
  Assorted crackers

1. In a large bowl, mix first 5 ingredients. Stir in the chicken, celery and almonds. Refrigerate, covered, at least 2 hours.
2. Serve with crackers.
2 TBSP.: *76 cal., 6g fat (1g sat. fat), 12mg chol., 71mg sod., 1g carb. (1g sugars, 0 fiber), 4g pro.*

STUFFED ASIAGO-BASIL MUSHROOMS

Even if you don't like mushrooms, you will have to try them again with these pretty appetizers, which taste divine. For a main dish, double the filling and use large portobellos.
—Lorraine Caland, Shuniah, ON

PREP: 25 MIN. • **BAKE:** 10 MIN.
MAKES: 2 DOZEN

- 24 baby portobello mushrooms (about 1 lb.), stems removed
- ½ cup reduced-fat mayonnaise
- ¾ cup shredded Asiago cheese
- ½ cup loosely packed basil leaves, stems removed
- ¼ tsp. white pepper
- 12 cherry tomatoes, halved
  Thinly sliced or shaved Parmesan cheese, optional

1. Preheat oven to 375°. Place mushroom caps in a greased 15x10x1-in. baking pan. Bake 10 minutes. Meanwhile, place mayonnaise, Asiago cheese, basil and pepper in a food processor; process until blended.
2. Drain juices from mushrooms. Fill each with 1 rounded tsp. mayonnaise mixture; top each with a tomato half.
3. Bake until lightly browned, 8-10 minutes. If desired, top with Parmesan cheese.
1 APPETIZER: *35 cal., 3g fat (1g sat. fat), 5mg chol., 50mg sod., 2g carb. (1g sugars, 0 fiber), 2g pro.*
Italian Sausage Mushrooms: Bake and drain mushroom caps as directed. Meanwhile, in a large skillet, cook 1 lb. bulk Italian sausage over medium heat until no longer pink; drain. In a bowl, mix 6 oz. softened cream cheese, 3 Tbsp. minced fresh parsley and the sausage; spoon into mushroom caps. Bake as directed. Sprinkle with an additional 1 Tbsp. parsley.

PUMPKIN PINWHEELS

Cream cheese, mozzarella and roasted red peppers make these spirited pinwheels devilishly delicious. They were a hit at my last Halloween party.
—Anndrea Bailey, Huntington Beach, CA

PREP: 15 MIN. + CHILLING • **BAKE:** 20 MIN. • **MAKES:** 32 PINWHEELS

- 2 pkg. (8 oz. each) cream cheese, softened
- 1 cup shredded part-skim mozzarella cheese
- ½ cup chopped roasted sweet red peppers, drained
- ¼ tsp. Italian seasoning
- ¼ tsp. garlic salt
- ¼ tsp. onion powder
- 2 tubes (8 oz. each) refrigerated crescent rolls
  Pretzel sticks, optional
  Fresh cilantro leaves, optional

1. Preheat oven to 350°. Beat cream cheese until smooth. Beat in mozzarella, red peppers and seasonings until blended. Unroll tubes of crescent dough and separate each into 2 rectangles; press perforations to seal.
2. Spread cheese mixture over each rectangle. Roll up jelly-roll style, starting with a short side; pinch seam to seal. Wrap and chill at least 1 hour.
3. Cut each roll crosswise into 8 slices; place on ungreased baking sheets, cut side down. Bake until golden brown, 20-22 minutes. If desired, decorate pinwheels with pretzel sticks and cilantro leaves to look like pumpkins.
1 PINWHEEL: *112 cal., 8g fat (3g sat. fat), 17mg chol., 204mg sod., 7g carb. (2g sugars, 0 fiber), 3g pro.*

ICED HONEYDEW MINT TEA

I grow mint in the garden on my balcony. In this minty tea, I blend two of my favorite beverages—Moroccan mint tea and honeydew agua fresca.
—Sarah Batt Throne, El Cerrito, CA

TAKES: 20 MIN. • **MAKES:** 10 SERVINGS

- 4 cups water
- 24 fresh mint leaves
- 8 green tea bags
- ⅔ cup sugar
- 5 cups diced honeydew melon
- 3 cups ice cubes
  Additional ice cubes

1. In a large saucepan, bring water to a boil; remove from heat. Add mint leaves and tea bags; steep, covered, 3-5 minutes according to taste, stirring occasionally. Discard mint and tea bags. Stir in sugar.
2. Place 2½ cups honeydew, 2 cups tea and 1½ cups ice in a blender; cover and process until blended. Serve over additional ice. Repeat with remaining ingredients.
1 CUP: *83 cal., 0 fat (0 sat. fat), 0 chol., 15mg sod., 21g carb. (20g sugars, 1g fiber), 0 pro.* **Diabetic exchanges:** *1 starch, ½ fruit.*

PUMPKIN
PINWHEELS

WARM ROASTED BEET SALAD
PAGE 22

Salads & Dressings

Refreshing mixes, hearty favorites and more...with these recipes you'll whip up salads and dressings that complement—or star in—any homemade meal.

ROASTED RED POTATO SALAD

PEA & CRAB PASTA SALAD

This pretty pasta salad is jazzed up with crab, spinach and peas. With crumbled feta and just the right amount of Italian dressing, it makes a hearty side dish or a satisfying main course served with bread alongside.
—Taste of Home *Test Kitchen*

TAKES: 30 MIN. • **MAKES:** 6 SERVINGS

- 2½ cups uncooked medium pasta shells
- 2½ cups fresh baby spinach
- 1 pkg. (10 oz.) frozen peas, thawed
- 1½ cups imitation crabmeat
- ¼ cup crumbled feta cheese
- ½ cup Italian salad dressing

Cook pasta according to the package directions. Meanwhile, in a large bowl, combine spinach, peas and crab. Drain pasta and rinse in cold water. Stir into spinach mixture. Sprinkle with cheese. Drizzle with dressing and toss to coat.
1⅓ CUPS: *285 cal., 5g fat (1g sat. fat), 6mg chol., 465mg sod., 46g carb. (5g sugars, 4g fiber), 13g pro.*

CHINESE SPINACH-ALMOND SALAD

My favorite salad combines power-packed spinach, a good source of vitamins A and K, with carrots, mushrooms, lean meat and crunchy heart-healthy almonds. The flavors work well with a light Asian dressing.
—Mary Ann Kieffer, Lawrence, KS

TAKES: 10 MIN. • **MAKES:** 4 SERVINGS

- 1 pkg. (6 oz.) fresh baby spinach
- 2 cups cubed cooked pork
- 1 cup bean sprouts
- 2 medium carrots, thinly sliced
- ½ cup sliced fresh mushrooms
- ¼ cup sliced almonds, toasted
- ½ cup reduced-fat sesame ginger salad dressing

In a bowl, combine the first 6 ingredients. Divide among 4 salad plates; drizzle each serving with 2 Tbsp. dressing. Serve the salad immediately.
1 SERVING: *244 cal., 11g fat (3g sat. fat), 63mg chol., 500mg sod., 12g carb. (6g sugars, 3g fiber), 24g pro.* **Diabetic exchanges:** *3 lean meat, 1 vegetable, 1 fat, ½ starch.*

ROASTED RED POTATO SALAD

I got this recipe from my sister-in-law and I've made it often at the request of friends and co-workers. It's quick and easy, just what I need in my busy life. I learned how to cook from the two best cooks I know—my mom, Arline, and my Grandma Etta.
—Ginger Cusano, Sandusky, OH

PREP: 40 MIN. + CHILLING
MAKES: 8 SERVINGS

- 2 lbs. red potatoes, cut into 1-in. cubes
- 1 medium onion, chopped
- 4 large hard-boiled eggs, sliced
- 6 bacon strips, cooked and crumbled
- 1 cup mayonnaise
- ½ tsp. salt
- ¼ tsp. pepper
  Paprika and minced fresh parsley, optional

1. Place the cubed potatoes in a greased 15x10x1-in. baking pan. Bake, uncovered, at 400° until tender and golden brown, stirring occasionally, 25-30 minutes. Cool for 15 minutes.
2. Transfer to a large bowl; add onion, eggs, bacon, mayonnaise, salt and pepper. Toss to coat. Cover and refrigerate potato salad for several hours or overnight. Sprinkle with paprika and parsley if desired.
¾ CUP: *355 cal., 27g fat (5g sat. fat), 120mg chol., 412mg sod., 20g carb. (3g sugars, 2g fiber), 7g pro.*

TEST KITCHEN TIP

When roasting potatoes, don't just go off the bake time in the recipe. If they're not tender yet, then keep on cookin'.

SALADS & DRESSINGS

LEMONY TORTELLINI BACON SALAD

Summer meals shouldn't be complicated. We love this simple salad on warm nights. Serve with a cool glass of iced tea or lemonade.
—Samantha Vicars, Kenosha, WI

TAKES: 20 MIN. • **MAKES:** 4 SERVINGS

- 2 cups frozen cheese tortellini (about 8 oz.)
- 4 cups fresh broccoli florets
- ¾ cup mayonnaise
- 1 Tbsp. balsamic vinegar
- 2 tsp. lemon juice
- ¾ tsp. dried oregano
- ¼ tsp. salt
- 1 pkg. (5 oz.) spring mix salad greens
- 4 bacon strips, cooked and crumbled

1. In a large saucepan, cook tortellini according to the package directions, adding broccoli during the last 5 minutes of cooking. Meanwhile, in a small bowl, mix the mayonnaise, vinegar, lemon juice, oregano and salt.
2. Drain tortellini and broccoli; gently rinse with cold water. Transfer to a large bowl. Add dressing; toss to coat. Serve over salad greens; sprinkle with bacon.
1 CUP SALAD WITH 2 CUPS GREENS: *484 cal., 40g fat (7g sat. fat), 32mg chol., 693mg sod., 21g carb. (3g sugars, 4g fiber), 11g pro.*

GROUND BEEF TACO SALAD

GROUND BEEF TACO SALAD

Everyone at our house loves this taco salad. In spring we look for something light and refreshing on the menu after the heavier comfort food of winter.
—Muriel Bertrand, Shoreview, MN

TAKES: 25 MIN. • **MAKES:** 2 SERVINGS

- ½ lb. ground beef
- ⅓ cup bean dip
- 1 tsp. chili powder
- ¼ tsp. salt
- 1 cup canned diced tomatoes plus 2 Tbsp. liquid
- 2 cups chopped lettuce
- ½ cup shredded cheddar cheese
- 2 green onions, sliced
- 2 Tbsp. sliced ripe olives
- ½ cup corn chips

1. In a large skillet, cook beef over medium heat until no longer pink; drain. Stir in the bean dip, chili powder, salt and tomato liquid. Remove from the heat.
2. In a large bowl, combine the tomatoes, lettuce, cheese, onions and olives. Add beef mixture; toss to coat. Top with chips. Serve salad immediately.
2 CUPS: *469 cal., 28g fat (12g sat. fat), 107mg chol., 1007mg sod., 25g carb. (5g sugars, 4g fiber), 32g pro.*

**LEMONY TORTELLINI
BACON SALAD**

CILANTRO BLUE CHEESE SLAW

CRANBERRY WALDORF GELATIN

We enjoy this easy-to-make salad in the fall when apples are in season. Their crisp freshness adds so much to a favorite dish.
—Debbie Short, Carlisle, IA

PREP: 15 MIN. + CHILLING • **MAKES:** 12 SERVINGS

1	envelope unflavored gelatin
1	cup cold water, divided
1	pkg. (3 oz.) cranberry gelatin
2	cups boiling water
1	can (14 oz.) whole-berry cranberry sauce
½	to 1 tsp. ground cinnamon
¼	tsp. ground ginger
⅛	to ¼ tsp. salt
2	medium tart apples, peeled and diced
1	cup chopped walnuts

Sprinkle unflavored gelatin over ¼ cup cold water; let stand for 5 minutes. In a bowl, dissolve softened gelatin and cranberry gelatin in boiling water. Stir in cranberry sauce until blended. Add the cinnamon, ginger, salt and remaining cold water. Cover and refrigerate until almost set. Fold in apples and walnuts. Pour into an ungreased 2½-qt. serving bowl. Refrigerate until firm.
¾ **CUP:** *156 cal., 6g fat (0 sat. fat), 0 chol., 50mg sod., 24g carb. (18g sugars, 1g fiber), 4g pro.*

CILANTRO BLUE CHEESE SLAW

Serve this slaw as a side dish to any meal, or use it to top your favorite fish taco recipe instead of lettuce and the usual toppings.
—Christi Dalton, Hartsville, TN

TAKES: 25 MIN. • **MAKES:** 8 SERVINGS

8	cups shredded cabbage
1	small red onion, halved and thinly sliced
⅓	cup minced fresh cilantro
1	jalapeno pepper, seeded and minced
¼	cup crumbled blue cheese
¼	cup fat-free mayonnaise
¼	cup reduced-fat sour cream
2	Tbsp. rice vinegar
2	Tbsp. lime juice
1	garlic clove, minced
1	tsp. sugar
1	tsp. grated lime zest
¾	tsp. salt
½	tsp. coarsely ground pepper

In a large bowl, combine the cabbage, onion, cilantro and jalapeno. In a small bowl, combine the remaining ingredients; pour over salad and toss to coat.
NOTE: Wear disposable gloves when cutting hot peppers; the oils can burn skin. Avoid touching your face.
¾ **CUP:** *63 cal., 2g fat (1g sat. fat), 6mg chol., 362mg sod., 9g carb. (5g sugars, 3g fiber), 3g pro.* **Diabetic exchanges:** *1 vegetable, ½ fat.*

CRANBERRY WALDORF GELATIN

QUINOA WILTED SPINACH SALAD

Get all the nutritious benefits of quinoa, spinach and cranberries paired with the crunchy texture of nuts in this easy and scrumptious salad. A flavorful dressing splashed with orange tops everything off.
—Sharon Ricci, Mendon, NY

TAKES: 30 MIN. • **MAKES:** 10 SERVINGS

- 2 cups water
- 1 cup quinoa, rinsed
- 1 pkg. (6 oz.) fresh baby spinach, torn
- ½ cup dried cranberries

DRESSING

- 3 Tbsp. olive oil
- 2 Tbsp. orange juice
- 1 Tbsp. red wine vinegar
- 1 Tbsp. maple syrup
- 1 garlic clove, minced
- ½ tsp. salt
- ⅛ tsp. pepper
- 1 green onion, finely chopped
- ½ cup chopped pecans, toasted

1. In a small saucepan, bring water to a boil. Add quinoa. Reduce heat; cover and simmer for about 12-15 minutes or until the water is absorbed. Remove from heat; fluff quinoa with a fork.

2. In a large bowl, combine the warm quinoa, spinach and cranberries. For the dressing, in a small bowl, whisk the oil, orange juice, vinegar, maple syrup, garlic, salt and pepper. Stir in onion. Pour over quinoa mixture and toss to coat. Sprinkle with pecans.

NOTE: Look for quinoa in the cereal, rice or organic food aisle.

¾ **CUP:** 171 cal., 9g fat (1g sat. fat), 0 chol., 136mg sod., 20g carb. (6g sugars, 2g fiber), 3g pro.

DRESSED-UP STEAK SALAD

DRESSED-UP STEAK SALAD

This sirloin gets its fresh taste from tomato, red onion and avocado. A little steak sauce helps the dressing complement the meat. To complete the meal, serve soft breadsticks and lemon sherbet.
—Taste of Home *Test Kitchen*

PREP: 15 MIN. + MARINATING • **BROIL:** 5 MIN.
MAKES: 2 SERVINGS

- ⅓ cup canola oil
- 2 Tbsp. lime juice
- 1 Tbsp. steak sauce
- 1 Tbsp. red wine vinegar
- ½ tsp. Dijon mustard
- ¼ tsp. salt

MARINADE

- 2 Tbsp. steak sauce
- 1 tsp. canola oil
- 1 tsp. lime juice
- ⅛ to ¼ tsp. hot pepper sauce

SALAD

- ½ lb. boneless beef sirloin steak
- 3 cups torn mixed salad greens
- 1 medium tomato, cut into wedges
- 1 small ripe avocado, peeled and cubed
- 2 slices red onion, separated into rings

1. In a jar with a tight-fitting lid, combine first 6 ingredients; shake well. Refrigerate until serving.

2. In a small bowl, combine marinade ingredients. Brush on both sides of steak; let stand for 30 minutes. Broil steak 4 in. from the heat until meat reaches desired doneness, 5-6 minutes on each side.

3. Meanwhile, on 2 plates, arrange greens, tomato, avocado and onion. Thinly slice steak; place on top of salads. Serve with salad dressing.

1 SERVING: 696 cal., 59g fat (9g sat. fat), 64mg chol., 834mg sod., 19g carb. (8g sugars, 7g fiber), 26g pro.

REUBEN SALAD IN A JAR

Amy Smith from Avon, Connecticut, shared her layered Reuben salad with us, and we couldn't resist making it extra portable. Get ready to be asked for the recipe.
—Taste of Home *Test Kitchen*

TAKES: 30 MIN. • **MAKES:** 4 SERVINGS

2	Tbsp. butter, melted
⅛	tsp. pepper
2	cups cubed rye bread
¾	cup Thousand Island salad dressing
2	cups chopped pastrami
1	cup sauerkraut, rinsed and well drained
1	large tomato, diced
8	green onions, thinly sliced
1	cup shredded Swiss cheese
1	pkg. (6 oz.) ready-to-serve salad greens

1. In a bowl, combine butter and pepper. Add bread cubes and toss to coat. Arrange in a single layer in an ungreased 15x10x1-in. baking pan. Bake at 400° until the croutons are golden brown, 8-10 minutes, stirring occasionally. Cool.

2. In each of four 1-qt. wide-mouth canning jars, divide and layer ingredients in the following order: salad dressing, pastrami, sauerkraut, tomato, green onions, cheese and salad greens. Cover and refrigerate until serving. Divide croutons among 4-oz. glass jars or other small containers; cover. To serve, transfer salads and croutons into bowls; toss to combine.

1 SERVING: *509 cal., 35g fat (13g sat. fat), 81mg chol., 1454mg sod., 24g carb. (10g sugars, 4g fiber), 24g pro.*

WARM ROASTED BEET SALAD

(SHOWN ON PAGE 16)
Beets shine in this hearty salad. It's beautiful on the plate, too. When I have it, I prefer to use hazelnut oil in this salad.
—Jill Anderson, Sleepy Eye, MN

PREP: 30 MIN. • **BAKE:** 40 MIN.
MAKES: 6 SERVINGS

8	fresh beets
	Cooking spray
1½	cups orange juice
1	shallot, chopped
2	Tbsp. olive oil
2	Tbsp. balsamic vinegar
1	tsp. minced fresh thyme or ¼ tsp. dried thyme
½	tsp. grated orange zest
⅛	tsp. salt
⅛	tsp. pepper
6	cups fresh arugula or baby spinach
3	Tbsp. crumbled blue cheese
3	Tbsp. chopped hazelnuts, toasted

1. Scrub and peel the beets. Cut into wedges; place on a baking sheet coated with cooking spray. Spritz the beets with additional cooking spray until coated. Bake at 350° for 40-50 minutes or until tender, turning occasionally.

2. Meanwhile, for dressing, heat orange juice over medium heat in a small saucepan. Bring to a boil. Reduce the heat; simmer, uncovered, until the liquid is syrupy and reduced to about ⅓ cup. Remove from heat. Whisk in the next 7 ingredients. Set dressing aside to cool.

3. Just before serving, place arugula in a large bowl. Drizzle with ¼ cup dressing; toss to coat. Divide mixture among 6 salad plates. Place beets in the same bowl; add the remaining dressing and toss to coat. Arrange on the plates. Sprinkle salads with blue cheese and hazelnuts.

1 SERVING: *147 cal., 8g fat (2g sat. fat), 3mg chol., 167mg sod., 17g carb. (12g sugars, 2g fiber), 4g pro.* **Diabetic exchanges:** *2 vegetable, 1½ fat, ½ fruit.*

REUBEN SALAD IN A JAR

CALIFORNIA AVOCADO SALAD

CALIFORNIA AVOCADO SALAD

Spread a little sunshine with this easy salad. Just four ingredients drizzled with orange yogurt dressing and you have a light lunch or a pretty side to serve with dinner.
—James Schend, Pleasant Prairie, WI

TAKES: 20 MIN. • **MAKES:** 8 SERVINGS

- 3 medium oranges, peeled and sectioned
- 2 medium ripe avocados, peeled and sliced
- ¼ cup toasted pine nuts
- 2 tsp. minced fresh rosemary
  Orange Yogurt Dressing

Arrange oranges and avocados on a platter; sprinkle with pine nuts and rosemary. Drizzle dressing over salad. Serve immediately.

½ **CUP:** *135 cal., 11g fat (1g sat. fat), 3mg chol., 129mg sod., 10g carb. (5g sugars, 3g fiber), 2g pro.* **Diabetic exchanges:** *2 fat, ½ fruit.*

ORANGE YOGURT DRESSING

Honey brings a hint of sweetness to this creamy citrus salad dressing. The orange flavor is a wonderful complement to fresh spinach. It's also terrific served over lettuce or fruit.
—Beverly Florence, Midwest City, OK

PREP: 10 MIN. + CHILLING • **MAKES:** ⅔ CUP

- ¼ cup reduced-fat mayonnaise
- ¼ cup fat-free plain yogurt
- 2 Tbsp. orange juice
- 2 tsp. honey
- 1 tsp. grated orange zest
- ¼ tsp. salt
  Dash white pepper

In a small bowl, whisk together all ingredients; cover and refrigerate for at least 1 hour.

2 **TBSP.:** *57 cal., 4g fat (1g sat. fat), 4mg chol., 220mg sod., 5g carb. (0 sugars, 0 fiber), 1g pro.* **Diabetic exchanges:** *1 fat.*

VIETNAMESE CRUNCHY
CHICKEN SALAD

VIETNAMESE CRUNCHY CHICKEN SALAD

When I lived in Cleveland, I dined at a really good Vietnamese restaurant. There was a dish that I couldn't get enough of. Because I had it so frequently, I figured out the components and flavors and created my own easy-to-make version.
—Erin Schillo, Northfield, OH

PREP: 30 MIN. + MARINATING
COOK: 10 MIN. • **MAKES:** 4 SERVINGS

- 3 Tbsp. olive oil
- 2 Tbsp. lime juice
- 1 Tbsp. minced fresh cilantro
- 1½ tsp. grated lime zest
- ½ tsp. salt
- ½ tsp. pepper
- ¼ tsp. cayenne pepper
- 1 lb. boneless skinless chicken breasts, cut into thin strips

DRESSING
- ½ cup olive oil
- ¼ cup lime juice
- 2 Tbsp. rice vinegar
- 2 Tbsp. sugar
- 1 Tbsp. grated lime zest
- ¾ tsp. salt
- ½ tsp. crushed red pepper flakes
- ¼ tsp. pepper

SALAD
- 5 cups thinly sliced cabbage (about 1 lb.)
- 1 cup minced fresh cilantro
- 1 cup julienned carrots
- 1 cup salted peanuts, coarsely chopped

1. In a large bowl, mix first 7 ingredients; add chicken and toss to coat. Refrigerate, covered, 30 minutes. In a small bowl, whisk dressing ingredients. In a large skillet over medium-high heat, stir-fry half the chicken mixture for 4-5 minutes or until no longer pink. Remove from the pan; repeat with the remaining chicken. Cool slightly.
2. In a large bowl, combine sliced cabbage, cilantro, carrots and chicken; toss mixture to combine. Add the peanuts and dressing; toss to coat. Serve immediately.

2 CUPS: 743 cal., 59g fat (9g sat. fat), 63mg chol., 1068mg sod., 25g carb. (12g sugars, 7g fiber), 35g pro.

STRAWBERRY-AVOCADO TOSSED SALAD

STRAWBERRY-AVOCADO TOSSED SALAD

Delicious and beautiful! Strawberries and avocado on top of romaine are drizzled with a honey vinaigrette dressing. Perfect with a grilled steak and crusty bread.
—Pam Nordahl, Edina, MN

TAKES: 25 MIN. • **MAKES:** 4 SERVINGS

- ¼ cup olive oil
- 8 tsp. sugar
- 8 tsp. honey
- 2 Tbsp. cider vinegar
- 2 tsp. lemon juice
- ¼ tsp. salt
- 4 cups torn romaine
- 2 medium ripe avocados, peeled and thinly sliced
- 20 fresh strawberries, sliced
- ¼ cup chopped pecans, toasted

1. In a small bowl, whisk together the oil, sugar, honey, vinegar, lemon juice and salt.
2. Divide romaine among 4 salad plates. Top each plate with avocado and strawberries. Drizzle with dressing. Sprinkle with pecans.

1 SERVING: 384 cal., 29g fat (4g sat. fat), 0 chol., 159mg sod., 33g carb. (24g sugars, 8g fiber), 3g pro.

HOW-TO

PDQ Avocados

When life hands you hard avocados, here's how to ripen them ASAP. Place them in a paper bag with an apple or banana. Poke the bag a few times with a toothpick or scissors, and let ripen at room temperature for a day or two. The more fruits (and ethylene gas they give off), the faster the results.

CUCUMBER MELON SALAD

BALSAMIC ASPARAGUS SALAD

Give yourself enough time to let the flavors blend for at least an hour when making this salad; that's one of the secrets to why it tastes so delicious. If you're short on time, use ½ cup prepared balsamic vinaigrette instead of making it from scratch.
—Dolores Brigham, Inglewood, CA

PREP: 20 MIN. + CHILLING
MAKES: 6 SERVINGS

- 2 lbs. fresh asparagus, trimmed and cut into 1-in. pieces
- ⅓ cup thinly sliced red onion
- ½ cup chopped sweet red pepper
- ¼ cup dried cranberries
- 3 Tbsp. olive oil
- 3 Tbsp. balsamic vinegar
- 1 Tbsp. lemon juice
- 1 Tbsp. Dijon mustard
- Dash salt and pepper
- 3 Tbsp. slivered almonds, toasted
- 3 Tbsp. chopped cooked bacon or bacon bits

1. In a large saucepan, bring 1 in. of water to a boil. Add asparagus; cover and boil for 3-4 minutes or until crisp-tender. Drain and immediately place asparagus in ice water. Drain and pat dry. Transfer to a large bowl; add the onion, red pepper and cranberries.
2. In a jar with a tight-fitting lid, combine the oil, vinegar, lemon juice, mustard, salt and pepper; shake well. Pour dressing over asparagus mixture; toss to coat. Cover and refrigerate for at least 1 hour. Just before serving, stir in almonds and bacon.
¾ **CUP:** *139 cal., 9g fat (1g sat. fat), 3mg chol., 208mg sod., 12g carb. (7g sugars, 2g fiber), 4g pro.* **Diabetic exchanges:** *2 vegetable, 2 fat.*

TEST KITCHEN TIP

It's important to cool the asparagus immediately after cooking—otherwise it continues to cook and gets soft and mushy.

CUCUMBER MELON SALAD

This colorful salad is tangy and delicious, and the unexpected combination is a pleasant surprise. You can use whatever type of melon you have on hand.
—Edie Farm, Farmington, NM

TAKES: 15 MIN. • **MAKES:** 2 SERVINGS

- 2 Tbsp. canola oil
- 1 Tbsp. lemon juice
- ½ tsp. sugar
- Dash pepper
- 1 unpeeled small cucumber
- 1 cup cubed melon of your choice

1. In a small bowl, combine the oil, lemon juice, sugar and pepper. Slice cucumber, then cut into quarters.
2. In a serving bowl, combine cucumber and melon. Pour dressing over all; toss gently to coat.
1½ **CUPS:** *159 cal., 14g fat (1g sat. fat), 0 chol., 4mg sod., 10g carb. (9g sugars, 1g fiber), 1g pro.* **Diabetic exchanges:** *3 fat, ½ starch.*

HOLIDAY SLAW WITH APPLE CIDER DRESSING

I found this refreshing twist on coleslaw at a local grocery store and tweaked it to fit my family's taste. You can substitute raisins for dried cranberries. When it's available, I use a prepared apple cider salad dressing to make this dish even easier!
—Susan Bickta, Kutztown, PA

PREP: 15 MIN. + CHILLING • **MAKES:** 8 SERVINGS

- 1 pkg. (14 oz.) coleslaw mix
- 1¼ cups chopped fresh kale
- 1 cup crumbled Gorgonzola cheese
- 1 cup dried cranberries
- ⅓ cup finely chopped red onion
- 1 cup mayonnaise
- ⅓ cup sugar
- ¼ cup thawed apple juice concentrate
- 3 Tbsp. cider vinegar
- ⅛ tsp. salt

Place first 5 ingredients in a large bowl. In another bowl, whisk remaining ingredients. Pour over coleslaw mix; toss to coat. Refrigerate, covered, at least 2 hours before serving.
¾ CUP: *316 cal., 24g fat (6g sat. fat), 15mg chol., 383mg sod., 23g carb. (18g sugars, 3g fiber), 4g pro.*

ISRAELI PEPPER TOMATO SALAD

HOLIDAY SLAW WITH APPLE CIDER DRESSING

ISRAELI PEPPER TOMATO SALAD

This Israeli salad, traditionally eaten at breakfast, lends itself to endless variety...you can add foods like olives, beets or potatoes.
—Sandy Long, Lees Summit, MO

PREP: 25 MIN. + CHILLING • **MAKES:** 9 SERVINGS

- 6 medium tomatoes, seeded and chopped
- 1 each medium green, sweet red and yellow peppers, chopped
- 1 medium cucumber, seeded and chopped
- 1 medium carrot, chopped
- 3 green onions, thinly slices
- 1 jalapeno pepper, seeded and chopped
- 2 Tbsp. each minced fresh cilantro, parsley, dill and mint
- ¼ cup lemon juice
- 2 Tbsp. olive oil
- 3 garlic cloves, minced
- ½ tsp. salt
- ¼ tsp. pepper

In a large bowl, combine the tomatoes, sweet peppers, cucumber, carrot, green onions, jalapeno and herbs. In a small bowl, whisk together the remaining ingredients. Pour over the tomato mixture; toss to coat evenly. Cover and refrigerate for at least 1 hour. Serve with a slotted spoon.
NOTE: Wear disposable gloves when cutting hot peppers; the oils can burn skin. Avoid touching your face.
1 CUP: *64 cal., 3g fat (0 sat. fat), 0 chol., 143mg sod., 8g carb. (5g sugars, 3g fiber), 2g pro.* **Diabetic exchanges:** *1 vegetable, ½ fat.*

QUICK AMBROSIA FRUIT SALAD

I mix in a little coconut and just enough marshmallows so it tastes like the creamy ambrosia I grew up with. Now everyone in my home loves it too.
—Trisha Kruse, Eagle, ID

TAKES: 10 MIN. • **MAKES:** 6 SERVINGS

- 1 can (8¼ oz.) fruit cocktail, drained
- 1 can (8 oz.) unsweetened pineapple chunks, drained
- 1 cup green grapes
- 1 cup seedless red grapes
- 1 cup miniature marshmallows
- 1 medium banana, sliced
- ¾ cup vanilla yogurt
- ½ cup sweetened shredded coconut

In a large bowl, combine all ingredients. Chill until serving.

¾ CUP: *191 cal., 4g fat (3g sat. fat), 2mg chol., 48mg sod., 40g carb. (34g sugars, 2g fiber), 3g pro.*

AVOCADO & GRAPEFRUIT SALAD

This simple and colorful salad is easy to make. We eat a lot of grapefruit so I was happy to come up with this pleasing combination. The honey in the dressing enhances the taste of both the grapefruit and the avocado.
—Marion Sell, Santa Maria, CA

TAKES: 20 MIN. • **MAKES:** 2 SERVINGS

- 4 Bibb or Boston lettuce leaves
- 1 medium grapefruit, peeled
- 1 medium ripe avocado, peeled and sliced
- 1 Tbsp. canola oil
- 1½ tsp. white wine vinegar
- ½ tsp. honey
- ⅛ tsp. salt

1. Place lettuce on two salad plates. Section the grapefruit over a bowl to reserve juice. Arrange grapefruit sections and avocado slices on lettuce.
2. In a small bowl, whisk the oil, vinegar, honey, salt and 1½ tsp. of the reserved grapefruit juice. Drizzle over the salads; serve immediately.

1 SERVING: *256 cal., 20g fat (2g sat. fat), 0 chol., 155mg sod., 20g carb. (11g sugars, 7g fiber), 3g pro.*

RANCH POTATO SALAD

I make this creamy potato salad with cheese, bacon and ranch salad dressing. My sister asked for the recipe as soon as she tried it.
—Lynn Breunig, Wind Lake, WI

PREP: 30 MIN. + CHILLING
MAKES: 8 SERVINGS

- 2 lbs. red potatoes
- 1 bottle (8 oz.) ranch salad dressing
- 1 cup shredded cheddar cheese
- 1 pkg. (2.8 oz.) bacon bits
- ¼ tsp. pepper
  Dash garlic powder

1. Place potatoes in a large saucepan and cover with water. Bring to a boil. Reduce heat; cover and simmer until tender, about 20-25 minutes.
2. In a large bowl, combine the remaining ingredients (dressing will be thick). Drain potatoes and cut into cubes; add to the dressing and gently toss to coat. Cover and refrigerate for 2 hours or until chilled. Refrigerate leftovers.

1 CUP: *316 cal., 22g fat (6g sat. fat), 27mg chol., 649mg sod., 20g carb. (2g sugars, 2g fiber), 9g pro.*

QUICK AMBROSIA FRUIT SALAD

WILTED SPINACH SALAD WITH BUTTERNUT SQUASH

WILTED SPINACH SALAD WITH BUTTERNUT SQUASH

This warm winter salad is packed with good-for-you spinach, squash and almonds. It feels so festive served at the holidays.
—Margee Berry, White Salmon, WA

PREP: 20 MIN. • **COOK:** 25 MIN.
MAKES: 4 SERVINGS

- 1   cup cubed peeled butternut squash
- ½   tsp. chili powder
- ½   tsp. salt, divided
- 4   tsp. olive oil, divided
- ⅓   cup balsamic vinegar
- 2   Tbsp. dry red wine or chicken broth
- 2   Tbsp. whole-berry cranberry sauce
- 5   cups fresh baby spinach
- 4   slices red onion
- ½   cup dried cranberries
- ⅓   cup slivered almonds, toasted
- ⅓   cup crumbled goat cheese
     Coarsely ground pepper, optional

1. In a small skillet, saute the squash, chili powder and ¼ tsp. salt in 2 tsp. oil until tender, 11-13 minutes. Set aside; keep the squash warm.

2. In a small saucepan, bring vinegar to a boil. Reduce heat; simmer for 4-6 minutes or until reduced to ¼ cup. Stir in the wine, cranberry sauce, and remaining oil and salt. Bring to a boil; cook 1 minute longer.

3. Place spinach on a serving platter; top with onion, cranberries and the squash mixture. Drizzle salad with warm dressing. Sprinkle with almonds, goat cheese and, if desired, pepper. Serve immediately.

1 SERVING: *228 cal., 12g fat (3g sat. fat), 12mg chol., 382mg sod., 28g carb. (17g sugars, 4g fiber), 5g pro.* **Diabetic exchanges:** *2 fat, 1½ starch, 1 vegetable.*

BLT SALAD

In my family of six, it's hard to find a vegetable or salad that everyone will eat, but they all rave about this one. With garden-fresh basil and tomatoes, the salad is simply amazing.
—Susie Clayton, South St. Paul, MN

TAKES: 25 MIN. • **MAKES:** 6 SERVINGS

- 1   lb. sliced bacon, cut into 1-in. pieces
- ¼   cup butter, cubed
- 4   slices white bread, crusts removed and cut into 1-in. cubes
- ½   cup mayonnaise
- 3   to 5 Tbsp. minced fresh basil
- 2   Tbsp. red wine vinegar
- ½   tsp. pepper
- ½   tsp. minced garlic
- 6   cups torn romaine
- 1½ cups grape tomatoes

1. In a large skillet, cook the bacon over medium heat until crisp. Using a slotted spoon, remove to paper towels; drain, reserving 2 Tbsp. drippings. Set bacon and drippings aside.

2. In another large skillet, melt butter. Add bread cubes; cook over medium heat for 4-5 minutes or until golden brown, stirring frequently. Remove to paper towels; cool.

3. For dressing, in a small bowl, whisk the mayonnaise, basil, vinegar, pepper, garlic and reserved drippings. In a large bowl, combine the romaine, tomatoes and bacon. Drizzle with dressing and toss to coat. Top with toasted bread cubes.

1 SERVING: *429 cal., 37g fat (12g sat. fat), 53mg chol., 743mg sod., 13g carb. (3g sugars, 2g fiber), 12g pro.*

SESAME, SUNFLOWER & CARROT SALAD

TANGY CILANTRO LIME CONFETTI SALAD

I love great salads that burst with flavor—the kind that make you feel like you're splurging without having to reach for that piece of chocolate cake. This is one of my favorites, and everyone I serve it to loves it as well.
—*Jasey McBurnett, Rock Springs, WY*

TAKES: 25 MIN. • **MAKES:** 6 SERVINGS

- 2   medium sweet orange peppers, chopped
- 2   medium ripe avocados, peeled and cubed
- 1   container (10½ oz.) cherry tomatoes, halved
- 1   cup fresh or frozen corn, thawed
- ½   medium red onion, finely chopped

DRESSING
- ¼   cup seasoned rice vinegar
- 3   Tbsp. lime juice
- 2   Tbsp. olive oil
- ½   cup fresh cilantro leaves
- 2   garlic cloves, halved
- 2   tsp. sugar
- ½   tsp. kosher salt
- ¼   tsp. pepper

Place the first 5 ingredients in a large bowl. Place the dressing ingredients in a blender; cover and process until creamy and light in color. Pour over vegetable mixture; toss to coat. Refrigerate, covered, up to 3 hours.

1 CUP: *187 cal., 12g fat (2g sat. fat), 0 chol., 526mg sod., 20g carb. (10g sugars, 5g fiber), 3g pro.* **Diabetic exchanges:** *2 vegetable, 2 fat, ½ starch.*

SESAME, SUNFLOWER & CARROT SALAD

I love the bright golden colors that make this a beautiful salad to serve, and a super healthy one to eat. It's a versatile side that goes with nearly everything!
—*Jessica Gerschitz, Jericho, NY*

PREP: 20 MIN. + CHILLING • **MAKES:** 8 SERVINGS

- 6   medium carrots
- ½   cup sesame seeds, toasted
- ½   cup sunflower kernels, toasted
- ½   cup sliced almonds, toasted
- ½   cup golden raisins

DRESSING
- ¼   cup reduced-fat mayonnaise
- ¼   cup lemon juice
- ¼   cup olive oil
- 2   Tbsp. honey mustard
- ½   tsp. salt

Shred carrots with a hand grater or in a food processor fitted with grating attachment. Place carrots in a large bowl with next 4 ingredients. In a small bowl, whisk dressing ingredients until blended. Pour dressing over the carrot mixture; toss to coat. Cover and refrigerate for at least 1 hour before serving.

½ CUP: *283 cal., 21g fat (3g sat. fat), 3mg chol., 335mg sod., 22g carb. (11g sugars, 5g fiber), 6g pro.*

TANGY CILANTRO LIME CONFETTI SALAD

CHICKEN & APPLE SALAD WITH GREENS

My favorite memory of eating this dish was when Mom made it for lunch on weekends when we were home from school, and we could have something other than brown-bag lunches. Happy memories of childhood days make this salad extra special.
—*Trisha Kruse, Eagle, ID*

TAKES: 30 MIN. • **MAKES:** 6 SERVINGS

VINAIGRETTE
- ¼ cup balsamic vinegar
- ¼ cup orange juice
- ¼ cup olive oil
- 2 Tbsp. lemon juice
- 2 Tbsp. reduced-sodium soy sauce
- 1 Tbsp. brown sugar
- 1 Tbsp. Dijon mustard
- ½ tsp. curry powder, optional
- ½ tsp. salt
- ¼ tsp. pepper
- ¼ tsp. ground ginger

SALAD
- 2 cups shredded cooked chicken
- 2 medium apples, chopped
- ½ cup thinly sliced red onion
- 10 cups torn mixed salad greens
- ½ cup chopped walnuts, toasted

In a large bowl, whisk the vinaigrette ingredients until blended. Add chicken, apples and onion; toss to coat. Just before serving, place greens on a large serving plate; top with chicken mixture. Sprinkle with walnuts.

NOTE: To toast nuts, bake in a shallow pan in a 350° oven for 5-10 minutes or cook in a skillet over low heat until lightly browned, stirring occasionally.

1 SERVING: *306 cal., 19g fat (3g sat. fat), 42mg chol., 549mg sod., 20g carb. (12g sugars, 4g fiber), 17g pro.*

ANTIPASTO
SALAD PLATTER

ANTIPASTO SALAD PLATTER

I used to work in a pizza shop where this salad was the most popular item on the menu. On the nights when it's just too hot to cook—or any night—it's the perfect quick fix.
—*Webbie Carvajal, Alpine, TX*

TAKES: 25 MIN. • **MAKES:** 8 SERVINGS

- 1½ cups cubed fully cooked ham
- 1 jar (10 oz.) pimiento-stuffed olives, drained and sliced
- 1 can (3.8 oz.) sliced ripe olives, drained
- 1 pkg. (3½ oz.) sliced pepperoni, quartered
- 8 cups shredded lettuce
- 10 to 12 cherry tomatoes, quartered
- 1 cup Italian salad dressing
- 1½ cups shredded part-skim mozzarella cheese

In a large bowl, combine the ham, olives and pepperoni. On a platter or individual salad plates, arrange the lettuce, olive mixture and cherry tomatoes. Drizzle with dressing; sprinkle with cheese.

1 SERVING: *342 cal., 29g fat (7g sat. fat), 41mg chol., 1830mg sod., 9g carb. (3g sugars, 2g fiber), 13g pro.*

CHICKEN PARMESAN BURGERS
PAGE 44

Soups & Sandwiches

Chow down on chili, cheesy broccoli soup, chowder and more with the comforting creations in this chapter. Add sandwiches for dunking or make them your mouthwatering main course.

COBB SALAD CLUB SANDWICH

You'll never have to choose between a salad and a sandwich again. With its generous ingredients piled club-style high, we affectionately call it the alpha Clobb sandwich!
—Carmell Childs, Clawson, UT

TAKES: 25 MIN. • **MAKES:** 2 SERVINGS

- 3 Tbsp. butter, softened
- 3 slices rustic Italian bread
- 3 slices cheddar or provolone cheese
- 2 pieces leaf lettuce
- 3 slices tomato
- 7 thin slices deli smoked peppered turkey breast
- ½ medium ripe avocado, peeled and sliced
- 3 Tbsp. blue cheese spread
- 7 thin slices deli oven-roasted chicken
- 7 thin slices deli ham
- 5 crisp cooked bacon strips
- 1 large hard-boiled egg, sliced

1. Spread butter over 1 side of each bread slice. Place 1 slice cheese on each unbuttered side of bread. Toast bread, butter side down, in a large skillet or electric griddle over medium-low heat until golden brown, 4-5 minutes.

2. Layer 1 toast with lettuce, tomato, turkey and avocado. Top with another toast and spread with blue cheese spread. Top with chicken, ham, bacon and egg. Top with remaining toast, cheese side down. Cut sandwich in half, secure with toothpicks and serve.

½ **SANDWICH:** 878 cal., 58g fat (26g sat. fat), 285mg chol., 2774mg sod., 32g carb. (5g sugars, 4g fiber), 58g pro.

CINNAMON WHISKEY BBQ CHICKEN WRAPS

Chicken, bacon, cheese and an amazing barbecue sauce make this a family favorite! The sauce can be made ahead and stored in the refrigerator.
—Jolene Martinelli, Fremont, NH

PREP: 40 MIN. • **GRILL:** 15 MIN.
MAKES: 4 SERVINGS

- ⅓ cup packed brown sugar
- ⅓ cup ketchup
- 2 Tbsp. cider vinegar
- 2 Tbsp. cinnamon whiskey
- ¾ tsp. Worcestershire sauce
- ¾ tsp. molasses
- 1 small garlic clove, minced
- ¼ tsp. pepper
- ⅛ tsp. cayenne pepper

WRAP
- 1 lb. boneless skinless chicken breast halves
- ½ tsp. salt
- ¼ tsp. pepper
- 1 cup shredded cheddar cheese
- ¼ cup prepared ranch salad dressing
- 4 flour tortillas (10 in.)
- 8 bacon strips, cooked and crumbled
  Shredded lettuce, optional

1. In a small saucepan, combine the first 9 ingredients. Bring to a boil. Reduce heat; simmer, covered, until thickened, 5-8 minutes. Reserve ¼ cup sauce for wraps.

2. Sprinkle chicken with salt and pepper; place on a greased grill rack. Grill, covered, over medium heat 7-8 minutes. Turn; grill until a thermometer reads 165°, 7-8 minutes longer, brushing occasionally with sauce. Top with cheese; grill, covered, until cheese is melted, 1-2 minutes longer. Let chicken stand 5 minutes before slicing into strips.

3. Spread dressing over tortillas. Top with chicken; drizzle with reserved sauce. Top with bacon and, if desired, lettuce. Fold in ends of tortillas; roll up.

1 **WRAP:** 697 cal., 30g fat (11g sat. fat), 109mg chol., 1770mg sod., 62g carb. (28g sugars, 3g fiber), 41g pro.

CARMELL CHILDS
Clawson, UT

COBB SALAD CLUB SANDWICH

ITALIAN CABBAGE SOUP

CREAMY CHICKEN SOUP

Kids won't think twice about eating the vegetables that are incorporated into this creamy and cheesy soup.
—LaVonne Lundgren, Sioux City, IA

TAKES: 30 MIN. • **MAKES:** 8 SERVINGS

    4   cups cubed cooked chicken breast
 3½   cups water
    2   cans (10¾ oz. each) condensed cream
        of chicken soup, undiluted
    1   pkg. (16 oz.) frozen mixed vegetables, thawed
    1   can (14½ oz.) diced potatoes, drained
    1   pkg. (16 oz.) Velveeta, cubed

In a Dutch oven, combine the first 5 ingredients. Bring to a boil. Reduce heat; cover and simmer until vegetables are tender, 8-10 minutes. Stir in cheese just until melted (do not boil).
1⅓ CUPS: *429 cal., 22g fat (11g sat. fat), 116mg chol., 1464mg sod., 23g carb. (6g sugars, 4g fiber), 33g pro.*

ITALIAN CABBAGE SOUP

After doing yardwork on a windy day, we love to come in for a light but hearty soup like this one. It's brimming with cabbage, veggies and white beans. Pass the oven-warmed bread!
—Jennifer Stowell, Deep River, IA

PREP: 15 MIN. • **COOK:** 6 HOURS • **MAKES:** 8 SERVINGS (2 QT.)

    4   cups chicken stock
    1   can (6 oz.) tomato paste
    1   small head cabbage (about 1½ lbs.), shredded
    4   celery ribs, chopped
    2   large carrots, chopped
    1   small onion, chopped
    1   can (15½ oz.) great northern beans, rinsed and drained
    2   garlic cloves, minced
    2   fresh thyme sprigs
    1   bay leaf
   ½   tsp. salt
        Shredded Parmesan cheese, optional

1. In a 5- or 6-qt. slow cooker, whisk together stock and tomato paste. Stir in vegetables, beans, garlic and seasonings. Cook, covered, on low until vegetables are tender, 6-8 hours.
2. Remove thyme sprigs and bay leaf. If desired, serve with cheese.
1 CUP: *111 cal., 0 fat (0 sat. fat), 0 chol., 537mg sod., 21g carb. (7g sugars, 6g fiber), 8g pro.* **Diabetic exchanges:** *1½ starch.*

CREAMY CHICKEN SOUP

SHRIMP CHOWDER

SHRIMP CHOWDER

*I simmer my rich and creamy shrimp soup
in the slow cooker. Because the chowder
is ready in less than four hours, it can be
prepared in the afternoon and served to
dinner guests that night.*
—Will Zunio, Gretna, LA

PREP: 15 MIN. • **COOK:** 3½ HOURS
MAKES: 12 SERVINGS (3 QT.)

½ cup chopped onion
2 tsp. butter
2 cans (12 oz. each) evaporated milk
2 cans (10¾ oz. each) condensed
   cream of potato soup, undiluted
2 cans (10¾ oz. each) condensed
   cream of chicken soup, undiluted
1 can (7 oz.) white or
   shoepeg corn, drained
1 tsp. Creole seasoning
½ tsp. garlic powder
2 lbs. peeled and deveined
   cooked small shrimp
3 oz. cream cheese, cubed

1. In a small skillet, saute onion in butter
until tender. In a 5-qt. slow cooker, combine
the onion, milk, soups, corn, Creole
seasoning and garlic powder.
2. Cover and cook on low for 3 hours. Stir in
shrimp and cream cheese. Cook 30 minutes
longer or until shrimp are heated through
and cheese is melted. Stir to blend.
NOTE: The following spices may be
substituted for 1 tsp. Creole seasoning:
¼ tsp. each salt, garlic powder and paprika;
and a pinch each of dried thyme, ground
cumin and cayenne pepper.
1 CUP: *202 cal., 8g fat (4g sat. fat), 169mg
chol., 745mg sod., 13g carb. (4g sugars, 1g
fiber), 20g pro.*

CUBAN ROASTED PORK SANDWICHES

For an incredible hot sandwich, slowly roast pork in a seasoned citrus marinade, then layer slices of meat with pickles, zippy mustard, ham and cheese.
—Taste of Home *Test Kitchen*

PREP: 20 MIN. + MARINATING
BAKE: 3½ HOURS + GRILLING
MAKES: 24 SERVINGS

- 1 boneless pork shoulder butt roast (5 to 6 lbs.)
- 4 garlic cloves, sliced
- 2 large onions, sliced
- 1 cup orange juice
- 1 cup lime juice
- 2 Tbsp. dried oregano
- 2 tsp. ground cumin
- 1 tsp. salt
- 1 tsp. pepper

SANDWICHES

- 4 loaves (1 lb. each) French bread
- ¾ cup butter, softened
- ½ to 1 cup yellow mustard
- 24 thin sandwich pickle slices
- 2¼ lbs. sliced deli ham
- 2¼ lbs. Swiss cheese, sliced

1. Cut sixteen 1-in. slits in pork; insert garlic slices. In a large bowl, combine the onions, orange juice, lime juice and seasonings. Pour 1½ cups marinade into another large bowl; add pork and turn to coat with marinade. Cover and refrigerate for at least 8 hours or overnight, turning pork occasionally. Cover and refrigerate the remaining marinade.
2. Drain pork, discarding the drained marinade. Place pork and the reserved marinade in a shallow roasting pan. Bake at 350° until tender, 3½-4 hours, basting occasionally. Let stand for 15 minutes before slicing.
3. Meanwhile, cut each loaf of bread in half lengthwise; flatten slightly. Spread cut side with butter; spread the crust side with mustard. Cut pork into thin slices. Layer pickles, pork, ham and cheese over the mustard. Replace tops so buttered side is outward. Cut each loaf into sixths.
4. Cook in batches on a panini maker or indoor grill for 4-5 minutes or until bread is browned and cheese is melted.
1 SANDWICH: *590 cal., 27g fat (15g sat. fat), 119mg chol., 1206mg sod., 47g carb. (5g sugars, 2g fiber), 39g pro.*

BACON CHEESEBURGERS WITH FRY SAUCE

In Utah, fry sauce is the beloved state condiment. We use it not just as a dip for fries, but also as a spread for hamburgers. Utah is known as the Beehive State, so I wanted to add honey as a special touch to my fry sauce.
—Elisabeth Larsen, Pleasant Grove, UT

PREP: 25 MIN. • **GRILL:** 10 MIN.
MAKES: 4 SERVINGS

- 1 tsp. Worcestershire sauce
- 1 garlic clove, minced
- ½ tsp. seasoned salt
- ¼ tsp. pepper
- 1 lb. ground beef
- 4 slices sharp cheddar cheese
- ¼ cup mayonnaise
- 2 Tbsp. ketchup
- 1 Tbsp. cider vinegar
- 1 Tbsp. honey
- 4 hamburger buns, split and toasted
- 8 cooked bacon strips
- ½ cup french-fried onions
  Lettuce leaves and sliced tomato, optional

1. In a large bowl, combine Worcestershire sauce, garlic, seasoned salt and pepper. Add beef; mix lightly but thoroughly. Shape into four ½-in.-thick patties.
2. Grill burgers, covered, over medium heat until a thermometer reads 160°, 5-7 minutes on each side. Top with cheese; grill, covered, until the cheese is melted, 1-2 minutes longer.
3. Meanwhile, in a small bowl, combine mayonnaise, ketchup, vinegar and honey; spread over cut sides of buns. Top bun bottoms with bacon, burgers, french-fried onions and, if desired, lettuce and tomato. Replace tops.
1 BURGER: *708 cal., 46g fat (16g sat. fat), 124mg chol., 1277mg sod., 33g carb. (10g sugars, 1g fiber), 39g pro.*

BACON CHEESEBURGERS WITH FRY SAUCE

SALMON SLIDERS WITH SUN-DRIED TOMATO SPREAD

SALMON SLIDERS WITH SUN-DRIED TOMATO SPREAD

My husband isn't a fan of salmon burgers, but he devoured these! The combination of feta, dill and fresh salmon on the toasted pretzel bun, topped with sun-dried tomato mayonnaise, changed his mind. The pickle adds tartness and crunch to balance the flavors and textures perfectly.
—*Arlene Erlbach, Morton Grove, IL*

PREP: 30 MIN. + COOLING • **COOK:** 10 MIN./BATCH
MAKES: 8 SERVINGS

- 1 jar (7 oz.) julienned oil-packed sun-dried tomatoes, drained and chopped
- ¼ cup orange juice
- ¾ cup mayonnaise
- 8 oz. crumbled feta cheese
- ⅓ cup crushed saltines
- 1 large egg, lightly beaten
- 3 Tbsp. finely chopped red onion
- 2 Tbsp. snipped fresh dill
- 1 lb. salmon fillet, skinned, cut into 1-in. cubes
- 2 Tbsp. olive oil
- 8 mini pretzel buns, toasted
- 16 hamburger dill pickle slices

1. Place tomatoes and orange juice in a small saucepan. Bring to a boil; reduce heat. Simmer, uncovered, until thickened, about 15 minutes. Cool completely. Transfer to a small bowl; stir in mayonnaise. Refrigerate until serving.
2. Meanwhile, in a large bowl, combine the feta, saltines, egg, red onion and dill. Place salmon in a food processor; pulse until coarsely chopped and add to the feta mixture. Mix lightly but thoroughly. Shape into eight 1-in.-thick patties.
3. In a large skillet, heat oil over medium-high heat. Add patties in batches; cook until golden brown, 3-4 minutes on each side. Serve on buns with mayonnaise mixture and pickles.
1 SLIDER: 515 cal., 35g fat (8g sat. fat), 68mg chol., 738mg sod., 31g carb. (3g sugars, 4g fiber), 20g pro.

PEANUT BUTTER, HONEY & PEAR OPEN-FACED SANDWICHES

I work a 12-hour night shift at a hospital, and when I come home in the morning, I don't feel like cooking a big breakfast. I love these sandwiches because they're versatile; sometimes I use apples instead of pears, and different cheeses, such as Brie or grated Parmesan.
—*L.J. Washington, Carpinteria, CA*

TAKES: 10 MIN. • **MAKES:** 4 SERVINGS

- ¼ cup chunky peanut butter
- 4 slices honey whole wheat bread, toasted
- 1 medium pear, thinly sliced
- ¼ tsp. salt
- 4 tsp. honey
- ½ cup shredded cheddar cheese

Spread peanut butter over toast slices. Top with pear, salt, honey and cheese. Place on a microwave-safe plate; microwave on high until cheese is melted, 20-25 seconds.
1 OPEN-FACED SANDWICH: 268 cal., 14g fat (4g sat. fat), 14mg chol., 446mg sod., 28g carb. (13g sugars, 4g fiber), 11g pro.

PEANUT BUTTER, HONEY & PEAR OPEN-FACED SANDWICHES

BACON & DATE GOAT CHEESE BURGERS

This burger is a rich and decadent combination of sweet and savory in every bite. If you can't find maple bacon in your local store, you can add 1½ tablespoons maple syrup to the spinach-goat cheese mixture in the food processor and use regular bacon.
—Sharon Michelle Anglin, Livingston, MT

PREP: 30 MIN. • **GRILL:** 10 MIN.
MAKES: 6 SERVINGS

- 2¾ cups fresh baby spinach, divided
- 1 pkg. (8 oz.) pistachios, shelled
- 2 Tbsp. lemon juice
- 2 garlic cloves, halved
- ½ to 1½ tsp. crushed red pepper flakes
- ¼ tsp. salt
- ¼ tsp. pepper
- 1 pkg. (5.3 oz.) fresh goat cheese, crumbled
- ¼ cup olive oil
- 1½ lbs. ground beef
- 1 pkg. (8 oz.) pitted dates, chopped
- 6 brioche hamburger buns, split
- ½ lb. maple-flavored bacon strips, cooked
- 1 medium red onion, sliced

1. Place 2 cups spinach, pistachios, lemon juice, garlic, pepper flakes, salt and pepper in a food processor; pulse until chopped. Add goat cheese; process until blended. Continue processing while gradually adding oil in a steady stream to reach a spreadable consistency. Refrigerate until serving.
2. Meanwhile, in a large bowl, combine beef and dates, mixing lightly but thoroughly. Shape into six ½-in.-thick patties. Place burgers on an oiled grill rack or in a greased 15x10x1-in. pan. Grill, covered, over medium heat or broil 4-5 in. from heat until a thermometer reads 160°, 4-5 minutes per side. Grill buns, cut sides down, over medium heat until toasted.
3. Top bun bottoms with remaining spinach, burgers, red onion and the bacon. Spread 4 tsp. goat cheese mixture over cut side of each bun top; place on burger. Cover and refrigerate remaining goat cheese mixture; save for another use.
1 BURGER: *804 cal., 45g fat (11g sat. fat), 118mg chol., 788mg sod., 67g carb. (34g sugars, 9g fiber), 39g pro.*

CRAB & ASPARAGUS SOUP

CRAB & ASPARAGUS SOUP

I get rave reviews from family and friends whenever I make this soup, but the biggest compliment was when my son called to ask for the recipe so he could make it for his roommates.
—Patti Bogetti, Magnolia, DE

PREP: 25 MIN. • **COOK:** 40 MIN.
MAKES: 6 SERVINGS

- 1¼ cups chopped sweet onion
- 1 celery rib, chopped
- 2 Tbsp. butter
- 2 Tbsp. all-purpose flour
- ½ tsp. seafood seasoning
- ¼ tsp. salt
- ¼ tsp. pepper
- ⅛ tsp. ground nutmeg
- 1 cup water
- 1½ tsp. chicken bouillon granules
- 2 medium red potatoes, cubed
- 8 oz. fresh asparagus, cut into ¾-in. pieces
- 2 cups half-and-half cream
- 1 can (6½ oz.) lump crabmeat, drained
- 2 tsp. minced fresh parsley

Optional toppings: Chopped fresh parsley and cracked pepper

1. In a large saucepan, saute onion and celery in butter. Stir in the flour, seafood seasoning, salt, pepper and nutmeg until blended; gradually add water and bouillon. Bring to a boil; cook and stir for 2 minutes or until thickened. Stir in potatoes. Reduce heat; simmer, uncovered, for 10 minutes.
2. Add asparagus; cook 8-12 minutes longer or until vegetables are tender. Stir in cream, crab and minced parsley; heat through. If desired, top with parsley and pepper.
¾ CUP: *257 cal., 12g fat (8g sat. fat), 78mg chol., 546mg sod., 22g carb. (6g sugars, 2g fiber), 12g pro.*

TEST KITCHEN TIP

In order to keep asparagus fresh longer, place the cut stems in a container of cold water—similar to flowers in a vase. Place the container in the refrigerator, changing the water at least once every 2 days.

The Elvis Sandwich
Top with ½ medium banana, sliced, and 1 bacon strip, cooked and crumbled.

Thai-Inspired Roast Beef Sandwich
Top with 2 thin slices deli roast beef, 1 tsp. chopped salted peanuts, ½ tsp. grated lime zest and ⅛ tsp. crushed red pepper flakes.

PB & YAY!

This time, put down the jelly and create an over-the-top peanut butter sandwich.

It's simple! To start, spread 2 Tbsp. creamy peanut butter over 1 slice of bread. We like the crusty bakery kind for stability, but take your pick. Then, get to topping!

Southern Peanut Butter Mayo Sandwich
Combine 1 Tbsp. each mayonnaise and creamy peanut butter; spread over bread instead of plain peanut butter to start. Top with 2 Tbsp. shredded cheddar.

Peanut Butter, Chicken & Basil Sandwich
Top with 3 Tbsp. shredded cooked chicken, 1 Tbsp. torn fresh basil and ⅛ tsp. sea salt. Drizzle with 1 tsp. extra virgin olive oil.

Peanut Butter, Apple & Raisin Sandwich
Top with ½ medium apple, thinly sliced, and 1 Tbsp. golden raisins. Sprinkle with ⅛ tsp. ground cinnamon.

Peanut Butter S'mores Sandwich
Place on a baking sheet; top with 1 Tbsp. milk chocolate chips and 2 Tbsp. miniature marshmallows. Broil 4-5 in. from heat until lightly browned, 30-60 seconds.

Peanut Butter, Strawberry & Honey Sandwich
Top with ¼ cup sliced fresh strawberries and 1 tsp. thinly sliced fresh mint; drizzle with 1 tsp. honey.

Peanut Butter, Krispies & Chocolate Sandwich
Top with 2 Tbsp. Rice Krispies and 1 tsp. grated dark chocolate candy bar.

Peanut Butter, Pickle & Potato Chip Sandwich
Top with 1 whole dill pickle, sliced, and 2 Tbsp. slightly crushed kettle-cooked potato chips.

Spicy Peanut Butter & Pork Sandwich
Layer with 2 Tbsp. shredded cooked pork and 1 tsp. Sriracha chili sauce. Sprinkle with curry powder; top with thinly sliced jalapeno pepper.

THE BEST EVER CHILI

My dad and my father-in-law are the gurus in our chili-loving clan. But after my honeymoon to New Mexico, inspired by the fresh and fragrant chile peppers at the Santa Fe farmers market, I felt it was time to introduce them to my spicy, meaty version with a touch of masa harina.
—Sarah Farmer, Waukesha, WI

PREP: 20 MIN. • **COOK:** 1 HOUR 20 MIN.
MAKES: 8 SERVINGS

- 3 dried ancho or guajillo chiles
- 1 to 2 cups boiling water
- 2 Tbsp. tomato paste
- 3 garlic cloves
- ¼ cup chili powder
- 1½ tsp. smoked paprika
- 2 tsp. ground cumin
- 1 lb. ground beef
- 1½ tsp. Montreal steak seasoning
- 2 lbs. beef tri-tip roast, cut into ½-in. cubes
- 2 tsp. salt, divided
- 2 tsp. coarsely ground pepper, divided
- 2 Tbsp. canola oil, divided
- 1 large onion, chopped (about 2 cups)
- 1 poblano pepper, seeded and chopped
- 1 tsp. dried oregano
- 1½ tsp. crushed red pepper flakes
- 3 cups beef stock
- 1 bottle (12 oz.) beer
- 2 cans (14½ oz. each) fire-roasted diced tomatoes, undrained
- 1 can (16 oz.) kidney beans, drained
- 3 Tbsp. masa harina
  American cheese slices, sour cream, shredded cheddar cheese, diced red onion and corn chips, optional

1. Combine chiles and enough boiling water to cover; let stand until softened, about 15 minutes. Drain, reserving ⅓ cup of the soaking liquid. Discard stems and seeds. Process chiles, tomato paste, garlic and reserved liquid until smooth.

2. In a small skillet, toast chili powder, paprika and cumin over medium heat until aromatic, 3-4 minutes; remove and set aside. In a Dutch oven, cook and stir ground beef and steak seasoning over medium-high heat until beef is no longer pink, about 5 minutes; remove and drain.

3. Sprinkle steak cubes with 1 tsp. each salt and pepper. In same Dutch oven, brown beef in batches in 1 Tbsp. oil over medium-high heat; remove and set aside. Saute onion and poblano pepper in the remaining 1 Tbsp. oil until tender, about 5 minutes. Stir in toasted spices, oregano and pepper flakes. Add the cooked meats along with stock, beer, tomatoes, beans, remaining salt and pepper, and chile paste mixture. Cook over medium heat for 20 minutes; reduce heat to low. Stir in masa; simmer 30-45 minutes longer. Serve with desired toppings.

FREEZE OPTION: Freeze cooled chili in freezer containers. To use, partially thaw in refrigerator overnight. Heat through in a saucepan, stirring occasionally; add a little broth or water if necessary.

1¾ CUPS: *473 cal., 20g fat (6g sat. fat), 103mg chol., 1554mg sod., 29g carb. (8g sugars, 7g fiber), 41g pro.*

THE BEST EVER CHILI

TEST KITCHEN TIP

While this chili is fantastic right out of the pot, as with a lot of soups, stews and other chilis, it tastes even better the next day.

FIG, CARAMELIZED ONION & GOAT CHEESE PANINI

CRANBERRY-WALNUT CHICKEN SALAD SANDWICHES

I made these simple yet special sandwiches for a birthday party. Tangy cranberries and crunchy celery pep up the chicken. Leftover turkey works well, too.
—Shannon Tucker, Land O' Lakes, FL

TAKES: 15 MIN. • **MAKES:** 8 SERVINGS

- ½ cup mayonnaise
- 2 Tbsp. honey Dijon mustard
- ¼ tsp. pepper
- 2 cups cubed rotisserie chicken
- 1 cup shredded Swiss cheese
- ½ cup chopped celery
- ½ cup dried cranberries
- ¼ cup chopped walnuts
- ½ tsp. dried parsley flakes
- 8 lettuce leaves
- 16 slices pumpernickel bread

1. In a large bowl, combine mayonnaise, mustard and pepper. Stir in the chicken, cheese, celery, cranberries, walnuts and parsley.

2. Place lettuce on 8 slices of bread; top each with ½ cup chicken salad. Top with remaining bread.
1 SANDWICH: *411 cal., 22g fat (5g sat. fat), 49mg chol., 469mg sod., 35g carb. (7g sugars, 5g fiber), 20g pro.*

FIG, CARAMELIZED ONION & GOAT CHEESE PANINI

A taste of this sandwich whisks you to the Italian countryside. It combines sweet honey, dried figs, tangy goat cheese, nutty Asiago and salty prosciutto. We often pack it in our picnic basket for summer or fall outings.
—Maria Brennan, Middlebury, CT

PREP: 1 HOUR • **GRILL:** 5 MIN./BATCH
MAKES: 6 SERVINGS

- 6 Tbsp. butter, divided
- 3 large onions, halved and thinly sliced
- 1 Tbsp. sugar
- ¼ tsp. salt
- 12 dried figs, sliced
- 1 cup water
- 3 Tbsp. honey
- 12 slices slices Italian bread (½ in. thick)
- 8 oz. Asiago cheese, sliced
- 12 thin slices prosciutto
- ¾ cup crumbled goat cheese
  Balsamic glaze, optional

1. In a large skillet, heat 2 Tbsp. butter over medium heat. Add onions, sugar and salt; cook and stir until softened, about 15 minutes. Reduce heat to medium-low; cook until onions are deep golden brown, 30-40 minutes, stirring occasionally.
2. Meanwhile, place figs, water and honey in a small saucepan. Bring to a boil; reduce heat. Simmer, uncovered, until liquid is almost evaporated, about 20 minutes.
3. Preheat panini maker or indoor electric grill. Layer 6 slices of bread with Asiago cheese, prosciutto, goat cheese, caramelized onions and figs; top with remaining bread. Spread outsides of sandwiches with remaining butter.
4. Cook sandwiches, covered, until bread is browned and the cheese is melted, 4-5 minutes. If desired, drizzle with balsamic glaze.
1 SANDWICH: *572 cal., 31g fat (18g sat. fat), 108mg chol., 1144mg sod., 52g carb. (25g sugars, 5g fiber), 26g pro.*

CHINESE SCALLION PANCAKE BEEF ROLLS

CHICKEN PARMESAN BURGERS

(SHOWN ON PAGE 32)

A restaurant-quality burger that's topped with marinara and loaded with cheese—what's not to love? Fresh basil adds even more flavor if you like.
—Brooke Petras, Alpine, CA

TAKES: 30 MIN. • **MAKES:** 4 SERVINGS

- 3 Tbsp. olive oil, divided
- 1 small onion, finely chopped
- 2 garlic cloves, minced
- ¾ cup marinara sauce, divided
- ½ cup finely chopped or shredded part-skim mozzarella cheese
- ½ cup dry bread crumbs
- 1 tsp. Italian seasoning
- 1 tsp. dried oregano
- ½ tsp. salt
- ½ tsp. pepper
- 1 lb. ground chicken
- 4 slices part-skim mozzarella cheese
- 4 hamburger buns, split and toasted
- ¼ cup shredded Parmesan cheese
  Fresh basil leaves, optional

1. In a large skillet, heat 1 Tbsp. oil over medium-high heat. Add onion; cook and stir until tender, about 3 minutes. Add garlic; cook 1 minute longer. Remove from heat; cool slightly.
2. In a large bowl, combine ¼ cup marinara sauce, chopped mozzarella cheese, bread crumbs, seasonings and onion mixture. Add the chicken; mix lightly but thoroughly. With wet hands, shape mixture into four ½-in.-thick patties.
3. In the same skillet, heat the remaining 2 Tbsp. oil over medium heat. Cook the burgers until a thermometer reads 165°, 4-5 minutes on each side. Top with sliced mozzarella cheese; cook, covered, until cheese is melted, 1-2 minutes.
4. Serve in buns; top with remaining ½ cup marinara sauce, Parmesan cheese and, if desired, basil leaves.
1 BURGER: *603 cal., 33g fat (10g sat. fat), 108mg chol., 1275mg sod., 41g carb. (8g sugars, 3g fiber), 38g pro.*

CHINESE SCALLION PANCAKE BEEF ROLLS

This is a favorite in our household, and it's perfect for using up leftover roast beef. The green onion cake dough is easy to make and cooks quickly. Then just reheat the sliced beef in a frying pan with a sweet and savory sauce.
—Carla Mendres, Winnipeg, MB

PREP: 45 MIN. + STANDING • **COOK:** 40 MIN.
MAKES: 8 SERVINGS

- 2½ cups all-purpose flour
- 1 tsp. salt
- 1 cup boiling water
- 1 bunch green onions, finely chopped
- ½ cup canola oil
- 1 Tbsp. sesame oil
- 1 small onion, thinly sliced
- 2 garlic cloves, minced
- 1 tsp. minced fresh gingerroot
- 1 pkg. (15 oz.) refrigerated beef roast au jus, drained and chopped, or 2 cups chopped cooked roast beef
- 3 Tbsp. soy sauce
- 2 Tbsp. hoisin sauce
- 1 Tbsp. honey

1. Place flour and salt in a large bowl; stir in boiling water until dough forms a ball. Turn onto a floured surface; knead until smooth and elastic, 4-6 minutes. Place in a large bowl; cover and let rest for 30 minutes.
2. Divide dough into 8 portions; roll each portion into an 8-in. circle. Sprinkle each with 1 Tbsp. green onion. Roll up jelly-roll style; holding 1 end of the rope, wrap dough around, forming a coil, pinching to seal. Flatten slightly. Roll each coil to ⅛-in. thickness.
3. In a large skillet, heat 1 Tbsp. canola oil. Cook pancakes, 1 at a time, over medium-high heat until golden brown, 2-3 minutes on each side, adding additional oil as needed; keep warm.
4. In the same skillet, heat sesame oil over medium-high heat. Add onion, garlic and ginger; cook and stir until tender, 5-6 minutes. Add the remaining ingredients; cook until heated through, 3-4 minutes longer. Spoon about ¼ cup beef mixture down center of each pancake. If desired, sprinkle with sliced green onions. Roll up tightly and serve.
1 ROLL: *390 cal., 20g fat (3g sat. fat), 32mg chol., 898mg sod., 37g carb. (5g sugars, 2g fiber), 16g pro.*

LOBSTER ROLLS

Mayonnaise infused with dill and lemon lends refreshing flavor to these super sandwiches. Try pan-toasting the buns in butter for something special.
—Taste of Home *Test Kitchen*

TAKES: 30 MIN. • **MAKES:** 8 SERVINGS

1	cup chopped celery
⅓	cup mayonnaise
2	Tbsp. lemon juice
½	tsp. dill weed
5	cups cubed cooked lobster meat (about 4 small lobsters)
8	hoagie rolls, split and toasted

In a large bowl, combine the celery, mayonnaise, lemon juice and dill weed. Gently stir in lobster. Serve on rolls.

1 SANDWICH: *354 cal., 12g fat (2g sat. fat), 133mg chol., 887mg sod., 36g carb. (5g sugars, 1g fiber), 25g pro.*

CHICKEN CORDON BLEU SOUP

LOBSTER ROLLS

CHICKEN CORDON BLEU SOUP

This is a wonderful addition to potlucks, and it comes together so easily! Cauliflower makes a nice, extra-creamy backdrop for the classic flavors of chicken cordon bleu you can eat with a spoon.
—Heidi Der, Stow, OH

PREP: 15 MIN. • **COOK:** 25 MIN. • **MAKES:** 6 SERVINGS (2 QT.)

2	Tbsp. butter
2	Tbsp. olive oil
1	small head cauliflower, coarsely chopped
1	medium onion, chopped
1	garlic clove, minced
3	Tbsp. all-purpose flour
2	cups chicken broth
2	cups shredded cooked chicken
2	cups half-and-half cream
1	cup finely cubed fully cooked ham
1	Tbsp. Dijon mustard
1	tsp. salt
½	tsp. pepper
2	cups shredded Swiss cheese

1. In a large saucepan, heat butter and oil over medium-high heat. Add cauliflower and onion; cook and stir until crisp-tender, 8-10 minutes. Add garlic; cook 1 minute longer. Stir in flour until blended; gradually whisk in broth. Bring to a boil, stirring constantly; cook and stir until cauliflower is tender, 12-15 minutes.
2. Puree soup using an immersion blender. Or, cool soup slightly and puree in batches in a blender; return to pan. Stir in chicken, cream, ham, mustard, salt and pepper; heat through. Stir in cheese until melted.

1⅓ CUPS: *481 cal., 32g fat (16g sat. fat), 141mg chol., 1254mg sod., 11g carb. (5g sugars, 1g fiber), 33g pro.*

HEARTY VEGETABLE SPLIT PEA SOUP

HEARTY VEGETABLE SPLIT PEA SOUP

This slow-cooked soup is my secret weapon on busy days. It's delicious served with oyster crackers that are tossed in a bit of melted butter and herbs and then lightly toasted in the oven.
—Whitney Jensen, Spring Lake, MI

PREP: 10 MIN. • **COOK:** 7 HOURS • **MAKES:** 8 SERVINGS (2 QT.)

- 1 pkg. (16 oz.) dried green split peas, rinsed
- 1 large carrot, chopped
- 1 celery rib, chopped
- 1 small onion, chopped
- 1 bay leaf
- 1½ tsp. salt
- ½ tsp. dried thyme
- ½ tsp. pepper
- 6 cups water

In a 3- or 4-qt. slow cooker, combine all ingredients. Cook, covered, on low 7-9 hours or until peas are tender. Stir before serving. Discard bay leaf.

FREEZE OPTION: Freeze cooled soup in freezer containers. To use, partially thaw in refrigerator overnight. Heat through in a saucepan, stirring occasionally; add water if necessary.

1 CUP: *202 cal., 1g fat (0 sat. fat), 0 chol., 462mg sod., 36g carb. (5g sugars, 15g fiber), 14g pro.* **Diabetic exchanges:** *2 starch, 1 lean meat.*

Pea Soup with Ham: Add 2 cups cubed cooked ham and 2 minced garlic cloves. Decrease water to 5 cups. Cook as directed. Stir in 1 cup milk; heat through.

Curried Ham & Split Pea Soup: Add 2 cups cubed cooked ham, 1 Tbsp. curry powder and 4 minced garlic cloves. Decrease water to 2 cups; add 4 cups reduced-sodium beef broth. Cook as directed.

SWEET & SPICY PEANUT BUTTER-BACON SANDWICHES

I craved peanut butter and bacon toast while pregnant. Then I sampled a friend's peanut butter with chile pepper in it and loved it. The little zip made the sandwich better.
—Carolyn Eskew, Dayton, OH

TAKES: 10 MIN. • **MAKES:** 2 SERVINGS

- ¼ cup peanut butter
- 4 slices cinnamon-raisin bread
- ⅛ tsp. cayenne pepper
- 4 crisp cooked bacon strips
- 2 tsp. honey

Spread peanut butter on 2 bread slices; sprinkle with cayenne. Top with bacon and drizzle with honey. Top with remaining bread.

1 SANDWICH: *461 cal., 26g fat (6g sat. fat), 23mg chol., 664mg sod., 43g carb. (15g sugars, 6g fiber), 21g pro.*

READER REVIEW

"I didn't have cinnamon-raisin bread, so I improvised. I usually sprinkle my peanut butter toast with cinnamon and hot pepper, so I just sprinkled on a few raisins after toasting my bread. Oh, my goodness...it was a mouthful of pleasure. I made the toast open-faced to cut down on the bread. Will definitely keep this method of peanut butter toast!"
—ANNRMS, TASTEOFHOME.COM

SWEET & SPICY PEANUT BUTTER-BACON SANDWICHES

STEAK SANDWICHES WITH QUICK-PICKLED VEGETABLES

This recipe is a Cambodian version of the classic Vietnamese dish banh mi. This sandwich has acidity from the pickled vegetables, freshness from the cucumber, spiciness from the sriracha mayo, and sweetness from the marinated beef.
—*Hudson Stiver, Bowen Island, BC*

PREP: 30 MIN. + MARINATING
COOK: 15 MIN. + STANDING
MAKES: 6 SERVINGS

- 1 cup white vinegar
- 1 Tbsp. sugar
- 1½ cups thinly sliced fresh carrots
- 1 small daikon radish, thinly sliced
- ¼ cup packed brown sugar
- ¼ cup rice vinegar
- ¼ cup soy sauce
- 1 beef top sirloin steak (1¼ lbs.)
- 1 Tbsp. olive oil
- 1 French bread baguette (10½ oz.), halved lengthwise
- ½ cup mayonnaise
- 2 Tbsp. Sriracha chili sauce
- ½ cup thinly sliced English cucumber
    Fresh cilantro leaves

1. Whisk white vinegar and sugar until sugar is dissolved. Add carrots and radish. Refrigerate at least 2 hours. Meanwhile, in a shallow dish, combine brown sugar, rice vinegar and soy sauce. Add beef and turn to coat. Refrigerate 1 hour, turning once. Drain beef, discarding marinade.
2. In a large skillet, heat oil over medium-high heat. Cook steak to desired doneness (for medium-rare, a thermometer should read 135°; medium, 140°; medium-well, 145°), 7-10 minutes on each side. Let rest 10 minutes before slicing.
3. Meanwhile, place the baguette on an ungreased baking sheet, cut sides up. Broil 3-4 in. from heat until golden brown, 3-4 minutes. Drain carrots and radish, reserving 1½ tsp. vinegar marinade. In a bowl, combine mayonnaise, chili sauce and reserved vinegar marinade; spread half over cut sides of baguette. Top with steak, cucumber, pickled vegetables and cilantro; replace top. Cut crosswise into 6 slices. Serve with remaining mayonnaise mixture.
1 SANDWICH: *430 cal., 20g fat (4g sat. fat), 40mg chol., 888mg sod., 37g carb. (9g sugars, 2g fiber), 25g pro.*

CHEESY BROCCOLI SOUP IN A BREAD BOWL

CHEESY BROCCOLI SOUP IN A BREAD BOWL

This creamy, rich, cheesy broccoli soup tastes just like one from a restaurant! My family requests it all the time. You can even make your own homemade bread bowls if you'd like.
—*Rachel Preus, Marshall, MI*

PREP: 15 MIN. • **COOK:** 30 MIN.
MAKES: 6 SERVINGS

- ¼ cup butter, cubed
- ½ cup chopped onion
- 2 garlic cloves, minced
- 4 cups fresh broccoli florets (about 8 oz.)
- 1 large carrot, finely chopped
- 3 cups chicken stock
- 2 cups half-and-half cream
- 2 bay leaves
- ½ tsp. salt
- ¼ tsp. ground nutmeg
- ¼ tsp. pepper
- ¼ cup cornstarch
- ¼ cup water or additional chicken stock
- 2½ cups shredded cheddar cheese
- 6 small round bread loaves (about 8 oz. each), optional
    Optional toppings: Crumbled cooked bacon, additional shredded cheddar cheese, ground nutmeg and pepper

1. In a 6-qt. stockpot, heat butter over medium heat; saute onion and garlic until tender, 6-8 minutes. Stir in broccoli, carrot, stock, cream and seasonings; bring to a boil. Simmer, uncovered, until vegetables are tender, 10-12 minutes.
2. Mix cornstarch and water until smooth; stir into soup. Bring to a boil, stirring occasionally; cook and stir until thickened, 1-2 minutes. Remove bay leaves. Stir in cheese until melted.
3. If using bread bowls, cut a slice off the top of each bread loaf; hollow out bottoms, leaving ¼-in.-thick shells (save removed bread for another use). Fill with soup just before serving.
4. If desired, serve soup with toppings.
1 CUP SOUP: *422 cal., 32g fat (19g sat. fat), 107mg chol., 904mg sod., 15g carb. (5g sugars, 2g fiber), 17g pro.*

**BACON-CHICKEN CLUB PIZZA
PAGE 61**

Quick Fixes

Your busy lifestyle doesn't have to get in the way of your cooking. With these recipes ready in half an hour or less, dinner can be homemade and delicious every night.

HADDOCK EN PAPILLOTE

CHICKEN WITH PINEAPPLE

I'm always on the lookout for low-fat recipes that are scrumptious, too, like this one. In this dish, the quick-cooking chicken breasts get a wonderful, sweet flavor from pineapple, honey and teriyaki sauce.
—Jenny Reece, Lowry, MN

TAKES: 20 MIN. • **MAKES:** 4 SERVINGS

- 4   boneless skinless chicken breast halves (4 oz. each)
- 1   Tbsp. all-purpose flour
- 1   Tbsp. canola oil
- 2   cans (8 oz. each) unsweetened pineapple chunks
- 1   tsp. cornstarch
- 1   Tbsp. honey
- 1   Tbsp. reduced-sodium teriyaki sauce or reduced-sodium soy sauce
- ⅛   tsp. pepper
     Hot cooked rice

1. Flatten the chicken to ¼-in. thickness. Place flour in a large shallow dish; add the chicken and turn to coat.
2. In a large skillet, brown the chicken over medium heat in oil until the juices run clear, 3-5 minutes on each side. Remove and keep warm. Drain pineapple, reserving ¼ cup juice. (Discard remaining juice or save for another use.)
3. In a small bowl, combine cornstarch and reserved juice until smooth. Gradually add to skillet. Stir in the honey, teriyaki sauce and pepper. Bring to a boil. Cook and stir until thickened, about 30 seconds. Add the pineapple and chicken; heat through. Serve with rice.
1 SERVING: *247 cal., 6g fat (1g sat. fat), 63mg chol., 135mg sod., 22g carb. (19g sugars, 1g fiber), 24g pro.* **Diabetic exchanges:** *3 lean meat, 1 fruit, ½ starch, ½ fat.*

HADDOCK EN PAPILLOTE

This is a great dish for entertaining. It's easy to prepare, yet impressive. You can also make up the bundles earlier in the day and then pop them in the oven 15 minutes before you want dinner on the table.
—Amanda Singleton, Rogersville, TN

TAKES: 30 MIN. • **MAKES:** 4 SERVINGS

- 1½ lbs. haddock or cod fillets, cut into 4 portions
- 4   Tbsp. dry white wine
- 2   tsp. snipped fresh dill or 1 tsp. dill weed
- 1   tsp. grated lemon zest
- ½   cup julienned carrot
- ½   cup julienned zucchini
- 4   Tbsp. slivered almonds, toasted
- 4   Tbsp. butter

1. Preheat oven to 375°. Place each fillet on a piece of heavy-duty foil or parchment (about 12 in. square) . Drizzle fillets with wine; sprinkle with dill and lemon zest. Top with carrot, zucchini and almonds; dot with butter. Fold foil or parchment around fish, sealing tightly.
2. Place packets on a baking sheet. Bake until fish just begins to flake easily with a fork, 10-12 minutes. Open foil carefully to allow steam to escape.
1 PACKET: *311 cal., 16g fat (8g sat. fat), 129mg chol., 219mg sod., 4g carb. (2g sugars, 1g fiber), 34g pro.*

TEST KITCHEN TIP

Looking for a knockout grilled supper? Make foil packets and grill for about 10 minutes. Any meaty fish will work nicely. Cod is a good substitute for the haddock.

BRAISED PORK LOIN CHOPS

An easy herb rub gives sensational taste to these pork chops.
The meat turns out tender and delicious.
—Marilyn Larsen, Port Orange, FL

TAKES: 30 MIN. • **MAKES:** 4 SERVINGS

1	garlic clove, minced
1	tsp. rubbed sage
1	tsp. dried rosemary, crushed
½	tsp. salt
⅛	tsp. pepper
4	boneless pork loin chops (½ in. thick and 4 oz. each)
1	Tbsp. butter
1	Tbsp. olive oil
¾	cup dry white wine or apple juice
1	Tbsp. minced fresh parsley

1. Mix first 5 ingredients; rub over both sides of pork chops. In a large nonstick skillet, heat butter and oil over medium-high heat; brown chops on both sides. Remove from pan.
2. In same pan, bring wine to a boil, stirring to loosen browned bits from pan. Cook, uncovered, until liquid is reduced to ½ cup. Add chops; return to a boil. Reduce heat; simmer, covered, until pork is tender, 6-8 minutes. Sprinkle with parsley.
1 PORK CHOP WITH 2 TBSP. SAUCE: *218 cal., 13g fat (5g sat. fat), 62mg chol., 351mg sod., 3g carb. (2g sugars, 0 fiber), 22g pro.* **Diabetic exchanges:** *3 lean meat, 1½ fat.*

BRAISED PORK LOIN CHOPS

MEXI-MAC SKILLET

MEXI-MAC SKILLET

My husband loves this recipe, and I love how simple it is to put together! Because you don't need to precook the macaroni, it's a timesaving dish.
—Maurane Ramsey, Fort Wayne, IN

TAKES: 30 MIN. • **MAKES:** 4 SERVINGS

1	lb. extra-lean ground beef (95% lean)
1	large onion, chopped
1¼	tsp. chili powder
1	tsp. dried oregano
¼	tsp. salt
1	can (14½ oz.) diced tomatoes, undrained
1	can (8 oz.) tomato sauce
1	cup fresh or frozen corn
½	cup water
⅔	cup uncooked elbow macaroni
½	cup shredded reduced-fat cheddar cheese

1. In a large nonstick skillet, cook and crumble beef with onion over medium-high heat until no longer pink, 5-7 minutes.
2. Stir in seasonings, tomatoes, tomato sauce, corn and water; bring to a boil. Stir in macaroni. Reduce heat; simmer, covered, until macaroni is tender, 15-20 minutes, stirring occasionally. Sprinkle with cheese.
1¼ CUPS: *318 cal., 10g fat (4g sat. fat), 75mg chol., 755mg sod., 28g carb. (9g sugars, 5g fiber), 32g pro.* **Diabetic exchanges:** *1 starch, 3 lean meat, 1 vegetable.*

HEARTY PITA TACOS

You don't need to skimp on flavor when trying to eat healthy. Our 9-year-old daughter enjoys helping us make these tasty tacos, and she likes eating them even more.
—Jamie Valocchi, Mesa, AZ

TAKES: 30 MIN. • **MAKES:** 6 SERVINGS

- 1 lb. lean ground beef (90% lean)
- 1 small sweet red pepper, chopped
- 2 green onions, chopped
- 1 can (16 oz.) kidney beans, rinsed and drained
- ¾ cup frozen corn
- ⅔ cup taco sauce
- 1 can (2¼ oz.) sliced ripe olives, drained
- ½ tsp. garlic salt
- ¼ tsp. onion powder
- ¼ tsp. dried oregano
- ¼ tsp. paprika
- ¼ tsp. pepper
- 6 whole wheat pita pocket halves
- 6 Tbsp. shredded reduced-fat cheddar cheese
  Optional: Sliced avocado and additional taco sauce

1. In a large skillet, cook the beef, red pepper and onions over medium heat until meat is no longer pink; drain. Stir in beans, corn, taco sauce, olives and seasonings; heat through.

2. Spoon ¾ cup beef mixture into each pita half. Sprinkle with cheese. Serve with avocado and additional taco sauce if desired.

1 SERVING: *339 cal., 10g fat (4g sat. fat), 52mg chol., 787mg sod., 38g carb. (4g sugars, 8g fiber), 26g pro.* **Diabetic exchanges:** *3 lean meat, 2½ starch.*

HEARTY PITA TACOS

EGG ROLL NOODLE BOWL

APPLESAUCE-GLAZED PORK CHOPS

These tasty, tender chops are glazed with a sweet, smoky apple-flavored sauce. They're on the table in no time at all, making them perfect for hectic weeknights.
—Brenda Campbell, Olympia, WA

TAKES: 30 MIN. • **MAKES:** 4 SERVINGS

    4   bone-in pork loin chops (½ in. thick and 7 oz. each)
    1   cup unsweetened applesauce
    ¼   cup packed brown sugar
    1   Tbsp. barbecue sauce
    1   Tbsp. Worcestershire sauce
    1   garlic clove, minced
    ½   tsp. salt
    ½   tsp. pepper

1. Preheat oven to 350°. Place pork chops in a large cast-iron or other ovenproof skillet. Mix remaining ingredients in a small bowl; spoon over chops.
2. Bake, uncovered, until a thermometer reads 145°, 20-25 minutes. Let stand for 5 minutes before serving.
1 CHOP: *295 cal., 9g fat (3g sat. fat), 86mg chol., 448mg sod., 23g carb. (21g sugars, 1g fiber), 30g pro.* **Diabetic exchanges:** *4 lean meat, 1 starch, ½ fruit.*
Pork Chops with Chili Sauce: Place chops in skillet; top each with an onion slice and green pepper ring. Spoon 1 bottle (12 oz.) chili sauce over top. Bake as directed.
Breaded Pork Chops: Beat 1 large egg in a shallow bowl; place ¾ cup seasoned bread crumbs in a second bowl. Dip chops in egg, then bread crumbs. Place in skillet and bake as directed. Serve with gravy if desired.

EGG ROLL NOODLE BOWL

We love Asian egg rolls, but they can be challenging to make. Simplify everything with this deconstructed egg roll made on the stovetop and served in a bowl.
—Courtney Stultz, Weir, KS

TAKES: 30 MIN. • **MAKES:** 4 SERVINGS

    1   Tbsp. sesame oil
    ½   lb. ground pork
    1   Tbsp. soy sauce
    1   garlic clove, minced
    1   tsp. ground ginger
    ½   tsp. salt
    ¼   tsp. ground turmeric
    ¼   tsp. pepper
    6   cups shredded cabbage (about 1 small head)
    2   large carrots, shredded (about 2 cups)
    4   oz. rice noodles
    3   green onions, thinly sliced
        Additional soy sauce, optional

1. In a large cast-iron or other heavy skillet, heat oil over medium-high heat; cook and crumble pork until browned, 4-6 minutes. Stir in soy sauce, garlic and seasonings. Add cabbage and carrots; cook until the vegetables are tender, stirring occasionally, 4-6 minutes longer.
2. Cook rice noodles according to package directions; drain and immediately add to pork mixture, tossing to combine. Sprinkle with green onions. If desired, serve with additional soy sauce.
1½ CUPS: *302 cal., 12g fat (4g sat. fat), 38mg chol., 652mg sod., 33g carb. (2g sugars, 4g fiber), 14g pro.* **Diabetic exchanges:** *2 medium-fat meat, 2 vegetable, 1½ starch, ½ fat.*

TEST KITCHEN TIP

Meatless Monday?

Try this dish with mushrooms, scrambled eggs or tofu instead of pork.

APPLESAUCE-GLAZED PORK CHOPS

LEMON-PARSLEY BAKED COD

LEMON-PARSLEY BAKED COD

After trying a few cod recipes, this was the first fish recipe that got two thumbs up from my picky "meat-only" eaters. The tangy lemon gives the cod some oomph.
—*Trisha Kruse, Eagle, ID*

TAKES: 30 MIN. • **MAKES:** 4 SERVINGS

- 3 Tbsp. lemon juice
- 3 Tbsp. butter, melted
- ¼ cup all-purpose flour
- ½ tsp. salt
- ¼ tsp. paprika
- ¼ tsp. lemon-pepper seasoning
- 4 cod fillets (6 oz. each)
- 2 Tbsp. minced fresh parsley
- 2 tsp. grated lemon zest

1. Preheat oven to 400°. In a shallow bowl, mix lemon juice and butter. In a separate shallow bowl, mix flour and seasonings. Dip fillets in lemon juice mixture, then in flour mixture to coat both sides; shake off excess.

2. Place in a 13x9-in. baking dish coated with cooking spray. Drizzle with remaining lemon juice mixture. Bake 12-15 minutes or until fish just begins to flake easily with a fork. Mix parsley and lemon zest; sprinkle over fish.

1 FILLET: *232 cal., 10g fat (6g sat. fat), 87mg chol., 477mg sod., 7g carb. (0 sugars, 0 fiber), 28g pro.* **Diabetic exchanges:** *4 lean meat, 2 fat, ½ starch.*

TEST KITCHEN TIP

Go for freshly squeezed lemon juice when preparing this dish. Bottled lemon juice, which is from concentrate, won't provide the same bright, fresh flavor. Buy 4 lemons to get the job done.

CREAMY SHRIMP PASTA

Whip up a restaurant favorite at home with our simple recipe. Jarred Alfredo sauce makes it a snap!
—*Taste of Home Test Kitchen*

TAKES: 20 MIN. • **MAKES:** 4 SERVINGS

- 1 pkg. (9 oz.) refrigerated fettuccine
- ½ lb. sliced fresh mushrooms
- ½ cup chopped onion
- 1 Tbsp. butter
- 1 jar (15 oz.) Alfredo sauce
- 1 pkg. (10 oz.) fresh baby spinach, chopped
- 1 lb. peeled and deveined cooked shrimp (31-40 per lb.)

Cook fettuccine according to the package directions. Saute mushrooms and onion in butter in a large skillet until tender. Stir in the Alfredo sauce, spinach and shrimp; heat through. Drain fettuccine; add to sauce and toss to coat.

1 SERVING: *519 cal., 18g fat (10g sat. fat), 244mg chol., 810mg sod., 50g carb. (3g sugars, 6g fiber), 39g pro.*

CREAMY CURRIED CHICKEN

This is a big hit in our house. My young son and daughter gobble it up. With its irresistible blend of curry and sweet coconut milk, it'll become a favorite with your family, too.
—Tracy Simiele, Chardon, OH

TAKES: 30 MIN. • **MAKES:** 4 SERVINGS

  1½ cups uncooked instant rice
  1   lb. boneless skinless chicken breasts, cut into 1-in. pieces
  2   tsp. curry powder
  ¾   tsp. salt
  ¼   tsp. pepper
  ½   cup chopped onion
  1   Tbsp. canola oil
  1   can (13.66 oz.) coconut milk
  2   Tbsp. tomato paste
  3   cups fresh baby spinach
  1   cup chopped tomato

1. Cook rice according to package directions. Meanwhile, sprinkle the chicken with curry, salt and pepper. In a large skillet, saute the chicken and onion in oil until chicken is no longer pink.
2. Stir in coconut milk and tomato paste. Bring to a boil. Reduce heat; simmer, uncovered, for 5 minutes or until thickened. Add spinach and tomato; cook 2-3 minutes longer or until spinach is wilted. Serve with rice.
1 CUP CHICKEN MIXTURE WITH ¾ CUP RICE: *508 cal., 27g fat (19g sat. fat), 63mg chol., 541mg sod., 39g carb. (6g sugars, 4g fiber), 29g pro.*

ONE-POT DINNER

CREAMY CURRIED CHICKEN

ONE-POT DINNER

Everyone comes back for seconds when I serve this well-seasoned skillet supper. I like the fact that it's on the table in just 30 minutes.
—Bonnie Morrow, Spencerport, NY

TAKES: 30 MIN. • **MAKES:** 5 SERVINGS

  ½   lb. ground beef
  1   medium onion, chopped
  1   cup chopped celery
  ¾   cup chopped green pepper
  2   tsp. Worcestershire sauce
  1   tsp. salt, optional
  ½   tsp. dried basil
  ¼   tsp. pepper
  2   cups uncooked medium egg noodles
  1   can (16 oz.) kidney beans, rinsed and drained
  1   can (14½ oz.) stewed tomatoes
  ¾   cup water
  1   beef bouillon cube

1. In a large saucepan or skillet, cook the beef, onion, celery and green pepper over medium heat until meat is no longer pink and vegetables are crisp-tender; drain. Add Worcestershire sauce, salt if desired, basil and pepper. Stir in the noodles, beans, tomatoes, water and bouillon.
2. Bring to a boil. Reduce heat; cover and simmer for 20 minutes or until noodles are tender, stirring occasionally.
1 CUP: *263 cal., 6g fat (2g sat. fat), 41mg chol., 535mg sod., 36g carb. (8g sugars, 7g fiber), 17g pro.*

MEDITERRANEAN PORK & ORZO

QUICK CHICKEN PICCATA

Laced with lemon and simmered in white wine, this stovetop entree is super easy and elegant. Almost any side—noodles, veggies or bread—tastes better next to this lovely chicken.
—Cynthia Heil, Augusta, GA

TAKES: 30 MIN. • **MAKES:** 4 SERVINGS

- ¼ cup all-purpose flour
- ½ tsp. salt
- ½ tsp. pepper
- 4 boneless skinless chicken breast halves (4 oz. each)
- ¼ cup butter, cubed
- ¼ cup white wine or chicken broth
- 1 Tbsp. lemon juice
  Minced fresh parsley, optional

1. In a shallow bowl, mix flour, salt and pepper. Pound chicken breasts with a meat mallet to ½-in. thickness. Dip chicken in flour mixture to coat both sides; shake off excess.
2. In a large skillet, heat butter over medium heat. Brown chicken on both sides. Add wine; bring to a boil. Reduce heat; simmer, uncovered, until chicken is no longer pink, 12-15 minutes. Drizzle with lemon juice. If desired, sprinkle with parsley.

1 CHICKEN BREAST HALF WITH ABOUT 1 TBSP. SAUCE: *265 cal., 14g fat (8g sat. fat), 93mg chol., 442mg sod., 7g carb. (0 sugars, 0 fiber), 24g pro.*

MEDITERRANEAN PORK & ORZO

On a really busy day, this meal-in-a-bowl is one of my top picks. It's quick to put together, leaving me a lot more time to relax at the table.
—Mary Relyea, Canastota, NY

TAKES: 30 MIN. • **MAKES:** 6 SERVINGS

- 1½ lbs. pork tenderloin
- 1 tsp. coarsely ground pepper
- 2 Tbsp. olive oil
- 3 qt. water
- 1¼ cups uncooked orzo pasta
- ¼ tsp. salt
- 1 pkg. (6 oz.) fresh baby spinach
- 1 cup grape tomatoes, halved
- ¾ cup crumbled feta cheese

1. Rub pork with pepper; cut into 1-in. cubes. In a large nonstick skillet, heat oil over medium heat. Add pork; cook and stir until no longer pink, 8-10 minutes.
2. Meanwhile, in a Dutch oven, bring water to a boil. Stir in orzo and salt; cook, uncovered, 8 minutes. Add spinach; cook until the orzo is tender and spinach is wilted, 45-60 seconds longer. Drain.
3. Add tomatoes to pork; heat through. Stir in the orzo mixture and feta cheese.

1⅓ CUPS: *372 cal., 11g fat (4g sat. fat), 71mg chol., 306mg sod., 34g carb. (2g sugars, 3g fiber), 31g pro.* **Diabetic exchanges:** *3 lean meat, 2 starch, 1 vegetable, 1 fat.*

QUICK CHICKEN PICCATA

BAKED SALMON CAKES

Made in muffin pans and served with sauce on the side, these little salmon patties make a fantastic light meal. You can also bake a double batch and freeze some for a quick lower-fat supper later on.
—Nikki Haddad, Germantown, MD

TAKES: 30 MIN. • **MAKES:** 4 SERVINGS

- 1   can (14¾ oz.) salmon, drained, bones and skin removed
- 1½ cups soft whole wheat bread crumbs
- ½   cup finely chopped sweet red pepper
- ½   cup egg substitute
- 3   green onions, thinly sliced
- ¼   cup finely chopped celery
- ¼   cup minced fresh cilantro
- 3   Tbsp. fat-free mayonnaise
- 1   Tbsp. lemon juice
- 1   garlic clove, minced
- ⅛   to ¼ tsp. hot pepper sauce

SAUCE
- 2   Tbsp. fat-free mayonnaise
- ¼   tsp. capers, drained
- ¼   tsp. dill weed
-     Dash lemon juice

1. In a large bowl, combine the first 11 ingredients. Place ⅓ cup salmon mixture into each of 8 muffin cups coated with cooking spray. Bake cakes at 425° until a thermometer reads 160°, 10-15 minutes.
2. Meanwhile, combine sauce ingredients. Serve with salmon.

1 SERVING: *266 cal., 9g fat (2g sat. fat), 48mg chol., 914mg sod., 17g carb. (5g sugars, 3g fiber), 28g pro.*

READER REVIEW

"I loved the baked method. It's so much easier and healthier than frying, yet the cakes were still perfectly crispy on the outside."
—RLLEWIS7, TASTEOFHOME.COM

SKILLET BEEF & MACARONI

SKILLET BEEF & MACARONI

I found this recipe 30 years ago on a can label. My family loved it, and I always received compliments when I took the dish to potluck suppers. Because it's so easy, it's a real timesaver for anyone with a busy schedule.
—Maxine Neuhauser, Arcadia, CA

TAKES: 30 MIN. • **MAKES:** 6 SERVINGS

- 1½ lbs. ground beef
- ½   cup chopped onion
- 2   cans (8 oz. each) tomato sauce
- 1   cup water
- 1   pkg. (7 oz.) macaroni
- ½   cup chopped green pepper
- 2   Tbsp. Worcestershire sauce
- 1   tsp. salt
- ¼   tsp. pepper

In a large skillet over medium-high heat, cook beef and onion until the meat is no longer pink; drain. Stir in the remaining ingredients; bring to a boil. Reduce heat; simmer, covered, until macaroni is tender, stirring occasionally, 20-25 minutes. Add more water if needed.

1 CUP: *317 cal., 11g fat (5g sat. fat), 56mg chol., 700mg sod., 29g carb. (3g sugars, 2g fiber), 25g pro.*

VEGETARIAN LINGUINE

SPINACH, SHRIMP & RICOTTA TACOS

I was looking for a new recipe for tacos, and this version was a perfect solution. With shrimp, green chiles, spinach and ricotta, it's made up of ingredients I love that aren't normally associated with traditional tacos.
—Priscilla Gilbert, Indian Harbour Beach, FL

TAKES: 30 MIN. • **MAKES:** 6 SERVINGS

- 1 carton (15 oz.) part-skim ricotta cheese
- 2 Tbsp. minced fresh cilantro
- 4 garlic cloves, minced, divided
- ¼ tsp. salt
- ⅛ tsp. pepper
- 1 Tbsp. canola oil
- 1 medium onion, chopped
- 1 lb. uncooked shrimp (31-40 per lb.), peeled and deveined
- 2 cans (4 oz. each) chopped green chiles
- ¼ tsp. crushed red pepper flakes
- 10 oz. fresh baby spinach (about 12 cups)
- 12 corn tortillas (6 in.), warmed
  Salsa and lime wedges

1. In a large bowl, combine ricotta, cilantro, half the minced garlic, salt and pepper; set mixture aside.
2. In a large skillet, heat oil over medium-high heat. Add onion; cook and stir until softened, 4-5 minutes. Add shrimp, green chiles and pepper flakes; cook 1 minute longer. Add spinach and remaining garlic; cook and stir until shrimp turn pink and spinach is wilted, 4-5 minutes.
3. Serve shrimp mixture in tortillas with ricotta mixture, salsa and lime wedges.
2 TACOS: 317 cal., 11g fat (4g sat. fat), 114mg chol., 468mg sod., 32g carb. (2g sugars, 5g fiber), 25g pro. **Diabetic exchanges:** *3 lean meat, 1½ starch, 1 vegetable, ½ fat.*

TEST KITCHEN TIP
If you happen to have any leftover shrimp, serve it over hot cooked pasta, polenta or quinoa. A little sprinkle of Parmesan cheese won't hurt, either.

VEGETARIAN LINGUINE

Looking for a tasty alternative to meat-and-potatoes meals? Try this colorful pasta dish. My oldest son came up with the stick-to-the-ribs supper that uses fresh mushrooms, zucchini and other veggies, as well as basil and provolone cheese.
—Jane Bone, Cape Coral, FL

TAKES: 30 MIN. • **MAKES:** 6 SERVINGS

- 6 oz. uncooked linguine
- 2 Tbsp. butter
- 1 Tbsp. olive oil
- 2 medium zucchini, thinly sliced
- ½ lb. fresh mushrooms, sliced
- 1 large tomato, chopped
- 2 green onions, chopped
- 1 garlic clove, minced
- ½ tsp. salt
- ¼ tsp. pepper
- 1 cup shredded provolone cheese
- 3 Tbsp. shredded Parmesan cheese
- 2 tsp. minced fresh basil

1. Cook linguine according to package directions. Meanwhile, in a large skillet, heat butter and oil over medium heat. Add zucchini and mushrooms; saute 3-5 minutes. Add tomato, onions, garlic and seasonings. Reduce heat; simmer, covered, about 3 minutes.
2. Drain linguine; add to the vegetable mixture. Sprinkle with cheeses and basil. Toss to coat.
1½ CUPS: 260 cal., 13g fat (7g sat. fat), 25mg chol., 444mg sod., 26g carb. (3g sugars, 2g fiber), 12g pro. **Diabetic exchanges:** *1½ starch, 1½ fat, 1 medium-fat meat, 1 vegetable.*

PRISCILLA GILBERT
Indian Harbour
Beach, FL

SPINACH, SHRIMP
& RICOTTA TACOS

BAKED TILAPIA

I've decided to cook healthier for my family, and that includes having more fish at home. This is a great recipe, and it's fast, too!
—Hope Stewart, Raleigh, NC

TAKES: 20 MIN. • **MAKES:** 4 SERVINGS

4	tilapia fillets (6 oz. each)
3	Tbsp. butter, melted
3	Tbsp. lemon juice
1½	tsp. garlic powder
⅛	tsp. salt
2	Tbsp. capers, drained
½	tsp. dried oregano
⅛	tsp. paprika

1. Place tilapia in an ungreased 13x9-in. baking dish. Combine butter, lemon juice, garlic powder and salt; pour over the fillets. Sprinkle with capers, oregano and paprika.
2. Bake, uncovered, at 425° for 10-15 minutes or until fish flakes easily with a fork.

1 FILLET: *224 cal., 10g fat (6g sat. fat), 106mg chol., 304mg sod., 2g carb. (0 sugars, 0 fiber), 32g pro.* **Diabetic exchanges:** *4 lean meat, 2 fat.*

CAESAR CHICKEN WITH FETA

BAKED TILAPIA

CAESAR CHICKEN WITH FETA

My tomatoey chicken is the perfect answer on those crazy days when supper has to be on the table in 30 minutes, tops (doesn't hurt that it's delicious, too).
—Denise Chelpka, Phoenix, AZ

TAKES: 10 MIN. • **MAKES:** 4 SERVINGS

4	boneless skinless chicken breast halves (4 oz. each)
½	tsp. salt
¼	tsp. pepper
2	tsp. olive oil
1	medium tomato, chopped
¼	cup creamy Caesar salad dressing
½	cup crumbled feta cheese

Sprinkle chicken with salt and pepper. In a large skillet, heat oil over medium-high heat. Brown chicken on one side. Turn chicken; add the tomato and salad dressing to skillet. Cook, covered, until a thermometer inserted in chicken reads 165°, 6-8 minutes. Sprinkle with feta cheese.

1 CHICKEN BREAST HALF WITH 3 TBSP. TOMATO MIXTURE: *262 cal., 16g fat (4g sat. fat), 76mg chol., 664mg sod., 2g carb. (1g sugars, 1g fiber), 26g pro.*

TACOS IN A BOWL

Here's a wonderful, oh-so-easy dish that young people will love. If you have leftover taco meat, kids can whip this up really quickly. Garnish each serving with sour cream and salsa for a little more southwestern flair.
—Sue Schoening, Sheboygan, WI

TAKES: 25 MIN. • **MAKES:** 2 SERVINGS

- ½ lb. lean ground beef (90% lean)
- 2 Tbsp. finely chopped onion
- ¾ cup canned diced tomatoes, drained
- 2 Tbsp. taco seasoning
- 1 cup water
- 1 pkg. (3 oz.) ramen noodles
- ¼ cup shredded cheddar or Mexican cheese blend
  Crushed tortilla chips, optional

1. In a small skillet, cook beef and onion over medium heat until meat is no longer pink; drain. Stir in the tomatoes, taco seasoning and water. Bring to a boil. Add ramen noodles (discard seasoning packet or save for another use). Cook and stir until noodles are tender, 3-5 minutes.

2. Spoon into serving bowls; sprinkle with cheese and tortilla chips if desired.

1 CUP: *480 cal., 21g fat (10g sat. fat), 85mg chol., 1279mg sod., 40g carb. (3g sugars, 2g fiber), 30g pro.*

BACON-CHICKEN CLUB PIZZA

(SHOWN ON PAGE 48)

Pizza topped with lettuce, tomatoes and dressing? Your family is in for a treat! Vegetables give the cheesy crust a cool and welcoming crunch.
—Debbie Reid, Clearwater, FL

TAKES: 25 MIN. • **MAKES:** 8 SLICES

- 1 prebaked 12-in. pizza crust
- 4 oz. cream cheese, softened
- 1 shallot, minced
- 2 cups shredded rotisserie chicken
- 1½ cups shredded Monterey Jack cheese
- 1 cup shredded sharp cheddar cheese
- 8 slices ready-to-serve fully cooked bacon, cut into 1-in. pieces
- ¼ cup sour cream
- 3 Tbsp. 2% milk
- 2 tsp. ranch salad dressing mix
- 1 cup shredded lettuce
- 1 plum tomato, seeded and chopped

1. Place crust on an ungreased pizza pan. Combine cream cheese and shallot; spread over crust. Top with the chicken, cheeses and bacon.

2. Bake at 425° for 12-15 minutes or until edges are lightly browned and the cheese is melted.

3. Meanwhile, in a small bowl, combine the sour cream, milk and dressing mix. Sprinkle lettuce and tomato over pizza; drizzle with the dressing.

1 SLICE: *444 cal., 25g fat (13g sat. fat), 84mg chol., 939mg sod., 26g carb. (1g sugars, 0 fiber), 28g pro.*

TACOS IN A BOWL

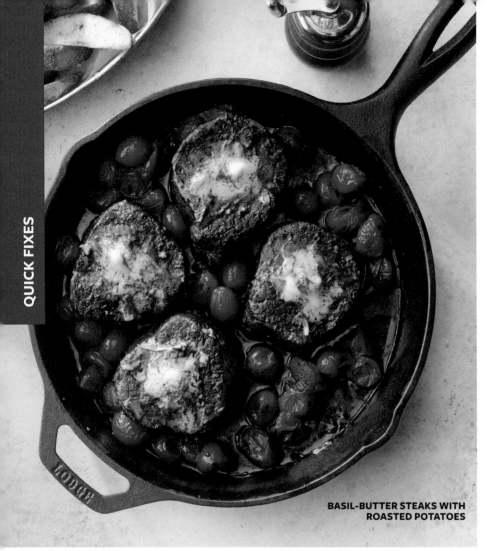

1 cup shredded zucchini
2 large eggs, lightly beaten
⅓ cup minced fresh parsley
1 tsp. lemon juice
½ tsp. salt
⅛ tsp. pepper
2 Tbsp. canola oil

1. In a large saucepan, heat the butter over medium-high heat. Add onion; cook and stir until tender. Remove from heat.
2. Add the light tuna, ½ cup bread crumbs, zucchini, eggs, parsley, lemon juice, salt and pepper to the onion mixture; mix lightly but thoroughly. Shape into six ½-in.-thick patties; coat with remaining bread crumbs.
3. In a large skillet, heat oil over medium heat. Add patties; cook 3 minutes on each side or until patties are golden brown and heated through.
2 FISH CAKES: *400 cal., 19g fat (5g sat. fat), 170mg chol., 1261mg sod., 31g carb. (4g sugars, 3g fiber), 26g pro.*

SKILLET HAM & RICE

Ham, rice and mushrooms make a tasty combination in this homey stovetop dish. It goes from start to finish in just 25 minutes.
—Susan Zivec, Regina, SK

TAKES: 25 MIN. • MAKES: 2 SERVINGS

1 tsp. olive oil
1 medium onion, chopped
1 cup sliced fresh mushrooms
1 cup cubed fully cooked ham
⅛ tsp. pepper
½ cup reduced-sodium chicken broth
¼ cup water
¾ cup uncooked instant rice
2 green onions, sliced
¼ cup shredded Parmesan cheese

1. In a large nonstick skillet, heat oil over medium-high heat; saute the onion and mushrooms until tender. Stir in the ham, pepper, broth and water; bring to a boil. Stir in rice. Reduce heat; simmer, covered, until rice is tender, about 5 minutes.
2. Fluff with a fork. Top with green onions and cheese.
1¼ CUPS: *322 cal., 8g fat (3g sat. fat), 49mg chol., 1168mg sod., 38g carb. (4g sugars, 2g fiber), 24g pro.*

BASIL-BUTTER STEAKS WITH ROASTED POTATOES

A few ingredients and 30 minutes are all you will need for this incredibly satisfying meal. A simple basil butter gives these steaks a very special taste.
—Taste of Home *Test Kitchen*

TAKES: 30 MIN. • MAKES: 4 SERVINGS

1 pkg. (15 oz.) frozen Parmesan and roasted garlic red potato wedges
4 beef tenderloin steaks (1¼ in. thick and 6 oz. each)
½ tsp. salt
½ tsp. pepper
5 Tbsp. butter, divided
2 cups grape tomatoes
1 Tbsp. minced fresh basil

1. Bake potato wedges according to the package directions.
2. Meanwhile, sprinkle steaks with salt and pepper. In a 10-in. cast-iron or other ovenproof skillet, brown steaks in 2 Tbsp.

BASIL-BUTTER STEAKS WITH ROASTED POTATOES

butter. Add tomatoes to skillet. Bake, uncovered, at 425° until meat reaches desired doneness, 15-20 minutes (for medium-rare, a thermometer should read 135°; medium, 140°; medium-well, 145°).
3. In a small bowl, combine the basil and remaining butter. Spoon over steaks and serve with potatoes.
1 SERVING: *538 cal., 29g fat (13g sat. fat), 112mg chol., 740mg sod., 27g carb. (2g sugars, 3g fiber), 41g pro.*

TUNA ZUCCHINI CAKES

Here's a great combination of seafood and garden vegetables. Friends tell me that they like that it's so colorful and pretty, not to mention so wonderful to eat!
—Billie Blanton, Kingsport, TN

TAKES: 25 MIN. • MAKES: 3 SERVINGS

1 Tbsp. butter
½ cup finely chopped onion
1 pouch (6.4 oz.) light tuna in water
1 cup seasoned bread crumbs, divided

BROCCOLI SHRIMP ALFREDO

After tasting fettuccine Alfredo at a restaurant, I tried to duplicate the recipe at home. You can't imagine how pleased I was when I came up with this delicious version. Not only does my family love the creamy dish, but my husband prefers it to the one at the restaurant!
—Rae Natoli, Kingston, NY

TAKES: 30 MIN. • **MAKES:** 4 SERVINGS

- 8 oz. uncooked fettuccine
- 1 lb. uncooked medium shrimp, peeled and deveined
- 3 garlic cloves, minced
- ½ cup butter, cubed
- 1 pkg. (8 oz.) cream cheese, cubed
- 1 cup whole milk
- ½ cup shredded Parmesan cheese
- 4 cups frozen broccoli florets
- ½ tsp. salt
  Dash pepper

1. Cook fettuccine according to package directions. Meanwhile, in a large skillet, saute shrimp and garlic in butter until shrimp turn pink. Remove and set aside.
2. In the same skillet, combine the cream cheese, milk and Parmesan cheese; cook and stir until cheeses are melted and mixture is smooth.
3. Place 1 in. of water in a saucepan; add broccoli. Bring to a boil. Reduce heat; cover and simmer for 6-8 minutes or until tender. Drain. Stir the broccoli, shrimp, salt and pepper into cheese sauce; heat through. Drain fettuccine; top with shrimp mixture.
1 SERVING: *809 cal., 50g fat (30g sat. fat), 271mg chol., 1030mg sod., 52g carb. (9g sugars, 4g fiber), 38g pro.*

TERIYAKI GLAZED CHICKEN

TERIYAKI GLAZED CHICKEN

I love to experiment with food. We're able to buy sweet onions grown on Maui, so I stir-fry them with chicken and carrots to create a tasty teriyaki meal.
—Kel Brenneman, Riverdale, CA

TAKES: 30 MIN. • **MAKES:** 4 SERVINGS

- 1 lb. boneless skinless chicken breast halves, cut into strips
- 3 Tbsp. canola oil, divided
- 4 medium carrots, julienned
- 1 medium sweet onion, julienned
- ½ cup soy sauce
- ¼ cup packed brown sugar
  Hot cooked rice
  Sesame seeds, toasted, optional
  Sliced green onions, optional

1. In a large skillet or wok, stir-fry chicken in 2 Tbsp. oil until no longer pink, 6-8 minutes. Remove chicken and set aside. In the same skillet, stir-fry carrots in remaining oil for 2 minutes. Add onion; stir-fry until vegetables are tender, 2-4 minutes longer.
2. Combine soy sauce and brown sugar; add to skillet. Bring to a boil. Return chicken to skillet. Boil until sauce is slightly thickened, about 5 minutes. Serve with rice. Sprinkle with sesame seeds and green onions if desired.
1 SERVING: *324 cal., 13g fat (2g sat. fat), 63mg chol., 1922mg sod., 23g carb. (20g sugars, 3g fiber), 28g pro.*

TEST KITCHEN TIP

A simple swap to reduced-sodium soy sauce will decrease sodium to about 1,200 milligrams per serving, but that's still high. To cut even more, replace some of the soy sauce with reduced-sodium broth or water.

BROCCOLI SHRIMP ALFREDO

SHRIMP PAD THAI

TENDER SWEET & SOUR PORK CHOPS

My best friend gave me the recipe for these delightful pork chops years ago. It's become one of my family's favorites, and I prepare them often.
—Gina Young, Lamar, CO

TAKES: 25 MIN. • **MAKES:** 6 SERVINGS

- 6   boneless pork loin chops (4 oz. each)
- ¾   tsp. pepper
- ½   cup water
- ⅓   cup cider vinegar
- ¼   cup packed brown sugar
- 2   Tbsp. reduced-sodium soy sauce
- 1   Tbsp. Worcestershire sauce
- 1   Tbsp. cornstarch
- 2   Tbsp. cold water

1. Sprinkle the pork chops with pepper. In a large skillet coated with cooking spray, cook pork over medium heat for 4-6 minutes on each side or until lightly browned. Remove pork chops and keep warm.
2. Add the water, cider vinegar, brown sugar, soy sauce and Worcestershire sauce to skillet; stir to loosen the browned bits. Bring to a boil. Combine cornstarch and cold water until smooth; stir into skillet. Bring to a boil; cook and stir for 2 minutes or until mixture is thickened.
3. Return chops to the pan. Reduce heat; cover and simmer for 4-5 minutes or until meat is tender.
1 PORK CHOP WITH 3 TBSP. SAUCE: *198 cal., 6g fat (2g sat. fat), 55mg chol., 265mg sod., 12g carb. (10g sugars, 0 fiber), 22g pro.* **Diabetic exchanges:** *3 lean meat, 1 starch.*

SHRIMP PAD THAI

You can make this yummy Thai classic in no time. Find fish sauce and chili garlic sauce in the Asian foods aisle of your grocery store.
—Elise Ray, Shawnee, KS

TAKES: 30 MIN. • **MAKES:** 4 SERVINGS

- 4   oz. uncooked thick rice noodles
- ½   lb. uncooked small shrimp, peeled and deveined
- 2   tsp. canola oil
- 1   large onion, chopped
- 1   garlic clove, minced
- 1   large egg, lightly beaten
- 3   cups coleslaw mix
- 4   green onions, thinly sliced
- ⅓   cup rice vinegar
- ¼   cup sugar
- 3   Tbsp. reduced-sodium soy sauce
- 2   Tbsp. fish sauce or additional reduced-sodium soy sauce
- 2   to 3 tsp. chili garlic sauce
- 2   Tbsp. chopped salted peanuts
     Chopped fresh cilantro leaves

1. Cook noodles according to package directions.
2. In a large nonstick skillet or wok, stir-fry the shrimp in oil until shrimp turn pink; remove and set aside. Add onion and garlic to the pan. Make a well in the center of the onion mixture; add egg. Stir-fry for 2-3 minutes or until egg is completely set.
3. Add the coleslaw mix, green onions, vinegar, sugar, soy sauce, fish sauce, chili garlic sauce and peanuts; heat through. Return shrimp to the pan and heat through. Drain noodles; toss with shrimp mixture. Garnish with cilantro.
1¼ CUPS: *338 cal., 7g fat (1g sat. fat), 115mg chol., 1675mg sod., 52g carb. (23g sugars, 3g fiber), 17g pro.*

TENDER SWEET &
SOUR PORK CHOPS

SAUCY MAC & CHEESE

I love the curly noodles in this creamy recipe. Cavatappi is a corkscrew pasta, also sold under the name cellentani, but any type of spiral pasta will work. This dish is fun to make and looks so pretty topped with extra cheese and crunchy, golden bread crumbs. I like to add ground pepper to my serving.
—Sara Martin, Brookfield, WI

TAKES: 25 MIN. • **MAKES:** 4 SERVINGS

- 2 cups cavatappi or spiral pasta
- 3 Tbsp. butter, divided
- ⅓ cup panko (Japanese) bread crumbs
- 2 Tbsp. all-purpose flour
- 1½ cups 2% milk
- ¾ lb. Velveeta, cubed
- ¼ cup shredded cheddar cheese

1. Cook pasta according to the package directions. Meanwhile, in a large nonstick skillet, melt 1 Tbsp. butter over medium-high heat. Add bread crumbs; cook and stir until golden brown. Remove to a small bowl and set aside.
2. In the same skillet, melt remaining butter. Stir in flour until smooth. Gradually add the milk; bring to a boil. Cook and stir until thickened, about 2 minutes. Reduce heat. Stir in Velveeta until melted.
3. Drain pasta; add to cheese mixture. Cook and stir until heated through, 3-4 minutes. Sprinkle with shredded cheddar cheese and bread crumbs.

1¼ CUPS: 661 cal., 36g fat (21g sat. fat), 121mg chol., 1267mg sod., 58g carb. (11g sugars, 2g fiber), 27g pro.

TEST KITCHEN TIP

Turn up the fun on pasta night by serving this family favorite as the main attraction in a mac-and-cheese bar. Make it hearty with meaty toppings like crumbled bacon, shredded rotisserie chicken or taco meat, and pile on the freshness with chopped tomatoes, bell peppers, green onions and more.

CRAB EGG FOO YONG

CRAB EGG FOO YONG

Enjoy a classic Chinese takeout dish without leaving your home. This makes a quick dinner and is as delicious as what you would get in any restaurant.
—Beverly Preston, Fond du Lac, WI

TAKES: 30 MIN. • **MAKES:** 4 SERVINGS

- 4 tsp. cornstarch
- 2 tsp. sugar
- 1 can (14½ oz.) reduced-sodium chicken broth
- 2 Tbsp. reduced-sodium soy sauce
- 1 Tbsp. white vinegar

EGG FOO YONG
- 2 Tbsp. all-purpose flour
- 4 large eggs
- 1 can (14 oz.) bean sprouts, drained
- 2 cans (6 oz. each) lump crabmeat, drained
- ⅓ cup thinly sliced green onions
- ⅛ tsp. garlic powder
- ⅛ tsp. pepper
- 3 Tbsp. vegetable oil

1. In a small saucepan, combine cornstarch and sugar. Stir in the broth, soy sauce and vinegar until smooth. Bring to a boil; cook and stir for 2 minutes or until thickened. Set aside and keep warm.
2. In a large bowl, whisk flour and eggs until smooth. Stir in bean sprouts, crab, onions, garlic powder and pepper. In a large skillet, heat oil. Drop crab mixture by ⅓ cupfuls into oil. Cook until for 2 minutes on each side or until golden brown. Serve with the sauce.

2 PATTIES WITH ⅓ CUP SAUCE: 297 cal., 16g fat (3g sat. fat), 269mg chol., 1159mg sod., 12g carb. (3g sugars, 2g fiber), 25g pro.

SPICY CORNED BEEF TACOS

Using leftovers in new and exciting ways is my favorite cooking challenge. These fun tacos take my favorite Reuben ingredients and turn them into something totally different—and completely delicious.
—Fay Moreland, Wichita Falls, TX

TAKES: 30 MIN. • **MAKES:** 6 SERVINGS

- 2 cups coleslaw mix
- 4 green onions, thinly sliced
- 2 jalapeno peppers, seeded and thinly sliced
- 1 cup Thousand Island salad dressing
- 1 to 2 Tbsp. Sriracha chili sauce
- 2 Tbsp. canola oil
- 3 cups chopped cooked corned beef
- 2 cups refrigerated diced potatoes with onion
- 12 flour tortillas (6 in.), warmed

1. In a small bowl, combine coleslaw mix, green onions and jalapenos. In another small bowl, whisk salad dressing and chili sauce until combined.
2. In a large skillet, heat oil over medium heat. Add corned beef and diced potatoes; cook and stir 8-10 minutes or until heated through. Serve in tortillas with coleslaw mixture and dressing mixture.

2 TACOS: *621 cal., 39g fat (9g sat. fat), 60mg chol., 1606mg sod., 48g carb. (8g sugars, 4g fiber), 16g pro.*

TEST KITCHEN TIP

Worried that your jalapenos are a little too spicy? After you slice them, toss them in ¼ cup vodka for about 10 minutes. It will remove a lot of the heat, leaving only the great jalapeno flavor.

BEEF BROCCOLI STIR-FRY

My family asks for this tasty stir-fry over and over again. I love it because it comes together so quickly, and it combines tender beef and good-for-you veggies in one dish.
—Ruth Stahl, Shepherd, MT

TAKES: 25 MIN. • **MAKES:** 4 SERVINGS

- ½ tsp. garlic powder
- 3 Tbsp. cornstarch, divided
- 2 Tbsp. plus ½ cup water, divided
- 1 lb. boneless beef top round steak, cut into thin 2-in. strips
- ¼ cup soy sauce
- 2 Tbsp. brown sugar
- 1 tsp. ground ginger
- 2 Tbsp. canola oil, divided
- 4 cups fresh broccoli florets
- 1 small onion, cut into thin wedges
  Hot cooked rice

1. Mix garlic powder and 2 Tbsp. each cornstarch and water; toss with beef. In a small bowl, mix soy sauce, brown sugar, ginger and the remaining cornstarch and water until smooth.
2. In a large skillet, heat 1 Tbsp. oil over medium-high heat; stir-fry the beef until browned, 2-3 minutes. Remove from pan.
3. In same pan, stir-fry broccoli and onion in remaining oil over medium-high heat until crisp-tender, 4-5 minutes. Stir soy sauce mixture; add to the pan. Cook and stir until thickened, 1-2 minutes. Return beef to pan; heat through. Serve with rice.

1 CUP: *291 cal., 11g fat (2g sat. fat), 63mg chol., 974mg sod., 18g carb. (9g sugars, 2g fiber), 30g pro.*

SPICY CORNED BEEF TACOS

CHICKEN BISCUIT SKILLET

SALMON SUPREME WITH GINGER SOY SAUCE

Served with asparagus, this is my favorite meal to prepare on Friday nights. It's light in calories and delicious, too.
—Agnes Ward, Stratford, ON

TAKES: 25 MIN. • **MAKES:** 4 SERVINGS

- 2 Tbsp. all-purpose flour
- 1 Tbsp. cornstarch
- 4 salmon fillets (4 oz. each)
- 1 Tbsp. canola oil
- ⅓ cup sherry or unsweetened apple juice
- 2 green onions, chopped
- ¼ cup minced fresh gingerroot
- 3 Tbsp. reduced-sodium soy sauce
- 2 Tbsp. honey
- 1 Tbsp. balsamic vinegar
- ½ tsp. garlic powder

1. In a shallow bowl, combine flour and cornstarch. Dip fillets in flour mixture. In a large nonstick skillet, cook salmon in oil over medium-high heat for 4-6 minutes on each side or until fish flakes easily with a fork. Remove and keep warm.
2. Add sherry, stirring to loosen browned bits from the pan. Add remaining ingredients; cook, stirring occasionally, for 2 minutes to allow flavors to blend. Serve with salmon.
1 FILLET WITH 2 TBSP. SAUCE: *319 cal., 16g fat (3g sat. fat), 67mg chol., 526mg sod., 15g carb. (10g sugars, 0 fiber), 24g pro.*

CHICKEN BISCUIT SKILLET

My mother always made this while we were growing up. Now I make it for my own husband and kids. I use the small-size biscuits because they brown up so nicely on top. I also add mushrooms to this recipe sometimes because my family loves 'em.
—Keri Boffeli, Monticello, IA

TAKES: 30 MIN. • **MAKES:** 6 SERVINGS

- 1 Tbsp. butter
- ⅓ cup chopped onion
- ¼ cup all-purpose flour
- 1 can (10½ oz.) condensed chicken broth, undiluted
- ¼ cup fat-free milk
- ⅛ tsp. pepper
- 2 cups shredded cooked chicken breast
- 2 cups frozen peas and carrots (about 10 oz.), thawed
- 1 tube (12 oz.) refrigerated buttermilk biscuits, quartered

1. Preheat oven to 400°. Melt butter in a 10-in. ovenproof skillet over medium-high heat. Add the onion; cook and stir until tender, 2-3 minutes.
2. In a small bowl, mix flour, broth, milk and pepper until smooth; stir into pan. Bring to a boil, stirring constantly; cook and stir until thickened, 1-2 minutes. Add the chicken and peas and carrots; heat through. Arrange biscuits over stew. Bake until biscuits are golden brown, 15-20 minutes.
1 SERVING: *320 cal., 11g fat (4g sat. fat), 42mg chol., 861mg sod., 36g carb. (4g sugars, 2g fiber), 22g pro.*

TEST KITCHEN TIP

This is a great use for leftover chicken. During the holiday season it can easily be made with turkey. The biscuits are plentiful, making this a hearty dish that's perfect for chilly weather.

SALMON SUPREME WITH GINGER SOY SAUCE

GRILLED BEEF &
BLUE CHEESE TACOS
PAGE 73

Main Dishes

Whether you're looking for the perfect entree to spice things up at the dinner table or a heartwarming classic for the family to gather around, discover everything you need on the following pages.

PARMESAN PORK ROAST

PARMESAN PORK ROAST

A wonderful sweet and savory flavor comes from just a few pantry staples in this easy roast.
—Karen Warner, Louisville, OH

PREP: 15 MIN. • **COOK:** 5½ HOURS • **MAKES:** 10 SERVINGS

- 1   boneless pork loin roast (4 lbs.)
- ⅔   cup grated Parmesan cheese
- ½   cup honey
- 3   Tbsp. soy sauce
- 2   Tbsp. dried basil
- 2   Tbsp. minced garlic
- 2   Tbsp. olive oil
- ½   tsp. salt
- 2   Tbsp. cornstarch
- ¼   cup cold water

1. Cut roast in half. Place in a 3-qt. slow cooker. In a small bowl, combine the cheese, honey, soy sauce, basil, garlic, oil and salt; pour over pork. Cover and cook on low for 5½-6 hours or until a thermometer reads 160°.
2. Remove meat to a serving platter; keep warm. Skim fat from cooking juices; transfer to a small saucepan. Bring liquid to a boil. Combine cornstarch and water until smooth. Gradually stir into pan. Bring to a boil; cook and stir for 2 minutes or until thickened. Slice roast; serve with gravy.
FREEZE OPTION: Cool pork and gravy. Freeze sliced pork and gravy in freezer containers. To use, partially thaw in refrigerator overnight. Heat through slowly in a covered skillet, stirring occasionally and adding a little broth or water if necessary.
5 OZ COOKED PORK: *330 cal., 13g fat (4g sat. fat), 95mg chol., 529mg sod., 15g carb. (14g sugars, 0 fiber), 38g pro.*

OVER-THE-BORDER SHRIMP ENCHILADAS

These enchiladas have a bit of a kick thanks to chili powder and green chiles, but the deliciously creamy sauce balances it all.
—Beverly O'Ferrall, Linkwood, MD

PREP: 20 MIN. • **BAKE:** 20 MIN. • **MAKES:** 8 SERVINGS

- 1   medium onion, chopped
- 2   Tbsp. olive oil
- ¾   lb. uncooked medium shrimp, peeled and deveined
- 1   can (4 oz.) chopped green chiles
- ½   tsp. chili powder
- ¼   tsp. salt
- ¼   tsp. ground cumin
- ¼   tsp. pepper
- 1   pkg. (8 oz.) cream cheese, cubed
- 8   flour tortillas (8 in.), warmed
- 1½ cups chunky salsa
- 1½ cups shredded Monterey Jack cheese

1. In a large skillet, saute onion in oil until tender. Add shrimp, green chiles, chili powder, salt, cumin and pepper. Cook until shrimp turn pink, 2-3 minutes. Stir in cream cheese until melted.
2. Place ⅓ cup shrimp mixture down the center of each tortilla. Roll up and place seam side down in a greased 13x9-in. baking dish. Pour salsa over the top; sprinkle with Monterey Jack cheese. Bake, uncovered, at 350° for 20-25 minutes or until heated through.
1 ENCHILADA: *417 cal., 23g fat (11g sat. fat), 102mg chol., 809mg sod., 32g carb. (3g sugars, 1g fiber), 19g pro.*

OVER-THE-BORDER
SHRIMP ENCHILADAS

MOM'S MEAT LOAF FOR 2

If you're looking for a small but mighty meal, here's a great fit. You'll love the old-fashioned flavor and scrumptious sauce. The recipe is easy to double for sandwiches the next day.
—Michelle Beran, Claflin, KS

PREP: 15 MIN. • **BAKE:** 40 MIN.
MAKES: 2 MINI MEAT LOAVES

- 1 large egg
- ¼ cup 2% milk
- ⅓ cup crushed saltines
- 3 Tbsp. chopped onion
- ¼ tsp. salt
- ⅛ tsp. rubbed sage
   Dash pepper
- ½ lb. lean ground beef (90% lean)
- ¼ cup ketchup
- 2 Tbsp. brown sugar
- ¼ tsp. Worcestershire sauce

1. In a large bowl, beat egg. Add the milk, cracker crumbs, onion, salt, sage and pepper. Crumble beef over mixture and mix well. Shape into 2 loaves; place in a shallow baking dish coated with cooking spray.
2. Combine the ketchup, brown sugar and Worcestershire sauce; spoon over loaves. Bake at 350° until no longer pink and a thermometer reads 160°, 40-45 minutes; drain.
1 SERVING: *337 cal., 12g fat (4g sat. fat), 162mg chol., 898mg sod., 31g carb. (18g sugars, 1g fiber), 27g pro.*

CHICKEN & ARTICHOKE LASAGNA

My family loves lasagna, and I love the slow cooker. I wanted to try something a little different from the classic lasagna we usually have. This recipe not only tastes incredible, it's convenient, too.
—Kelly Silvers, Edmond, OK

PREP: 30 MIN. • **COOK:** 3 HOURS + STANDING
MAKES: 8 SERVINGS

- 2 cans (14 oz. each) water-packed artichoke hearts, drained and finely chopped
- 1 cup shredded Parmesan cheese, divided
- ¼ cup loosely packed basil leaves, finely chopped
- 3 garlic cloves, minced, divided
- 1 lb. ground chicken
- 1 Tbsp. canola oil
- 1 cup finely chopped onion
- ¾ tsp. salt
- ½ tsp. pepper
- ½ cup white wine
- 1 cup half-and-half cream
- 1 pkg. (8 oz.) cream cheese, softened
- 1 cup shredded Monterey Jack cheese
- 1 large egg
- 1½ cups 2% cottage cheese
- 9 no-cook lasagna noodles
- 2 cups shredded part-skim mozzarella cheese
   Prepared pesto, optional
   Additional basil, optional

1. Fold two 18-in. square pieces of foil into thirds. Crisscross strips and place strips on bottom and up sides of a 6-qt. slow cooker. Coat strips with cooking spray. Combine artichoke hearts, ½ cup Parmesan cheese, basil and 2 garlic cloves.

2. In a large skillet, crumble chicken over medium heat 6-8 minutes or until no longer pink; drain. Set chicken aside. Add canola oil and onion; cook and stir just until tender, 6-8 minutes. Add the salt, pepper and remaining garlic; cook 1 minute longer. Stir in wine. Bring to a boil; cook until liquid is reduced by half, 4-5 minutes. Stir in cream, cream cheese and Monterey Jack cheese. Return chicken to pan. Combine egg, cottage cheese and remaining Parmesan.
3. Spread ¾ cup meat mixture into slow cooker. Layer with 3 noodles (breaking noodles as necessary to fit), ¾ cup meat mixture, ½ cup cottage cheese mixture, 1 cup artichoke mixture and ½ cup of mozzarella cheese. Repeat layers twice; top with remaining mozzarella cheese. Cook, covered, on low until noodles are tender, 3-4 hours. Remove slow cooker insert and let stand 30 minutes. If desired, serve with pesto and sprinkle with additional basil.
1 SERVING: *588 cal., 34g fat (18g sat. fat), 144mg chol., 1187mg sod., 31g carb. (6g sugars, 1g fiber), 36g pro.*

CHICKEN & ARTICHOKE LASAGNA

**GRILLED PORK TENDERLOIN
WITH CHERRY SALSA MOLÉ**

GRILLED PORK TENDERLOIN WITH CHERRY SALSA MOLÉ

The combination of pork and cherries has long been a favorite of mine. The hint of spice and chocolate in the salsa mole makes the combination even more special.
—Roxanne Chan, Albany, CA

PREP: 25 MIN. • **GRILL:** 15 MIN. + STANDING
MAKES: 6 SERVINGS

- 2 pork tenderloins (¾ lb. each)
- 1 Tbsp. canola oil
- ½ tsp. salt
- ¼ tsp. ground cumin
- ¼ tsp. chili powder
- 1 cup pitted fresh or frozen dark sweet cherries, thawed, chopped
- 1 jalapeno pepper, seeded and minced
- ½ cup finely chopped peeled jicama
- 1 oz. semisweet chocolate, grated
- 2 Tbsp. minced fresh cilantro
- 1 green onion, thinly sliced
- 1 Tbsp. lime juice
- 1 tsp. honey
   Salted pumpkin seeds or pepitas

1. Brush tenderloins with oil; sprinkle with salt, cumin and chili powder. Grill, covered, over medium heat until a thermometer reads 145°, 15-20 minutes, turning occasionally. Let stand 10-15 minutes.
2. Meanwhile, combine cherries, jalapeno, jicama, chocolate, cilantro, green onion, lime juice and honey. Slice pork; serve with cherry salsa and pumpkin seeds.

3 OZ. COOKED PORK WITH ¼ CUP SALSA: *218 cal., 8g fat (3g sat. fat), 64mg chol., 248mg sod., 11g carb. (9g sugars, 2g fiber), 23g pro.* **Diabetic exchanges:** *3 lean meat, ½ starch, ½ fat.*

CRUNCHY BAKED CHICKEN

I've fixed this dish many times for company, and I've never had anyone fail to ask for the recipe. The leftovers—if there are any—are very good heated up in the microwave.
—Elva Jean Criswell, Charleston, MS

PREP: 15 MIN. • **BAKE:** 50 MIN.
MAKES: 6 SERVINGS

- 1 large egg
- 1 Tbsp. whole milk
- 1 can (2.8 oz.) french-fried onions, crushed
- ¾ cup grated Parmesan cheese
- ¼ cup dry bread crumbs
- 1 tsp. paprika
- ½ tsp. salt
   Dash pepper
- 1 broiler/fryer chicken (3 to 4 lbs.), cut up
- ¼ cup butter, melted

1. In a shallow bowl, whisk egg and milk. In another shallow bowl, combine the onions, cheese, bread crumbs, paprika, salt and pepper. Dip chicken in egg mixture, then roll in onion mixture.
2. Place in a greased 13x9-in. baking dish. Drizzle with butter. Bake, uncovered, at 350° for 50-60 minutes or until juices run clear.

1 SERVING: *418 cal., 28g fat (11g sat. fat), 148mg chol., 423mg sod., 8g carb. (1g sugars, 0 fiber), 32g pro.*

GRILLED BEEF & BLUE CHEESE TACOS

(SHOWN ON PAGE 68)

Everyone loves the tangy sauce that goes with these sizzling steak tacos. For an authentic feel, I like to wrap the tortillas in foil and steam them while the steak and onions are cooking.
—Lois Szydlowski, Tampa, FL

PREP: 25 MIN. • **GRILL:** 10 MIN.
MAKES: 6 SERVINGS

- 2 medium red onions, cut into ¼-in. slices
- 2 Tbsp. canola oil
- ½ tsp. salt, divided
- 1 beef top sirloin steak (1½ lbs.)
- ¼ cup soy sauce
- 2 Tbsp. Worcestershire sauce
- 1 Tbsp. brown sugar
- 1 Tbsp. balsamic vinegar
- 1 garlic clove, minced
- ¼ tsp. pepper
- 12 flour tortillas (6 in.), warmed
- 1 cup crumbled blue cheese

1. Brush onions with oil; sprinkle with ¼ tsp. salt. Sprinkle steak with remaining salt. Grill onions and steak, covered, over medium heat until meat reaches desired doneness (for medium-rare, a thermometer should read 135°; medium, 140°; medium-well, 145°), and onions are tender, 4-6 minutes per side. Let steak and onions stand 5 minutes.
2. Meanwhile, in a large bowl, combine soy sauce, Worcestershire, brown sugar, vinegar, garlic and pepper. Halve onion slices; cut steak thinly across grain. Add onions and steak to soy mixture; toss to coat. Serve in tortillas with blue cheese.
2 TACOS: 524 cal., 23g fat (9g sat. fat), 63mg chol., 1576mg sod., 41g carb. (6g sugars, 4g fiber), 36g pro.

TEST KITCHEN TIP
No sirloin? Flank or skirt steak may be used instead.

ONE-POT SPAGHETTI DINNER

All you need is one pot to make this meal that features a simple homemade sauce. Allspice adds a unique taste, but you can substitute Italian seasoning if you prefer.
—Carol Benzel-Schmidt, Stanwood, WA

PREP: 10 MIN. • **COOK:** 25 MIN.
MAKES: 4 SERVINGS

- 1 lb. lean ground beef (90% lean)
- 1¾ cups sliced fresh mushrooms
- 3 cups tomato juice
- 1 can (14½ oz.) no-salt-added diced tomatoes, drained
- 1 can (8 oz.) no-salt-added tomato sauce
- 1 Tbsp. dried minced onion
- ½ tsp. salt
- ½ tsp. garlic powder
- ½ tsp. ground mustard
- ¼ tsp. pepper
- ⅛ tsp. ground allspice
- ⅛ tsp. ground mace, optional
- 6 oz. uncooked multigrain spaghetti, broken into pieces
  Fresh mozzarella cheese pearls or shaved Parmesan cheese, optional

1. In a Dutch oven, cook ground beef and mushrooms over medium heat until meat is no longer pink; drain. Add the tomato juice, diced tomatoes, tomato sauce, onion and seasonings.
2. Bring to a boil. Stir in spaghetti. Simmer, covered, 12-15 minutes or until spaghetti is tender. If desired, serve with cheese.
1½ CUPS: 414 cal., 10g fat (4g sat. fat), 71mg chol., 925mg sod., 48g carb. (15g sugars, 6g fiber), 33g pro.

ONE-POT SPAGHETTI DINNER

MONGOLIAN CHICKEN

Here's a fun, different way to make chicken. It has a lot of flavor and a bit of heat for good measure.
—Mary Ann Lee, Clifton Park, NY

PREP: 20 MIN. + MARINATING
COOK: 15 MIN. • **MAKES:** 4 SERVINGS

- ¼ cup reduced-sodium soy sauce
- 2 Tbsp. cornstarch
- 1 Tbsp. brown sugar
- 1½ lbs. boneless skinless chicken breasts, cut into thin strips
- ¼ cup sherry
- ¼ cup hoisin sauce
- 3 Tbsp. minced fresh cilantro
- 1 Tbsp. sugar
- 1 tsp. Mongolian Fire oil or sesame oil
- 2 Tbsp. canola oil, divided
- 2 cups fresh pea pods, cut into thirds
- 3 plum tomatoes, seeded and cut into 1-in. pieces
- 1 garlic clove, minced
- 1 Tbsp. minced fresh gingerroot
  Hot cooked rice

1. In a shallow dish, combine the soy sauce, cornstarch and brown sugar. Add the chicken; turn to coat. Let stand at room temperature for 30 minutes.
2. Meanwhile, in a small bowl, combine the sherry, hoisin, cilantro, sugar and Mongolian Fire oil until smooth; set aside. Drain chicken and discard marinade.
3. In a large skillet or wok, stir-fry chicken in 1 Tbsp. canola oil until no longer pink. Remove and keep warm. Stir-fry the pea pods, tomatoes, garlic and ginger in remaining oil until vegetables are crisp-tender, 2-4 minutes.
4. Add sherry mixture to the pan. Bring to a boil; cook and stir until slightly thickened, about 2 minutes. Add the chicken; heat through. Serve with rice.

1½ CUPS: *376 cal., 13g fat (2g sat. fat), 94mg chol., 651mg sod., 23g carb. (14g sugars, 3g fiber), 38g pro.*

TUNA & PEA CASSEROLE

Turn to this recipe when you want a tuna casserole that's a little different—the horseradish adds extra flavor. This dish is a tried-and-true favorite in our family.
—Jackie Smulski, Lyons, IL

PREP: 20 MIN. • **BAKE:** 40 MIN.
MAKES: 6 SERVINGS

- 8 oz. uncooked egg noodles
- 2 cans (10¾ oz. each) condensed cream of mushroom soup, undiluted
- ½ cup mayonnaise
- ½ cup 2% milk
- 2 to 3 tsp. prepared horseradish
- ½ tsp. dill weed
- ⅛ tsp. pepper
- 1 cup frozen peas, thawed
- 1 can (4 oz.) mushroom stems and pieces, drained
- 1 small onion, chopped
- 1 jar (2 oz.) diced pimientos, drained
- 2 cans (6 oz. each) tuna, drained and flaked
- ¼ cup dry bread crumbs
- 1 Tbsp. butter, melted

1. Cook noodles according to package directions. Meanwhile, in a large bowl, combine the soup, mayonnaise, milk, horseradish, dill and pepper. Stir in the peas, mushrooms, onion, pimientos and tuna.
2. Drain noodles; stir into soup mixture. Transfer to a greased 2-qt. baking dish. Toss bread crumbs and butter; sprinkle over the top.
3. Bake, uncovered, at 375° until bubbly, 40-45 minutes.

1¼ CUPS: *505 cal., 25g fat (5g sat. fat), 66mg chol., 1196mg sod., 45g carb. (5g sugars, 5g fiber), 24g pro.*

MONGOLIAN CHICKEN

PEACH-GLAZED RIBS

SNEAKY TURKEY MEATBALLS

Like most kids, mine refuse to eat certain veggies. In order to get healthy foods into their diets, I have to be sneaky sometimes. The veggies in this recipe keep the meatballs moist while providing nutrients—and I'm happy to say my kids love 'em.
—Courtney Stultz, Weir, KS

PREP: 15 MIN. • **BAKE:** 20 MIN. • **MAKES:** 6 SERVINGS

- ¼ head cauliflower, broken into florets
- ½ cup finely shredded cabbage
- 1 Tbsp. potato starch or cornstarch
- 1 Tbsp. balsamic vinegar
- 1 tsp. sea salt
- 1 tsp. dried basil
- ½ tsp. pepper
- 1 lb. ground turkey
  Optional: Barbecue sauce and chopped fresh basil leaves

1. Preheat oven to 400°. Place cauliflower in a food processor; pulse until finely chopped. Transfer to a large bowl. Add the cabbage, potato starch, vinegar, salt, basil and pepper.
2. Add turkey; mix lightly but thoroughly. With ice cream scoop or wet hands, shape into 1½-in. balls. Place meatballs on a greased rack in a 15x10x1-in. baking pan. Bake for 20-24 minutes or until cooked through. If desired, toss meatballs with barbecue sauce and top with basil.
2 MEATBALLS: 125 cal., 6g fat (1g sat. fat), 50mg chol., 370mg sod., 4g carb. (1g sugars, 1g fiber), 15g pro. **Diabetic exchanges:** *2 medium-fat meat.*

PEACH-GLAZED RIBS

For a mouthwatering alternative to the usual barbecue sauce for ribs, try this slightly spicy recipe at your next picnic. The peaches add just the right touch of sweetness and a lovely color.
—Sharon Taylor, Columbia, SC

PREP: 15 MIN. • **GRILL:** 1¼ HOURS • **MAKES:** 6 SERVINGS

- 3 to 4 lbs. pork baby back ribs, cut into serving-size pieces
- 1 can (15¼ oz.) peach halves, drained
- ⅓ cup soy sauce
- ¼ cup canola oil
- ¼ cup honey
- 2 Tbsp. brown sugar
- 1 tsp. sesame seeds, toasted
- 1 garlic clove, peeled
- ¼ tsp. ground ginger

1. Prepare grill for indirect heat, using a drip pan. Place ribs over drip pan. Grill, covered, over indirect medium heat for 60 minutes, turning occasionally.
2. Meanwhile, in a blender, combine the remaining ingredients; cover and process until smooth. Baste ribs.
3. Grill until meat is tender and juices run clear, 15-20 minutes longer, basting occasionally with remaining sauce.
1 SERVING: 568 cal., 40g fat (13g sat. fat), 122mg chol., 930mg sod., 25g carb. (23g sugars, 1g fiber), 28g pro.

SNEAKY TURKEY MEATBALLS

ENCHILADA CASSER-OLÉ!

LINGUINE WITH HERBED CLAM SAUCE

This impressive pasta looks and tastes so much like fancy restaurant fare, you'll want to serve it to guests, which I often do. But the dish is so easy to prepare that you can enjoy it just about anytime.
—Carolee Snyder, Hartford City, IN

PREP: 20 MIN. • COOK: 15 MIN.
MAKES: 4 SERVINGS

  1 can (10 oz.) whole baby clams
  1 can (6½ oz.) minced clams
  ½ cup finely chopped onion
  ¼ cup olive oil
  ¼ cup butter
  ⅓ cup minced fresh parsley
  4 garlic cloves, minced
  2 Tbsp. cornstarch
  ½ cup white wine or chicken broth
  ¼ cup minced fresh basil
     or 4 tsp. dried basil
     Dash pepper
     Dash cayenne pepper
     Hot cooked linguine
     Shredded Parmesan cheese

1. Drain baby and minced clams, reserving juice; set clams and juice aside. In a large skillet, saute onion in oil and butter until tender. Add parsley and garlic; cook and stir for 2 minutes. Add drained clams; cook 2 minutes longer.

2. Combine cornstarch and clam juice until smooth; stir into skillet with wine or broth. Bring to a boil; cook and stir for 1-2 minutes or until thickened. Stir in the basil, pepper and cayenne. Serve sauce over linguine; sprinkle with Parmesan cheese.

1⅔ CUPS: 357 cal., 25g fat (9g sat. fat), 61mg chol., 970mg sod., 11g carb. (1g sugars, 1g fiber), 17g pro.

ENCHILADA CASSER-OLÉ!

We love every kind of Mexican food, but my husband especially adores this casserole. I'm happy that it combines all our favorite ingredients in one dish.
—Marsha Wills, Homosassa, FL

PREP: 25 MIN. • BAKE: 30 MIN.
MAKES: 8 SERVINGS

  1 lb. lean ground beef (90% lean)
  1 large onion, chopped
  2 cups salsa
  1 can (15 oz.) black beans, rinsed and drained
  ¼ cup reduced-fat Italian salad dressing
  2 Tbsp. reduced-sodium taco seasoning
  ¼ tsp. ground cumin
  6 flour tortillas (8 in.)
  ¾ cup reduced-fat sour cream
  1 cup shredded reduced-fat Mexican cheese blend
  1 cup shredded lettuce
  1 medium tomato, chopped
  ¼ cup minced fresh cilantro

1. In a large skillet, cook beef and onion over medium heat until meat is no longer pink; drain. Stir in the salsa, black beans, dressing, taco seasoning and cumin. Place 3 tortillas in an 11x7-in. baking dish coated with cooking spray. Layer with half of the meat mixture, sour cream and cheese. Repeat layers.

2. Cover and bake at 400° for 25 minutes. Uncover; bake until heated through, 5-10 minutes longer. Let stand 5 minutes; top with lettuce, tomato and cilantro.

1 PIECE: 357 cal., 12g fat (5g sat. fat), 45mg chol., 864mg sod., 37g carb. (6g sugars, 3g fiber), 23g pro. **Diabetic exchanges:** *3 lean meat, 2 starch, 1 vegetable, 1 fat.*

POTATO-TOPPED GROUND BEEF SKILLET

The depth of flavor in this recipe is amazing. I never have any leftovers when I take it to potlucks. I love recipes that I can cook and serve in the same skillet. If your butcher has chili grind beef, which is coarsely ground, go for that. It lends an extra meaty texture.
—Fay A. Moreland, Wichita Falls, TX

PREP: 25 MIN. • **COOK:** 45 MIN.
MAKES: 8 SERVINGS

- 2 lbs. lean ground beef (90% lean)
- ½ tsp. salt
- ¼ tsp. pepper
- 1 Tbsp. olive oil
- 1 large onion, chopped
- 4 medium carrots, sliced
- ½ lb. sliced fresh mushrooms
- 4 garlic cloves, minced
- 2 Tbsp. all-purpose flour
- 2 tsp. herbes de Provence
- 1¼ cups dry red wine or reduced-sodium beef broth
- 1 can (14½ oz.) reduced-sodium beef broth

TOPPING
- 1¼ lbs. red potatoes (about 4 medium), cut into ¼-in. slices
- 1 Tbsp. olive oil
- ¼ tsp. salt
- ⅛ tsp. pepper
- ⅓ cup shredded Parmesan cheese
  Minced fresh parsley, optional

1. In a broiler-safe 12-in. skillet, cook and crumble beef over medium-high heat until no longer pink, 6-8 minutes. Stir in salt and pepper; remove from pan.
2. In same pan, heat oil over medium-high heat; saute onion, carrots, mushrooms and garlic until onion is tender, 4-6 minutes. Stir in flour and herbs; cook 1 minute. Stir in wine; bring to a boil. Cook 1 minute, stirring to loosen browned bits from pan. Add beef and broth; return to a boil. Reduce heat; simmer, covered, until flavors are blended, about 30 minutes, stirring occasionally. Remove from heat.
3. Meanwhile, place potatoes in a large saucepan; add water to cover. Bring to a boil. Reduce heat; cook, uncovered, until tender, 10-12 minutes. Drain; cool slightly.

4. Preheat broiler. Arrange potatoes over stew, overlapping slightly; brush lightly with oil. Sprinkle with salt and pepper, then cheese. Broil 5-6 in. from heat until potatoes are lightly browned, 6-8 minutes. Let stand 5 minutes. If desired, sprinkle with parsley.
1¼ CUPS: *313 cal., 14g fat (5g sat. fat), 74mg chol., 459mg sod., 18g carb. (4g sugars, 3g fiber), 26g pro.* **Diabetic exchanges:** *3 lean meat, 1 vegetable, ½ starch, ½ fat.*

POTATO-TOPPED
GROUND BEEF SKILLET

**GINGER-CURRY
CHICKEN TACOS**

BLUEBERRY CHOPS
WITH CINNAMON SWEET
POTATOES

*A sweet and spicy combo is the perfect
accent for meaty chops. With a fresh green
veggie on the side, this is a hearty summer
meal. It's easy, yet impressive enough to
serve to company.*
—Laura Davis, Chincoteague, VA

PREP: 40 MIN. • **GRILL:** 10 MIN.
MAKES: 4 SERVINGS

- 1 cup fresh or frozen blueberries
- ¼ cup water
- 3 Tbsp. brown sugar
- 1 Tbsp. red wine vinegar
- 1 Tbsp. chopped chipotle
   peppers in adobo sauce

SWEET POTATOES
- 1½ lbs. sweet potatoes (about
   2 medium), peeled and
   cut into 1-in. cubes
- 2 Tbsp. butter
- 1 Tbsp. packed brown sugar
- 1 Tbsp. half-and-half cream
- ¼ tsp. kosher salt
- ¼ tsp. ground cinnamon

PORK
- 4 pork rib chops (1 in. thick
   and 8 oz. each)
- 2 tsp. kosher salt
- 1 tsp. coarsely ground pepper

1. For sauce, combine first 5 ingredients
in a small saucepan; bring to a boil over
medium-high heat. Reduce the heat;
simmer, uncovered, until liquid is reduced
by half, 8-10 minutes. Remove from heat;
keep warm.
2. Place sweet potatoes and enough water
to cover in a large saucepan; bring to a boil.
Reduce heat; cook, uncovered, until the
potatoes are tender, 10-15 minutes. Drain;
return to pan. Mash potatoes until smooth,
adding butter, brown sugar, cream, salt and
cinnamon. Cover; keep warm.
3. Meanwhile, preheat grill or broiler.
Sprinkle pork chops with salt and pepper.
Grill, covered, over medium heat or broil
4 in. from heat on a broiler pan until a
thermometer reads 145°, 4-6 minutes
per side. Remove from heat; let stand,
covered, 5 minutes. Serve over sweet
potatoes; top with sauce.
1 SERVING: *520 cal., 16g fat (8g sat. fat),
90mg chol., 1216mg sod., 61g carb. (34g
sugars, 6g fiber), 32g pro.*

GINGER-CURRY
CHICKEN TACOS

*I love tacos (who doesn't?), but I wanted
to put my own unique twist on them by
incorporating some Indian flavors. These
ginger-curry versions hit the spot!*
—Michael Cohen, Los Angeles, CA

PREP: 25 MIN. • **COOK:** 10 MIN.
MAKES: 4 SERVINGS

- ⅔ cup chopped cucumber
- ⅔ cup chopped peeled mango
- ⅓ cup chopped red onion
- ½ serrano pepper, seeded and sliced
- 3 Tbsp. lime juice, divided
- ¼ tsp. salt, divided
- ⅛ tsp. pepper, divided
- ⅓ cup fat-free plain Greek yogurt
- ½ tsp. minced fresh gingerroot
- ⅛ tsp. curry powder

TACOS
- 1 tsp. canola oil
- 1 lb. boneless skinless chicken
   breasts, cut into ½-in. cubes
- 1 tsp. curry powder
- ⅛ tsp. salt

- ⅛ tsp. pepper
- 4 naan flatbreads, halved, or
   8 corn tortillas (6 in.), warmed
- 1½ tsp. minced fresh mint
   Lime wedges

1. In a small bowl, combine the cucumber,
mango, red onion, serrano pepper, 2 Tbsp.
lime juice, ⅛ tsp. salt and dash of pepper. In
another small bowl, combine the yogurt,
ginger, curry powder, remaining lime juice,
and remaining salt and pepper.
2. In a large nonstick skillet, heat oil over
medium-high heat. Sprinkle chicken with
curry, salt and pepper. Cook chicken until
no longer pink, 6-8 minutes. Serve in naan
halves with mango slaw, yogurt sauce and
mint. Garnish with lime wedges.
2 TACOS: *335 cal., 8g fat (2g sat. fat), 68mg
chol., 768mg sod., 36g carb. (9g sugars, 2g
fiber), 30g pro.* **Diabetic exchanges:** *3 lean
meat, 2 starch.*

TEST KITCHEN TIP

Curry powders vary in heat level, so
it's better to start out on the lighter
side and add more only after tasting.

**GINGER-CURRY
CHICKEN TACOS**

LAURA DAVIS
Chincoteague, VA

BLUEBERRY CHOPS WITH
CINNAMON SWEET POTATOES

ROASTED HONEY MUSTARD CHICKEN

I love a good roasted chicken, and this one is easy and delicious. After a quick prep, the marinade does its magic in the fridge until time for roasting. It's fun to dress up the dish based on whatever vegetables are fresh and in season at the market.
—Kara Brook, Owings Mills, MD

PREP: 20 MIN. + MARINATING
BAKE: 1¾ HOURS + STANDING
MAKES: 6 SERVINGS

- ¾ cup honey
- ⅓ cup extra virgin olive oil
- ⅓ cup Dijon mustard
- ¼ cup lemon juice
- 3 Tbsp. chicken seasoning
- 7 garlic cloves, minced
- 1 broiler/fryer chicken (3 to 4 lbs.)

VEGETABLES

- 1½ lbs. baby red potatoes
- 1 lb. carrots, cut into 1-in. pieces
- 3 to 4 fresh rosemary sprigs
- 2 Tbsp. extra virgin olive oil
- 1 tsp. chicken seasoning
- ½ tsp. salt
- ¼ tsp. pepper
- 1 medium lemon, sliced

1. In a small bowl, whisk first 6 ingredients until blended. Pour 1 cup marinade into a large bowl or shallow dish. Add the chicken and turn to coat. Refrigerate for at least 3 hours, turning occasionally. Cover and refrigerate the remaining marinade to use for basting.

2. Drain chicken, discarding marinade in bowl. Preheat oven to 450°. Place chicken on a rack in a shallow roasting pan, breast side up. Tuck wings under chicken; tie drumsticks together.

3. Roast 15 minutes. Meanwhile, in a large bowl, combine potatoes, carrots, rosemary, oil, chicken seasoning, salt and pepper. Add vegetables to roasting pan; reduce oven setting to 350°.

4. Roast until a thermometer inserted in thickest part of thigh reads 170°-175°, 1½-1¾ hours, adding the lemon slices during the last 15 minutes of roasting and brushing occasionally with reserved marinade. Cover loosely with foil if chicken browns too quickly.

5. Remove chicken from oven; tent with foil. Let stand 15 minutes before carving; discard rosemary sprigs.

5 OZ. COOKED CHICKEN WITH 1 CUP VEGETABLES: *654 cal., 31g fat (7g sat. fat), 104mg chol., 919mg sod., 58g carb. (32g sugars, 4g fiber), 36g pro.*

ROASTED HONEY MUSTARD CHICKEN

CLAMBAKE PACKETS

I've long been a fan of things prepared in a foil packet—we'll make them quite a bit when out on the boat or camping. This one, with fresh seafood, sausage, corn on the cob and potatoes, tastes like summer on the shore.
—Laura Davis, Chincoteague, VA

PREP: 20 MIN. • **GRILL:** 25 MIN.
MAKES: 6 SERVINGS

- 1½ lbs. uncooked shell-on shrimp (16-20 per lb.)
- 1½ lbs. red potatoes, quartered
- 26 fresh littleneck clams
- 3 medium ears sweet corn, cut into 1-in. slices
- ¾ lb. smoked kielbasa or fully cooked andouille sausage links, cut into 1-in. slices
- ¼ cup olive oil
- 1 Tbsp. seafood seasoning
- 1 medium lemon, sliced

1. Divide shrimp, potatoes, clams, corn and sausage on 6 pieces of heavy-duty foil (about 18 in. square). Drizzle with oil; sprinkle with seafood seasoning. Top with lemon slices. Fold foil around mixture, sealing tightly.

2. Grill, covered, over medium-high heat until clams open and vegetables are tender, 25-30 minutes. Open the foil carefully to allow steam to escape. Discard any unopened clams.

1 PACKET: *526 cal., 28g fat (7g sat. fat), 197mg chol., 894mg sod., 32g carb. (5g sugars, 3g fiber), 37g pro.*

PRESSURE-COOKER CUBAN ROPA VIEJA

CHICKEN CORDON BLEU

The addition of bacon in this cordon bleu recipe makes it one of my favorite comforting recipes. I've cooked it for both friends and family, and everyone's a fan.
—Jim Wick, Orlando, FL

PREP: 15 MIN. • **BAKE:** 40 MIN. • **MAKES:** 4 SERVINGS

- 4 boneless skinless chicken breast halves (8 oz. each)
- 2 Tbsp. butter, softened
- 1 tsp. dried thyme
- 4 thin slices fully cooked ham
- 4 thin slices Swiss cheese
- 8 bacon strips
- 2 large eggs
- ½ cup 2% milk
- ½ cup all-purpose flour
- ¾ cup dry bread crumbs
- ½ tsp. garlic powder
- 1 tsp. dried oregano
- ¼ cup shredded Parmesan cheese

1. Flatten chicken breasts to ⅛-in. thickness; spread butter on the insides. Sprinkle with thyme. Top with a slice of ham and Swiss cheese; roll up tightly. Wrap each with 2 slices of bacon and secure with toothpicks.
2. In a small bowl, beat eggs and milk. Place flour in another bowl. Combine the bread crumbs, garlic powder, oregano and cheese. Dip each chicken breast into egg mixture; dip into flour to coat. Dip each again into egg mixture, then coat with crumbs.
3. Place on a greased baking sheet. Bake, uncovered, at 350° for 40-45 minutes or until chicken juices run clear.
1 CHICKEN BREAST HALF: *654 cal., 27g fat (11g sat. fat), 280mg chol., 961mg sod., 30g carb. (3g sugars, 2g fiber), 70g pro.*

PRESSURE-COOKER CUBAN ROPA VIEJA

This recipe offers a great authentic Cuban taste that can be prepared at home. I love having this as a go-to recipe for a weeknight meal.
—Melissa Pelkey Hass, Waleska, GA

PREP: 25 MIN. • **COOK:** 20 MIN. + RELEASING • **MAKES:** 8 SERVINGS

- 6 bacon strips, chopped
- 2 beef flank steaks (1 lb. each), cut in half
- 1 can (28 oz.) crushed tomatoes
- 2 cups beef stock
- 1 can (6 oz.) tomato paste
- 5 garlic cloves, minced
- 1 Tbsp. ground cumin
- 2 tsp. dried thyme
- ¾ tsp. salt
- ½ tsp. pepper
- 1 medium onion, thinly sliced
- 1 medium sweet pepper, sliced
- 1 medium green pepper, sliced
- ¼ cup minced fresh cilantro
  Hot cooked rice

1. Select saute setting on a 6-qt. electric pressure cooker and adjust for high heat; add bacon. Cook bacon until crisp, stirring occasionally. Remove with a slotted spoon; drain on paper towels.
2. In drippings, brown steak in batches. Return bacon to pressure cooker. In a large bowl, combine tomatoes, beef stock, tomato paste, garlic, seasonings, onions and peppers; pour over meat. Lock lid; close pressure-release valve. Adjust to pressure-cook on high for 12 minutes. Allow pressure to naturally release for 10 minutes, then quick-release any remaining pressure.
3. Shred beef with 2 forks; return to pressure cooker. Stir in cilantro. Remove with a slotted spoon; serve with rice.
1 SERVING: *335 cal., 17g fat (6g sat. fat), 68mg chol., 765mg sod., 17g carb. (9g sugars, 4g fiber), 29g pro.*

CHICKEN CORDON BLEU

PRESSURE-COOKER CRANBERRY
MUSTARD PORK LOIN

PRESSURE-COOKER CRANBERRY MUSTARD PORK LOIN

This dressed-up pork loin is so easy that you only have to spend a few minutes preparing it. It's a family favorite because it is so tasty, and a favorite of mine because it's so fast and easy!
—Laura Cook, Wildwood, MO

PREP: 15 MIN. • **COOK:** 30 MIN. + RELEASING • **MAKES:** 8 SERVINGS

- 1   boneless pork loin roast (2 lbs.)
- 1   can (14 oz.) whole-berry cranberry sauce
- ¼   cup Dijon mustard
- 3   Tbsp. packed brown sugar
- 3   Tbsp. lemon juice
- 1   Tbsp. cornstarch
- ¼   cup cold water

1. Place roast in a 6-qt. electric pressure cooker. Combine the cranberry sauce, mustard, brown sugar and lemon juice; pour over roast. Lock lid; close pressure-release valve. Adjust to pressure-cook on high for 25 minutes. Allow pressure to naturally release for 10 minutes, then quick-release any remaining pressure. Remove roast and keep warm. Press cancel.
2. Strain cooking juices into a 2-cup measuring cup; add enough water to measure 2 cups. Return juices to the pressure cooker. Select saute setting and adjust for medium heat; bring liquid to a boil. In a small bowl, mix cornstarch and water until smooth; gradually stir into cooking juices. Cook and stir until sauce is thickened, 1-2 minutes. Press cancel. Serve sauce with pork.
1 SERVING: *255 cal., 6g fat (2g sat. fat), 56mg chol., 236mg sod., 28g carb. (19g sugars, 1g fiber), 22g pro.*

SAUSAGE & SQUASH PENNE

I love using frozen cooked winter squash because the hard work—peeling, chopping and cooking—is all done for me.
—Jennifer Roberts, South Burlington, VT

TAKES: 30 MIN. • **MAKES:** 4 SERVINGS

- 2   cups uncooked penne pasta
- 1   pkg. (12 oz.) frozen cooked winter squash
- 2   Tbsp. olive oil
- 3   cooked Italian sausage links (4 oz. each), sliced
- 1   medium onion, chopped
- ¼   cup grated Parmesan cheese
- ¼   tsp. salt
- ¼   tsp. dried parsley flakes
- ¼   tsp. pepper
     Additional grated Parmesan cheese and minced fresh parsley, optional

1. Cook pasta and squash according to package directions. Meanwhile, in a large skillet, heat oil over medium heat. Add sausage and onion; cook and stir until sausage is browned and onion is tender; keep warm.
2. In a small bowl, mix the cooked squash, cheese, salt, parsley and pepper until blended. Drain pasta; transfer to a serving plate. Spoon squash mixture over pasta; top with sausage mixture. Sprinkle with additional cheese and parsley.
¾ CUP PASTA WITH ½ CUP SAUSAGE AND ¼ CUP SQUASH: *468 cal., 26g fat (8g sat. fat), 40mg chol., 705mg sod., 41g carb. (4g sugars, 4g fiber), 19g pro.*

SAUSAGE & SQUASH PENNE

SLOW-COOKED
STUFFED PEPPERS

SLOW-COOKED STUFFED PEPPERS

*My favorite kitchen appliance is the slow
cooker, and I use mine more than anyone else
I know. Here's a tasty, good-for-you dish.*
—Michelle Gurnsey, Lincoln, NE

PREP: 15 MIN. • **COOK:** 3 HOURS
MAKES: 4 SERVINGS

- 4 medium sweet red peppers
- 1 can (15 oz.) black beans,
  rinsed and drained
- 1 cup shredded pepper jack cheese
- ¾ cup salsa
- 1 small onion, chopped
- ½ cup frozen corn
- ⅓ cup uncooked converted
  long grain rice
- 1¼ tsp. chili powder
- ½ tsp. ground cumin
  Reduced-fat sour cream, optional

1. Cut and discard tops from peppers;
remove seeds. In a large bowl, mix beans,
cheese, salsa, onion, corn, rice, chili powder
and cumin; spoon into peppers. Place the
peppers in a 5-qt. slow cooker coated with
cooking spray.

2. Cook, covered, on low until peppers are
tender and filling is heated through, 3-4
hours. If desired, serve with sour cream.
1 STUFFED PEPPER: *317 cal., 10g fat
(5g sat. fat), 30mg chol., 565mg sod.,
43g carb. (6g sugars, 8g fiber), 15g pro.*
Diabetic exchanges: *2 starch, 2 lean meat,
2 vegetable, 1 fat.*

SIMPLE CHICKEN ENCHILADAS

*This recipe is so quick and easy, and I always
receive a ton of compliments. It quickly
becomes a favorite of friends whenever I
share the recipe. Modify the spiciness with
the intensity of the salsa you use.*
—Kristi Black, Harrison Township, MI

PREP: 20 MIN. • **BAKE:** 25 MIN.
MAKES: 5 SERVINGS

- 1 can (10 oz.) enchilada sauce, divided
- 4 oz. cream cheese, cubed
- 1½ cups salsa
- 2 cups cubed cooked chicken
- 1 can (15 oz.) pinto beans,
  rinsed and drained
- 1 can (4 oz.) chopped green chiles
- 10 flour tortillas (6 in.)
- 1 cup shredded Mexican cheese blend

Optional: Shredded lettuce, chopped
tomato, sour cream and sliced ripe
olives

1. Spoon ½ cup enchilada sauce into a
greased 13x9-in. baking dish. In a large
saucepan, cook and stir the cream cheese
and salsa over medium heat for 2-3 minutes
or until blended. Stir in the chicken, beans
and chiles.

2. Place about ⅓ cup of chicken mixture
down the center of each tortilla. Roll up and
place seam side down over sauce. Top with
remaining enchilada sauce; sprinkle with
shredded cheese.

3. Cover and bake at 350° for 25-30 minutes
or until heated through. Serve with lettuce,
tomato, sour cream and olives if desired.
2 ENCHILADAS: *468 cal., 13g fat (6g sat. fat),
75mg chol., 1394mg sod., 51g carb. (6g
sugars, 8g fiber), 34g pro.*

> **TEST KITCHEN TIP**
>
> Any beans can be used in
> this recipe in place of the pinto
> beans—for example, black beans
> or kidney beans.

MANDY RIVERS
Lexington, SC

SOUTHERN
SHRIMP & GRITS

SOUTHERN
SHRIMP & GRITS

A southern specialty, sometimes called breakfast shrimp, this dish is also great for dinner—especially when company's coming. It's down-home comfort food at its finest.
—Mandy Rivers, Lexington, SC

PREP: 15 MIN. • **COOK:** 20 MIN.
MAKES: 4 SERVINGS

- 2 cups reduced-sodium chicken broth
- 2 cups 2% milk
- ⅓ cup butter, cubed
- ¾ tsp. salt
- ½ tsp. pepper
- ¾ cup uncooked old-fashioned grits
- 1 cup shredded cheddar cheese

SHRIMP
- 8 thick-sliced bacon strips, chopped
- 1 lb. uncooked medium shrimp, peeled and deveined
- 3 garlic cloves, minced
- 1 tsp. Cajun or blackened seasoning
- 4 green onions, chopped

1. In a large saucepan, bring the broth, milk, butter, salt and pepper to a boil. Slowly stir in grits. Reduce heat. Cover and cook for 12-14 minutes or until thickened, stirring occasionally. Stir in cheese until melted. Set aside and keep warm.

2. In a large skillet, cook bacon strips over medium heat until crisp. Remove to paper towels with a slotted spoon; drain skillet, reserving 4 tsp. drippings. Saute shrimp, garlic and seasoning in drippings until shrimp turn pink. Serve with grits and sprinkle with onions.

1 CUP GRITS WITH ½ CUP SHRIMP MIXTURE: *674 cal., 42g fat (22g sat. fat), 241mg chol., 1845mg sod., 33g carb. (7g sugars, 1g fiber), 41g pro.*

Quickly Separate and
Peel Garlic Cloves

Place the head of garlic in one bowl and smash with the bottom of a similar-sized bowl. You can also smash between two cutting boards.

Put the whole crushed bulb in a hard-sided bowl with a similar-sized bowl over the top. Metal is best, but you can use glass or even a firm plastic food storage container with a lid. A jar works, too, but it takes longer to shake. Shake vigorously for 10-15 seconds to separate the papery outer layer from the garlic cloves.

The cloves are peeled and the skins can be easily discarded.

❄ PESTO-CHICKEN PENNE CASSEROLES

Pesto and Alfredo sauce give bold flavors to this rich pasta. This recipe makes two casseroles, so you can have one for dinner tonight and freeze one for later.
—Laura Kayser, Ankeny, IA

PREP: 20 MIN. • **BAKE:** 40 MIN.
MAKES: 2 CASSEROLES (6 SERVINGS EACH)

- 1   pkg. (16 oz.) penne pasta
- 6   cups cubed cooked chicken
- 4   cups shredded Italian cheese blend
- 3   cups fresh baby spinach
- 1   can (15 oz.) crushed tomatoes
- 1   jar (15 oz.) Alfredo sauce
- 1½ cups 2% milk
- 1   jar (8.1 oz.) prepared pesto
- ½   cup seasoned bread crumbs
- ½   cup grated Parmesan cheese
- 1   Tbsp. olive oil

1. Cook pasta according to package directions. Meanwhile, in a large bowl, combine the chicken, cheese blend, spinach, tomatoes, Alfredo sauce, milk and pesto. Drain pasta and add to chicken mixture; toss to coat.
2. Transfer to 2 greased 8-in. square baking dishes. In a small bowl, combine the bread crumbs, Parmesan cheese and oil; sprinkle over casseroles.
3. Cover and freeze 1 casserole for up to 3 months. Cover and bake remaining casserole at 350° for 40-45 minutes or until bubbly.
TO USE FROZEN CASSEROLE: Thaw in the refrigerator overnight. Remove from the refrigerator 30 minutes before baking. Cover and bake at 350° for 50-60 minutes or until bubbly.
1⅓ CUPS: 612 cal., 30g fat (13g sat. fat), 111mg chol., 829mg sod., 41g carb. (3g sugars, 3g fiber), 42g pro.

SESAME GINGER BEEF SKEWERS

My family loves the flavors of these zippy kabobs. They're perfect for a laid-back cookout in the backyard.
—Jasey McBurnett, Rock Springs, WY

PREP: 20 MIN. + MARINATING
GRILL: 5 MIN. • **MAKES:** 6 SERVINGS

- 1   beef flank steak (1½ lbs.)
- 1   cup rice vinegar
- 1   cup soy sauce
- ¼   cup packed brown sugar
- 2   Tbsp. minced fresh gingerroot
- 6   garlic cloves, minced
- 3   tsp. sesame oil
- 2   tsp. Sriracha chili sauce or
     1 tsp. hot pepper sauce
- ½   tsp. corn starch
     Optional: Sesame seeds and thinly sliced green onions

1. Cut beef into ¼-in.-thick strips. In a large bowl, whisk the first 7 ingredients until blended. Pour 1 cup marinade into a shallow dish. Add beef; turn to coat. Refrigerate, covered, 2-8 hours. Cover and refrigerate remaining marinade.
2. Drain beef, discarding marinade in dish. Thread beef onto 12 metal or soaked wooden skewers. Grill kabobs, covered, over medium-high heat or broil 4 in. from heat until meat reaches desired doneness (for medium-rare, a thermometer should read 135°; medium, 140°; medium-well, 145°), 4-5 minutes, turning occasionally and basting frequently using ½ cup of reserved marinade.
3. To make glaze, bring remaining marinade (about ¾ cup) to a boil; whisk in ½ tsp. cornstarch. Cook, whisking constantly until thickened, 1-2 minutes. Brush kabobs with glaze just before serving. If desired, top with sesame seeds and sliced green onions.
2 KABOBS: 264 cal., 10g fat (4g sat. fat), 54mg chol., 1480mg sod., 18g carb. (15g sugars, 0 fiber), 24g pro.

SESAME GINGER BEEF SKEWERS

CONTEST-WINNING
EGGPLANT PARMESAN

CONTEST-WINNING EGGPLANT PARMESAN

Because my recipe calls for baking eggplant instead of frying it, it's much healthier! The prep time is a little longer than for some recipes, but the Italian flavors and rustic elegance are well worth it.
—Laci Hooten, McKinney, TX

PREP: 40 MIN. • **COOK:** 25 MIN.
MAKES: 8 SERVINGS

- 3 large eggs, beaten
- 2½ cups panko (Japanese) bread crumbs
- 3 medium eggplants, cut into ¼-in. slices
- 2 jars (4½ oz. each) sliced mushrooms, drained
- ½ tsp dried basil
- ⅛ tsp. dried oregano
- 2 cups shredded part-skim mozzarella cheese
- ½ cup grated Parmesan cheese
- 1 jar (28 oz.) spaghetti sauce

1. Preheat oven to 350°. Place eggs and bread crumbs in separate shallow bowls. Dip eggplant in eggs, then coat in crumbs. Place on baking sheets coated with cooking spray. Bake 15-20 minutes or until tender and golden brown, turning once.
2. In a small bowl, combine mushrooms, basil and oregano. In another bowl, combine mozzarella and Parmesan.
3. Spread ½ cup sauce into a 13x9-in. baking dish coated with cooking spray. Layer with a third of the mushroom mixture, a third of the eggplant, ¾ cup sauce and a third of the cheese mixture. Repeat layers twice.
4. Bake, uncovered, at 350° until casserole is heated through and cheese is melted, 25-30 minutes.
1 SERVING: *305 cal., 12g fat (5g sat. fat), 102mg chol., 912mg sod., 32g carb. (12g sugars, 9g fiber), 18g pro.*

READER REVIEW

"The only difference between my recipe and this one— I saute fresh mushrooms instead of using canned. Awesome recipe, especially with a chunky garden veggie sauce."
DIANNE, TASTEOFHOME.COM

CALIFORNIA CHICKEN CLUB PIZZA

CALIFORNIA CHICKEN CLUB PIZZA

Inspired by the California Club pizza from California Pizza Kitchen, I decided to whip up my own version. It's loaded with tons of fresh veggies, so that means it has to be good for you, right?
—Robert Pickart, Chicago, IL

PREP: 25 MIN. • **BAKE:** 10 MIN.
MAKES: 4 SERVINGS

- 1 Tbsp. cornmeal
- 1 loaf (1 lb.) frozen pizza dough, thawed
- 1 cup shredded mozzarella cheese
- 1 cup ready-to-use grilled chicken breast strips
- 4 bacon strips, cooked and crumbled
- 2 cups shredded romaine
- 1 cup fresh arugula
- ¼ cup mayonnaise
- 1 Tbsp. lemon juice
- 1 tsp. grated lemon zest
- ½ tsp. pepper
- 1 medium tomato, thinly sliced
- 1 medium ripe avocado, peeled and sliced
- ¼ cup loosely packed basil leaves, chopped

1. Preheat oven to 450°. Grease a 14-in. pizza pan; sprinkle with cornmeal. On a floured surface, roll dough into a 13-in. circle. Transfer to prepared pan; build up edges slightly. Sprinkle with cheese, chicken, and bacon. Bake until crust is lightly browned, 10-12 minutes.
2. Meanwhile, place romaine and arugula in a large bowl. In a small bowl, combine mayonnaise, lemon juice, lemon zest and pepper. Pour over lettuces; toss to coat. Arrange over warm pizza. Top with tomato, avocado and basil. Serve immediately.
2 SLICES: *612 cal., 30g fat (7g sat. fat), 51mg chol., 859mg sod., 59g carb. (4g sugars, 5g fiber), 29g pro.*

CREAMY SCALLOP CREPES

These savory crepes feel so elegant for a special dinner. I like to add ¼ teaspoon of fresh dill to the crepe batter before refrigerating it.
—Doreen Kelly, Hatboro, PA

PREP: 45 MIN. + CHILLING • **BAKE:** 15 MIN.
MAKES: 6 SERVINGS

  2 large egg whites
  1 large egg
1½ cups fat-free milk
  1 cup all-purpose flour
  ½ tsp. salt
  2 Tbsp. unsalted butter, melted
FILLING
  1 lb. bay scallops
  ½ cup white wine or reduced-sodium chicken broth
  ⅛ tsp. white pepper
  1 lb. sliced fresh mushrooms
  4 green onions, sliced
  2 Tbsp. butter
  ¼ cup all-purpose flour
  ⅔ cup fat-free evaporated milk
  ½ cup shredded reduced-fat Swiss cheese
     Sliced green onions, optional

1. In a small bowl, beat the egg whites, egg and milk. Combine flour and salt; add to milk mixture and mix well. Cover and refrigerate for 1 hour.
2. Brush an 8-in. nonstick skillet lightly with melted butter; heat. Stir crepe batter; pour 2 Tbsp. into center of skillet. Lift and tilt pan to coat bottom evenly. Cook until top appears dry; turn and cook 15-20 seconds longer. Remove to a wire rack. Repeat with the remaining batter, brushing skillet with melted butter as needed. When cool, stack crepes with waxed paper or paper towels in between.
3. In a large nonstick skillet, bring the scallops, wine and pepper to a boil. Reduce heat; simmer until scallops are firm and opaque, 3-4 minutes. Drain, reserving cooking liquid; set liquid and scallops aside.
4. In the same skillet, saute mushrooms and green onions in butter until almost tender. Sprinkle with flour; stir until blended. Gradually stir in evaporated milk and cooking liquid. Bring to a boil; cook and stir until thickened, about 2 minutes. Remove from the heat. Stir in cheese and scallops.
5. Spread ⅓ cup filling down the center of each crepe; roll up and place in a 13x9-in. baking dish coated with cooking spray. Cover and bake at 350° until heated through, 12-15 minutes.
2 CREPES: *331 cal., 10g fat (6g sat. fat), 76mg chol., 641mg sod., 33g carb. (9g sugars, 2g fiber), 24g pro.* **Diabetic exchanges:** *3 lean meat, 2 starch, 2 fat.*

PRESSURE-COOKER CHICKEN CACCIATORE

My husband and I own and operate a busy farm. There are days when there's just no time left for cooking! It's really nice to be able to come into the house at night and have dinner ready in just a few minutes.
—Aggie Arnold-Norman, Liberty, PA

PREP: 15 MIN. • **COOK:** 15 MIN. + RELEASING
MAKES: 6 SERVINGS

  2 medium onions, thinly sliced
  1 broiler/fryer chicken (3 to 4 lbs.), cut up and skin removed
  2 garlic cloves, minced
  1 to 2 tsp. dried oregano
  1 tsp. salt
  ½ tsp. dried basil
  ¼ tsp. pepper
  1 bay leaf
  1 can (14½ oz.) diced tomatoes, undrained
  1 can (8 oz.) tomato sauce
  1 can (4 oz.) mushroom stems and pieces, drained
  ¼ cup white wine or water
     Hot cooked pasta

Place onions in a 6-qt. electric pressure cooker. Add the next 11 ingredients. Lock lid; close pressure-release valve. Adjust to pressure-cook on high for 15 minutes. When finished cooking, allow pressure to naturally release for 10 minutes, then quick-release any remaining pressure. Discard bay leaf. Serve chicken with sauce over pasta.
1 SERVING: *207 cal., 6g fat (2g sat. fat), 73mg chol., 787mg sod., 11g carb. (6g sugars, 3g fiber), 27g pro.*

CREAMY SCALLOP CREPES

SENATE BEAN POTPIE

The flavors from a classic Senate bean soup inspired this hearty potpie with a crumbly cornbread topping.
—Janice Elder, Charlotte, NC

PREP: 30 MIN. • **BAKE:** 20 MIN. + STANDING
MAKES: 6 SERVINGS

- 2 Tbsp. canola oil
- 2 medium carrots, chopped
- 2 celery ribs, chopped
- 1 medium onion, chopped
- 1½ cups cubed fully cooked ham
- 3 Tbsp. all-purpose flour
- 1 can (14½ oz.) chicken broth
- 2 cans (15½ oz. each) navy or other white beans, rinsed and drained
- ¼ tsp. salt
- ¼ tsp. pepper
- 1 pkg. (8½ oz.) cornbread/muffin mix
- ½ cup 2% milk
- 1 large egg, lightly beaten
- 2 green onions, finely chopped
- ¼ cup minced fresh parsley
- 2 Tbsp. butter, melted

1. Preheat oven to 425°. In a 10-in. ovenproof skillet, heat oil over medium-high heat. Add carrots, celery and onion; cook and stir 6-8 minutes or until tender. Add ham. Stir in flour until blended; gradually stir in broth. Bring to a boil, stirring constantly; cook and stir until thickened, 1-2 minutes.

2. Add beans, salt and pepper; return to a boil. In a small bowl, combine muffin mix, milk, egg, green onions, parsley and melted butter; stir just until blended. Spoon evenly over bean mixture (dish will be full).

3. Bake 20-25 minutes or until topping is golden brown. Let stand 15 minutes.

1 SERVING: *513 cal., 17g fat (5g sat. fat), 66mg chol., 1619mg sod., 67g carb. (12g sugars, 12g fiber), 24g pro.*

SLOW-COOKER TURKEY BREAST

Here's an easy recipe to try when you're craving turkey. It uses pantry ingredients, which is handy.
—Maria Juco, Milwaukee, WI

PREP: 10 MIN. • **COOK:** 5 HOURS
MAKES: 14 SERVINGS

- 1 bone-in turkey breast (6 to 7 lbs.), skin removed
- 1 Tbsp. olive oil
- 1 tsp. dried minced garlic
- 1 tsp. seasoned salt
- 1 tsp. paprika
- 1 tsp. Italian seasoning
- 1 tsp. pepper
- ½ cup water

Brush turkey with oil. Combine the garlic, seasoned salt, paprika, Italian seasoning and pepper; rub over turkey. Transfer to a 6-qt. slow cooker; add water. Cover and cook on low for 5-6 hours or until tender.

4 OZ. COOKED TURKEY: *174 cal., 2g fat (0 sat. fat), 101mg chol., 172mg sod., 0 carb. (0 sugars, 0 fiber), 37g pro.* **Diabetic exchanges:** *4 lean meat.*

Lemon-Garlic Turkey Breast: Combine ¼ cup minced fresh parsley, 8 minced garlic cloves, 4 tsp. grated lemon zest, 2 tsp. salt-free lemon-pepper seasoning and 1½ tsp. salt; rub over turkey breast. Add water and cook as directed.

**PRESSURE-COOKER
MEDITERRANEAN
CHICKEN ORZO**

PRESSURE-COOKER MEDITERRANEAN CHICKEN ORZO

Orzo pasta with chicken, olives and herbes de Provence has the bright flavors of Mediterranean cuisine. Here's a bonus: Leftovers reheat well.
—Thomas Faglon, Somerset, NJ

PREP: 15 MIN. • **COOK:** 5 MIN. + STANDING
MAKES: 6 SERVINGS

- 6 boneless skinless chicken thighs (about 1½ lbs.), cut into 1-in. pieces
- 2 cups reduced-sodium chicken broth
- 2 medium tomatoes, chopped
- 1 cup sliced pitted green olives, drained
- 1 cup sliced pitted ripe olives, drained
- 1 large carrot, halved lengthwise and chopped
- 1 small red onion, finely chopped
- 1 Tbsp. grated lemon zest
- 3 Tbsp. lemon juice
- 2 Tbsp. butter
- 1 Tbsp. herbes de Provence
- 1 cup uncooked orzo pasta

1. In a 6-qt. electric pressure cooker, combine the first 11 ingredients; stir to combine. Lock lid; close pressure-release valve. Adjust to pressure-cook on high for 8 minutes. Quick-release pressure.
2. Add orzo. Lock lid; close pressure-release valve. Adjust to pressure-cook on low for 3 minutes. Allow pressure to naturally release for 4 minutes, then quick-release any remaining pressure. Let stand for 8-10 minutes before serving.
NOTE: Look for herbes de Provence in the spice aisle.
1 SERVING: *415 cal., 19g fat (5g sat. fat), 86mg chol., 941mg sod., 33g carb. (4g sugars, 3g fiber), 27g pro.*

SLOW-COOKER POT ROAST

I work full time, so this slow-cooked pot roast is a favorite when I want a hearty home-cooked meal. It's a comfort to walk in and smell this simmering roast that I know will be tender and delicious.
—Gina Jackson, Ogdensburg, NY

PREP: 15 MIN. • **COOK:** 6 HOURS
MAKES: 8 SERVINGS

- 1 cup warm water
- 1 Tbsp. beef base
- ½ lb. sliced fresh mushrooms
- 1 large onion, coarsely chopped
- 3 garlic cloves, minced
- 1 boneless beef chuck roast (3 lbs.)
- ½ tsp. pepper
- 1 Tbsp. Worcestershire sauce
- ¼ cup butter, cubed
- ⅓ cup all-purpose flour
- ¼ tsp. salt

1. In a 5- or 6-qt. slow cooker, whisk water and beef base; add mushrooms, onion and garlic. Sprinkle roast with pepper; transfer to slow cooker. Drizzle with Worcestershire sauce. Cook, covered, on low 6-8 hours or until meat is tender.
2. Remove roast to a serving platter; tent with foil. Strain cooking juices, reserving vegetables. Skim fat from cooking juices. In a large saucepan, melt butter over medium heat. Stir in flour and salt until smooth; gradually whisk in cooking juices. Bring to a boil, stirring constantly; cook and stir 1-2 minutes or until thickened. Stir in cooked vegetables. Serve with roast.
NOTE: Look for beef base near the broth and bouillon.
5 OZ. COOKED MEAT WITH ½ CUP GRAVY: *380 cal., 22g fat (10g sat. fat), 126mg chol., 467mg sod., 8g carb. (2g sugars, 1g fiber), 35g pro.*

DID YOU KNOW?

Worcestershire sauce was originally considered a mistake. In 1835, an English lord commissioned two chemists to duplicate a sauce he had tried in India. The pungent batch was disappointing and wound up in their cellar. When the pair stumbled upon the aged concoction two years later, they were pleasantly surprised by its unique taste.

LASAGNA TOSS

This easy dish tastes just like lasagna without all the layering prep work. It's perfect for busy weeknights!
—Sharon Martin, Denver, PA

PREP: 15 MIN. • **BAKE:** 20 MIN. • **MAKES:** 6 SERVINGS

   1 lb. ground beef
   ½ cup chopped onion
   1 garlic clove, minced
   ½ tsp. salt
   1¾ cups spaghetti sauce
   6 oz. spiral noodles, cooked and drained
   1 cup small curd 4% cottage cheese
   2 cups shredded part-skim mozzarella cheese, divided
      Grated Parmesan cheese
      Minced fresh basil

1. Preheat oven to 350°. In a large skillet, brown beef with onion, garlic and salt. Stir in spaghetti sauce; simmer until heated. Remove 1 cup meat sauce; set aside. Stir noodles into the remaining sauce. Place half of the noodle mixture in a greased 2-qt. casserole. Cover with cottage cheese and 1 cup of mozzarella cheese.
2. Add remaining noodle mixture; top with reserved meat sauce and remaining 1 cup mozzarella cheese. Sprinkle with Parmesan cheese. Cover; bake for 20-25 minutes. Let stand 5 minutes before serving. If desired, sprinkle with basil.
1½ CUPS: 436 cal., 19g fat (9g sat. fat), 74mg chol., 885mg sod., 34g carb. (10g sugars, 3g fiber), 31g pro.

LASAGNA TOSS

ALMOND PORK CHOPS WITH HONEY MUSTARD

ALMOND PORK CHOPS WITH HONEY MUSTARD

I love how crunchy almonds and sweet mustard sauce jazz up this tender pork dish. Usually I double the recipe. One chop per person is never enough for my crowd of grown children and grandkids.
—Lily Julow, Lawrenceville, GA

TAKES: 30 MIN. • **MAKES:** 4 SERVINGS

   ½ cup smoked almonds
   ½ cup dry bread crumbs
   2 large eggs
   ⅓ cup all-purpose flour
   ¼ tsp. salt
   ⅛ tsp. pepper
   4 boneless pork loin chops (1 in. thick and 6 oz. each)
   2 Tbsp. olive oil
   2 Tbsp. butter
   ½ cup reduced-fat mayonnaise
   ¼ cup honey
   2 Tbsp. Dijon mustard

1. In a food processor, process the almonds until finely chopped. Transfer to a shallow bowl; add bread crumbs. In another bowl, beat the eggs. In a large bowl, combine flour, salt and pepper. Add 1 pork chop at a time and toss to coat. Dip in eggs, then coat with almond mixture.
2. Preheat oven to 400°. In a large skillet over medium heat, cook chops in oil and butter until lightly browned, 2-3 minutes on each side. Transfer to a rimmed baking sheet; bake, uncovered, until a thermometer inserted in pork reads 145°, about 10-15 minutes. Meanwhile, in a small bowl, combine the mayonnaise, honey and mustard. Serve with pork chops.
1 PORK CHOP WITH ABOUT 3 TBSP. SAUCE: 642 cal., 40g fat (11g sat. fat), 204mg chol., 659mg sod., 31g carb. (20g sugars, 2g fiber), 39g pro.

CHEDDAR BEEF ENCHILADAS

CHEDDAR BEEF ENCHILADAS

I created these enchiladas to satisfy several picky eaters in our house. They were an instant hit and are now in my weekly rotation. I like that we can enjoy this meal twice by freezing half for a busy day.
—Stacy Cizek, Conrad, IA

PREP: 30 MIN. • **BAKE:** 20 MIN.
MAKES: 2 CASSEROLES (3 SERVINGS EACH)

- 1   lb. ground beef
- 1   envelope taco seasoning
- 1   cup water
- 2   cups cooked rice
- 1   can (16 oz.) refried beans
- 2   cups shredded cheddar cheese, divided
- 12 flour tortillas (8 in.), warmed
- 1   jar (16 oz.) salsa
- 1   can (10¾ oz.) condensed cream of chicken soup, undiluted

1. In a large skillet, cook beef over medium heat until no longer pink; drain. Stir in taco seasoning and water. Bring to a boil. Reduce heat; simmer, uncovered, for 5 minutes. Stir in rice. Cook and stir until liquid is evaporated.
2. Spread about 2 Tbsp. refried beans, ¼ cup beef mixture and 1 Tbsp. cheese down the center of each tortilla; roll up. Place seam side down in 2 greased 13x9-in. baking dishes.
3. Combine salsa and soup; pour down the center of enchiladas. Sprinkle with remaining cheese.
4. Bake 1 casserole, uncovered, at 350° for 20-25 minutes or until heated through and cheese is melted. Cover and freeze remaining casserole for up to 3 months.
TO USE FROZEN CASSEROLE: Thaw in the refrigerator overnight. Cover and bake at 350° for 30 minutes. Uncover; bake 5-10 minutes longer or until heated through and cheese is melted.
2 ENCHILADAS: *840 cal., 33g fat (14g sat. fat), 88mg chol., 2242mg sod., 95g carb. (4g sugars, 7g fiber), 37g pro.*

HERBED CHICKEN WITH WILD RICE

My family is always busy, so it's nice when we can come home to a meal that's already prepared and ready to eat. Just open up a bag of salad and dinner is ready!
—Becky Gifford, Conway, AR

PREP: 20 MIN. • **COOK:** 4 HOURS • **MAKES:** 6 SERVINGS

- 1   pkg. (6 oz.) long grain and wild rice mix
- 6   boneless skinless chicken breast halves (5 oz. each)
- 1   Tbsp. canola oil
- 1   tsp. butter
- ½   lb. sliced fresh mushrooms
- 1   can (10¾ oz.) condensed cream of chicken soup, undiluted
- 1   cup water
- 3   bacon strips, cooked and crumbled
- 1   tsp. dried parsley flakes
- ½   tsp. dried thyme
- ¼   tsp. dried tarragon

1. Place rice in a 5-qt. slow cooker; set aside seasoning packet. In a large skillet, brown chicken in oil and butter. Add to slow cooker. In the same skillet, saute mushrooms until tender; place over chicken.
2. In a small bowl, combine the soup, water, bacon, herbs and contents of seasoning packet. Pour over top. Cover and cook on low for 4-5 hours or until chicken is tender.
1 SERVING: *351 cal., 11g fat (3g sat. fat), 88mg chol., 890mg sod., 27g carb. (1g sugars, 1g fiber), 35g pro.*

HERBED CHICKEN
WITH WILD RICE

MACARONI TACO BAKE

Comforting mac and cheese with a touch of taco flavoring and tortilla-chip crunch...no wonder everyone loves it! It's a fun change of pace from regular macaroni.
—Elizabeth King, Duluth, MN

PREP: 30 MIN. • **BAKE:** 15 MIN.
MAKES: 8 SERVINGS

- 2 pkg. (7¼ oz. each) macaroni and cheese dinner mix
- 1 lb. ground beef
- 1 cup chunky salsa
- 2 cups crushed tortilla chips
- 1 can (2¼ oz.) sliced ripe olives, drained
- 2 cups shredded Mexican cheese blend
  Sour cream, optional

1. Prepare macaroni and cheese according to package directions. Meanwhile, in a large skillet, cook beef until no longer pink; drain. Stir in salsa; set aside.

2. Spread macaroni into a greased 13x9-in. baking dish. Layer with beef mixture, chips and olives; sprinkle with cheese.

3. Bake, uncovered, at 350° until heated through, 15-20 minutes. Serve with sour cream if desired.

1¼ CUPS: *597 cal., 33g fat (17g sat. fat), 105mg chol., 991mg sod., 48g carb. (7g sugars, 1g fiber), 28g pro.*

PRESSURE-COOKER SAUERBRATEN

One of my all-time favorite German dishes is sauerbraten, but I don't love that it normally takes five to 10 days to make. Using an electric pressure cooker, I think I've captured that same distinctive flavor in less than two hours.
—James Schend, Pleasant Prairie, WI

PREP: 20 MIN. + STANDING • **COOK:** 20 MIN.
MAKES: 4 SERVINGS

- 4 whole cloves
- 4 whole peppercorns
- 1 bay leaf
- ½ cup water
- ½ cup white vinegar
- 2 tsp. sugar
- ½ tsp. salt
  Dash ground ginger
- 1 lb. boneless beef top round steak, cut into 1-in. cubes

PRESSURE-COOKER SAUERBRATEN

- 3 medium carrots, cut into ½-in. slices
- 2 celery ribs, cut into ½-in. slices
- 1 small onion, chopped
- ⅓ cup crushed gingersnaps
  Hot cooked egg noodles
  Chopped fresh parsley and coarsely ground pepper, optional

1. Place cloves, peppercorns and bay leaf on a double thickness of cheesecloth; bring up corners of cloth and tie with kitchen string to form a bag. In a large bowl, combine the water, vinegar, sugar, salt and ginger. Add the cubed beef and spice bag; let stand at room temperature for 30 minutes.

2. Transfer to a 6-qt. electric pressure cooker. Add the carrots, celery and onion. Lock lid; close the pressure-release valve.

Adjust to pressure-cook on high for 10 minutes. When finished cooking, quick-release pressure. Select saute setting and adjust for high heat; bring liquid to a boil. Discard spice bag. Stir in gingersnaps; cook and stir until thickened, about 3 minutes. Serve with egg noodles. If desired, top with parsley and pepper.

FREEZE OPTION: Freeze cooled sauerbraten in freezer containers. To use, partially thaw in refrigerator overnight. Heat through in a saucepan, stirring occasionally and adding a little broth or water if necessary.

1 CUP: *228 cal., 5g fat (2g sat. fat), 63mg chol., 436mg sod., 18g carb. (8g sugars, 2g fiber), 27g pro.* **Diabetic exchanges:** *3 lean meat, 1 starch, 1 vegetable.*

**TURKEY & APPLE
ARUGULA SALAD IN A JAR
PAGE 107**

Meal Planner

Who said leftovers can't be new and exciting? Here are fresh ways to impress with the same ingredient the next day, and the day after that! Your family might not even know the difference.

Chicken on the Fly

Throw some chicken on the grill to prep four delicious dinners for super breezy weeknights. Start with Grilled Buttermilk Chicken. Then turn the leftovers into a potpie, chicken Wellington or a cool salad.

CHICKEN BISCUIT POTPIE

This hearty meal in one takes just 10 minutes to assemble before popping it in the oven.
—Dorothy Smith, El Dorado, AR

PREP: 10 MIN. • **BAKE:** 25 MIN.
MAKES: 4 SERVINGS

1⅔ cups frozen mixed
    vegetables, thawed
1½ cups cubed cooked chicken
1 can (10¾ oz.) condensed cream
    of chicken soup, undiluted
¼ tsp. dried thyme
1 cup biscuit/baking mix
½ cup whole milk
1 large egg

1. In a large bowl, combine the vegetables, chicken, soup and thyme. Pour into an ungreased deep-dish 9-in. pie plate. Combine the biscuit mix, milk and egg; spoon over chicken mixture.
2. Bake potpie at 400° until golden brown, 25-30 minutes.

1 SERVING: *376 cal., 14g fat (4g sat. fat), 103mg chol., 966mg sod., 38g carb. (5g sugars, 5g fiber), 23g pro.*

GRILLED BUTTERMILK CHICKEN

I created this recipe years ago after one of our farmers market customers, a chef, shared the idea of marinating chicken in buttermilk. The chicken is easy to prepare and always turns out moist and delicious! I bruise the thyme sprigs by twisting them before adding to the buttermilk mixture; this tends to release the oils in the leaves and flavor the chicken better.
—Sue Gronholz, Beaver Dam, WI

PREP: 10 MIN. + MARINATING • **GRILL:** 10 MIN.
MAKES: 12 SERVINGS

1½ cups buttermilk
4 fresh thyme sprigs
4 garlic cloves, halved
½ tsp. salt
12 boneless skinless chicken
    breast halves (about 4½ lbs.)

1. Place the buttermilk, thyme, garlic and salt in a large bowl or shallow dish. Add chicken and turn to coat. Refrigerate for 8 hours or overnight, turning occasionally.
2. Drain chicken, discarding marinade. Grill, covered, over medium heat until a thermometer reads 165°, 5-7 minutes per side.

1 CHICKEN BREAST HALF: *189 cal., 4g fat (1g sat. fat), 95mg chol., 168mg sod., 1g carb. (1g sugars, 0 fiber), 35g pro.* **Diabetic exchanges:** *5 lean meat.*

TEST KITCHEN TIP

Make Your Own Buttermilk

Combine 1 Tbsp. lemon juice or white vinegar plus enough milk to measure 1 cup. Stir, then let stand for 5 minutes.

CHICKEN BISCUIT POTPIE

GRILLED BUTTERMILK CHICKEN

SUE GRONHOLZ
Beaver Dam, WI

FLAKY CHICKEN WELLINGTON

FLAKY CHICKEN WELLINGTON

This cozy chicken Wellington takes a classic recipe and makes it super easy! I like to cook the chicken a day or so ahead to make it even simpler to throw together on busy nights.
—Kerry Dingwall, Wilmington, NC

PREP: 30 MIN. • **BAKE:** 15 MIN.
MAKES: 6 SERVINGS

- 2   cups cubed cooked chicken
- 1   pkg. (10 oz.) frozen chopped spinach, thawed and squeezed dry
- 3   hard-boiled large eggs, chopped
- ½   cup finely chopped dill pickles
- ⅓   cup finely chopped celery
- 2   tubes (8 oz. each) refrigerated crescent rolls
- 2   tsp. prepared mustard, divided
- 1   cup sour cream
- 2   Tbsp. dill pickle juice

1. Preheat oven to 350°. In a large bowl, combine the first 5 ingredients. Unroll 1 tube of the crescent dough into 1 long rectangle; press perforations to seal.
2. Spread half the mustard over dough; top with half the chicken mixture to within ¼ in. of edges. Roll up jelly-roll style, starting with a long side; pinch seam to seal. Place cut side down on a parchment-lined baking sheet. Cut slits in the top. Repeat with the remaining crescent dough, mustard and chicken mixture.
3. Bake until golden brown, 15-20 minutes. Meanwhile, combine sour cream and pickle juice; serve with pastries.

FREEZE OPTION: Cover and freeze unbaked pastries on a parchment-lined baking sheet until firm. Transfer to a freezer container; return to freezer. To use, bake the pastries on a parchment-lined baking sheet in a preheated 350° oven until golden brown, 30-35 minutes. Prepare sauce as directed.

⅓ **PASTRY WITH ABOUT 3 TBSP. SAUCE:** *495 cal., 28g fat (6g sat. fat), 144mg chol., 830mg sod., 37g carb. (10g sugars, 2g fiber), 25g pro.*

CHICKEN, NECTARINE & AVOCADO SALAD

CHICKEN, NECTARINE & AVOCADO SALAD

This summery salad comes together very quickly. Using granola adds crunch and makes it different. I've tried using a few different types of granola, and our favorites have been mixtures with a lot of nuts and that aren't extremely sweet. This is not the time for your chocolate granola!
—Elisabeth Larsen, Pleasant Grove, UT

TAKES: 15 MIN. • **MAKES:** 4 SERVINGS

- 6   oz. fresh baby spinach (about 8 cups)
- 2   medium nectarines, thinly sliced
- 2   cups cubed cooked chicken
- 1   cup crumbled feta cheese
- ½   cup poppy seed salad dressing
- 1   medium ripe avocado, peeled and sliced
- 1   cup granola with fruit and nuts

In a large bowl, combine the baby spinach, nectarines, chicken and feta. Drizzle with dressing; toss to coat. Top with avocado and granola. Serve immediately.

1½ **CUPS:** *561 cal., 32g fat (7g sat. fat), 87mg chol., 539mg sod., 38g carb. (18g sugars, 7g fiber), 30g pro.*

HOW-TO

Shred Chicken & Turkey Fast

Make fast work of shredding poultry with your stand mixer's paddle attachment. Refrigerate or freeze the meat in 2-cup quantities so it's easy to use in recipes. Use in any recipe that calls for cubed or shredded meat.

Suppertime Stretch

Spice up Taco Tuesday when you serve Seasoned Taco Meat and all the fixin's. Then turn the extra beef into any of these delicious foods—no one will know it's leftovers. Make a kid-friendly taco pizza, tasty pinwheel apps or an amazing breakfast-for-dinner.

MEAT-AND-POTATO QUICHE

This hearty dish is welcome anytime, of course, but our family especially enjoys it at breakfast! It just seems to get the day off to an extra good start.
—Esther Beachy, Hutchinson, KS

PREP: 20 MIN. • **BAKE:** 30 MIN.
MAKES: 6 SERVINGS

- 3 Tbsp. canola oil
- 3 cups shredded peeled potatoes, well drained
- 1 cup shredded part-skim mozzarella cheese
- ¾ cup prepared taco meat
- ¼ cup chopped onion
- 1 cup heavy whipping cream
- 5 large eggs
- ½ tsp. salt
- ⅛ tsp. pepper

1. Combine oil and potatoes in a 10-in. pie plate. Press mixture down evenly to form a crust. Bake at 425° until lightly browned, about 10 minutes.

2. Layer with the mozzarella, taco meat and onion. Whisk together the cream, eggs, salt and pepper; pour over beef mixture. Bake until a knife inserted in center comes out clean, about 30 minutes.
1 PIECE: *377 cal., 29g fat (13g sat. fat), 242mg chol., 356mg sod., 18g carb. (3g sugars, 2g fiber), 12g pro.*

SEASONED TACO MEAT

I got this recipe from the restaurant where I work. Everyone in town loves the blend of different seasonings. Now the secret is out!
—Denise Mumm, Dixon, IA

PREP: 10 MIN. • **COOK:** 35 MIN.
MAKES: 6½ CUPS

- 3 lbs. ground beef
- 2 large onions, chopped
- 2 cups water
- 5 Tbsp. chili powder
- 2 tsp. salt
- 1 tsp. ground cumin
- ¾ tsp. garlic powder
- ¼ to ½ tsp. crushed red pepper flakes

In a large skillet or Dutch oven, cook beef and onion over medium heat until meat is no longer pink; drain. Add water and seasonings. Bring to a boil. Reduce heat; simmer, uncovered, until the water is evaporated, about 15 minutes.
¼ CUP: *113 cal., 7g fat (3g sat. fat), 35mg chol., 277mg sod., 2g carb. (1g sugars, 1g fiber), 10g pro.*

MEAT-AND-POTATO QUICHE

SEASONED TACO MEAT

SPICY EGG BAKE

TACO PIZZA SQUARES

Your gang will come running the minute you take this zesty pizza out of the oven. I top a refrigerated pizza dough with taco meat, tomatoes and cheese to bring a full-flavored fiesta to the table.
—Sarah Vovos, Middleton, WI

TAKES: 25 MIN. • **MAKES:** 10 SERVINGS

- 1 tube (13.8 oz.) refrigerated pizza crust
- 1 can (8 oz.) pizza sauce
- 2 cups prepared taco meat
- 2 medium tomatoes, seeded and chopped
- 2 cups shredded mozzarella cheese
  Optional: Shredded lettuce and sour cream

Unroll pizza dough and place in a 15x10x1-in. baking pan. Spread with the pizza sauce; sprinkle with the taco meat, tomatoes and cheese. Bake at 400° until crust is golden brown, 15-20 minutes. Top with shredded lettuce and sour cream if desired.

1 PIECE: *259 cal., 11g fat (5g sat. fat), 40mg chol., 660mg sod., 23g carb. (4g sugars, 2g fiber), 17g pro.*

SPICY EGG BAKE

This family favorite makes a wonderful morning meal served with muffins and fresh fruit. It's also a great way to use up extra taco meat. Adjust the heat by choosing a hotter or milder salsa.
—Michelle Jibben, Springfield, MN

TAKES: 30 MIN. • **MAKES:** 8 SERVINGS

- 1 tube (8 oz.) refrigerated crescent rolls
- 10 large eggs
- ⅓ cup water
- 3 Tbsp. butter
- 1½ cups prepared taco meat
- 1 cup shredded cheddar cheese
- 1 cup shredded Monterey Jack cheese
- 1 cup salsa

1. Unroll crescent roll dough into a greased 13x9-in. baking dish. Seal seams and perforations; set aside.
2. In a small bowl, whisk the eggs and water. In a large skillet, heat butter until hot. Add egg mixture; cook and stir over medium heat until eggs are almost set. Remove from the heat.
3. Sprinkle taco meat over dough. Layer with eggs, cheeses and salsa. Bake, uncovered, at 375° until bubbly and cheese is melted, 14-16 minutes.

1 PIECE: *481 cal., 32g fat (14g sat. fat), 327mg chol., 981mg sod., 19g carb. (4g sugars, 3g fiber), 30g pro.*

TACO PIZZA SQUARES

MEAL PLANNER

TACO PINWHEELS

TACO PINWHEELS

These pinwheels come together quickly when you start with leftover taco meat. They make a great party appetizer served with salsa, or a fun lunch option with a salad on the side.
—Cindy Reams, Philipsburg, PA

PREP: 15 MIN. + CHILLING
MAKES: 3 DOZEN PINWHEELS

- 4   oz. cream cheese, softened
- ¾   cup prepared taco meat
- ¼   cup finely shredded cheddar cheese
- ¼   cup salsa
- 2   Tbsp. mayonnaise
- 2   Tbsp. chopped ripe olives
- 2   Tbsp. finely chopped onion
- 5   flour tortillas (8 in.), room temperature
- ½   cup shredded lettuce
     Additional salsa

1. In a small bowl, beat the cream cheese until smooth. Stir in the taco meat, cheese, salsa, mayonnaise, olives and onion. Spread over tortillas. Sprinkle with lettuce; roll up tightly. Wrap in plastic and refrigerate for at least 1 hour.
2. Unwrap and cut into 1-in. pieces. Serve with additional salsa.
1 PINWHEEL: *51 cal., 3g fat (1g sat. fat), 6mg chol., 84mg sod., 4g carb. (0 sugars, 0 fiber), 2g pro.*

Now We're Talking Turkey

Bone-in turkey breast makes a winning roasted dinner with just 10 minutes of easy prep. The next day, turn those tasty leftovers into a hearty stew, a big 13x9 casserole, or a so-stylish salad in a jar.

TURKEY-SWEET POTATO STEW

A batch of this soup brings the nostalgic flavors and heartwarming feel of the holidays at any time of year.
—Radine Kellogg, Fairview, IL

PREP: 20 MIN. • **COOK:** 30 MIN.
MAKES: 4 SERVINGS

- 2 medium sweet potatoes, peeled and cubed
- 2 cups water
- 2 tsp. sodium-free chicken bouillon granules
- 1 can (14¾ oz.) cream-style corn
- 1 Tbsp. minced fresh sage
- ¼ tsp. pepper
- 1 Tbsp. cornstarch
- 1 cup 2% milk
- 2 cups cubed cooked turkey breast

1. In a large saucepan, combine potatoes, water and bouillon; bring to a boil. Reduce heat; cook, covered, until the potatoes are tender, 10-15 minutes.
2. Stir in the corn, sage and pepper; heat through. In a small bowl, mix cornstarch and milk until smooth; stir into soup. Bring to a boil; cook and stir until thickened, 1-2 minutes. Stir in turkey; heat through.
1½ CUPS: 275 cal., 3g fat (1g sat. fat), 65mg chol., 374mg sod., 39g carb. (13g sugars, 3g fiber), 26g pro. **Diabetic exchanges:** *3 lean meat, 2½ starch.*

ROSEMARY TURKEY BREAST

I season turkey with a blend of rosemary, garlic and paprika. Because I rub half of the mixture directly on the meat under the skin, I can remove the skin before serving and not sacrifice flavor. The result is an entree that's lower in fat, yet delicious—the perfect meal.
—Dorothy Pritchett, Wills Point, TX

PREP: 10 MIN.
BAKE: 1½ HOURS + STANDING
MAKES: 15 SERVINGS

- 2 Tbsp. olive oil
- 8 to 10 garlic cloves, peeled
- 3 Tbsp. chopped fresh rosemary or 3 tsp. dried rosemary, crushed
- 1 tsp. salt
- 1 tsp. paprika
- ½ tsp. coarsely ground pepper
- 1 bone-in turkey breast (5 lbs.)

1. In a food processor, combine the oil, garlic cloves, rosemary, salt, paprika and pepper; cover and process until garlic is coarsely chopped.
2. With your fingers, carefully loosen the skin from both sides of the turkey breast. Spread half of the garlic mixture over the meat under the skin. Smooth skin over meat and secure to underside of breast with toothpicks. Spread remaining garlic mixture over turkey skin.
3. Place turkey breast on a rack in a shallow roasting pan. Bake, uncovered, at 325° until a thermometer reads 170°, 1½-2 hours. Let stand for 15 minutes before slicing. Discard the toothpicks.
4 OZ. COOKED TURKEY: 148 cal., 3g fat (0 sat. fat), 78mg chol., 207mg sod., 1g carb. (0 sugars, 0 fiber), 29g pro. **Diabetic exchanges:** *4 lean meat.*

TURKEY-SWEET POTATO STEW

ROSEMARY TURKEY BREAST

TURKEY LATTICE PIE

TURKEY LATTICE PIE

With its pretty lattice crust, this cheesy baked dish is as eye-catching as it is tasty. It's easy to make, too, since it uses crescent roll dough.
—Lorraine Naig, Emmetsburg, IA

PREP: 20 MIN. • **BAKE:** 20 MIN.
MAKES: 12 SERVINGS

- 3 tubes (8 oz. each) refrigerated crescent rolls
- 4 cups cubed cooked turkey
- 1½ cups shredded cheddar or Swiss cheese
- 3 cups frozen chopped broccoli, thawed and drained
- 1 can (10¾ oz.) condensed cream of chicken soup, undiluted
- 1⅓ cups whole milk
- 2 Tbsp. Dijon mustard
- 1 Tbsp. dried minced onion
- ½ tsp. salt
  Dash pepper
- 1 large egg, lightly beaten

1. Preheat oven to 375°. Unroll 2 tubes of crescent roll dough; separate into rectangles. Place the rectangles in an ungreased 15x10x1-in. baking pan. Press onto the bottom and ¼ in. up the sides of pan to form a crust, sealing seams and perforations. Bake 5-7 minutes or until light golden brown.
2. Meanwhile, in a large bowl, combine the turkey, cheese, broccoli, soup, milk, mustard, onion, salt and pepper. Spoon over crust.
3. Unroll the remaining dough; divide into rectangles. Seal perforations. Cut each rectangle into four 1-in. strips. Using strips, make a lattice design on top of the turkey mixture. Brush with egg. Bake casserole 17-22 minutes longer or until top crust is golden brown and filling is bubbly.
1 PIECE: *396 cal., 20g fat (4g sat. fat), 81mg chol., 934mg sod., 30g carb. (8g sugars, 2g fiber), 24g pro.*

TURKEY & APPLE
ARUGULA SALAD IN A JAR

TURKEY & APPLE ARUGULA SALAD IN A JAR

Join the jarred salad craze with this adaptation of a turkey and apple salad inspired by a recipe from Nancy Heishman of Las Vegas.
—Taste of Home *Test Kitchen*

TAKES: 20 MIN. • **MAKES:** 4 SERVINGS

- ½ cup orange juice
- 3 Tbsp. red wine vinegar
- 1 to 3 Tbsp. sesame oil
- 2 Tbsp. minced fresh chives
- ¼ tsp. salt
- ¼ tsp. coarsely ground pepper

SALAD

- 4 cups cubed cooked turkey
- 4 tsp. curry powder
- ½ tsp. coarsely ground pepper
- ¼ tsp. salt
- 1 large apple, chopped
- 1 Tbsp. lemon juice
- 1 cup green grapes, halved
- 1 can (11 oz.) mandarin oranges, drained
- ½ cup pomegranate seeds or dried cranberries
- ½ cup chopped walnuts
- 4 cups fresh arugula or baby spinach

1. In a small bowl, whisk first 6 ingredients. Place turkey in a large bowl; sprinkle with the seasonings and toss to combine. In a separate bowl, toss chopped apple with lemon juice.
2. In each of four 1-qt. wide-mouth canning jars, divide and layer the ingredients in the following order: orange juice mixture, seasoned turkey, apple, grapes, oranges, pomegranate seeds, walnuts and fresh arugula. Cover and refrigerate until serving. Transfer salads into bowls; toss to combine.
1 SERVING: *471 cal., 19g fat (3g sat. fat), 141mg chol., 453mg sod., 33g carb. (25g sugars, 5g fiber), 45g pro.*

**BEST EVER SWEET PICKLES
PAGE 114**

Side Dishes & Condiments

Enrich your meals with this collection of sides, condiments and more that will have everyone asking for another helping. From sweet jams to savory grains and flavorful butters —even tasty veggies to win over the kids— we've got you covered.

CORN & BROCCOLI
IN CHEESE SAUCE

VANILLA PEAR BERRY JAM

*This is the first jam that I came up with on
my own—and it turned out pretty well!*
—Rachel Creech, Marion, IN

PREP: 30 MIN. • **PROCESS:** 10 MIN.
MAKES: 7 HALF-PINTS

- 4 cups fresh strawberries, hulled
- 2 cups chopped peeled ripe
  pears (about 2 medium)
- 2 Tbsp. lemon juice
- 1 pkg. (1¾ oz.) powdered fruit pectin
- 6 cups sugar
- 2 Tbsp. vanilla extract

1. Crush strawberries; transfer to a Dutch
oven. Stir in pears, lemon juice and pectin.
Bring to a full rolling boil over high heat,
stirring constantly. Stir in sugar; return to
a full rolling boil. Boil for 1 minute, stirring
constantly. Remove from heat; skim off
foam. Stir in vanilla.
2. Ladle hot mixture into 7 hot half-pint
jars, leaving ¼-in. headspace. Remove air
bubbles and adjust headspace, if necessary,
by adding hot mixture. Wipe rims. Center
lids on jars; screw on the bands until
fingertip tight.
3. Place jars into canner, ensuring that they
are completely covered with water. Bring to
a boil; process for 10 minutes. Remove jars
and cool.
NOTE: The processing time listed is for
altitudes of 1,000 feet or less. Add 1 minute
to the processing time for each 1,000 feet of
additional altitude.
2 TBSP.: *91 cal., 0 fat (0 sat. fat), 0 chol.,
0 sod., 23g carb. (23g sugars, 0 fiber), 0 pro.*

CORN & BROCCOLI
IN CHEESE SAUCE

*This veggie side is a solid standby. Because
it's made in a slow cooker, there's more room
in the oven. My daughter likes to add leftover
ham to hers.*
—Joyce Johnson, Uniontown, OH

PREP: 10 MIN. • **COOK:** 3 HOURS
MAKES: 8 SERVINGS

- 1 pkg. (16 oz.) frozen corn, thawed
- 1 pkg. (16 oz.) frozen broccoli
  florets, thawed
- 4 oz. reduced-fat Velveeta, cubed
- ½ cup shredded cheddar cheese
- 1 can (10¼ oz.) reduced-fat
  reduced-sodium condensed cream
  of chicken soup, undiluted
- ¼ cup fat-free milk

1. In a 4-qt. slow cooker, combine corn,
broccoli and cheeses. In a small bowl,
combine soup and milk; pour over
vegetable mixture.
2. Cover and cook on low until heated
through, 3-4 hours. Stir before serving.
¾ CUP: *148 cal., 5g fat (3g sat. fat), 16mg
chol., 409mg sod., 21g carb. (4g sugars, 3g
fiber), 8g pro.* **Diabetic exchanges:** *1 starch,
1 medium-fat meat.*

HOMEMADE PEAR HONEY

Pear honey is an old recipe that's been passed down through families. We especially like it with hot biscuits and butter. It's also good on pound cake or even ice cream. Make sure the pears you use are very firm.
—Charlotte McDaniel, Jacksonville, AL

PREP: 20 MIN. • **COOK:** 45 MIN. • **MAKES:** 6 HALF-PINTS

- 8 medium pears, peeled and quartered
- 4 cups sugar
- 1 can (20 oz.) crushed pineapple, drained

1. Place pears in a food processor; process until finely chopped. In a Dutch oven, combine pears and sugar; bring to a boil. Reduce heat; simmer, uncovered, 45 minutes, stirring occasionally. Stir in pineapple; cook and stir 5 minutes longer.
2. Remove from heat. Ladle hot liquid into 6 hot half-pint jars; wipe rims. Seal and allow to cool. Refrigerate up to 2 weeks.
2 TBSP.: *91 cal., 0 fat (0 sat. fat), 0 chol., 1mg sod., 24g carb. (22g sugars, 1g fiber), 0 pro.*

HOMEMADE PEAR HONEY

**ASPARAGUS WITH
TARRAGON LEMON SAUCE**

ASPARAGUS WITH
TARRAGON LEMON SAUCE

With its fresh taste and minimal prep work, this is a recipe I'm sure you'll love.
—Patricia Swart, Galloway, NJ

TAKES: 15 MIN. • **MAKES:** 6 SERVINGS

- 2 lbs. fresh asparagus, trimmed
- 3 Tbsp. olive oil
- 1 tsp. all-purpose flour
- 3 Tbsp. fat-free milk
- 1 Tbsp. lemon juice
- 2 tsp. minced fresh tarragon
  Dash salt

1. Place asparagus in a steamer basket; place in a large saucepan over 1 in. of water. Bring to a boil; cover and steam for 3-5 minutes or until crisp-tender. Drain.
2. Meanwhile, in a small saucepan, combine olive oil and flour. Gradually stir in milk until smooth. Bring to a boil; cook and stir for 1 minute or until thickened. Remove from the heat. Stir in lemon juice, tarragon and salt. Serve with asparagus.
1 SERVING: *83 cal., 7g fat (1g sat. fat), 0 chol., 36mg sod., 4g carb. (2g sugars, 1g fiber), 2g pro.* **Diabetic exchanges:** *1 vegetable, 1 fat.*

SIDE DISHES & CONDIMENTS

SPANISH HOMINY

I received this recipe from a good friend who is a fabulous cook. The colorful side dish gets its zesty flavor from spicy canned tomatoes with green chiles.
—Donna Brockett, Kingfisher, OK

PREP: 15 MIN. • **COOK:** 6 HOURS • **MAKES:** 12 SERVINGS

4   cans (15½ oz. each) hominy, rinsed and drained
1   can (14½ oz.) diced tomatoes, undrained
1   can (10 oz.) diced tomatoes and green chiles, undrained
1   can (8 oz.) tomato sauce
¾   lb. bacon strips, diced
1   large onion, chopped
1   medium green pepper, chopped

1. In a 5-qt. slow cooker, combine the hominy, tomatoes and tomato sauce.
2. In a large skillet, cook bacon until crisp; remove with a slotted spoon to paper towels. Drain drippings from pan; reserve 1 Tbsp.
3. In the same skillet, saute onion and green pepper in drippings until tender. Stir onion mixture and bacon into hominy mixture. Cover and cook on low until heated through, 6-8 hours.
¾ CUP: *150 cal., 5g fat (2g sat. fat), 11mg chol., 1039mg sod., 20g carb. (2g sugars, 5g fiber), 6g pro.*

SPANISH HOMINY

TEXAS-STYLE SPANISH RICE

A Mexican friend gave me the original version of this fragrant rice recipe, but I've modified the spices to suit my family's tastes. It has become a favorite side at our house; see if it doesn't do the same at yours!
—Melissa Pride, Plano, TX

PREP: 10 MIN. • **COOK:** 25 MIN. • **MAKES:** 6 SERVINGS

¼   cup chopped onion
¼   cup chopped green pepper
2   Tbsp. canola oil
1   cup uncooked long grain rice
½   cup tomatoes with green chiles
¼   tsp. ground turmeric
1   tsp. ground cumin
½   tsp. salt
¼   tsp. garlic powder
2   cups water
2   to 3 Tbsp. chopped fresh cilantro, optional

In a skillet, saute the onion and green pepper in oil for about 2 minutes. Add rice and stir until coated with oil. Add tomatoes, turmeric, cumin, salt, garlic powder and water; bring to a boil. Reduce heat and simmer, covered, about 20 minutes or until liquid is absorbed. Add cilantro if desired.
¾ CUP: *166 cal., 5g fat (1g sat. fat), 0 chol., 279mg sod., 27g carb. (2g sugars, 1g fiber), 3g pro.*

TEXAS-STYLE SPANISH RICE

MISO-BUTTERED SUCCOTASH

The miso paste used in this super simple dish gives depth and a hint of savoriness to canned or fresh vegetables. To brighten the flavor profile even more, you could add a splash of your favorite white wine.
—William Milton III, Clemson, SC

TAKES: 20 MIN. • **MAKES:** 6 SERVINGS

- 2 tsp. canola oil
- 1 small red onion, chopped
- 2 cans (15¼ oz. each) whole kernel corn, drained
- 1½ cups frozen shelled edamame, thawed
- ½ medium sweet red pepper, chopped (about ½ cup)
- 2 Tbsp. unsalted butter, softened
- 1 tsp. white miso paste
- 3 green onions, thinly sliced Coarsely ground pepper

1. In a large skillet, heat oil over medium-high heat. Add red onion; cook and stir until crisp-tender, about 2-3 minutes. Add corn, edamame and red pepper. Cook until vegetables reach desired tenderness, 4-6 minutes longer.

2. In a small bowl, mix butter and miso paste until combined; stir into pan until melted. Sprinkle with green onions and pepper before serving.

¾ CUP: *193 cal., 9g fat (3g sat. fat), 10mg chol., 464mg sod., 20g carb. (11g sugars, 6g fiber), 8g pro.*

> **TEST KITCHEN TIP**
>
> Try mixing a bit of leftover miso paste into your favorite cold spreads—mix it with mayonnaise, cream cheese or sour cream— to boost flavor. It can give salad dressings and marinades a lift, too.

MISO-BUTTERED SUCCOTASH

MINTY SUGAR SNAP PEAS

BEST EVER SWEET PICKLES
(SHOWN ON PAGE 108)

When I was a kid, I always looked forward to the homemade jams and jellies my granny made from her farm-grown berries. Our urban backyard doesn't have room for a berry patch, but we have a trellis for growing cucumbers. I pack away these sweet pickles every summer.
—Ellie Martin Cliffe, Milwaukee, WI

PREP: 1 HOUR + STANDING
PROCESS: 10 MIN. • **MAKES:** 4 PINTS

 9   cups sliced pickling cucumbers
 1   large sweet onion, halved
     and thinly sliced
 ¼   cup canning salt
 1   cup sugar
 1   cup water
 1   cup white vinegar
 ½   cup cider vinegar
 2   Tbsp. mustard seed
 1   tsp. celery seed
 ½   tsp. whole peppercorns
 4   bay leaves
 12 garlic cloves, crushed

1. In a large nonreactive bowl, combine cucumbers, onion and salt. Cover with crushed ice and mix well. Let stand 3 hours. Drain; rinse and drain thoroughly.
2. In a Dutch oven, combine sugar, water, vinegars, mustard seed, celery seed and peppercorns. Bring to a boil, stirring to dissolve sugar. Add cucumber mixture; return to a boil, stirring occasionally. Reduce heat; simmer, uncovered, 4-5 minutes or until heated through.
3. Carefully ladle hot mixture into 4 hot wide-mouth 1-pint jars, leaving ½-in. headspace. Add 3 garlic cloves and 1 bay leaf to each jar. Remove air bubbles and, if necessary, adjust headspace by adding hot pickling liquid. Wipe rims. Center lids on jars; screw on bands until fingertip tight.
4. Place jars into canner with simmering water, ensuring that they are completely covered with water. Bring to a boil; process for 10 minutes. Remove jars and cool.
¼ CUP: 35 cal., 0 fat (0 sat. fat), 0 chol., 175mg sod., 8g carb. (7g sugars, 0 fiber), 0 pro.

MINTY SUGAR SNAP PEAS
Fresh mint adds a lively touch to cooked sugar snap peas. It's also nice on green beans or carrots.
—Alice Kaldahl, Ray, ND

TAKES: 10 MIN. • **MAKES:** 4 SERVINGS

 3   cups fresh sugar snap peas, trimmed
 ¼   tsp. sugar
 2   to 3 Tbsp. minced fresh mint
 2   Tbsp. butter

Place 1 in. of water in a large skillet. Add peas and sugar; bring to a boil. Reduce heat; simmer, covered, until peas are crisp-tender, 4-5 minutes; drain. Stir in mint and butter.
¾ CUP: 102 cal., 6g fat (4g sat. fat), 15mg chol., 45mg sod., 9g carb. (4g sugars, 3g fiber), 4g pro. **Diabetic exchanges:** *2 vegetable, 1½ fat.*

Grilling Marinades

Prepare to become a pit master. Mix up a sauce in a shallow dish, toss in the main ingredient and let it rest in the fridge for up to the max marinating time.

1 Huli Huli
1 cup packed **brown sugar**, ¾ cup **ketchup**, ¾ cup **reduced-sodium soy sauce**, ⅓ cup **sherry** or **chicken broth**, 2½ tsp. minced **fresh gingerroot** and 1½ tsp. minced **garlic**.
—*Sharon Boling, San Diego, CA*

2 Northwoods
6 Tbsp. **maple syrup**, 6 Tbsp. **balsamic vinegar**, ¾ tsp. **salt** and ¾ tsp. coarsely **ground pepper**.
—*Nicholas King, Duluth, MN*

3 Honey-Garlic
¼ cup **lemon juice**, ¼ cup **honey**, 2 Tbsp. **soy sauce** and 2 minced **garlic cloves**.
—*Helen Carpenter, Albuquerque, NM*

4 Orange-Spice
½ cup thawed **orange juice concentrate**, ¼ cup **honey**, ¼ cup **soy sauce**, 1 tsp. **Chinese five-spice powder** and ½ tsp. **garlic powder**.
—*Debra Stevens, Lutz, FL*

5 Ranch
2 cups **sour cream**, 1 envelope **ranch salad dressing mix**, 4 tsp. **lemon juice**, 4 tsp. **Worcestershire sauce**, 2 tsp. **celery salt**, 2 tsp. **paprika**, 1 tsp. **garlic salt** and 1 tsp. **pepper**.
—*Barbee Decker, Whispering Pines, NC*

6 Heavenly Greek
⅓ cup **lemon juice**, 2 Tbsp. **olive oil**, 4 tsp. grated **lemon zest**, 2 minced **garlic cloves**, 1 tsp. **dried oregano**, ¼ tsp. **salt** and ¼ tsp. **pepper**.
—*Meagan Jensen, Reno, NV*

7 Southwest Chili
2 Tbsp. **olive oil**, 1 Tbsp. **chili powder**, 1 tsp. **garlic salt**, 1 tsp. **ground coriander**, 1 tsp. **dried oregano**, ½ tsp. **ground cumin** and ½ tsp. **pepper**.
—*Lindsay Matuszak, Reno, NV*

8 Balsamic Mustard
1¼ cups **balsamic vinaigrette**, 4 tsp. **ground mustard**, 2¼ tsp. **Worcestershire sauce** and 2 minced **garlic cloves**.
—*Gail Garcelon, Beaverton, OR*

9 Ginger-Peach
¼ cup **peach preserves**, 1 Tbsp. **lemon juice**, 1 Tbsp. finely chopped **crystallized ginger**, 2 tsp. grated **lemon zest** and ⅛ tsp. **ground cloves**.
—*Jacqueline Correa, Landing, NJ*

10 Tangy Barbecue
1 cup **barbecue sauce**, ½ cup **burgundy wine** or **beef broth** and ¼ cup **lemon juice**.
—*Beverly Dietz, Surprise, AZ*

Match the Marinade	
Beef	8 hours
Pork	6 hours
Chicken	4 hours
Fruit	1 hour
Seafood	30 minutes

**LEMON-PARMESAN
BROILED ASPARAGUS**

CILANTRO GINGER CARROTS

Peppery-sweet ginger and cooling cilantro have starring roles in this colorful side of crisp-tender carrots. They go from pan to plate in a twinkling.
—Taste of Home *Test Kitchen*

TAKES: 15 MIN. • **MAKES:** 4 SERVINGS

- 1 Tbsp. butter
- 1 lb. fresh carrots, sliced diagonally
- 1½ tsp. minced fresh gingerroot
- 2 Tbsp. chopped fresh cilantro
- ½ tsp. salt
- ¼ tsp. pepper

In a large skillet, heat butter over medium-high heat. Add carrots; cook and stir 4-6 minutes or until crisp-tender. Add ginger; cook 1 minute longer. Stir in cilantro, salt and pepper.
½ **CUP:** *73 cal., 3g fat (2g sat. fat), 8mg chol., 396mg sod., 11g carb. (5g sugars, 3g fiber), 1g pro.* **Diabetic exchanges:** *1 vegetable, ½ fat.*

LEMON-PARMESAN BROILED ASPARAGUS

These special spears are packed with flavor, thanks to the lemon-garlic dressing they're tossed in before roasting. It's a simple, quick side that goes with almost anything.
—Tina Mirilovich, Johnstown, PA

TAKES: 15 MIN. • **MAKES:** 4 SERVINGS

- ¼ cup mayonnaise
- 4 tsp. olive oil
- 1½ tsp. grated lemon zest
- 1 garlic clove, minced
- ½ tsp. seasoned salt
- ½ tsp. pepper
- 1 lb. fresh asparagus, trimmed
- 2 Tbsp. shredded Parmesan cheese
  Lemon wedges, optional

1. Preheat broiler. In large bowl, combine the first 6 ingredients. Add asparagus; toss to coat. Place in a single layer on a wire rack over a foil-lined 15x10x1-in. baking pan.
2. Broil 5-6 in. from heat 5-7 minutes or until tender and lightly browned. Transfer to a serving platter; sprinkle with Parmesan cheese. If desired, serve with lemon wedges.
1 SERVING: *156 cal., 15g fat (3g sat. fat), 3mg chol., 309mg sod., 3g carb. (1g sugars, 1g fiber), 2g pro.* **Diabetic exchanges:** *3 fat, 1 vegetable.*

TEST KITCHEN TIP

In order to keep asparagus fresh longer, place the cut stems in a container of cold water—similar to flowers in a vase. Place the container in the refrigerator, changing the water at least once every 2 days.

CILANTRO GINGER CARROT

CAULIFLOWER DILL KUGEL

I enjoy cauliflower and kugel, so it made sense to combine the two into one special dish. The ricotta cheese adds a distinctive creaminess and lightness to the kugel, while shallots and herbs deepen the flavors.
—*Arlene Erlbach, Morton Grove, IL*

PREP: 30 MIN. • **BAKE:** 35 MIN. + STANDING
MAKES: 8 SERVINGS

5   Tbsp. butter, divided
1½   cups thinly sliced shallots
4   large eggs
2   cups whole-milk ricotta cheese
1   cup minced fresh parsley, divided
½   cup shredded Gruyere
    or Swiss cheese
¼   cup dill weed, divided
3   tsp. grated lemon zest, divided
¼   tsp. salt, divided
⅛   tsp. pepper
1   pkg. (16 oz.) frozen cauliflower,
    thawed and patted dry
¾   cup panko (Japanese) bread crumbs
½   tsp. garlic powder

1. Preheat oven to 375°. In a large skillet, heat 3 Tbsp. butter over medium-high heat. Add shallots; cook and stir until golden brown, 3-5 minutes. Remove and set aside.

2. In a large bowl, mix eggs, ricotta cheese, ¾ cup parsley, Gruyere cheese, 3 Tbsp. dill, 2 tsp. lemon zest, ⅛ tsp. salt and the pepper. Stir in cauliflower and shallots. Transfer to a greased 8-in. square baking dish.

3. In the same skillet, heat remaining butter. Add bread crumbs; cook and stir until lightly browned, 2-3 minutes. Stir in the garlic powder and the remaining parsley, dill, lemon zest and salt. Sprinkle over the cauliflower mixture.

4. Bake, uncovered, until set, 35-45 minutes. Let stand 10 minutes before cutting. Refrigerate leftovers.

1 PIECE: *289 cal., 19g fat (11g sat. fat), 147mg chol., 343mg sod., 16g carb. (7g sugars, 3g fiber), 16g pro.*

**HASSELBACK
SWEET POTATOES**

HASSELBACK SWEET POTATOES

My family and friends love the warm, inviting flavors of the luscious citrus butter, smooth cream cheese, sweet dates, fresh sage and toasted pecans that surround and capture the deliciousness of sweet potato in every bite.
—Brenda Watts, Gaffney, SC

PREP: 30 MIN. • **BAKE:** 70 MIN.
MAKES: 6 SERVINGS

- 6 medium sweet potatoes
- ½ cup unsalted butter, melted
- 2 Tbsp. brown sugar
- 2 Tbsp. orange juice
- 2 tsp. grated orange zest
- ½ tsp. kosher salt
- ½ tsp. coarsely ground pepper
- 6 oz. cream cheese, softened
- 12 pitted dates, chopped
- 12 fresh sage leaves, chopped
- ½ cup chopped pecans
     Fresh sage, chopped, optional

1. Preheat oven to 425°. Cut thin slices lengthwise from bottom of sweet potatoes to allow them to lie flat; discard slices. Place potatoes flat side down; cut crosswise into ⅛-in. slices, leaving them intact at the bottom. Arrange sweet potatoes in a greased 13x9-in. baking pan.
2. In a small bowl, whisk together butter, brown sugar, orange juice and orange zest. Spoon half the butter mixture evenly over sweet potatoes; sprinkle with salt and pepper. Combine cream cheese, dates and sage; spread between potato slices.

3. Bake, covered, until potatoes are just becoming tender, 45-50 minutes. Remove pan from oven and uncover; spoon the remaining butter mixture over potatoes and top with pecans. Return to oven and bake until potatoes are completely tender and topping is golden brown, 25-30 minutes longer. If desired, serve with chopped fresh sage.
1 SWEET POTATO: *552 cal., 32g fat (16g sat. fat), 69mg chol., 271mg sod., 64g carb. (34g sugars, 8g fiber), 6g pro.*

5i

BOURBON PEACH JAM

Bourbon has been popular at our house since we visited Kentucky's Bourbon Trail a few years ago. This jam reminds me of that fun trip with every bite.
—Katie Ferrier, Houston, TX

PREP: 70 MIN. • **PROCESS:** 10 MIN.
MAKES: 3 HALF-PINTS

- 4 cups finely chopped peeled fresh peaches (about 6 medium)
- 1½ cups packed brown sugar
- 1 cup sugar
- 1 Tbsp. lemon juice
- 3 Tbsp. bourbon or 3 tsp. vanilla or bourbon extract

1. In a large saucepan, combine peaches, sugars and lemon juice; bring to a boil. Reduce heat; simmer, uncovered, until mixture is thick and a thermometer reads 220°, about 60 minutes. Remove from heat; skim off foam. Stir in bourbon.
2. Ladle hot mixture into 3 hot half-pint jars, leaving ¼-in. headspace. Remove air bubbles and adjust headspace, if necessary, by adding hot mixture. Wipe rims. Center lids on jars; screw on bands until fingertip tight.
3. Place jars in canner, ensuring that they are completely covered with water. Bring to a boil; process for 10 minutes. Remove jars and cool.
NOTE: The processing time listed is for altitudes of 1,000 feet or less. Add 1 minute to the processing time for each 1,000 feet of additional altitude.
2 TBSP.: *88 cal., 0 fat (0 sat. fat), 0 chol., 4mg sod., 23g carb. (22g sugars, 0 fiber), 0 pro.*

BADGER STATE STUFFING

Your family will love the contrasting sweet, savory, and slightly tart flavors in this spin on a Thanksgiving classic. Feel free to use your favorite beer or dried fruit to make the dish your own.
—*Andrea Fetting, Franklin, WI*

PREP: 35 MIN. • **BAKE:** 50 MIN. + STANDING
MAKES: 8 CUPS

- ½ lb. bacon strips, diced
- ½ lb. sliced fresh mushrooms
- 1 medium onion, diced
- 1 cup chopped celery (about 3 stalks)
- 1 cup chopped carrot (about 4 medium carrots)
- 2 garlic cloves, minced
- 1 can (8 oz.) sauerkraut, rinsed and well drained
- ½ cup amber beer or chicken broth
- 5 cups cubed sourdough bread (½-in. cubes)
- 1 cup dried cherries or dried cranberries
- 1 large egg
- 1¼ cups chicken broth
- 3 Tbsp. minced fresh parsley
- 1 tsp. poultry seasoning
- ½ tsp. pepper

1. Preheat oven to 350°. In a large skillet, cook bacon over medium heat until crisp, stirring occasionally. Remove with a slotted spoon; drain on paper towels. Discard drippings, reserving 3 Tbsp. in pan.

2. Add mushrooms, onion, celery and carrot to the drippings; cook and stir over medium-high heat until tender, 8-10 minutes. Add garlic; cook 1 minute longer. Stir in sauerkraut and beer. Bring to a boil; cook, uncovered, until liquid is reduced by half.

3. In a large bowl, combine bread cubes, cherries, bacon and sauerkraut mixture. In a small bowl, whisk egg, broth, parsley, poultry seasoning and pepper. Gradually stir into bread mixture.

4. Transfer to a greased 2-qt. baking dish. Bake, covered, 20 minutes. Uncover; bake until lightly browned, 30-35 minutes longer. Let stand 10 minutes before serving.

1 CUP: *271 cal., 11g fat (4g sat. fat), 39mg chol., 700mg sod., 35g carb. (18g sugars, 3g fiber), 9g pro.*

BADGER STATE STUFFING

SIDE DISHES & CONDIMENTS

BRUSSELS SPROUTS WITH PECANS & HONEY

I know what you're thinking—but even the kids will eat these slightly sweet and nutty Brussels sprouts like candy. My family always turned their noses up at Brussels sprouts until they tried these. Now they request the dish often.
—Deborah Latimer, Loveland, CO

PREP: 25 MIN. • **BAKE:** 10 MIN.
MAKES: 6 SERVINGS

- ½ cup pecan halves, coarsely chopped
- ¼ cup butter
- 1 Tbsp. olive oil
- 1½ lbs. fresh Brussels sprouts, halved
- 2 Tbsp. brown sugar
- 2 Tbsp. sherry or unsweetened apple juice
- 2 Tbsp. heavy whipping cream
- 2 Tbsp. honey
  Coarsely ground pepper

1. Preheat oven to 400°. Place pecans in a 10-in. ovenproof skillet. Bake until lightly browned, stirring occasionally, 5-7 minutes. Remove and set aside.
2. In the same pan, heat butter and oil over medium-high heat. Add the Brussels sprouts; cook and stir until crisp-tender, 8-10 minutes. Stir in the brown sugar, sherry and cream until blended. Top with pecans; drizzle with honey.
3. Bake, uncovered, until Brussels sprouts are browned and tender, 8-10 minutes. Sprinkle with pepper before serving.
½ CUP: 253 cal., 18g fat (7g sat. fat), 26mg chol., 121mg sod., 21g carb. (13g sugars, 5g fiber), 4g pro.

PINA COLADA JAM

If you like pina coladas, you'll love this! But here's the kicker: The secret ingredient is fresh zucchini.
—Taste of Home *Test Kitchen*

PREP: 15 MIN. • **COOK:** 20 MIN. + COOLING
MAKES: 7 HALF-PINTS

- 6 cups sugar
- 6 cups shredded peeled zucchini
- 1 can (8 oz.) crushed pineapple, undrained
- ¼ cup lime juice
- 2 pkg. (3 oz. each) pineapple gelatin
- 1 tsp. rum extract

1. Rinse 7 half-pint jars and lids with boiling water. Dry thoroughly.
2. In a Dutch oven, combine sugar, zucchini, pineapple and lime juice. Bring to a boil. Boil 10 minutes, stirring constantly. Remove from heat; stir in gelatin and extract until gelatin is dissolved.
3. Immediately fill all containers to within ½ in. of tops. Wipe off top edges of containers. Cool completely before covering with lids.
4. Refrigerate up to 3 weeks or freeze up to 1 year. Thaw frozen jam in refrigerator before serving.
2 TBSP.: 100 cal., 0 fat (0 sat. fat), 0 chol., 8mg sod., 25g carb. (25g sugars, 0 fiber), 0 pro.

READER REVIEW

"Absolutely delicious! Easy to make...came out just perfect. Will make nice gifts to give to friends."
—COCOLAMUS, TASTEOFHOME.COM

BRUSSELS SPROUTS WITH PECANS & HONEY

PRESSURE-COOKER CINNAMON APPLESAUCE

Homemade applesauce is a breeze in the Instant Pot. A few minutes of prep and a short cook time will put this cinnamon applesauce on the table very quickly!
—Ally Billhorn, Wilton, IA

PREP: 20 MIN. • **COOK:** 5 MIN. + RELEASING
MAKES: 8 CUPS

- 5 lbs. apples (about 15 medium), peeled and chopped
- 1 cup water
- ⅓ cup sugar
- 2 tsp. ground cinnamon
- ½ tsp. ground nutmeg
- ⅛ tsp. salt

1. Combine all ingredients in a 6-qt. electric pressure cooker. Lock lid; close pressure-release valve. Adjust to pressure-cook on high for 5 minutes. Let pressure release naturally.
2. Mash apples with a potato masher or use an immersion blender until blended. Serve warm or store in airtight container in the refrigerator.
⅔ CUP: *101 cal., 0 fat (0 sat. fat), 0 chol., 25mg sod., 26g carb. (22g sugars, 3g fiber), 0 pro.*

THE BEST MARINARA SAUCE

I developed this recipe with a friend to make the most of a bumper crop of tomatoes. Now, we like to make huge batches—we're talking 220 pounds of tomatoes huge—and then give jars as gifts along with a pound of pasta around the holidays. Knowing this sauce is made from the heart with the best possible ingredients makes me feel good about giving it to my family and friends.
—Shannon Norris, Cudahy, WI

PREP: 1 HOUR + SIMMERING
PROCESS: 40 MIN. • **MAKES:** 9 CUPS

- 3 Tbsp. olive oil
- 1 cup chopped onion
- ⅓ cup minced garlic, divided
- 12 lbs. plum tomatoes, quartered
- 2 cups water
- 1¼ cups minced fresh basil, divided
- ¼ cup minced fresh oregano
- ¼ cup tomato paste

THE BEST MARINARA SAUCE

SHANNON NORRIS
Cudahy, WI

- 2 tsp. kosher salt
- 1 tsp. coarsely ground pepper
- ¼ cup plus 1½ tsp. lemon juice

1. In a stockpot, heat oil over medium heat. Add onion; cook and stir until softened, 3-4 minutes. Add 2 Tbsp. garlic; cook 1 minute longer. Add tomatoes, water and ½ cup basil; bring to a boil. Reduce heat; simmer, covered, until the tomatoes are completely broken down and soft, about 1 hour, stirring occasionally.
2. Press tomato mixture through a food mill into a large bowl; discard skins and seeds. Return tomato mixture to stockpot; add ½ cup of remaining basil, oregano and remaining garlic. Bring to a boil. Reduce heat; simmer, uncovered, until thickened, 3½-4 hours, stirring occasionally. Add tomato paste and remaining ¼ cup basil; season with salt and pepper.
3. Add 1 Tbsp. plus 1½ tsp. lemon juice to each of 3 hot 1½-pint jars. Ladle hot mixture into jars, leaving ½-in. headspace. Remove air bubbles and adjust headspace, if necessary, by adding hot mixture. Wipe rims. Center lids on jars; screw on bands until fingertip tight.
4. Place jars into canner with simmering water, ensuring that they are completely covered with water. Bring to a boil; process for 40 minutes. Remove jars and cool.
¾ CUP: *131 cal., 4g fat (1g sat. fat), 0 chol., 348mg sod., 22g carb. (13g sugars, 6g fiber), 5g pro.* **Diabetic exchanges:** *1½ starch, 1 fat.*

CINNAMON-ORANGE
HONEY BUTTER

CINNAMON-ORANGE HONEY BUTTER

This is such a delicious butter spread for afternoon tea or with a dessert bread. Just mix it up and get ready for the compliments.
—Mary Bates, Cleveland, OH

TAKES: 5 MIN. • **MAKES:** ¾ CUP

- ½ cup butter, softened
- ¼ cup honey
- 1 to 2 tsp. orange zest
- ½ tsp. ground cinnamon

In a small bowl, combine all ingredients. Serve immediately. Refrigerate leftovers.
1 TBSP.: *89 cal., 8g fat (5g sat. fat), 20mg chol., 77mg sod., 6g carb. (6g sugars, 0 fiber), 0 pro.*

Maple Butter: Combine softened butter with 2 Tbsp. maple syrup, 1 tsp. minced fresh parsley and a dash pepper.

Rosemary-Lemon Butter: Combine softened butter with 4 tsp. grated lemon zest, 4 tsp. minced fresh rosemary and a dash pepper.

Herb Butter: Combine softened butter with 2 tsp. minced fresh chives, 2 tsp. minced fresh parsley, 2 tsp. minced fresh basil, ⅛ tsp. salt, ⅛ tsp. paprika and a dash pepper.

Curry Butter: Combine softened butter with 1½ tsp. curry powder, ½ tsp. ground cumin and ¼ tsp. crushed red pepper flakes.

HOMEMADE STEAK SEASONING

Here's the perfect seasoning for your favorite cut.
—Sarah Farmer, Waukesha, WI

TAKES: 5 MIN. • **MAKES:** ABOUT ⅓ CUP

- 2 Tbsp. coarsely ground pepper
- 2 Tbsp. kosher salt
- 2 tsp. onion powder
- 2 tsp. dried minced garlic
- 2 tsp. paprika
- 2 tsp. crushed coriander seeds
- 2 tsp. crushed red pepper flakes

In a small bowl, combine all ingredients. Store in an airtight container in a cool, dry place for up to 1 year.
½ TSP.: *3 cal., 0 fat (0 sat. fat), 0 chol., 360mg sod., 1g carb. (0 sugars, 0 fiber), 0 pro.*

EASY BEANS & POTATOES WITH BACON

EASY BEANS & POTATOES WITH BACON

I created this recipe because I love the combination of green beans with bacon. It's smart when company is coming because you can start the side dish in the slow cooker and continue preparing the rest of the dinner.
—Barbara Brittain, Santee, CA

PREP: 15 MIN. • **COOK:** 6 HOURS
MAKES: 10 SERVINGS

- 8 bacon strips, chopped
- 1½ lbs. fresh green beans, trimmed and cut into 2-in. pieces (about 4 cups)
- 4 medium potatoes, peeled and cut into ½-in. cubes
- 1 small onion, halved and sliced
- ¼ cup reduced-sodium chicken broth
- ½ tsp. salt
- ¼ tsp. pepper

1. In a large skillet, cook bacon over medium heat until crisp, stirring occasionally. Remove to paper towels with a slotted spoon; drain, reserving 1 Tbsp. drippings. Cover and refrigerate bacon until serving.

2. In a 5-qt. slow cooker, combine the remaining ingredients; stir in reserved drippings. Cover and cook on low for 6-8 hours or until potatoes are tender. Stir in bacon; heat through.
¾ CUP: *116 cal., 4g fat (1g sat. fat), 8mg chol., 256mg sod., 17g carb. (3g sugars, 3g fiber), 5g pro.* **Diabetic exchanges:** *1 starch, 1 fat.*

5i LIME SALT

Perk up any dish with a sprinkle of this zippy lime salt. It amplifies steak tacos, grilled pineapple, sweet potato fries and more.
—James Schend, Pleasant Prairie, WI

PREP: 5 MIN. • **BAKE:** 30 MIN. + COOLING • **MAKES:** ½ CUP

- ½ cup sea salt
- 1 Tbsp. grated lime zest

1. Preheat oven to 225°. Mix salt and lime zest until well combined; spread into a parchment-lined 15x10-1-in. baking pan.
2. Bake until mixture is dry, about 30 minutes. Cool completely in pan. Store in an airtight container at room temperature.
¼ **TSP.:** *0 cal., 0 fat (0 sat. fat), 0 chol., 480mg sod., 0 carb. (0 sugars, 0 fiber), 0 pro.*

LIME SALT

CARROT, PARSNIP & POTATO GRATIN

CARROT, PARSNIP & POTATO GRATIN

Thanks to a challenge in the Taste of Home *community a few years back, my husband and I tried parsnips and discovered that we liked them! In fact, I now grow them in my garden and have fun experimenting with them. This recipe is one of my experiments, and it turned out to be something we really enjoy!*
—Sue Gronholz, Beaver Dam, WI

PREP: 20 MIN. • **BAKE:** 50 MIN. • **MAKES:** 8 SERVINGS

- 1 lb. medium carrots, thinly sliced
- ½ lb. medium parsnips, peeled and thinly sliced
- ½ lb. Yukon Gold potatoes, peeled and thinly sliced
- 1 small onion, halved and sliced
- 2 garlic cloves, minced
- 1½ tsp. minced fresh rosemary
- ½ tsp. salt
- ½ tsp. ground nutmeg
- 1 cup half-and-half cream
- ¼ cup heavy whipping cream

Preheat oven to 400°. In a large bowl, combine all ingredients. Transfer to a greased 3-qt. baking dish. Cover and bake until vegetables are tender, 40-45 minutes. Uncover and bake until cream has thickened and is beginning to turn golden brown, 10-15 minutes longer. Let stand 5-10 minutes before serving.
¾ **CUP:** *141 cal., 6g fat (4g sat. fat), 23mg chol., 208mg sod., 19g carb. (6g sugars, 3g fiber), 3g pro.*

BRUSSELS SPROUTS BROWN BETTY

I had the idea to make a savory version of the family-favorite brown Betty, using vegetables in place of fruit while keeping the classic crunchy bread crumb topping.
—Shauna Havey, Roy, UT

PREP: 30 MIN. • **BAKE:** 40 MIN.
MAKES: 8 SERVINGS

- 1½ lbs. fresh Brussels sprouts, sliced
- 1 small onion, chopped
- 4 garlic cloves, minced
- 2 Tbsp. olive oil
- 1 tsp. salt
- ½ tsp. pepper
- 1½ cups shredded Swiss cheese
- 1 cup heavy whipping cream
- 8 bacon strips, cooked and crumbled
- 3 slices whole wheat bread, torn
- 2 Tbsp. butter, melted
  Minced fresh thyme, optional

1. Preheat oven to 425°. In a large bowl, combine the first 6 ingredients; toss to coat. Transfer to a greased 13x9-in. baking dish. Bake, uncovered, 20 minutes. Stir in the cheese, cream and bacon. Bake until casserole is bubbly and starting to brown, 12-15 minutes longer.
2. Meanwhile, place the bread in a food processor or blender. Cover and pulse until crumbs form. Transfer to a small bowl; stir in butter. Sprinkle over casserole. Bake until golden brown, 8-10 minutes longer. If desired, top with thyme before serving.
¾ CUP: 301 cal., 25g fat (13g sat. fat), 62mg chol., 554mg sod., 9g carb. (3g sugars, 3g fiber), 12g pro.

PINEAPPLE KIWI JAM

Pineapple, kiwi and a hint of lime blend nicely in this unique combination. It's especially good slathered on biscuits.
—Sondra Rogers, Columbus, IN

PREP: 20 MIN. • **COOK:** 15 MIN. + STANDING
MAKES: 8 HALF-PINTS

- 4 kiwifruit, peeled and thinly sliced
- 3 cups sugar
- 1 can (8 oz.) crushed pineapple, undrained
- ¼ cup lime juice
- 1 pouch (3 oz.) liquid fruit pectin
- 3 drops green food coloring, optional

1. In a 2-qt. microwave-safe bowl, combine the kiwi, sugar, pineapple and lime juice. Microwave, uncovered, on high until the mixture comes to a full rolling boil, 7-10 minutes, stirring every 2 minutes. Stir in pectin. Add food coloring if desired.
2. Pour into jars or freezer containers and cool to room temperature, about 1 hour. Cover and let stand overnight or until set, but not longer than 24 hours. Refrigerate or freeze.
2 TBSP.: 83 cal., 0 fat (0 sat. fat), 0 chol., 1mg sod., 22g carb. (20g sugars, 0 fiber), 0 pro.

PINEAPPLE KIWI JAM

BUTTERNUT-PINEAPPLE CRUMBLE

I tried this sweet and crunchy casserole out on my 80-year-old parents, and they loved it! Butternut squash now has a place at our holiday table year after year.
—Barbara Busch, Henrico, VA

PREP: 30 MIN. • **BAKE:** 35 MIN.
MAKES: 6 SERVINGS

- 1 medium butternut squash (4 lbs.), peeled and cubed
- 1 can (8 oz.) unsweetened crushed pineapple, drained
- 1 carton (8 oz.) spreadable honey nut cream cheese
- 2 Tbsp. butter, melted
- ½ tsp. ground cinnamon
- ½ tsp. ground nutmeg

TOPPING
- 10 shortbread cookies, crushed
- ¼ cup butter, melted
- 1 Tbsp. sugar
- ¾ cup honey-roasted sliced almonds

1. Preheat oven to 350°. Place squash in a large saucepan; add water to cover. Bring to a boil. Cook, covered, until tender, 15-20 minutes. Drain; cool slightly. Process in a food processor until slightly chunky. Add pineapple, cream cheese, butter, cinnamon and nutmeg; process until smooth. Transfer to a greased 8-in. square dish.

2. For topping, combine crushed cookies, butter and sugar; sprinkle over squash mixture. Top with almond slices. Bake, uncovered, until edges are lightly browned, 35-40 minutes.

1 CUP: *521 cal., 31g fat (14g sat. fat), 54mg chol., 445mg sod., 59g carb. (24g sugars, 11g fiber), 8g pro.*

TEST KITCHEN TIP

This dish is silky and smooth, but if you want a little different texture, you can skip pureeing the pineapple.

BUTTERNUT-PINEAPPLE CRUMBLE

BASIL SALT

SPICED CHERRY CHUTNEY

My fruity chutney gets deep flavor from ginger, cardamom, allspice and balsamic vinegar. It tastes amazing on grilled chicken or pork.
—Lily Julow, Lawrenceville, GA

PREP: 20 MIN. • **COOK:** 50 MIN. • **MAKES:** 1¼ CUPS

- 3 cups fresh or frozen pitted tart cherries, thawed
- 1 large sweet onion, finely chopped
- 1 small green pepper, chopped
- 1 small sweet red pepper, chopped
- ⅓ cup packed brown sugar
- ¼ cup balsamic vinegar
- 2 tsp. minced fresh gingerroot
- 1½ tsp. grated orange zest
- ½ tsp. ground cardamom
- ¼ tsp. salt
- ¼ tsp. crushed red pepper flakes
- ¼ tsp. ground allspice

In a large saucepan, combine all ingredients. Bring to a boil. Reduce heat; simmer, uncovered, for 45-50 minutes or until vegetables are tender and mixture achieves desired thickness, stirring occasionally. Serve warm or chilled. Refrigerate leftovers.
2 TBSP.: 73 cal., 0 fat (0 sat. fat), 0 chol., 66mg sod., 18g carb. (15g sugars, 1g fiber), 1g pro.

⑤ⱼ

BASIL SALT

This basil-infused salt adds a touch of herbal brightness to everything from corn on the cob to sliced tomatoes to fresh watermelon.
—James Schend, Pleasant Prairie, WI

PREP: 5 MIN. • **BAKE:** 30 MIN. + COOLING • **MAKES:** ¼ CUP

- ¼ cup coarse sea salt
- ¼ cup loosely packed basil leaves

1. Preheat oven to 225°. Place salt and basil in a small food processor; pulse until very finely chopped. Spread into a parchment-lined 15x10x1-in. baking pan.
2. Bake until mixture appears dry, about 30 minutes. Remove from oven; cool completely in pan. Store in an airtight container at room temperature.
¼ TSP.: 0 cal., 0 fat (0 sat. fat), 0 chol., 480mg sod., 0 carb. (0 sugars, 0 fiber), 0 pro.

SPICED CHERRY CHUTNEY

ELISABETH LARSEN
Pleasant Grove, UT

AIR-FRYER GARLIC-ROSEMARY
BRUSSELS SPROUTS

AIR-FRYER GARLIC-ROSEMARY BRUSSELS SPROUTS

This is my go-to Thanksgiving side dish. It's healthy and easy, and it doesn't take very much time to make. I usually season my turkey with fresh rosemary, then use leftover herbs for this standout.
—Elisabeth Larsen, Pleasant Grove, UT

TAKES: 30 MIN. • **MAKES:** 4 SERVINGS

3   Tbsp. olive oil
2   garlic cloves, minced
½   tsp. salt
¼   tsp. pepper
1   lb. Brussels sprouts, trimmed and halved

½   cup panko (Japanese) bread crumbs
1½ tsp. minced fresh rosemary

1. Preheat air fryer to 350°. Place the first 4 ingredients in a small microwave-safe bowl; microwave on high 30 seconds.
2. Toss Brussels sprouts with 2 Tbsp. oil mixture. Place all the Brussels sprouts in fryer basket and cook 4-5 minutes. Stir sprouts. Continue to air-fry until sprouts are lightly browned and near desired tenderness, about 8 minutes longer, stirring halfway through cooking time.
3. Toss bread crumbs with rosemary and the remaining oil mixture; sprinkle over sprouts. Continue cooking until crumbs are browned and sprouts are tender, 3-5 minutes. Serve immediately.

¾ **CUP:** *164 cal., 11g fat (1g sat. fat), 0 chol., 342mg sod., 15g carb. (3g sugars, 4g fiber), 5g pro.* **Diabetic exchanges:** *2 fat, 1 vegetable, ½ starch.*

TEST KITCHEN TIP

In our testing, we have found that cook times vary dramatically among brands of air fryers. As a result, we provide wider than normal ranges on suggested cook times. Begin checking at the first time listed and adjust as needed.

GINGER BLUEBERRY JAM

When I was very young, I watched my grandma make this jam in the kitchen. As I sneaked blueberries to snack, she picked me up and told me that if I wanted any more, I'd need to learn to make this jam!
—Jill Drury, River Forest, IL

PREP: 25 MIN. • **PROCESS:** 10 MIN.
MAKES: 4 HALF-PINTS

- 3 cups fresh blueberries
- 4 cups sugar
- 1 Tbsp. pomegranate juice
- 1½ tsp. lemon juice
- 1 pouch (3 oz.) liquid fruit pectin
- 2 Tbsp. finely chopped crystallized ginger
- ½ tsp. ground ginger

1. In a Dutch oven, mash the blueberries. Stir in sugar, pomegranate juice and lemon juice. Bring to a full rolling boil over high heat, stirring constantly. Stir in pectin. Return to a full rolling boil. Boil and stir for 1 full minute. Stir in crystallized and ground ginger.

2. Remove from the heat; skim off foam. Ladle hot mixture into 4 hot sterilized half-pint jars, leaving ¼-in. headspace. Remove air bubbles; wipe rims. Center lids on jars; screw on bands until fingertip tight. Process for 10 minutes in a boiling-water canner.

NOTE: The processing time listed is for altitudes of 1,000 feet or less. Add 1 minute to the processing time for each 1,000 feet of additional altitude.

2 TBSP.: 108 cal., 0 fat (0 sat. fat), 0 chol., 1mg sod., 28g carb. (27g sugars, 0 fiber), 0 pro.

HONEY-THYME BUTTER

Laced with honey and fresh thyme, this butter is perfect for either sweet or savory dishes. It's amazing on bread and rolls fresh out of the oven but equally as good on a stack of blueberry pancakes.
—Taste of Home *Test Kitchen*

TAKES: 5 MIN. • **MAKES:** 1¼ CUPS

- ½ cup butter, softened
- ⅓ cup honey
- 2 tsp. fresh thyme leaves

In a small bowl, beat the butter until light and fluffy. Add the honey and thyme; beat just until blended. Store in refrigerator.

1 TBSP.: 58 cal., 5g fat (3g sat. fat), 12mg chol., 37mg sod., 5g carb. (5g sugars, 0 fiber), 0 pro.

HONEY-THYME BUTTER

5i SRIRACHA SALT

Add a hint of subtle spice when you sprinkle this kicked-up salt on foods like eggs, grilled chicken, roasted veggies or popcorn.
—*James Schend, Pleasant Prairie, WI*

PREP: 5 MIN. + STANDING • **MAKES:** ½ CUP

- ½ cup kosher salt
- 5 tsp. Sriracha chili sauce
- ½ tsp. lime juice

Combine salt, chili sauce and lime juice; spread into a parchment-lined 15x10x1-in. baking pan. Let stand at least 8 hours or overnight. Store in an airtight container at room temperature.

¼ TSP.: *0 cal., 0 fat (0 sat. fat), 0 chol., 488mg sod., 0 carb. (0 sugars, 0 fiber), 0 pro.*

THREE-BERRY FREEZER JAM

Give in to temptation and buy fresh berries in bulk. You'll be glad you did when you transform those ripe little gems into a sweet spread that can also get you out of a gift-giving jam.
—*Shannon Becker, Burton, OH*

PREP: 20 MIN. + STANDING • **COOK:** 10 MIN.
MAKES: 6 HALF-PINTS

- 2 cups fresh strawberries
- 2 cups fresh raspberries
- 2 cups fresh blackberries
- 5¼ cups sugar
- 2 Tbsp. lemon juice
- 1 pkg. (1¾ oz.) powdered fruit pectin
- ¾ cup water

1. In a food processor, process berries in batches until finely chopped. Transfer to a large bowl. Stir in sugar and lemon juice. Let stand for 10 minutes, stirring occasionally.

2. In a small saucepan, combine the fruit pectin and water. Bring to a boil; cook and stir for 1 minute. Add to fruit mixture; stir constantly until sugar is dissolved, 4-5 minutes.

3. Pour into jars or freezer containers, leaving ½-in. headspace. Cover and let stand overnight or until set, but not longer than 24 hours. Refrigerate for up to 3 weeks or freeze for up to 12 months.

2 TBSP.: *92 cal., 0 fat (0 sat. fat), 0 chol., 0 sod., 24g carb. (23g sugars, 1g fiber), 0 pro.*

SRIRACHA SALT

CHEDDAR SPIRALS

Our kids love this cheesy pasta and will sample a spoonful right from the slow cooker when they walk by. Sometimes I add cocktail sausages, sliced Polish sausage or cubed ham to make it into a hearty dinner.
—Heidi Ferkovich, Park Falls, WI

PREP: 20 MIN. • **COOK:** 2½ HOURS
MAKES: 15 SERVINGS (¾ CUP EACH)

- 1 pkg. (16 oz.) spiral pasta
- 2 cups half-and-half cream
- 1 can (10¾ oz.) condensed cheddar cheese soup, undiluted
- ½ cup butter, melted
- 4 cups shredded cheddar cheese

Cook pasta according to package directions; drain. In a 5-qt. slow cooker, combine the cream, soup and butter until smooth; stir in the cheese and pasta. Cover and cook on low for 2½ hours or until cheese is melted.

¾ CUP: *260 cal., 19g fat (13g sat. fat), 67mg chol., 415mg sod., 12g carb. (2g sugars, 1g fiber), 10g pro.*

READER REVIEW

"My entire family loves this recipe. I decreased the butter to 1 tablespoon. I love to add cooked chicken and different veggies to it to make an easy on-the-go dinner."
—IMASKA, TASTEOFHOME.COM

ROOT VEGETABLE PAVÉ

This is a stunning side dish to serve company. The robust blend features earthy root vegetables in a lightly herbed cream sauce. It's a perfect make-ahead dish for special occasions.
—Carla Mendres, Winnipeg, MB

PREP: 40 MIN.
BAKE: 1¾ HOURS + STANDING
MAKES: 8 SERVINGS

- 3 medium russet potatoes, peeled
- 2 large carrots
- 2 medium turnips, peeled
- 1 large onion, halved
- 1 medium fennel bulb, fronds reserved
- ½ cup all-purpose flour

ROOT VEGETABLE PAVÉ

- 1 cup heavy whipping cream
- 1 Tbsp. minced fresh thyme, plus more for topping
- 1 Tbsp. minced fresh rosemary
- ½ tsp. salt
- ½ tsp. pepper, plus more for topping
- 1 cup shredded Asiago cheese, divided

1. Preheat the oven to 350°. With a mandoline or vegetable peeler, cut the first 5 ingredients into very thin slices. Transfer to a large bowl; toss with flour. Stir in the cream, thyme, 1 Tbsp. rosemary, salt and pepper.

2. Place half of the vegetable mixture into a greased 9-in. springform pan. Sprinkle with ½ cup cheese. Top with remaining vegetable mixture. Place pan on a baking sheet and cover with a double thickness of foil.

3. Bake until vegetables are tender and easily pierced with a knife, 1¾-2 hours. Remove from oven and top foil with large canned goods as weights. Let stand 1 hour. Remove cans, foil and rim from pan before cutting. Top with remaining cheese. Add reserved fennel fronds and, as desired, additional fresh thyme and pepper. Refrigerate leftovers.

1 SLICE: *248 cal., 15g fat (9g sat. fat), 46mg chol., 216mg sod., 23g carb. (4g sugars, 2g fiber), 7g pro.*

AUNT BETTY'S
BLUEBERRY MUFFINS
PAGE 143

Breads, Rolls & Muffins

Sometimes all you need is fresh bread and butter to make a good meal a great one. On these pages, explore an assortment of baked delights no one will be able to resist.

SWISS CHEESE BREAD

ROLLED BUTTERMILK BISCUITS

*I scribbled down this recipe when our family visited The Farmers'
Museum in Cooperstown, New York, more than 25 years ago. I must
have gotten it right, because these biscuits turn out great every time.*
—*Patricia Kile, Elizabethtown, PA*

PREP: 20 MIN. • **BAKE:** 15 MIN. • **MAKES:** 8 BISCUITS

- 2   cups all-purpose flour
- 3   tsp. baking powder
- ½   tsp. baking soda
- ¼   tsp. salt
- 3   Tbsp. cold butter
- ¾   to 1 cup buttermilk
- 1   Tbsp. fat-free milk

1. In a large bowl, combine the flour, baking powder, baking soda
and salt; cut in butter until mixture resembles coarse crumbs. Stir
in enough buttermilk just to moisten dough.
2. Turn onto a lightly floured surface; knead 3-4 times. Pat or roll
to ¾-in. thickness. Cut with a floured 2½-in. biscuit cutter. Place in
a large ungreased cast-iron or other ovenproof skillet.
3. Brush with milk. Bake at 450° until golden brown, 12-15 minutes.
1 BISCUIT: *162 cal., 5g fat (3g sat. fat), 12mg chol., 412mg sod.,
25g carb. (1g sugars, 1g fiber), 4g pro.* **Diabetic exchanges:**
1½ starch, 1 fat.

SWISS CHEESE BREAD

*This bread will receive rave reviews, whether you serve it as an
appetizer or with a meal. For real convenience, you can make it
ahead of time and freeze it!*
—*Karla Boice, Mahtomedi, MN*

TAKES: 30 MIN. • **MAKES:** 20 SERVINGS

- 1   loaf French bread (20 in.)
- 1   cup butter, softened
- 2   cups shredded Swiss cheese
- ¾   tsp. celery seed
- ¾   tsp. garlic powder
- 3   Tbsp. dried parsley flakes

1. Cut bread in half crosswise. Make diagonal cuts, 1 in. apart,
through bread but not through bottom. Combine all remaining
ingredients. Spread half the butter mixture between bread slices.
Spread remaining mixture over top and sides of bread.
2. Place bread on double thickness of foil; cover loosely with more
foil. Bake at 425° for 20-30 minutes. For last 5 minutes, remove
foil covering bread to allow it to brown.
1 PIECE: *187 cal., 13g fat (8g sat. fat), 34mg chol., 231mg sod., 12g
carb. (1g sugars, 1g fiber), 6g pro.*

ROLLED BUTTERMILK BISCUITS

GLUTEN-FREE BANANA BREAD

Tired of gluten-free baked goods that are dry and crumbly? This banana bread tastes like the real thing and goes over well with everyone.
—Gladys Arnold, Pittsburgh, PA

PREP: 20 MIN. • **BAKE:** 45 MIN. + COOLING
MAKES: 2 LOAVES (12 SLICES EACH)

- 2 cups gluten-free all-purpose baking flour
- 1 tsp. baking soda
- ¼ tsp. salt
- 4 large eggs, room temperature
- 2 cups mashed ripe bananas (4-5 medium)
- 1 cup sugar
- ½ cup unsweetened applesauce
- ⅓ cup canola oil
- 1 tsp. vanilla extract
- ½ cup chopped walnuts

1. In a large bowl, combine the flour, baking soda and salt. In a small bowl, whisk the eggs, bananas, sugar, applesauce, oil and vanilla. Stir into dry ingredients just until moistened.

2. Transfer to two 8x4-in. loaf pans coated with cooking spray. Sprinkle with walnuts. Bake at 350° for 45-55 minutes or until a toothpick inserted in the center comes out clean. Cool for 10 minutes before removing from pans to wire racks.

NOTE: Read all ingredient labels for possible gluten content prior to use. Ingredient formulas can change, and production facilities vary among brands. If you're concerned that your brand may contain gluten, contact the company.

1 SLICE: *140 cal., 6g fat (1g sat. fat), 35mg chol., 89mg sod., 21g carb. (11g sugars, 2g fiber), 3g pro.* **Diabetic exchanges:** *1 starch, 1 fat.*

CANDY CANE CHOCOLATE MINI LOAVES

Having a bunch of leftover candy canes after the holidays inspired me to use them up by adding them to a chocolate bread. Coffee and cocoa intensify the flavor.
—Shelly Platten, Amherst, WI

PREP: 25 MIN. • **BAKE:** 35 MIN. + COOLING
MAKES: 8 MINI LOAVES (6 SLICES EACH)

CANDY CANE CHOCOLATE MINI LOAVES

- ¼ cup butter, softened
- 1⅔ cups packed brown sugar
- 4 large egg whites, room temperature
- 2 large eggs, room temperature
- ¾ cup strong brewed coffee
- ½ cup vanilla yogurt
- ¼ cup canola oil
- 1 Tbsp. vanilla extract
- ¼ tsp. peppermint extract
- 3½ cups all-purpose flour
- ¾ cup baking cocoa
- 1½ tsp. baking soda
- ½ tsp. salt
- 1½ cups buttermilk
- 1 cup (6 oz.) miniature semisweet chocolate chips

TOPPING
- 2 oz. white baking chocolate, melted
- 3 Tbsp. crushed candy canes

1. Preheat oven to 350°. Coat eight 5¾x3x2-in. loaf pans with cooking spray. In a large bowl, beat butter and brown sugar until crumbly, about 2 minutes. Add egg whites, eggs, coffee, yogurt, oil and extracts until blended.

2. In another bowl, whisk flour, cocoa, baking soda and salt; add to brown sugar mixture alternately with buttermilk, beating well after each addition. Fold in miniature chocolate chips.

3. Transfer to prepared pans. Bake until a toothpick inserted in center comes out clean, 35-40 minutes. Cool 10 minutes before removing from pans to wire racks to cool completely.

4. Drizzle melted white baking chocolate over loaves. Sprinkle with crushed candies.

1 SLICE: *122 cal., 4g fat (2g sat. fat), 11mg chol., 99mg sod., 20g carb. (11g sugars, 1g fiber), 2g pro.*

ZUCCHINI APPLE BREAD

GARLIC HERB BUBBLE LOAF

I adapted an old sour cream bread recipe for this deliciously different pull-apart loaf that smells heavenly while baking. It has a light crust, tender interior and lots of herb and butter flavor. We think it's wonderful with a bowl of hot potato soup.
—Katie Crill, Priest River, ID

PREP: 25 MIN. + RISING • **BAKE:** 35 MIN.
MAKES: 18 SERVINGS

- ½ cup water (70° to 80°)
- ½ cup sour cream
- 2 Tbsp. butter, softened
- 3 Tbsp. sugar
- 1½ tsp. salt
- 3 cups bread flour
- 2¼ tsp. active dry yeast

GARLIC HERB BUTTER
- ¼ cup butter, melted
- 4 garlic cloves, minced
- ¼ tsp. each dried oregano, thyme and rosemary, crushed

1. In bread machine pan, place the first 7 ingredients in order suggested by manufacturer. Select dough setting (check dough after 5 minutes of mixing; add 1-2 Tbsp. of water or flour if needed).
2. When cycle is completed, turn dough onto a lightly floured surface. Cover and let rest for 15 minutes. Divide dough into 36 pieces. Shape each piece into a ball. In a shallow bowl, combine butter, garlic and herbs. Dip each ball in mixture; place in an ungreased 9x5-in. loaf pan. Cover and let rise in a warm place until doubled, about 45 minutes.
3. Bake at 375° for 35-40 minutes or until golden brown (cover loosely with foil if bread browns too quickly). Remove from pan to a wire rack. Serve warm.
NOTE: We recommend you do not use a bread machine's time-delay feature for this recipe.
1 SERVING: *141 cal., 6g fat (3g sat. fat), 12mg chol., 230mg sod., 19g carb. (2g sugars, 1g fiber), 3g pro.*

ZUCCHINI APPLE BREAD

Farmers markets are loaded with zucchini and apples in fall. Use them both to make this tender quick bread.
—Kathy Strawser, Dunkirk, NY

PREP: 30 MIN. • **BAKE:** 55 MIN. + COOLING
MAKES: 3 LOAVES (12 SLICES EACH)

- 4 cups all-purpose flour
- 3 tsp. baking soda
- 1½ tsp. ground cinnamon
- ½ tsp. ground nutmeg
- ¼ tsp. salt
- 5 large eggs, room temperature
- 1½ cups vegetable oil
- 2 cups sugar
- 1 cup packed brown sugar
- 1 tsp. vanilla extract
- 2 cups shredded zucchini
- 1½ cups chopped pecans
- 1 cup grated peeled apples

1. In a large bowl, combine the flour, baking soda, cinnamon, nutmeg and salt. In a large bowl, beat the eggs until frothy. Add the oil, sugars and vanilla; beat until blended. Stir into dry ingredients just until moistened. Fold in the zucchini, pecans and apples.
2. Transfer to 3 greased 8x4-in. loaf pans. Bake at 350° for 55-60 minutes or until a toothpick inserted in the center comes out clean. Cool for 10 minutes before removing from pans to wire racks.
1 SLICE: *246 cal., 14g fat (2g sat. fat), 30mg chol., 133mg sod., 29g carb. (18g sugars, 1g fiber), 3g pro.*

BERRY CREAM MUFFINS

If you can't decide which berries to use in these muffins, you can't go wrong using half raspberries and half blueberries!
—Linda Gilmore, Hampstead, MD

PREP: 15 MIN. • **BAKE:** 20 MIN. • **MAKES:** ABOUT 2 DOZEN

- 4 cups all-purpose flour
- 2 cups sugar
- 1¼ tsp. baking powder
- 1 tsp. baking soda
- 1 tsp. salt
- 3 cups fresh or frozen raspberries or blueberries
- 4 large eggs, lightly beaten, room temperature
- 2 cups sour cream
- 1 cup canola oil
- 1 tsp. vanilla extract

1. In a large bowl, combine the flour, sugar, baking powder, baking soda and salt; add fresh or frozen berries and toss gently. Combine the eggs, sour cream, oil and vanilla; mix well. Stir into the dry ingredients just until moistened.
2. Fill greased muffin cups two-thirds full. Bake at 400° until a toothpick inserted in the center comes out clean, 20-25 minutes. Cool for 5 minutes before removing from pans to a wire rack. Serve warm.
NOTE: If using frozen berries, do not thaw before adding to batter.
1 MUFFIN: *481 cal., 23g fat (6g sat. fat), 84mg chol., 330mg sod., 60g carb. (31g sugars, 3g fiber), 7g pro.*

CHEESY GARLIC HERB QUICK BREAD

CHEESY GARLIC HERB QUICK BREAD

This just might be the perfect bread to go along with any dish. The sharp cheddar cheese makes it irresistible.
—Taste of Home *Test Kitchen*

PREP: 15 MIN. • **BAKE:** 25 MIN. • **MAKES:** 1 LOAF (12 SLICES)

- 3 cups all-purpose flour
- 3 Tbsp. sugar
- 1 Tbsp. baking powder
- 2 tsp. Italian seasoning
- 1 tsp. garlic powder
- ½ tsp. salt
- 1 large egg, room temperature
- 1 cup fat-free milk
- ⅓ cup canola oil
- 1 cup shredded sharp cheddar cheese

1. Preheat oven to 350°. In a large bowl, whisk together first 6 ingredients. In another bowl, whisk together egg, milk and oil. Stir in cheese and add to flour mixture; stir just until moistened.
2. Spoon batter into a greased 9-in. cast-iron skillet. Bake at 350° until a toothpick inserted in center comes out clean, 25-30 minutes.
1 SLICE: *233 cal., 10g fat (2g sat. fat), 25mg chol., 175mg sod., 29g carb. (4g sugars, 1g fiber), 7g pro.*

> **TEST KITCHEN TIP**
>
> For muffins, prepare batter as directed. Spoon batter into 9 greased muffin tins and bake at 350° until a toothpick inserted in center comes out clean, 25-30 minutes.

BERRY CREAM MUFFINS

GERMAN CHOCOLATE RING

This recipe is modeled after German chocolate cake, which is my favorite. No wonder I enjoy making this sweet bread!
—Anne Frederick, New Hartford, NY

PREP: 30 MIN. + RISING
BAKE: 20 MIN. + COOLING
MAKES: 24 SERVINGS

- 1¼ cups sweetened shredded coconut, divided
- 1 cup (6 oz.) semisweet chocolate chips, divided
- ¾ cup chopped pecans
- 3 large eggs, room temperature, divided use
- 4½ to 5 cups all-purpose flour
- ½ cup sugar
- 1 tsp. salt
- 1 pkg. (¼ oz.) active dry yeast
- 1 cup whole milk
- 5 Tbsp. butter, divided

1. Combine 1 cup coconut, ¾ cup chocolate chips, pecans and 1 egg; set aside. In large bowl, combine 1 cup flour, sugar, salt and yeast. In small saucepan, heat milk and 4 Tbsp. butter to 120°-130°; add to flour mixture, beating until smooth. Add the remaining eggs and enough remaining flour to form a soft dough.

2. Turn dough onto a lightly floured surface. Knead until dough is smooth and elastic, 6-8 minutes. Place in greased bowl, turning once to grease top. Cover; let rise in a warm place until doubled, about 1 hour.

3. Punch dough down; turn onto lightly floured surface. Roll dough into 18x10-in. rectangle. Melt the remaining butter and brush over dough; spread with reserved chocolate mixture.

4. Roll up dough jelly-roll style, starting with a long side; pinch seam to seal. Place seam side down on greased baking sheet. Pinch ends together to form a ring.

5. With scissors, cut from outside edge two-thirds of the way toward center of ring at 1-in. intervals. Separate strips slightly; twist to allow filling to show. Cover and let rise until doubled, about 1 hour.

6. Bake at 350° for 20-25 minutes or until golden brown. Sprinkle with remaining chocolate chips; let stand for 5 minutes. Spread melted chocolate chips; sprinkle with remaining coconut. Carefully remove from pan to a wire rack to cool.

1 SLICE: *222 cal., 10g fat (5g sat. fat), 34mg chol., 149mg sod., 30g carb. (11g sugars, 2g fiber), 4g pro.*

POPOVERS FOR 2

This recipe has been handed down through my family, and I've had it for almost 50 years. My husband and I especially like these popovers for a late breakfast, but they're also great with soup or salad. Simply served with butter and honey, they're delicious anytime.
—Alpha Wilson, Roswell, NM

PREP: 10 MIN. + STANDING • **BAKE:** 30 MIN.
MAKES: 4 POPOVERS

- ½ cup 2% milk
- 1 large egg
- ½ cup all-purpose flour
- ¼ tsp. salt
- ¼ tsp. poultry seasoning, optional

Let the milk and egg stand at room temperature for 30 minutes. Combine all ingredients in a bowl; beat just until smooth. Pour into 4 greased 6-oz. custard cups; place on a baking sheet. Bake at 425° for 15 minutes. Reduce heat to 350° (do not open door). Bake 15-20 minutes longer or until popovers are deep golden brown (do not underbake). Serve warm.

2 POPOVERS: *180 cal., 4g fat (2g sat. fat), 98mg chol., 360mg sod., 27g carb. (3g sugars, 1g fiber), 8g pro.* **Diabetic exchanges:** *2 starch.*

GERMAN CHOCOLATE RING

STOLLEN BUTTER ROLLS

STOLLEN BUTTER ROLLS

Our family enjoys my stollen so much that it's just too good to be served only during the holidays. I created this buttery, less sweet dinner roll so we can satisfy our stollen cravings anytime.
—Mindy White, Nashville, TN

PREP: 45 MIN. + RISING • **BAKE:** 15 MIN.
MAKES: 2 DOZEN

  1 pkg. (¼ oz.) active dry yeast
  ¼ cup warm water (110° to 115°)
  1 cup 2% milk
  2 large eggs, room temperature
  ½ cup butter, softened
  1 Tbsp. sugar
  1 tsp. salt
  4¼ to 4¾ cups all-purpose flour
  ¾ cup chopped mixed candied fruit
  ¾ cup dried currants
  ½ cup cold butter, cut into
      24 pieces (1 tsp. each)

1. In a small bowl, dissolve yeast in warm water. In a large bowl, combine milk, eggs, butter, sugar, salt, yeast mixture and 3 cups flour; beat on medium speed until smooth. Stir in enough remaining flour to form a soft dough (dough will be sticky).
2. Turn dough onto a floured surface; knead until smooth and elastic, about 6-8 minutes. Place in a greased bowl, turning once to grease the top. Cover and let rise in a warm place until doubled, about 1 hour.
3. Punch dough down; turn onto a floured surface. Knead candied fruit and currants into dough (knead in more flour if necessary). Divide and shape into 24 balls; flatten slightly. Place 1 tsp. cold butter in center of each circle. Fold circles in half over butter; press edges to seal. Place in a greased 15x10x1-in. baking pan. Cover and let rise in a warm place until doubled, about 45 minutes.
4. Preheat oven to 375°. Bake rolls until golden brown, 15-20 minutes. Cool in pan 5 minutes; serve warm.
FREEZE OPTION: Freeze cooled rolls in airtight containers. To use, microwave each roll on high until warmed, 30-45 seconds.
1 ROLL: *198 cal., 9g fat (5g sat. fat), 37mg chol., 178mg sod., 28g carb. (9g sugars, 1g fiber), 4g pro.*

FRENCH ONION DROP BISCUITS

These simple biscuits have a golden color and mild onion flavor. They're so fast to fix.
—Galelah Dowell, Fairland, OK

TAKES: 20 MIN. • **MAKES:** 1 DOZEN

  2 cups biscuit/baking mix
  1 carton (8 oz.) French onion dip
  ¼ cup 2% milk

1. In a large bowl, combine baking mix and French onion dip. Stir in milk just until moistened. Drop by rounded tablespoonfuls 2 in. apart onto a baking sheet coated with cooking spray.
2. Bake at 450° for 10-14 minutes or until golden brown. Serve warm.
1 BISCUIT: *121 cal., 6g fat (3g sat. fat), 0 chol., 382mg sod., 14g carb. (1g sugars, 0 fiber), 2g pro.*

ENGLISH MUFFIN BREAD

FOCACCIA BARESE

This focaccia has been in my mom's family for several generations. It is one of my most requested recipes. Whenever I am invited to a party, I am not allowed to attend unless I bring it!
—Dora Travaglio, Mount Prospect, IL

PREP: 30 MIN. + RISING • **BAKE:** 30 MIN.
MAKES: 8 SERVINGS

- 1⅛ tsp. active dry yeast
- ¾ cup warm water (110° to 115°), divided
- ½ tsp. sugar
- ⅓ cup mashed potato flakes
- 1½ tsp. plus 2 Tbsp. olive oil, divided
- ¼ tsp. salt
- 1¾ cups bread flour

TOPPING

- 2 medium tomatoes, thinly sliced
- ¼ cup pitted Greek olives, halved
- 1½ tsp. minced fresh or dried oregano
- ½ tsp. coarse salt

1. In a large bowl, dissolve yeast in ½ cup warm water. Add sugar; let stand 5 minutes. Add the potato flakes, 1½ tsp. oil, salt, 1 cup flour and remaining water. Beat until smooth. Stir in enough remaining flour to form a soft dough.
2. Turn onto a floured surface; knead until smooth and elastic, 6-8 minutes. Place in a greased bowl, turning once to grease the top. Cover and let rise in a warm place until doubled, about 1 hour. Punch dough down. Cover and let rest for 10 minutes.
3. Place 1 Tbsp. olive oil in a 10-in. cast-iron or other ovenproof skillet; tilt pan to evenly coat. Add dough; shape to fit pan. Cover and let rise until doubled, about 30 minutes.
4. With fingertips, make several dimples over top of dough. Brush with remaining Tbsp. of oil. Blot tomato slices with paper towels. Arrange tomato slices and olives over dough; sprinkle with oregano and salt.
5. Bake at 375° for 30-35 minutes or until golden brown.
1 SLICE: *142 cal., 4g fat (0 sat. fat), 0 chol., 269mg sod., 24g carb. (1g sugars, 1g fiber), 4g pro.* **Diabetic exchanges:** *1½ starch, ½ fat.*

ENGLISH MUFFIN BREAD

Many years ago, a good friend gave me her mother's recipe for this delightful bread, and I've made it ever since. It's perfect for a hearty breakfast, especially when smothered with your favorite jam.
—Jane Zielinski, Rotterdam Junction, NY

PREP: 15 MIN. + RISING • **BAKE:** 35 MIN.
MAKES: 2 LOAVES (12 SLICES EACH)

- 5 cups all-purpose flour, divided
- 2 pkg. (¼ oz. each) active dry yeast
- 1 Tbsp. sugar
- 2 tsp. salt
- ¼ tsp. baking soda
- 2 cups warm whole milk (120° to 130°)
- ½ cup warm water (120° to 130°)
  Cornmeal

1. In a large bowl, combine 2 cups flour, yeast, sugar, salt and baking soda. Add warm milk and water; beat on low speed for 30 seconds, scraping bowl occasionally. Beat on high for 3 minutes.
2. Stir in remaining flour (batter will be stiff). Do not knead. Grease two 8x4-in. loaf pans. Sprinkle pans with cornmeal. Spoon batter into the pans and sprinkle cornmeal on top. Cover and let rise in a warm place until doubled, about 45 minutes.
3. Bake at 375° for 35 minutes or until loaves are golden brown. Remove from pans immediately and cool on wire racks. Slice and toast.
1 SLICE: *111cal., 1g fat (0 sat. fat), 2mg chol., 219mg sod., 22g carb. (2g sugars, 1g fiber), 4g pro.*

FOCACCIA BARESE

MAKEOVER CHEDDAR BISCUITS

MAKEOVER CHEDDAR BISCUITS

These biscuits have a cheesy richness that everyone will love. I like to serve them with steaming bowls of chili or a hearty beef soup.
—Alicia Rooker, Milwaukee, WI

TAKES: 30 MIN. • MAKES: 15 BISCUITS

- 1 cup all-purpose flour
- 1 cup cake flour
- 1½ tsp. baking powder
- ¾ tsp. salt
- ½ tsp. garlic powder, divided
- ¼ tsp. baking soda
- 4 Tbsp. cold butter, divided
- ⅓ cup finely shredded cheddar cheese
- 1 cup buttermilk
- ½ tsp. dried parsley flakes

1. In a large bowl, combine the flours, baking powder, salt, ¼ tsp. garlic powder and baking soda. Cut in 3 Tbsp. butter until mixture resembles coarse crumbs; add cheese. Stir in the buttermilk just until moistened.
2. Drop by 2 tablespoonfuls 2 in. apart onto baking sheets coated with cooking spray. Bake at 425° until golden brown, 10-12 minutes. Melt the remaining butter; stir in parsley and the remaining garlic powder. Brush over biscuits. Serve warm.
1 BISCUIT: *106 cal., 4g fat (3g sat. fat), 11mg chol., 233mg sod., 14g carb. (1g sugars, 0 fiber), 3g pro.*

BUTTER DIPS

I like these breadsticks because I can whip them up in a hurry if company drops in unexpectedly. Because my husband is a minister, this happens quite often. Most folks are amazed that a recipe this easy can taste so good!
—Elaine Norton, Lansing, MI

PREP: 25 MIN. • BAKE: 15 MIN. • MAKES: 32 BREADSTICKS

- 2½ cups all-purpose flour
- 1 Tbsp. sugar
- 3½ tsp. baking powder
- 1½ tsp. salt
- ½ to 1 cup shredded sharp cheddar cheese
- 1 cup whole milk
- ⅓ cup butter, melted

TOPPINGS
- Sesame seeds, garlic salt, onion salt or celery salt

1. In large bowl, combine the flour, sugar, baking powder, salt and cheese; add milk. Stir slowly with fork. When dough clings together, turn onto well-floured surface. On a floured surface, knead gently 10 times. Roll dough into 12x8-in. rectangle.
2. Cut dough in half lengthwise with sharp knife, then into 16 strips. Place butter in a 13x9-in. baking pan. Dip both sides of strips in melted butter. Place 2 rows in pan. Sprinkle with topping of your choice. Bake at 450° for 12-15 minutes. Serve immediately.
1 BREADSTICK: *65 cal., 3g fat (2g sat. fat), 8mg chol., 188mg sod., 8g carb. (1g sugars, 0 fiber), 2g pro.*

BUTTER DIPS

AUNT BETTY'S BLUEBERRY MUFFINS

(SHOWN ON PAGE 132)

My Aunt Betty bakes many items each Christmas, but I look forward to these mouthwatering muffins the most.
—Sheila Raleigh, Kechi, KS

PREP: 15 MIN. • **BAKE:** 20 MIN.
MAKES: ABOUT 1 DOZEN

- ½ cup old-fashioned oats
- ½ cup orange juice
- 1 large egg, room temperature
- ½ cup canola oil
- ½ cup sugar
- 1½ cups all-purpose flour
- 1¼ tsp. baking powder
- ½ tsp. salt
- ¼ tsp. baking soda
- 1 cup fresh or frozen blueberries

TOPPING

- 2 Tbsp. sugar
- ½ tsp. ground cinnamon

1. In a large bowl, combine oats and orange juice; let stand for 5 minutes. Beat in the egg, oil and sugar until blended. Combine the flour, baking powder, salt and baking soda; stir into oat mixture just until moistened. Fold in blueberries.
2. Fill greased or paper-lined muffin cups two-thirds full. Combine topping ingredients; sprinkle over batter. Bake at 400° for 20-25 minutes or until a toothpick inserted in the center comes out clean. Cool for 5 minutes before removing from pan to a wire rack. Serve warm.
NOTE: If using frozen blueberries, use without thawing them to avoid discoloring the batter.
1 SERVING: *208 cal., 10g fat (1g sat. fat), 18mg chol., 172mg sod., 28g carb. (13g sugars, 1g fiber), 3g pro.*

CRANBERRY ORANGE ALMOND QUICK BREAD

CRANBERRY ORANGE ALMOND QUICK BREAD

You can customize this bread to your family's specific tastes. Try dried apricots and pecans, or dried blueberries and hazelnuts.
—Taste of Home *Test Kitchen*

PREP: 15 MIN. • **BAKE:** 40 MIN. + COOLING
MAKES: 1 LOAF (12 SLICES)

- 3 cups all-purpose flour
- 3 Tbsp. sugar
- 1 Tbsp. baking powder
- ½ tsp. salt
- 1 cup dried cranberries
- ½ cup sliced almonds, toasted
- 1 large egg, room temperature
- 1 cup fat-free milk
- ⅓ cup canola oil
- ¾ tsp. grated orange zest
- ¾ tsp. almond extract

1. Preheat oven to 350°. In a large bowl, whisk together first 4 ingredients; stir in cranberries and almonds. In another bowl, whisk together egg, milk, oil, zest and extract. Add to flour mixture; stir just until moistened.
2. Transfer to a 9x5-in. loaf pan coated with cooking spray. Bake until a toothpick inserted in center comes out clean, 40-50 minutes. Cool in pan 10 minutes before removing to a wire rack to cool.
1 SLICE: *258 cal., 9g fat (1g sat. fat), 16mg chol., 234mg sod., 40g carb. (14g sugars, 2g fiber), 5g pro.*

HAZELNUT DATE PUMPKIN BREAD

🄔 EXTRA QUICK YEAST ROLLS

Making homemade rolls usually takes a lot of ingredients and time, but this recipe makes it so simple. They come together quickly and they freeze well, too.
—Eleanor Paine, Junction City, OR

PREP: 20 MIN. + RISING • **BAKE:** 10 MIN.
MAKES: 2 DOZEN

- 1 pkg. (¼ oz.) quick-rise yeast
- 1 Tbsp. sugar
- ¾ cup warm water (110° to 115°)
- 2½ cups biscuit/baking mix

1. Dissolve yeast and sugar in warm water. Stir in biscuit mix and turn out onto a lightly floured surface. Knead until smooth and elastic, about 5 minutes.
2. Divide and shape dough into 24 small balls. Place on greased baking sheet. Cover and let rise in a warm place until doubled, about 30 minutes.

3. Bake rolls at 400° until golden brown, 10-15 minutes.
1 ROLL: *54 cal., 2g fat (1g sat. fat), 0 chol., 158mg sod., 8g carb. (1g sugars, 0 fiber), 1g pro.*

❄ HAZELNUT DATE PUMPKIN BREAD

In the fall when the leaves are changing, baking fever takes over. This tender pumpkin bread will make your home smell delicious. The crunchy hazelnuts and sweet dates make it feel extra special.
—Lorraine Caland, Shuniah, ON

PREP: 25 MIN. • **BAKE:** 50 MIN. + COOLING
MAKES: 3 LOAVES (12 SLICES EACH)

- 5 cups all-purpose flour
- 2½ cups sugar
- 4 tsp. baking soda
- 1¾ tsp. ground cinnamon
- 1½ tsp. salt
- ¾ tsp. ground ginger
- ¾ tsp. ground cardamom

- 2 large eggs, room temperature
- 1 can (29 oz.) solid-pack pumpkin
- 1 cup 2% milk
- 1 cup canola oil
- 1 tsp. vanilla extract
- 2 cups chopped hazelnuts
- 2 cups chopped dates

1. Preheat oven to 350°. In a large bowl, whisk the first 7 ingredients. In a stand mixer, beat eggs, pumpkin, milk, oil and vanilla until blended. Beat in flour mixture just until moistened. Fold in hazelnuts and dates.
2. Transfer to 3 greased 8x4-in. loaf pans. Bake until a toothpick inserted in center comes out clean, 50-55 minutes. Cool in pans 10 minutes before removing to wire racks to cool.
FREEZE OPTION: Securely wrap cooled loaves in foil, then freeze. To use, thaw at room temperature.
1 SLICE: *252 cal., 11g fat (1g sat. fat), 11mg chol., 247mg sod., 37g carb. (21g sugars, 2g fiber), 4g pro.*

PUMPKIN PAN ROLLS

Serve these spicy-sweet pumpkin rolls for dinner—or any time of day—and get ready to hear a chorus of yums in your kitchen!
—Linnea Rein, Topeka, KS

PREP: 20 MIN. + RISING • **BAKE:** 20 MIN.
MAKES: 20 ROLLS

- ¾ cup whole milk
- ⅓ cup packed brown sugar
- 5 Tbsp. butter, divided
- 1 tsp. salt
- 2 pkg. (¼ oz. each) active dry yeast
- ½ cup warm water (110° to 115°)
- 2 to 2½ cups all-purpose flour
- 1½ cups whole wheat flour
- ½ cup solid-pack pumpkin
- ½ tsp. ground cinnamon
- ¼ tsp. ground ginger
- ¼ tsp. ground nutmeg

1. In a small saucepan, heat the milk, brown sugar, 4 Tbsp. butter and salt to 110°-115°; set aside.

2. In a large bowl, dissolve yeast in warm water. Stir in milk mixture. Add 1½ cups all-purpose flour, whole wheat flour, pumpkin, cinnamon, ginger and nutmeg. Beat until smooth. Add enough remaining all-purpose flour to form a soft dough.

3. Turn onto a floured surface; knead until smooth and elastic, 6-8 minutes. Place in a greased bowl, turning once to grease top. Cover and let rise in a warm place until doubled, about 1 hour.

4. Punch dough down. Divide into 20 pieces; shape into balls. Place in a greased 13x9-in. baking pan. Cover and let rise 30 minutes or until doubled.

5. Preheat oven to 375°. Melt remaining butter; brush over dough. Bake 20-25 minutes or until golden brown. Remove from pan to a wire rack. Serve warm.

1 ROLL: *124 cal., 3g fat (2g sat. fat), 9mg chol., 154mg sod., 21g carb. (5g sugars, 2g fiber), 3g pro.* **Diabetic exchanges:** *1½ starch, ½ fat.*

HERB QUICK BREAD

This simple bread is especially good with soups and stews, but slices are also tasty alongside fresh, green salads. The herbs make it a flavorful treat any time of the year.
—Donna Roberts, Manhattan, KS

PREP: 15 MIN. • **BAKE:** 40 MIN. + COOLING
MAKES: 1 LOAF (16 SLICES)

- 3 cups all-purpose flour
- 3 Tbsp. sugar
- 1 Tbsp. baking powder
- 3 tsp. caraway seeds
- ½ tsp. salt
- ½ tsp. ground nutmeg
- ½ tsp. dried thyme
- 1 large egg, room temperature
- 1 cup fat-free milk
- ⅓ cup canola oil

1. Preheat oven to 350°. In a large bowl, whisk together first 7 ingredients. In another bowl, whisk together egg, milk and oil. Add to the flour mixture; stir just until moistened.

2. Transfer to a 9x5-in. loaf pan coated with cooking spray. Bake until a toothpick inserted in center of bread comes out clean, 40-50 minutes. Cool in pan for 10 minutes before removing to a wire rack to cool.

TO MAKE MUFFINS: Pour the batter into 9 greased muffin cups; bake at 350°until a toothpick in the center comes out clean, about 20 minutes.

1 SLICE: *147 cal., 5g fat (1g sat. fat), 12mg chol., 160mg sod., 21g carb. (3g sugars, 1g fiber), 3g pro.* **Diabetic exchanges:** *1½ starch, 1 fat.*

HERB QUICK BREAD

**RASPBERRY-BANANA
BREAKFAST TACOS
PAGE 166**

Breakfast & Brunch

Start your mornings off right! Follow these recipes to wake your loved ones with the tempting aromas of bacon sizzling and sweet apples, peaches and berries baking into waffles, pancakes or French toast.

CAST-IRON SKILLET STEAK

SO-HEALTHY SMOOTHIES

This tastes like a milk shake, but it doesn't have all the fat. My husband and I look forward to it in the mornings. It's so good for you, and it will keep you energized for hours.
—Jessica Gerschitz, Jericho, NY

TAKES: 15 MIN. • **MAKES:** 4 SERVINGS

1   cup fat-free milk
¼   cup orange juice
2   Tbsp. vanilla yogurt
1   Tbsp. honey
1   small banana, sliced and frozen
⅔   cup frozen blueberries
½   cup chopped peeled mango, frozen
1¼ cups frozen unsweetened sliced peaches

In a blender, combine all ingredients; cover and process until smooth. Pour into chilled glasses; serve immediately.
¾ CUP: *107 cal., 1g fat (0 sat. fat), 2mg chol., 38mg sod., 24g carb. (21g sugars, 2g fiber), 3g pro.* **Diabetic exchanges:** *1 fruit, ½ starch.*

CAST-IRON SKILLET STEAK

If you've never cooked steak at home, it can be a little intimidating. That's why I came up with this basic recipe that's so simple, you can enjoy steak for any meal during the week—even breakfast.
—James Schend, Pleasant Prairie, WI

PREP: 5 MIN. + STANDING • **COOK:** 5 MIN. • **MAKES:** 2 SERVINGS

1   Tbsp. kosher salt, divided
1   beef New York strip or ribeye steak (1 lb.), 1 in. thick

1. Remove steak from refrigerator and sprinkle with 2 tsp. salt; let stand 45-60 minutes.
2. Preheat a cast-iron skillet over high heat until extremely hot, 4-5 minutes. Sprinkle remaining 1 tsp. salt in bottom of skillet; pat beef dry with paper towels. Place steak into skillet and cook until steak is easily moved, 1-2 minutes; flip, placing steak in a different section of the skillet. Cook 30 seconds and then begin moving steak, occasionally pressing slightly to ensure even contact with the skillet.
3. Continue turning and flipping until cooked to desired degree of doneness (for medium-rare, a thermometer should read 135°; medium, 140°; medium-well, 145°), 1-2 minutes.
6 OZ. COOKED BEEF: *494 cal., 36g fat (15g sat. fat), 134mg chol., 2983mg sod., 0 carb. (0 sugars, 0 fiber), 40g pro.*

SO-HEALTHY SMOOTHIES

SPINACH QUICHE WITH POTATO CRUST

While this recipe is delicious using ingredients exactly as listed, it's also a smart way to make the most of any leftover potatoes and veggies. Use 2½ cups leftover mashed potatoes and whatever cooked vegetables you have on hand. You can also substitute ½ pound Italian sausage for the bacon.
—Heather King, Frostburg, MD

PREP: 25 MIN. • **BAKE:** 55 MIN. + STANDING
MAKES: 8 SERVINGS

- 1   pkg. (24 oz.) refrigerated mashed potatoes
- 2   Tbsp. olive oil, divided
- 8   oz. sliced fresh mushrooms
- 2   garlic cloves, minced
- 5   oz. frozen chopped spinach, thawed and squeezed dry (about ½ cup)
- 6   bacon strips, cooked and crumbled, or ⅓ cup bacon bits
- 2   tsp. minced fresh rosemary or ½ tsp. dried rosemary, crushed
- 4   large eggs
- 1   cup 2% milk
- ¼   tsp. pepper
- 1   cup shredded cheddar cheese

1. Preheat oven to 350°. Press mashed potatoes onto bottom and up sides of a greased 9-in. deep-dish pie plate. Brush with 1 Tbsp. oil. Bake 30 minutes or until edges are golden brown.
2. Meanwhile, in a large skillet, heat remaining oil over medium-high heat. Add mushrooms; cook and stir 3-4 minutes or until tender. Add garlic; cook 1 minute longer. Remove from heat. Stir in spinach, bacon and rosemary; spoon over crust. In a small bowl, whisk eggs, milk and pepper until blended; add cheese. Pour over mushroom mixture.
3. Bake 25-30 minutes longer or until golden brown and a knife inserted in the center comes out clean. Let stand 10 minutes before cutting.
1 PIECE: *284 cal., 17g fat (7g sat. fat), 126mg chol., 495mg sod., 13g carb. (3g sugars, 1g fiber), 12g pro.*

APPLE PIE RICOTTA WAFFLES

APPLE PIE RICOTTA WAFFLES

I had apples and ricotta cheese to use up, so instead of making a pie I decided to do something different. The results were these fluffy, tender waffles with just a hint of sweetness.
—Teri Rasey, Cadillac, MI

PREP: 25 MIN. • **COOK:** 10 MIN./BATCH
MAKES: 6 SERVINGS

- ¼   cup butter
- 6   medium apples, peeled and chopped
- 2   Tbsp. sugar
- 1   Tbsp. honey
- 1   tsp. ground cinnamon
- 1   tsp. vanilla extract

WAFFLES

- 2   cups all-purpose flour
- 2   Tbsp. quick-cooking grits
- 1   Tbsp. cornstarch
- 1   tsp. baking soda
- ½   tsp. salt
- 2   large eggs, room temperature
- 2   cups buttermilk
- 1   cup reduced-fat ricotta cheese
- ½   cup canola oil
- 2   tsp. vanilla extract
- 1½ cups fat-free vanilla Greek yogurt
       Fresh blueberries, optional

1. In a large skillet, melt butter over medium-high heat. Add apples, sugar, honey, cinnamon and vanilla; cook and stir until apples are crisp-tender, 10-12 minutes. Remove from heat and keep warm.
2. Preheat waffle maker. In a large bowl, whisk flour, grits, cornstarch, baking soda and salt. In another bowl, whisk eggs, buttermilk, ricotta, oil and vanilla until blended. Add to dry ingredients; stir just until moistened.
3. Bake waffles according to the manufacturer's directions until golden brown. Serve with apple topping, yogurt and, if desired, blueberries.
1 TOPPED WAFFLE: *633 cal., 31g fat (8g sat. fat), 96mg chol., 709mg sod., 70g carb. (31g sugars, 4g fiber), 18g pro.*

CHEDDAR-BUTTERNUT
SQUASH CLAFOUTIS

CHEDDAR-BUTTERNUT SQUASH CLAFOUTIS

I came up with this savory version of French clafoutis, and I could have eaten the whole pan myself! I shared it for dinner with a salad, and my friends loved it. I dreamed of being in Paris with every scrumptious bite.
—Joseph A. Sciascia, San Mateo, CA

PREP: 20 MIN. • **COOK:** 50 MIN. + STANDING
MAKES: 6 SERVINGS

- 3 cups cubed peeled butternut squash
- 2 tsp. olive oil
- 1 tsp. minced fresh rosemary or ½ tsp. dried rosemary, crushed
- 1 tsp. minced fresh thyme or ½ tsp. dried thyme
- ½ tsp. kosher salt
- ¼ tsp. coarsely ground pepper
- 4 large eggs
- 1½ cups 2% milk
- ½ cup all-purpose flour
- ¼ tsp. cayenne pepper
- 2 cups shredded sharp white cheddar cheese
- ¼ cup grated Parmesan and Romano cheese blend
- 1 Tbsp. butter
- 1 Tbsp. minced fresh chives

1. Preheat oven to 400°.
2. Place butternut squash in a 12-in. cast-iron skillet. Drizzle with oil. Sprinkle with rosemary, thyme, salt and pepper; toss to coat. Roast until just tender, 15-20 minutes. Remove from the pan and keep warm.
3. In a large bowl, whisk eggs, milk, flour and cayenne; stir in cheeses. Place butter in same skillet; place skillet in oven until butter is melted, 1-2 minutes. Carefully tilt pan to coat bottom and sides with butter. Pour egg mixture into skillet; top with roasted squash.
4. Bake until puffed and edges are browned, 30-35 minutes. Let stand 15 minutes before cutting. Sprinkle with chives and additional Parmesan and Romano cheese blend.

1 PIECE: *357 cal., 22g fat (11g sat. fat), 176mg chol., 586mg sod., 22g carb. (5g sugars, 2g fiber), 19g pro.*

PUMPKIN CREAM OF WHEAT

This autumn-inspired breakfast tastes like pumpkin pie—without the guilt! Double the recipe if you feel like sharing.
—Amy Bashtovoi, Sidney, NE

TAKES: 10 MIN. • **MAKES:** 1 SERVING

- ½ cup 2% milk
- ¼ cup half-and-half cream
- 3 Tbsp. Cream of Wheat
- ¼ cup canned pumpkin
- 2 tsp. sugar
- ⅛ tsp. ground cinnamon
  Additional 2% milk

In a small microwave-safe bowl, combine the milk, cream and Cream of Wheat. Microwave, uncovered, on high for 1 minute; stir until blended. Cover and cook for 1-2 minutes or until thickened, stirring every 30 seconds. Stir in pumpkin, sugar and cinnamon. Serve with additional milk.

1 CUP: *314 cal., 9g fat (6g sat. fat), 39mg chol., 96mg sod., 46g carb. (18g sugars, 4g fiber), 10g pro.*

RHUBARB FRITTERS

I got this recipe from my niece's son. Since we live in apple country, we've enjoyed apple fritters for many years. This rhubarb treat is a nice change for spring when apples are few and rhubarb is plentiful.
—Helen Budinock, Wolcott, NY

TAKES: 30 MIN. • **MAKES:** ABOUT 3 DOZEN

- 1 cup all-purpose flour
- 1 cup plus 1 Tbsp. sugar, divided
- ½ tsp. salt
- 2 large eggs, room temperature, separated
- ½ cup 2% milk
- 1 Tbsp. butter, melted
- 2 cups finely chopped fresh or frozen rhubarb, thawed and drained
  Oil for deep-fat frying
  Confectioners' sugar

1. In a large bowl, combine flour, 1 cup sugar and the salt. In a small bowl, whisk egg yolks, milk and butter. Gradually add to dry ingredients, stirring until smooth.
2. Toss rhubarb with the remaining sugar; gently stir into batter. In a small bowl, beat egg whites until stiff. Fold into batter.
3. In a deep cast-iron skillet or deep-fat fryer, heat oil to 375°. Drop batter by tablespoonfuls into oil. Fry a few at a time, turning with a slotted spoon until golden brown. Drain on paper towels. Dust with confectioners' sugar. Serve warm.

NOTE: If using frozen rhubarb, measure rhubarb while still frozen, then thaw completely. Drain in a colander, but do not press liquid out.
1 FRITTER: *66 cal., 3g fat (1g sat. fat), 12mg chol., 41mg sod., 9g carb. (6g sugars, 0 fiber), 1g pro.*

RHUBARB FRITTERS

TOP THAT!

There's more than one way to dress up a waffle, and our staff doesn't hold back.

Bananas Foster Waffles
I love waffles topped with bananas Foster or the four B's (sliced bananas, butter, brown sugar and booze). I also like to fold crumbled bacon bits into the batter.
—Rashanda Cobbins, Food Editor

Coffee Butter Waffles
The best waffle I've ever had was topped with caramelized bacon, maple syrup and coffee butter.
—Maggie Knoebel, Culinary Assistant

Lemon & Blueberry Waffles
I eat waffles with lemon curd and a blueberry sauce I make by simmering blueberries with a little water, sugar and a sprig of thyme. Remove from heat and stir in a tablespoon or two of butter. Top with whipped cream and lemon zest.
—Jeanne Ambrose, Former Content Director

Nutella Waffles
I top my waffles with peanut butter, Nutella, bananas and a sprinkling of crushed peanuts. *Mmm.*
—Beth Tomkiw, Chief Content Officer

Over-Easy Waffles
I like to dress a waffle with an over-easy egg (one whole egg, one egg white), sprinkle it with sea salt and freshly ground pepper, then add a generous splash of maple syrup over it all.
—Deb Mulvey, Copy Chief

Spiced Waffles
I add cinnamon, nutmeg, cardamom, vanilla and almond extract to the batter. For the topping, I make a strawberry, rhubarb and orange sauce every spring and freeze it in small containers.
—*Linda Kast,*
Reminisce *Deputy Editor*

Churro Waffles
I make a churro-inspired version: I top waffles with cinnamon whipped cream and dulce de leche sauce.
—*Justin Williams,*
Culinary Assistant

Chocolate Peanut Fluff Waffles
Try adding chocolate chips to the batter, then top the waffles with banana slices and add a dollop of peanut butter fluff (equal parts peanut butter and marshmallow fluff and a touch of honey).
—*Rachel Maidl,*
Birds & Blooms *Editor*

PB&J Waffles
I like to spread mine with peanut or almond butter for some protein. Then I top them with fresh berries—kind of like a PB&J.
—*Shannon Norris,*
Senior Food Stylist

Croque-Madame Waffles
One of my favorite waffle combos ever was a savory croque-madame waffle—bechamel sauce, sliced ham and an over-easy egg.
—*Joe Hrdina,* Country *Designer*

SLOW-COOKER BREAKFAST BURRITOS

VEGETABLE FRITTATA

This fresh-tasting dish is an easy all-in-one meal. The bacon, eggs and hash browns make it hearty, while the fresh veggies add a hint of color.
—Alice Parker, Moultrie, GA

PREP: 20 MIN. • **BAKE:** 15 MIN.
MAKES: 6 SERVINGS

- 4 bacon strips, cut into ½-in. pieces
- 2 cups frozen shredded hash browns, thawed
- 1 cup chopped fresh broccoli
- ½ cup chopped green pepper
- ½ cup chopped red onion
- ½ to 1 tsp. dried rosemary, crushed
- 6 large eggs
- 3 Tbsp. water
- ½ tsp. salt
- ¼ tsp. pepper
- ¼ tsp. paprika

1. In an 8-in. ovenproof skillet, cook the bacon until crisp. Drain, reserving 2 Tbsp. drippings in the skillet. Remove bacon to paper towel.
2. Add hash browns, broccoli, green pepper, onion and rosemary to the skillet; cover and cook over low heat until hash browns are golden brown and vegetables are tender, about 10 minutes. Remove from the heat and set aside.
3. In a large bowl, whisk the eggs, water, salt and pepper; pour over hash browns. Top with bacon and paprika. Bake, uncovered, at 350° for 12-15 minutes or until eggs are completely set.

1 PIECE: 169 cal., 11g fat (4g sat. fat), 221mg chol., 378mg sod., 7g carb. (2g sugars, 1g fiber), 9g pro.

SLOW-COOKER BREAKFAST BURRITOS

Prep these tasty, hearty burritos the night before for a quick breakfast in the morning, or let them cook while you are away on a weekend afternoon for an easy supper.
—Anna Miller, Churdan, IA

PREP: 25 MIN.
COOK: 3¾ HOURS + STANDING
MAKES: 12 SERVINGS

- 1 pkg. (12 oz.) uncooked breakfast sausage links
- 1 pkg. (28 oz.) frozen O'Brien potatoes, thawed
- 2 cups shredded sharp cheddar cheese
- 12 large eggs
- ½ cup 2% milk
- ¼ tsp. seasoned salt
- ⅛ tsp. pepper
- 12 flour tortillas (6 in.)
  Optional toppings: Salsa, sliced jalapenos, chopped tomatoes, sliced green onions, cubed avocado

1. Remove sausage from casings. In a large skillet, cook sausage over medium heat until no longer pink, 8-10 minutes, breaking into crumbles; drain.
2. In a greased 4- or 5-qt. slow cooker, layer potatoes, sausage and cheese. In a large bowl, whisk eggs, milk, seasoned salt and pepper until blended; pour over top.
3. Cook, covered, on low 3¾-4¼ hours or until eggs are set and a thermometer reads 160°. Uncover and let stand 10 minutes. Serve in tortillas with toppings of your choice.

1 BURRITO: 382 cal., 21g fat (9g sat. fat), 221mg chol., 711mg sod., 29g carb. (2g sugars, 3g fiber), 18g pro.

MUSTARD HAM STRATA

I had this at a bed-and-breakfast years ago. The innkeepers were kind enough to give me the recipe, and I've made it many times since.
—Dolores Zornow, Poynette, WI

PREP: 15 MIN. + CHILLING • **BAKE:** 45 MIN. • **MAKES:** 12 SERVINGS

- 12 slices day-old bread, crusts removed, cubed
- 1½ cups cubed fully cooked ham
- 1 cup chopped green pepper
- ¾ cup shredded cheddar cheese
- ¾ cup shredded Monterey Jack cheese
- ⅓ cup chopped onion
- 7 large eggs
- 3 cups whole milk
- 3 tsp. ground mustard
- 1 tsp. salt

1. In a 13x9-in. baking dish coated with cooking spray, layer bread cubes, ham, green pepper, cheeses and onion. In a large bowl, combine eggs, milk, mustard and salt. Pour over top. Cover and refrigerate overnight.

2. Remove from the refrigerator 30 minutes before baking. Preheat oven to 325°. Bake, uncovered, 45-50 minutes or until a knife inserted in the center comes out clean. Let stand 5 minutes before cutting.

1 PIECE: *198 cal., 11g fat (5g sat. fat), 153mg chol., 648mg sod., 11g carb. (4g sugars, 1g fiber), 13g pro.* **Diabetic exchanges:** *2 medium-fat meat, 1 starch.*

MUSTARD HAM STRATA

POWER BERRY SMOOTHIE BOWL

POWER BERRY SMOOTHIE BOWL

While you can't taste the spinach in these smoothies, you get all its nutrients with big berry flavor.
—Christine Hair, Odessa, FL

TAKES: 10 MIN. • **MAKES:** 3 SERVINGS

- ½ cup orange juice
- ½ cup pomegranate juice
- 1 container (6 oz.) mixed berry yogurt
- 1 cup frozen unsweetened strawberries
- 1 cup fresh baby spinach
- ½ medium ripe frozen banana, sliced
- ½ cup frozen unsweetened blueberries
- 2 Tbsp. ground flaxseed
  Sliced fresh strawberries, fresh blueberries, flax seeds and granola, optional

In a blender, combine the first 8 ingredients; cover and process for 30 seconds or until smooth. Pour into chilled bowls; top as desired. Serve immediately.

1 CUP: *172 cal., 3g fat (0 sat. fat), 3mg chol., 47mg sod., 35g carb. (28g sugars, 4g fiber), 5g pro.*

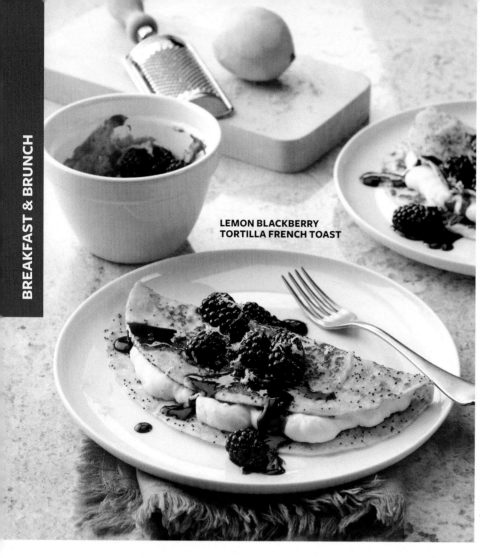

LEMON BLACKBERRY TORTILLA FRENCH TOAST

MAPLE-WALNUT STICKY BUNS

Mmm! These ooey-gooey goodies will have everyone licking maple syrup from their fingers—and reaching for seconds. The yeast dough chills overnight.
—Nancy Foust, Stoneboro, PA

PREP: 45 MIN. + RISING • **BAKE:** 30 MIN.
MAKES: 2 DOZEN

- 1 pkg. (¼ oz.) active dry yeast
- 1 cup warm water (110° to 115°)
- ½ cup mashed potatoes (without added milk and butter)
- 1 large egg, room temperature
- 2 Tbsp. shortening
- 2 Tbsp. sugar
- 1 tsp. salt
- 3 to 3½ cups all-purpose flour

TOPPING
- 1 cup maple syrup
- ¾ cup coarsely chopped walnuts

FILLING
- ⅓ cup sugar
- 1½ tsp. ground cinnamon
- 3 Tbsp. butter, softened

1. In a small bowl, dissolve yeast in warm water. In a large bowl, combine potatoes, egg, shortening, sugar, salt, yeast mixture and 1 cup flour; beat on medium speed until smooth. Stir in enough remaining flour to form a soft dough.
2. Turn dough onto a floured surface; knead until smooth and elastic, 6-8 minutes. Place in a greased bowl, turning once to grease the top. Cover and refrigerate overnight.
3. Pour syrup into a greased 13x9-in. baking dish; sprinkle with walnuts. In a small bowl, mix sugar and cinnamon. Punch down dough; turn onto a lightly floured surface. Roll into a 24x8-in. rectangle. Spread with butter to within ½ in. of edges; sprinkle with cinnamon sugar. Roll up jelly-roll style, starting with a long side; pinch seam to seal. Cut into 24 slices.
4. Place in prepared baking dish, cut side down. Cover with a kitchen towel; let rise in a warm place until doubled, about 30 minutes. Preheat oven to 350°.
5. Bake 30-35 minutes or until golden brown. Cool 5 minutes before inverting buns onto a platter.

1 BUN: *159 cal., 5g fat (1g sat. fat), 13mg chol., 114mg sod., 26g carb. (12g sugars, 1g fiber), 3g pro.*

LEMON BLACKBERRY TORTILLA FRENCH TOAST

This no-fuss twist on crepes is tart-sweet with a creamy lemon filling and juicy blackberries. Think of this as a cross between thin French toast, light crepes and crispy quesadillas.
—Arlene Erlbach, Morton Grove, IL

PREP: 25 MIN. • **COOK:** 5 MIN./BATCH
MAKES: 6 SERVINGS

- 1 pkg. (8 oz.) cream cheese, softened
- 6 Tbsp. lemon curd, divided
- 2 tsp. grated lemon zest
- ⅛ tsp. almond extract
- 2 large eggs
- 2 Tbsp. heavy whipping cream
- 1 Tbsp. poppy seeds
- 3 Tbsp. butter
- 6 flour tortillas (6 in.)
- 1⅓ cups fresh blackberries
- ¼ cup seedless blackberry spreadable fruit
  Additional grated lemon zest, optional

1. In a small bowl, beat the cream cheese, 3 Tbsp. lemon curd, lemon zest and almond extract until fluffy. Set aside.
2. In a shallow bowl, whisk eggs, cream and remaining lemon curd until blended; stir in poppy seeds. In a large skillet, heat 1 Tbsp. butter over medium heat. Dip both sides of a tortilla in egg mixture, allowing excess to drip off. Place in skillet; toast until golden brown, 2-3 minutes on each side. Remove to a wire rack. Repeat with remaining tortillas, greasing pan as needed.
3. Spread about 3 Tbsp. cream cheese mixture over each tortilla to within ¼ in. of edges. Fold tortillas in half over filling. In a microwave-safe bowl, combine the blackberries and spreadable fruit; microwave, covered, at 50% power until warmed, 2-3 minutes, stirring once. Serve with tortillas and, if desired, additional lemon zest.

1 FILLED TORTILLA: *445 cal., 27g fat (15g sat. fat), 134mg chol., 403mg sod., 42g carb. (21g sugars, 3g fiber), 8g pro.*

FIESTA SCRAMBLED EGGS

I love to fix this spicy scrambled egg dish for friends and family. It's almost a meal in itself, but I serve it with muffins or biscuits, fresh fruit juice and coffee.
—Kay Kropff, Canyon, TX

TAKES: 30 MIN. • **MAKES:** 6 SERVINGS

- ½ cup chopped onion
- ¼ cup chopped sweet red pepper
- 1 jalapeno pepper, seeded and chopped
- 8 bacon strips, cooked and crumbled
- 8 large eggs, lightly beaten
- 1 cup shredded cheddar cheese, divided
- ½ tsp. salt
- ⅛ tsp. pepper
  Salsa

In a large nonstick skillet, saute the onion and peppers until tender. Sprinkle with bacon. Pour eggs over the top; sprinkle with ½ cup cheese, salt and pepper. Cook over medium heat, stirring occasionally, until eggs are completely set. Sprinkle with remaining cheese. Serve with salsa.

NOTE: Wear disposable gloves when cutting hot peppers; the oils can burn skin. Avoid touching your face.

¾ CUP: 222 cal., 16g fat (8g sat. fat), 311mg chol., 529mg sod., 3g carb. (2g sugars, 0 fiber), 15g pro.

CHOCOLATE CHIP PANCAKES

Chocolate lovers in my household rush to breakfast when I whip up these irresistible pancakes. The batter calls for both chocolate milk and miniature chocolate chips. We top the finished flapjacks with butter and fruit, and my daughter says they're one of her all-time favorites.
—Laura Rader, Fergus Falls, MN

TAKES: 30 MIN.
MAKES: ABOUT 8 PANCAKES

- 1 cup all-purpose flour
- 1 Tbsp. sugar
- 2 tsp. baking powder
- ¼ tsp. salt
- 1 large egg, room temperature
- 1 cup chocolate milk
- 2 Tbsp. canola oil
- ½ tsp. vanilla extract
- ¼ cup miniature semisweet chocolate chips
  Sliced strawberries and bananas

In a bowl, combine flour, sugar, baking powder and salt. In another bowl, beat the egg, milk, oil, vanilla and chocolate chips. Add to dry ingredients and mix well. Pour batter by ¼ cupfuls onto a lightly greased hot griddle (stir batter before pouring each batch). Turn when bubbles form on top of pancakes. Cook until the second side is brown. Top with strawberries and bananas.

4 PANCAKES: 413 cal., 18g fat (6g sat. fat), 81mg chol., 537mg sod., 54g carb. (21g sugars, 3g fiber), 10g pro.

FIESTA SCRAMBLED EGGS

**RHUBARB COMPOTE
WITH YOGURT & ALMONDS**

RHUBARB COMPOTE
WITH YOGURT & ALMONDS

My Grandma Dot used to make rhubarb compote and always had some in the freezer when I came to visit. This breakfast is a tribute to her. No two stalks of rhubarb are exactly alike, so make sure to taste the compote before you chill it. It should be tart, but sometimes it needs a little extra sugar.
—Michael Hoffman, Brooklyn, NY

PREP: 10 MIN. • **COOK:** 15 MIN. + CHILLING • **MAKES:** 6 SERVINGS

- 2   cups finely chopped fresh rhubarb
- ¼   cup sugar
- 2   Tbsp. water
- 3   cups reduced-fat plain Greek yogurt
- 2   Tbsp. honey
- ¾   cup sliced almonds, toasted

1. In a small saucepan, combine rhubarb, sugar and water. Bring to a boil. Reduce heat; simmer, uncovered, 10-15 minutes or until rhubarb is tender, stirring occasionally. Transfer to a bowl; cool slightly. Refrigerate until cold.
2. In a small bowl, whisk yogurt and honey until blended. Spoon into serving dishes. Top with compote; sprinkle with almonds.
NOTE: To toast nuts, bake in a shallow pan in a 350° oven for 5-10 minutes or cook in a skillet over low heat until lightly browned, stirring occasionally.
**½ CUP YOGURT WITH ABOUT 2 TBSP. COMPOTE AND 2 TBSP.
ALMONDS:** *218 cal., 8g fat (2g sat. fat), 7mg chol., 49mg sod., 23g carb. (20g sugars, 2g fiber), 14g pro.* **Diabetic exchanges:** *1 starch, 1 reduced-fat milk, 1 fat.*

AUTUMN POWER PORRIDGE

This rib-sticking porridge is made with oats and protein-rich quinoa. The additions of pumpkin, maple syrup, dried cranberries and walnuts make it a kid-friendly breakfast.
—Jennifer Wickes, Pine Beach, NJ

PREP: 15 MIN. • **COOK:** 30 MIN. • **MAKES:** 4 SERVINGS

- 3   cups water
- ¾   cup steel-cut oats
- ½   cup quinoa, rinsed
- ¼   tsp. salt
- ¾   cup canned pumpkin
- 1   tsp. pumpkin pie spice
- 3   Tbsp. agave nectar or maple syrup
- ½   cup dried cranberries
- ⅓   cup coarsely chopped walnuts, toasted
     Milk, optional

1. In a large saucepan, combine the water, oats, quinoa and salt. Bring to a boil. Reduce heat; cover and simmer for 20 minutes.
2. Stir in the pumpkin, pie spice and agave nectar. Remove from the heat; cover and let stand for 5 minutes or until water is absorbed and grains are tender. Stir in cranberries and walnuts. Serve with milk if desired.
NOTE: Steel-cut oats are also known as Scotch oats or Irish oatmeal.
1 CUP: *361 cal., 10g fat (1g sat. fat), 0 chol., 155mg sod., 65g carb. (24g sugars, 7g fiber), 9g pro.*

AUTUMN POWER PORRIDGE

CRESCENT ZUCCHINI PIE

Friends will rave over the tender crust in this delicious brunch bake. You get to decide whether you'll let them in on the secret!
—Zelda DeHoedt, Cedar Rapids, IA

PREP: 20 MIN. • **BAKE:** 20 MIN.
MAKES: 6 SERVINGS

- 1   tube (8 oz.) refrigerated crescent rolls
- 2   tsp. Dijon mustard
- 4   cups sliced zucchini
- 1   cup chopped onion
- 6   Tbsp. butter, cubed
- 2   large eggs, lightly beaten
- 1   cup shredded part-skim mozzarella cheese
- 1   cup shredded Colby-Monterey Jack cheese
- 2   Tbsp. dried parsley flakes
- ½   tsp. salt
- ½   tsp. pepper
- ¼   tsp. dried basil
- ¼   tsp. dried oregano

1. Separate roll dough into 8 triangles and place in a greased 9-in. deep-dish pie plate with points toward the center. Press dough onto the bottom and up the sides of the plate to form a crust; seal seams. Spread with mustard.
2. In a large skillet, saute the zucchini and onion in butter until tender. In a large bowl, combine the eggs, cheeses, seasonings and zucchini mixture. Pour into crust.
3. Bake at 375° for 20-25 minutes or until a knife inserted in the center comes out clean. Cover edges loosely with foil if crust browns too quickly.
FREEZE OPTION: Securely wrap and freeze cooled pie in plastic wrap and foil. To use, partially thaw in refrigerator overnight. Remove from refrigerator 30 minutes before baking. Preheat oven to 350°. Unwrap pie; reheat in oven until heated through and a thermometer inserted in center reads 165°.
1 PIECE: *413 cal., 30g fat (16g sat. fat), 128mg chol., 849mg sod., 22g carb. (6g sugars, 1g fiber), 15g pro.*

SOUTHERN HASH BROWNS & HAM SHEET-PAN BAKE

COLLEEN DELAWDER
Herndon, VA

SOUTHERN HASH BROWNS & HAM SHEET-PAN BAKE

Why not take the convenience of sheet-pan cooking and apply it to breakfast? I love how easily this meal comes together.
—Colleen Delawder, Herndon, VA

PREP: 15 MIN. • **BAKE:** 35 MIN.
MAKES: 4 SERVINGS

- 1   pkg. (20 oz.) refrigerated shredded hash brown potatoes
- 3   Tbsp. olive oil
- ½   tsp. salt
- ½   tsp. pepper
- ¼   cup apple jelly
- ¼   cup apricot preserves
- 1   Tbsp. horseradish sauce
- 1   tsp. Dijon mustard
- ¼   tsp. garlic powder
- ¼   tsp. onion powder
- 2   cups cubed fully cooked ham
- 4   large eggs
- 2   green onions, finely chopped

1. Preheat oven to 400°. Place potatoes in a greased 15x10x1-in. baking pan. Drizzle with oil; sprinkle with salt and pepper. Toss to coat. Bake until edges are golden brown, 25-30 minutes.
2. In a small bowl, combine jelly, preserves, horseradish sauce, Dijon, garlic powder and onion powder. Pour over potatoes; add ham. Toss to coat.
3. With the back of a spoon, make 4 wells in potato mixture. Break an egg into each well. Bake until egg whites are completely set and yolks begin to thicken but are not hard, 10-12 minutes. Sprinkle with green onions and additional pepper.
1 SERVING: *483 cal., 19g fat (4g sat. fat), 228mg chol., 1340mg sod., 55g carb. (23g sugars, 3g fiber), 24g pro.*

**PEPPERONI & SAUSAGE
DEEP-DISH PIZZA QUICHE**

UPSIDE-DOWN
APPLE BACON PANCAKE

*I frequently cook Sunday brunch for
my husband and myself, and I'm always
experimenting with new recipes. Apples
picked from our tree were the inspiration
behind this sweet and savory pancake, which
my husband quickly declared a keeper.*
—Sue Gronholz, Beaver Dam, WI

PREP: 30 MIN. • **BAKE:** 20 MIN.
MAKES: 4 SERVINGS

- 4   bacon strips, chopped
- 1   large apple, peeled and sliced
- 2   Tbsp. brown sugar
- ½   tsp. ground cinnamon
- 1   cup all-purpose flour
- 2   Tbsp. sugar
- 1½   tsp. baking powder
- 1   large egg, room temperature
- ¾   cup 2% milk
- 1   Tbsp. butter, melted
- ½   tsp. vanilla extract
       Optional toppings: Confectioners'
       sugar and maple syrup

1. Preheat oven to 375°.
2. In an 8-in. cast-iron or ovenproof skillet,
cook bacon over medium heat until crisp.
Using a slotted spoon, remove bacon to
paper towels to drain, reserving drippings.
3. Add apples to drippings; cook and stir
over medium-high heat until crisp-tender,
2-3 minutes. Remove from heat. Sprinkle
with bacon, brown sugar and cinnamon.
4. In a large bowl, combine flour, sugar and
baking powder. In a small bowl, combine
egg, milk, butter and vanilla; stir into dry
ingredients just until moistened. Pour
over apples.
5. Bake pancake until lightly browned,
20-25 minutes. Invert onto a serving plate.
If desired, dust with confectioners' sugar
and serve with syrup.
*1 PIECE: 371 cal., 16g fat (7g sat. fat), 76mg
chol., 430mg sod., 46g carb. (20g sugars, 2g
fiber), 10g pro.*

PEPPERONI & SAUSAGE
DEEP-DISH PIZZA QUICHE

*Try this savory quiche for a hearty change-of-
pace breakfast. It makes a wonderful lunch
or dinner, too.*
—Donna Chesney, Naples, FL

PREP: 20 MIN. • **COOK:** 40 MIN.
MAKES: 8 SERVINGS

- 2   cups shredded mozzarella
       cheese, divided
- 1   cup shredded sharp cheddar cheese
- 4   large eggs
- 4   oz. cream cheese, softened
- ⅓   cup 2% milk
- ¼   cup grated Parmesan cheese
- ½   tsp. garlic powder
- ½   tsp. Italian seasoning
- ½   lb. bulk Italian sausage
- ½   cup pizza sauce
- 1   cup chopped pepperoni
       Fresh basil, optional

1. Preheat oven to 350°. Sprinkle 1 cup
mozzarella and cheddar cheese in a greased
13x9-in. baking dish. In a small bowl, beat
eggs, cream cheese, milk, Parmesan, garlic
powder and Italian seasoning; pour into
dish. Bake 30 minutes.
2. Meanwhile, in a small skillet, cook
sausage over medium heat until no longer
pink, 5-6 minutes, breaking into crumbles;
drain. Spread pizza sauce over egg mixture;
top with sausage, pepperoni and remaining
1 cup mozzarella cheese. Bake until golden
brown and bubbly, 10-15 minutes longer.
Let stand 5 minutes before serving. Top
with fresh basil if desired.
*1 PIECE: 409 cal., 34g fat (16g sat. fat),
177mg chol., 971mg sod., 5g carb. (2g
sugars, 0 fiber), 21g pro.*

**UPSIDE-DOWN
APPLE BACON PANCAKE**

OPEN-FACED FRICO EGG SANDWICH

The layer of melted and crisped cheese—the frico—is what makes this creamy sandwich unique. If you like spicy aoli, add two large cloves of garlic.
—*Julie Solis, Congers, NY*

TAKES: 30 MIN. • **MAKES:** 4 SERVINGS

- ¼ cup mayonnaise
- 1 Tbsp. olive oil
- 1 garlic clove, minced
- ⅛ tsp. salt
  Dash pepper
- ½ cup shredded Parmesan cheese
- 4 large eggs
- 4 slices Italian bread (1 in. thick), lightly toasted
- ½ cup sandwich giardiniera, drained and finely chopped
- 4 thin slices tomato
  Minced fresh parsley

1. For aioli, in a small bowl, combine the mayonnaise, olive oil, garlic, salt and pepper; set aside.
2. Sprinkle Parmesan into large nonstick skillet; heat over medium heat. Cook just until melted, about 2 minutes. Break eggs, 1 at a time, into a custard cup or saucer, then gently slide into pan over Parmesan. Immediately reduce heat to low. To prepare eggs sunny-side up, cover pan and cook until the yolks thicken but are not hard, 4-5 minutes.
3. Spread aioli over toasted bread. Top with giardiniera, tomato and egg. Sprinkle with parsley.
1 SANDWICH: *408 cal., 23g fat (5g sat. fat), 194mg chol., 1188mg sod., 33g carb. (3g sugars, 2g fiber), 16g pro.*

OPEN-FACED FRICO EGG SANDWICH

PUFF PANCAKE WITH BOURBON PEACHES

I could make this breakfast every weekend when we are smack dab in the middle of peach season.
—*James Schend, Pleasant Prairie, WI*

PREP: 20 MIN. • **COOK:** 20 MIN.
MAKES: 6 SERVINGS

- 1 Tbsp. butter
- 3 large eggs, room temperature, lightly beaten
- ½ cup 2% milk
- 1 tsp. vanilla extract
- ⅛ tsp. salt
- ½ cup all-purpose flour
- 1 cup water
- 4 Tbsp. bourbon or peach nectar, divided
- 2 Tbsp. honey
- 2 Tbsp. peach preserves
- 3 cups sliced peeled peaches (about 5 medium) or frozen unsweetened sliced peaches

1. Preheat oven to 400°. Place butter in a 9-in. deep-dish pie plate; heat in oven 2-3 minutes or until butter is melted. Meanwhile, in a small bowl, whisk eggs, milk, vanilla and salt until blended; gradually whisk in flour. Remove pie plate from oven; tilt carefully to coat bottom and sides with butter. Immediately pour in egg mixture. Bake pancake until puffed and browned, 18-22 minutes.
2. Meanwhile, in a large saucepan, combine the water, 3 Tbsp. bourbon, honey and preserves. Bring to a boil; reduce heat. Add peaches; cook and stir for 3-4 minutes or until tender. Remove peaches to a bowl; set aside. Bring sauce mixture to a boil; cook and stir until reduced to ½ cup. Remove from heat; stir in peaches and remaining 1 Tbsp. bourbon.
3. Remove pancake from oven. Serve immediately with warm peach sauce.
1 SERVING: *192 cal., 5g fat (2g sat. fat), 100mg chol., 110mg sod., 27g carb. (17g sugars, 1g fiber), 6g pro.*

SWEET POTATO DUTCH BABY WITH PRALINE SYRUP

This recipe reminds me of my favorite Dutch baby breakfast from when I was a child. The puffed pancakes and sweet praline syrup are so comforting morning or evening.
—Angela Spengler, Niceville, FL

PREP: 10 MIN. • **COOK:** 30 MIN.
MAKES: 6 SERVINGS

- 4 Tbsp. butter, divided
- 3 large eggs, room temperature
- ½ cup 2% milk
- ¼ cup mashed canned sweet potatoes in syrup, mashed
- ½ cup all-purpose flour
- ¼ tsp. salt
- ½ cup maple syrup
- ¼ cup chopped pecans

1. Preheat oven to 400°. Place 2 Tbsp. butter in a 10-in. ovenproof skillet. Place in oven until butter is melted, 4-5 minutes; carefully swirl to coat evenly.
2. Meanwhile, in a large bowl, whisk eggs, milk and sweet potatoes until blended. Whisk in flour and salt. Pour into hot skillet. Bake until puffed and sides are golden brown and crisp, 20-25 minutes.
3. In a small saucepan, combine syrup, pecans and remaining 2 Tbsp. butter. Cook and stir over medium heat until butter is melted. Remove pancake from oven; serve immediately with syrup.
1 SERVING: 261 cal., 14g fat (6g sat. fat), 115mg chol., 210mg sod., 30g carb. (19g sugars, 1g fiber), 5g pro.

SAVORY MUSTARD CHICKEN & STUFFING WAFFLES

Adding mustard to the chicken coating adds a tang that's amazing with the savory waffles and sweet maple syrup.
—John Ginn, Carlisle, PA

PREP: 20 MIN. • **COOK:** 40 MIN.
MAKES: 8 SERVINGS

- 1 pkg. (6 oz.) stuffing mix
- 4 large eggs
- ¼ cup yellow mustard
- ½ cup all-purpose flour
- 1 tsp. salt
- 1 tsp. pepper

SAVORY MUSTARD CHICKEN & STUFFING WAFFLES

- 8 boneless skinless chicken thighs (about 2 lbs.)
  Oil for frying

WAFFLES
- 1¾ cups all-purpose flour
- 2 Tbsp. sugar
- 3 tsp. baking powder
- 1¾ cups 2% milk
- 2 large eggs, room temperature
- ½ cup butter, melted
- 2 tsp. vanilla extract
  Maple syrup

1. Prepare stuffing mix according to the package directions; cool.
2. Meanwhile, in a shallow bowl, mix eggs and mustard. Place flour, salt and pepper in another shallow bowl. Dip chicken thighs in flour mixture to coat both sides; shake off excess. Dip in egg mixture, then again in the flour mixture, patting to help the coating adhere.

3. In an electric skillet, heat ½ in. oil to 375°. Fry chicken thighs, a few at a time, until golden brown and a thermometer reads at least 170°, 2-3 minutes on each side. Drain on paper towels and keep warm.
4. Preheat waffle maker. In a large bowl, whisk flour, sugar and baking powder. In another bowl, whisk milk, eggs, butter and vanilla until blended. Add to dry ingredients; stir just until moistened. Stir in the prepared stuffing.
5. Bake waffles according to manufacturer's directions until golden brown. Serve with chicken and syrup.
1 PIECE OF CHICKEN WITH 2 WAFFLES: 691 cal., 43g fat (16g sat. fat), 219mg chol., 1074mg sod., 44g carb. (7g sugars, 2g fiber), 32g pro.

SHAKSHUKA BREAKFAST PIZZA

SHAKSHUKA BREAKFAST PIZZA

I turned traditional shakshuka into an exciting brunch pizza. Its sweet, spicy and crunchy ingredients make it perfect for morning, noon or night.
—*Phillipe Sobon, Harwood Heights, IL*

PREP: 35 MIN. • **BAKE:** 15 MIN. • **MAKES:** 6 SERVINGS

- 1   Tbsp. olive oil
- 1   large onion, thinly sliced
- 1   Tbsp. ground cinnamon
- 1   Tbsp. paprika
- 2   tsp. ground cumin
- 2   garlic cloves, minced
- ⅛   tsp. cayenne pepper
- 1   can (14½ oz.) whole plum tomatoes, undrained
- 1   tsp. hot pepper sauce
- ½   tsp. salt
- ¼   tsp. pepper
- 1   loaf (1 lb.) frozen pizza dough, thawed
- 6   large eggs
- ½   cup crumbled feta cheese

1. Preheat oven to 400°. In a large saucepan, heat oil over medium-high heat. Add onion; cook and stir until tender, 4-5 minutes. Add cinnamon, paprika, cumin, garlic and cayenne; cook 1 minute longer. Stir in tomatoes, hot sauce, salt and pepper; cook and stir over medium heat until thickened, about 10 minutes.
2. Meanwhile, grease a 12-in. pizza pan. Roll dough to fit pan. Pinch edge to form a rim. Bake until edge is lightly browned, 10-12 minutes.
3. Spread crust with the tomato mixture. Using a spoon, make 6 indentations in tomato mixture; carefully break an egg into each. Sprinkle with feta. Bake until egg whites are completely set and yolks begin to thicken but are not hard, 12-15 minutes.
1 SLICE: 336 cal., 12g fat (3g sat. fat), 191mg chol., 654mg sod., 41g carb. (4g sugars, 5g fiber), 16g pro.

ALMOND-CHAI GRANOLA

Whether you snack on it by the handful or eat it with milk or yogurt, you'll be happy that you found this granola recipe.
—*Rachel Preus, Marshall, MI*

PREP: 20 MIN. • **BAKE:** 1¼ HOURS • **MAKES:** 8 CUPS

- 2   chai tea bags
- ¼   cup boiling water
- 3   cups quick-cooking oats
- 2   cups almonds, coarsely chopped
- 1   cup sweetened shredded coconut
- ½   cup honey
- ¼   cup olive oil
- ⅓   cup sugar
- 2   tsp. vanilla extract
- ¾   tsp. salt
- ¾   tsp. ground cinnamon
- ¾   tsp. ground nutmeg
- ¼   tsp. ground cardamom

1. Preheat oven to 250°. Steep tea bags in boiling water 5 minutes. Meanwhile, combine oats, almonds and coconut. Discard tea bags; stir remaining ingredients into tea. Pour tea mixture over the oat mixture; mix well to coat.
2. Spread evenly in a greased 15x10-in. rimmed pan. Bake until golden brown, stirring every 20 minutes, about 1¼ hours. Cool completely without stirring; store in an airtight container.
½ CUP: 272 cal., 16g fat (3g sat. fat), 0 chol., 130mg sod., 29g carb. (16g sugars, 4g fiber), 6g pro. **Diabetic exchanges:** *3 fat, 2 starch.*

ALMOND-CHAI GRANOLA

WALNUT GLAZED BACON

Once you taste this bacon, you may never want to go back to the plain kind. It's just right for anyone who loves the flavor combination of salty and sweet.
—Heather Cardeiro, King of Prussia, PA

PREP: 10 MIN. • **BAKE:** 25 MIN.
MAKES: 12 BACON STRIPS

½ cup finely chopped walnuts
¼ cup dark brown sugar
1 tsp. all-purpose flour
12 thick-sliced bacon strips

In a small bowl, combine the walnuts, brown sugar and flour. Place bacon on a greased broiler pan; sprinkle with walnut mixture. Bake at 350° until golden brown, 25-30 minutes.

1 BACON STRIP: *110 cal., 8g fat (2g sat. fat), 10mg chol., 251mg sod., 5g carb. (5g sugars, 0 fiber), 5g pro.*

ORANGE CHEESECAKE BREAKFAST ROLLS

These yummy rolls are a nice change of pace from the typical brown sugar and cinnamon kind. They make a nice treat for breakfast or brunch.
—Hannah Cobb, Owings Mills, MD

PREP: 50 MIN. + RISING • **BAKE:** 25 MIN.
MAKES: 2 DOZEN

2 pkg. (¼ oz. each) active dry yeast
¾ cup warm water (110° to 115°)
1¾ cups warm 2% milk (110° to 115°)
1 cup sugar
2 large eggs, room temperature
3 Tbsp. butter, melted
1½ tsp. salt
7 to 8 cups all-purpose flour
FILLING
1 pkg. (8 oz.) cream cheese, softened
½ cup sugar
1 Tbsp. thawed orange juice concentrate
½ tsp. vanilla extract
GLAZE
2 cups confectioners' sugar
3 Tbsp. orange juice
1 tsp. grated orange zest

ORANGE CHEESECAKE BREAKFAST ROLLS

1. In a large bowl, dissolve yeast in warm water. Add the milk, sugar, eggs, butter, salt and 5 cups flour. Beat until smooth. Stir in enough remaining flour to form a firm dough.

2. Turn onto a floured surface; knead until smooth and elastic, 6-8 minutes. Place in a greased bowl, turning once to grease the top. Cover and let rise in a warm place until doubled, about 1 hour.

3. In a small bowl, beat cream cheese, sugar, orange juice concentrate and vanilla until smooth. Punch dough down. Turn onto a lightly floured surface; divide in half. Roll 1 portion into an 18x7-in. rectangle. Spread half of the filling to within ½ in. of edges.

4. Roll up jelly-roll style, starting with a long side; pinch seam to seal. Cut into 12 slices; place cut side down in a greased 13x9-in. baking pan. Repeat with remaining dough and filling. Cover and let rise until doubled, about 30 minutes.

5. Preheat oven to 350°. Bake rolls for 25-30 minutes or until golden brown. Combine confectioners' sugar, orange juice and zest; drizzle over warm rolls. Refrigerate leftovers.

TO MAKE AHEAD: Prepare, shape and place rolls in baking pans as directed. Cover and refrigerate overnight. Remove rolls from the refrigerator and let stand for 30 minutes. Bake and glaze as directed.

1 ROLL: *284 cal., 6g fat (3g sat. fat), 33mg chol., 201mg sod., 52g carb. (24g sugars, 1g fiber), 6g pro.*

HAM & CHEDDAR BRUNCH RING

It's surprisingly easy to transform ordinary breakfast standbys into a next-level brunch centerpiece. This looks and smells so good, you might have to fend off guests en route from oven to table. Dig in!
—James Schend, Pleasant Prairie, WI

PREP: 25 MIN. • **BAKE:** 20 MIN.
MAKES: 8 SERVINGS

1   tube (8 oz.) refrigerated crescent rolls
10 pieces thinly sliced deli ham
1   cup shredded cheddar cheese, divided
11 large eggs, divided use
¾   cup roasted sweet red peppers, drained and chopped
4   green onions, thinly sliced
1   Tbsp. olive oil
1   tsp. minced garlic
2   tsp. sesame seeds, optional
    Chopped fresh parsley, optional

1. Preheat oven to 375°. Unroll crescent dough and separate into triangles. On an ungreased 12-in. pizza pan, arrange triangles in a ring with points toward the outside and wide ends overlapping to create a 3-in.-diameter hole in the center. Press overlapping dough to seal. Fold ham slices lengthwise and place on top of each triangle. Sprinkle with half the cheese.
2. In a large bowl, beat 10 eggs; add chopped peppers. In a large skillet, cook green onions in oil over medium heat until tender, 2-3 minutes. Add garlic; cook for 30 seconds. Pour in egg mixture; cook and stir until eggs are thickened and no liquid egg remains. Spoon egg mixture over cheese on wide end of triangles; sprinkle with remaining cheese. Fold pointed ends of triangles over filling, tucking points under to form a ring with a small hole in the center (filling will be visible). Beat remaining egg; brush over pastry. If desired, sprinkle with sesame seeds.
3. Bake until golden brown and heated through, 20-25 minutes. If desired, top with parsley to serve.
1 SERVING: *313 cal., 19g fat (5g sat. fat), 282mg chol., 735mg sod., 15g carb. (5g sugars, 0 fiber), 19g pro.*

RASPBERRY-BANANA BREAKFAST TACOS

(SHOWN ON PAGE 146)
My sweet take on breakfast tacos swaps in pancakes instead of tortillas! They're so easy and absolutely delicious. Choose fruits and berries depending on what's in season.
—Joan Hallford, North Richland Hills, TX

PREP: 25 MIN. • **COOK:** 5 MIN./BATCH
MAKES: 4 SERVINGS

¾   cup all-purpose flour
¾   cup whole wheat flour
3   Tbsp. sugar
2   tsp. baking powder
¾   tsp. ground cinnamon
½   tsp. salt
1   large egg, room temperature
1   cup 2% milk
2   Tbsp. canola oil
1   tsp. vanilla extract
⅓   cup cream cheese, softened
3   Tbsp. vanilla yogurt
1   small banana, sliced
1   cup fresh raspberries

1. Whisk together flours, sugar, baking powder, cinnamon and salt. Combine egg, milk, canola oil and vanilla; stir into the dry ingredients just until moistened.
2. Preheat a griddle over medium heat. Lightly grease griddle. Pour batter by ½ cupfuls onto griddle; cook until bubbles on top begin to pop and bottoms are golden brown. Turn; cook until second side is golden brown.
3. Meanwhile, beat together cream cheese and yogurt. Spread over pancakes; top with banana and raspberries. Fold up.
1 TACO: *429 cal., 17g fat (6g sat. fat), 71mg chol., 651mg sod., 59g carb. (19g sugars, 6g fiber), 11g pro.*

HAM & CHEDDAR BRUNCH RING

SAUSAGE & EGGS OVER CHEDDAR-PARMESAN GRITS

PETITE SAUSAGE QUICHES

You won't be able to eat just one of these miniature quiches. Filled with savory sausage, Swiss cheese and a dash of cayenne, the cuties will disappear fast from the brunch table.
—Dawn Stitt, Hesperia, MI

PREP: 25 MIN. • **BAKE:** 30 MIN. • **MAKES:** 3 DOZEN

- 1 cup butter, softened
- 6 oz. cream cheese, softened
- 2 cups all-purpose flour

FILLING

- 6 oz. bulk Italian sausage
- 1 cup shredded Swiss cheese
- 1 Tbsp. minced chives
- 1 large egg
- ½ cup half-and-half cream
- ¼ tsp. salt
  Dash cayenne pepper

1. Preheat oven to 375°. Beat butter, cream cheese and flour until smooth. Shape tablespoonfuls of dough into 36 balls; press onto the bottom and up the sides of greased miniature muffin cups.
2. In a large skillet, cook sausage over medium heat until no longer pink; drain and crumble. Sprinkle sausage, Swiss cheese and chives into muffin cups. Beat egg, cream, salt and pepper until blended; pour into shells.
3. Bake until browned, 28-30 minutes (for a browner bottom crust, bake on a lower rack). Serve warm.
1 QUICHE: 100 cal., 8g fat (4g sat. fat), 26mg chol., 95mg sod., 6g carb. (0 sugars, 0 fiber), 2g pro.

SAUSAGE & EGGS OVER CHEDDAR-PARMESAN GRITS

These creamy grits topped with Italian sausage, peppers, onions and a fried egg on top are total comfort food. Perfect for brunch or dinner, they are easy to put together and will satisfy a hungry crew.
—Debbie Glasscock, Conway, AR

PREP: 20 MIN. • **COOK:** 20 MIN. • **MAKES:** 6 SERVINGS

- 1 lb. bulk Italian sausage
- 1 large sweet onion, chopped
- 1 medium sweet yellow pepper, chopped
- 1 medium sweet red pepper, chopped
- 6 cups water
- 1½ cups quick-cooking grits
- 1 cup shredded sharp cheddar cheese
- ½ cup shredded Parmesan cheese
- 2 Tbsp. half-and-half cream
- ½ tsp. salt
- ¼ tsp. pepper
- 2 tsp. olive oil
- 6 large eggs
  Hot pepper sauce, optional

1. In a Dutch oven, cook sausage, onion, yellow pepper and red pepper over medium heat until sausage is no longer pink and vegetables are tender, 6-8 minutes, breaking up sausage into crumbles; drain.
2. Meanwhile, in a large saucepan, bring water to a boil. Slowly stir in grits. Reduce heat to medium-low; cook, covered, until thickened, about 5 minutes, stirring occasionally. Remove from heat. Stir in cheeses, cream, salt and pepper; keep warm.
3. In a large skillet, heat oil over medium-high heat. Break eggs, 1 at a time, into pan; reduce heat to low. Cook until whites are set and yolks begin to thicken, turning once if desired. Divide grits among 6 serving bowls; top with sausage mixture and eggs. If desired, serve with pepper sauce.
1 SERVING: 538 cal., 32g fat (12g sat. fat), 253mg chol., 972mg sod., 38g carb. (5g sugars, 3g fiber), 26g pro.

PETITE SAUSAGE QUICHES

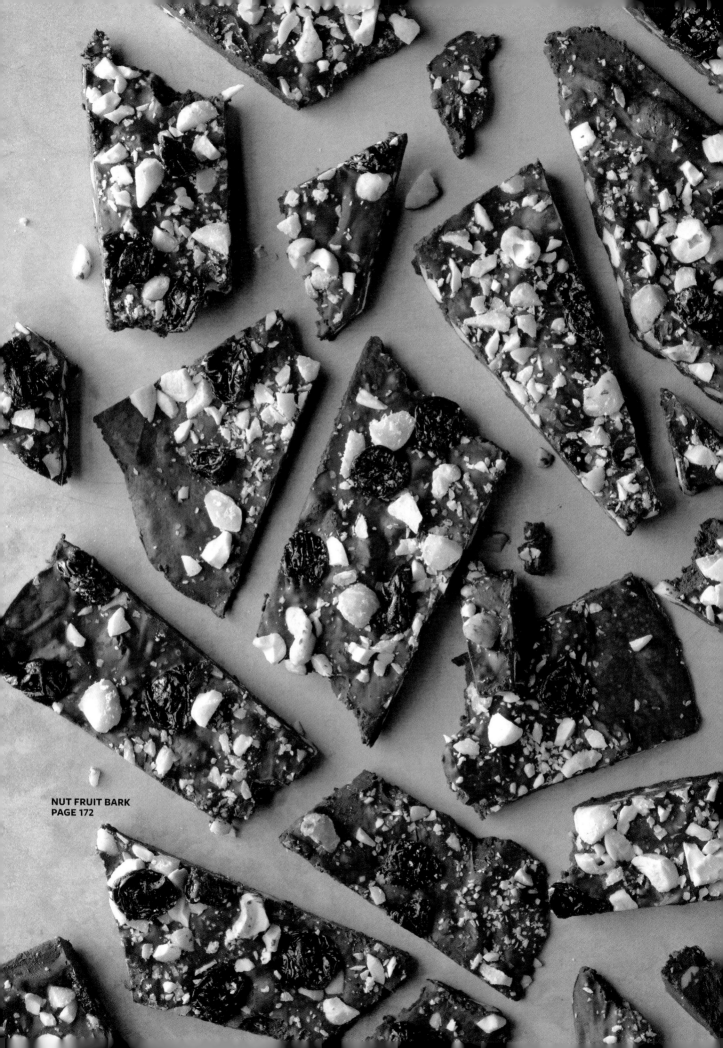

NUT FRUIT BARK
PAGE 172

Cookies, Bars & Candies

As scrumptious snacks or as crowd-pleasing desserts, these sweets are ideal for any occasion. You'll find they're easy to make—but hard to put down once you get a taste!

LEMON BLUEBERRY
WHOOPIE PIES

LEMON BLUEBERRY
WHOOPIE PIES

*These whoopie pies have it all: Soft, cakelike
cookies are studded with tart and juicy
blueberries and filled with tangy cream
cheese frosting. I take them to family and
school events and they are always the first
thing gone! Be sure to continually scrape the
sides of the bowl with a spatula while making
the batter and frosting.*
—Kathy Martino, Pittsburgh, PA

PREP: 30 MIN.
BAKE: 10 MIN./BATCH + COOLING
MAKES: 1 DOZEN

- ½ **cup butter, softened**
- ½ **cup sugar**
- 1 **large egg, room temperature**
- 1 **tsp. vanilla extract**
- 1¼ **cups plus 1 Tbsp.
  all-purpose flour, divided**
- ½ **tsp. baking powder**
- ¼ **tsp. baking soda**
- ¼ **tsp. salt**
- ¼ **cup buttermilk**
- 1 **cup fresh or frozen blueberries**
- 2 **tsp. grated lemon zest**

FILLING
- ¼ **cup butter, softened**
- ¼ **cup cream cheese, softened**
- 1 **Tbsp. honey**
- 1 **tsp. grated lemon zest**
- ½ **tsp. vanilla extract**
- 1½ **cups confectioners' sugar**

1. Preheat oven to 350°. Line baking sheets
with silicone baking mats or parchment.
2. In a large bowl, cream butter and sugar
until light and fluffy. Beat in egg and vanilla.
In another bowl, whisk 1¼ cups flour,
baking powder, baking soda and salt;
add to creamed mixture alternately with
buttermilk, beating well after each addition.
In another bowl, toss blueberries and
lemon zest with remaining flour; gently
fold into dough.

3. Drop dough by tablespoonfuls 2 in. apart
onto prepared baking sheets. Bake until
edges just begin to brown, 10-12 minutes.
Cool on pans 2 minutes. Remove to wire
racks to cool completely.
4. For filling, in a large bowl, beat butter
and cream cheese until blended. Beat in
honey, lemon zest and vanilla. Gradually
beat in confectioners' sugar until smooth.
Spread on bottoms of half of the cookies;
cover with remaining cookies. Refrigerate
in an airtight container.

FREEZE OPTION: Freeze whoopie pies in
freezer containers (do not stack). To use,
thaw before serving.

NOTE: If using frozen blueberries, use
without thawing to avoid discoloring
the batter.

1 WHOOPIE PIE: *281 cal., 14g fat (8g sat. fat),
51mg chol., 218mg sod., 38g carb. (26g
sugars, 1g fiber), 3g pro.*

CHOCOLATE BILLIONAIRES

I received this recipe from a friend while living in Texas. When we moved, I was sure to take the recipe with me. Everyone raves about these chocolate and caramel candies.
—June Humphrey, Strongsville, OH

PREP: 45 MIN. + CHILLING • **MAKES:** ABOUT 2 LBS.

- 1 pkg. (14 oz.) caramels
- 3 Tbsp. water
- 1½ cups chopped pecans
- 1 cup Rice Krispies
- 3 cups milk chocolate chips
- 1½ tsp. shortening

1. Line 2 baking sheets with waxed paper; grease the paper and set aside. In a large heavy saucepan, combine the caramels and water; cook and stir over low heat until smooth. Stir in pecans and cereal until coated. Drop by teaspoonfuls onto prepared pans. Refrigerate for 10 minutes or until firm.

2. Meanwhile, in a microwave, melt the chocolate chips and shortening; stir until smooth. Dip candy into chocolate, coating all sides; allow excess to drip off. Place on prepared pans. Refrigerate until set. Store in an airtight container.

1 OZ.: *172 cal., 10g fat (4g sat. fat), 4mg chol., 51mg sod., 20g carb. (17g sugars, 1g fiber), 2g pro.*

GUMDROP FUDGE

GUMDROP FUDGE

Making candy is one of my favorite things to do during the holidays. This sweet white fudge is as easy to put together as it is beautiful to serve.
—Jennifer Short, Omaha, NE

PREP: 20 MIN. + CHILLING • **MAKES:** ABOUT 3 LBS. (81 PIECES)

- 1½ lbs. white candy coating, coarsely chopped
- 1 can (14 oz.) sweetened condensed milk
- ⅛ tsp. salt
- 1½ tsp. vanilla extract
- 1½ cups chopped gumdrops

1. Line a 9-in. square pan with foil; set aside. In a heavy saucepan, combine the candy coating, milk and salt. Cook and stir over low heat until candy coating is melted. Remove from the heat; stir in vanilla and gumdrops.

2. Spread into prepared pan. Cover and refrigerate until firm. Using foil, remove fudge from the pan; cut into 1-in. squares. Store in an airtight container at room temperature.

1 PIECE: *74 cal., 3g fat (2g sat. fat), 2mg chol., 11mg sod., 12g carb. (11g sugars, 0 fiber), 0 pro.*

CHOCOLATE BILLIONAIRES

CHEWY GERMAN CHOCOLATE COOKIES

When I want a cookie that's as chewy as a brownie, this is the recipe I reach for. Coffee granules add the right amount of mocha flavor.
—*Darlene Brenden, Salem, OR*

PREP: 25 MIN. • **BAKE:** 10 MIN./BATCH
MAKES: 4 DOZEN

- 12 oz. German sweet chocolate, chopped
- 2 Tbsp. shortening
- 1 tsp. instant coffee granules
- 3 large eggs, room temperature
- 1¼ cups sugar
- 1 tsp. vanilla extract
- 1 cup all-purpose flour
- ½ tsp. baking powder
- ½ tsp. salt
- ½ cup chopped pecans
- 48 pecan halves
  Confectioners' sugar, optional

1. Preheat oven to 350° In a microwave, melt chocolate and shortening; stir until smooth. Stir in coffee granules; cool and set aside.

2. In a large bowl, beat eggs and sugar until light and lemon-colored. Beat in cooled chocolate and the vanilla. Combine the flour, baking powder and salt; add to chocolate mixture and mix well. Stir in chopped pecans.

3. Working quickly, drop dough by tablespoonfuls 2 in. apart onto greased baking sheets. Place a pecan half in the center of each. Bake until cookies are set, 10-12 minutes. Cool for 1 minute before removing to wire racks. If desired, dust with confectioners' sugar.

1 COOKIE: *98 cal., 5g fat (2g sat. fat), 12mg chol., 34mg sod., 9g carb. (7g sugars, 1g fiber), 1g pro.*

NUT FRUIT BARK

(SHOWN ON PAGE 168)

Here's a sophisticated version of fruit bark. Dark chocolate turns into a rich mocha flavor with the espresso powder. If you're a fan of sweet-salty tidbits, make sure to use the sea salt.
—*Thomas Faglon, Somerset, NJ*

PREP: 15 MIN. + CHILLING • **MAKES:** 1½ LBS.

- 1 lb. dark chocolate, coarsely chopped
- 1 tsp. instant espresso powder
- ½ cup dried cherries or blueberries, divided
- ½ cup macadamia nuts, chopped and divided
- ½ cup chopped cashews, divided
- ½ tsp. coarse sea salt, optional

1. Line bottom and sides of a 15x10x1-in. baking pan with parchment; grease the paper and set aside.

2. In a double boiler or metal bowl over hot water, melt chocolate; stir until smooth. Stir in espresso powder and half of the cherries and nuts. Spread into prepared pan; top with remaining cherries and nuts (pan will not be full). Sprinkle with salt if desired. Refrigerate for 30 minutes or until firm.

3. Break into pieces. Store in an airtight container.

1 OZ.: *147 cal., 10g fat (5g sat. fat), 1mg chol., 26mg sod., 14g carb. (11g sugars, 2g fiber), 2g pro.*

CHEWY GERMAN
CHOCOLATE COOKIES

BEN'S ENGLISH TOFFEE

I've been cooking since I was very young, and I first made this toffee recipe when I was 12 years old. I love to prepare desserts—candy is my favorite.
—Ben Lohse, Worcester, PA

PREP: 20 MIN. • **COOK:** 30 MIN. + STANDING
MAKES: 1¾ LBS.

- 2 tsp. plus ½ cup butter, divided
- 1¾ cups sugar
- ⅛ tsp. cream of tartar
- 1 cup heavy whipping cream
- 1 tsp. rum extract
- 1 cup milk chocolate chips
- 1 cup mixed nuts, chopped and toasted

1. Grease a 15x10x1-in. pan with 2 tsp. butter; set aside.
2. In a large heavy saucepan, combine sugar and cream of tartar; stir in cream and remaining butter. Cook and stir over medium heat until a candy thermometer reads 300° (hard-crack stage). Remove from the heat; stir in extract. Quickly pour into prepared pan. Let stand at room temperature until cool.
3. In a microwave, melt chocolate chips; stir until smooth. Spread over toffee. Sprinkle with nuts. Let stand until set, about 1 hour. Break into pieces. Store in an airtight container.

NOTE: We recommend that you test your candy thermometer before each use by bringing water to a boil; the thermometer should read 212°. Adjust your recipe temperature up or down based on your test.
1 OZ.: *171 cal., 11g fat (5g sat. fat), 22mg chol., 66mg sod., 18g carb. (16g sugars, 1g fiber), 2g pro.*

SKILLET CHOCOLATE CHUNK WALNUT BLONDIES

Put these beauties out at a potluck and you'll find only crumbs on your platter when it's time to head home. Everyone will ask who made those scrumptious blondies, so be sure to bring copies of the recipe!
—Peggy Woodward, Shullsburg, WI

PREP: 15 MIN. • **BAKE:** 30 MIN.
MAKES: 3 BLONDIES (6 SERVINGS EACH)

- 1 cup butter, melted
- 2 cups packed brown sugar
- 2 tsp. vanilla extract

SKILLET CHOCOLATE CHUNK WALNUT BLONDIES

- 2 large eggs, room temperature
- 2 cups all-purpose flour
- ½ cup ground walnuts
- 1 tsp. baking powder
- ½ tsp. salt
- ⅛ tsp. baking soda
- 1 cup chopped walnuts, toasted
- 1 cup semisweet chocolate chunks

1. Preheat oven to 350°. Grease three 6½-in. cast-iron skillets.
2. In a large bowl, mix butter, brown sugar and vanilla until blended. Add 1 egg at a time, whisking to blend after each addition. In another bowl, mix flour, ground walnuts, baking powder, salt and baking soda; stir into butter mixture. Fold in walnuts and chocolate chunks.

3. Spread into skillets. Bake until a toothpick inserted in center comes out with moist crumbs and top is golden, 30-35 minutes. Cool slightly; serve warm.
1 SERVING: *262 cal., 15g fat (7g sat. fat), 36mg chol., 149mg sod., 32g carb. (22g sugars, 1g fiber), 3g pro.*

> **TEST KITCHEN TIP**
> ### Don't have mini skillets?
> Grab your trusty 13x9-in. baking pan instead. Simply line it with parchment and grease it before adding the batter. Then bake 30-35 minutes or until a toothpick inserted in center comes out with moist crumbs and the top is golden brown.

**PEANUT BUTTER
PRETZEL BARS**

PEANUT BUTTER
PRETZEL BARS

*My secret to these rich no-bake bites?
Pretzels in the crust. They add a salty crunch
to the classic peanut butter-chocolate
pairing. The irresistible treats were the
first to sell out at our PTA bake sale!*
—Jennifer Beckman, Falls Church, VA

PREP: 15 MIN. + CHILLING
MAKES: 4 DOZEN

  1 **pkg. (16 oz.) miniature pretzels**
1½ **cups butter, melted**
1½ **cups peanut butter**
  3 **cups confectioners' sugar**
  2 **cups (12 oz.) semisweet
     chocolate chips**
  1 **Tbsp. shortening**

1. Line a 13x9-in. baking pan with foil,
letting ends extend up sides. Set aside
1½ cups pretzels for topping. Pulse
remaining pretzels in a food processor
until fine crumbs form. In a large bowl, mix
butter, peanut butter, confectioners' sugar
and pretzel crumbs.
2. Press into prepared pan. In a microwave,
melt chocolate chips and shortening; stir
until smooth. Spread over peanut butter
layer. Break reserved pretzels and sprinkle
over top; press down gently. Refrigerate,
covered, until set, about 1 hour. Lifting with
foil, remove from pan. Cut into 48 bars.
1 PIECE: *201 cal., 13g fat (6g sat. fat), 15mg
chol., 233mg sod., 22g carb. (12g sugars,
1g fiber), 3g pro.*

❄ VANILLA-BUTTER
SUGAR COOKIES

*These are one of my favorite cookies to bake
for Christmas. The dough recipe is versatile
and you can use it for other holidays, too.
Children like to help with decorating.*
—Cynthia Ettel, Glencoe, MN

PREP: 35 MIN. + CHILLING
BAKE: 10 MIN./BATCH + COOLING
MAKES: ABOUT 7 DOZEN

1½ **cups butter, softened**
1½ **cups sugar**
  2 **large eggs, room temperature**
  2 **Tbsp. vanilla extract**
  4 **cups all-purpose flour**
  1 **tsp. salt**
  1 **tsp. baking soda**
  1 **tsp. cream of tartar**
FROSTING
1½ **cups confectioners' sugar**
  3 **Tbsp. butter, softened**
  1 **Tbsp. vanilla extract**
  1 **to 2 Tbsp. whole milk
     Food coloring, optional
     Colored sugar**

1. Cream butter and granulated sugar until
light and fluffy. Beat in eggs and vanilla. In
another bowl, whisk flour, salt, baking soda
and cream of tartar. Gradually beat into
creamed mixture. Refrigerate, covered, for
30 minutes.
2. Preheat oven to 350°. On a lightly floured
surface, roll dough to ¼-in. thickness. Cut
with floured 2½-in. cookie cutters. Place
1 in. apart on ungreased baking sheets.
Bake 10-12 minutes. Cool on wire racks.
3. For frosting, beat confectioners' sugar,
butter, vanilla and enough milk to reach
desired consistency. If desired, add a few
drops of food coloring. Cut a small hole
in the tip of a pastry bag or in a corner of
a food-safe plastic bag; transfer frosting
to bag. Pipe decorations. Sprinkle with
colored sugar.
FREEZE OPTION: Freeze undecorated
cookies, layered between waxed paper,
in freezer containers. To use, thaw and
decorate as desired.
1 COOKIE: *80 cal., 4g fat (2g sat. fat),
14mg chol., 74mg sod., 10g carb. (6g sugars,
0 fiber), 1g pro.*

**VANILLA-BUTTER
SUGAR COOKIES**

SUNDAE FUNDAY BARK

KIM BANICK
Turner, OR

SUNDAE FUNDAY BARK

Any occasion is the right time to serve this easy-to-make bark. The fruits—packed with flavor but not overly sweet—go so well with the white candy base. A dark chocolate drizzle adds a lot of fun.
—Kim Banick, Turner, OR

PREP: 20 MIN. + CHILLING • **MAKES:** 1 LB.

  1 pkg. (10 to 12 oz.) white baking chips
 ¼ cup freeze-dried pineapple
 ¼ cup dried banana chips,
      coarsely chopped
 ¼ cup freeze-dried strawberry slices
 ¼ cup dried cherries
 ⅓ cup salted peanuts, coarsely chopped
 ¼ cup dark chocolate chips, melted

1. Line a 15x10x1-in. pan with parchment. In a microwave, melt baking chips; stir until smooth. Spread into a 12x8-in. rectangle in prepared pan. Sprinkle with fruits and peanuts; press into melted chips.
2. Refrigerate until firm, about 30 minutes. Break or cut bark into pieces. Drizzle dark chocolate over the bark before or after dividing into pieces. Store between layers of waxed paper in an airtight container.
1 OZ.: 152 cal., 9g fat (5g sat. fat), 4mg chol., 27mg sod., 17g carb. (16g sugars, 1g fiber), 2g pro.

APPLE KUCHEN BARS

This recipe is about family, comfort and simplicity. My mom made them, and now I bake them in my own kitchen. I make double batches to pass along the love!
—Elizabeth Monfort, Celina, OH

PREP: 35 MIN. • **BAKE:** 1 HOUR + COOLING
MAKES: 2 DOZEN

  3 cups all-purpose flour, divided
 ¼ tsp. salt
1½ cups cold butter, divided
  4 to 5 Tbsp. ice water
  8 cups thinly sliced peeled tart
      apples (about 8 medium)
  2 cups sugar, divided
  2 tsp. ground cinnamon

1. Preheat oven to 350°. Place 2 cups flour and salt in a food processor; pulse until blended. Add 1 cup butter; pulse until butter is the size of peas. While pulsing, add just enough ice water to form moist crumbs. Press mixture onto bottom of a greased 13x9-in. baking pan. Bake until edges are lightly browned, 20-25 minutes. Cool on a wire rack.
2. In a large bowl, combine apples, 1 cup sugar and cinnamon; toss to coat. Spoon over crust. Place remaining flour, butter and sugar in food processor; pulse until coarse crumbs form. Sprinkle over apples. Bake until golden brown and apples are tender, 60-70 minutes. Cool completely on a wire rack. Cut into 24 bars.
1 BAR: 240 cal., 12g fat (7g sat. fat), 30mg chol., 106mg sod., 33g carb. (21g sugars, 1g fiber), 2g pro.

HOW-TO

Get Things Settled

Next time you open a new bag of flour, save yourself some mess with this trick. Slap the top of the bag a couple of times before opening it. This settles the flour so it doesn't spray out when you open the bag.

CHOCOLATE MINCEMEAT BARS

Mincemeat is just so classic for holiday desserts. Even people who say they don't care for the taste will love these tender chocolate bars—I promise.
—Darlene Berndt, South Bend, IN

PREP: 15 MIN. • **BAKE:** 20 MIN. • **MAKES:** 3 DOZEN

- ½ cup shortening
- 1 cup sugar
- 3 large eggs, room temperature
- 2 cups all-purpose flour
- 2 tsp. baking soda
- 1¾ cups mincemeat
- 2 cups (12 oz.) semisweet chocolate chips
   Confectioners' sugar

1. In a large bowl, cream shortening and sugar until light and fluffy. Add 1 egg at a time, beating well after each addition. Combine flour and baking soda; gradually add to the creamed mixture and mix well. Beat in mincemeat. Stir in chocolate chips.

2. Spread into a greased 15x10x1-in. baking pan. Bake at 375° for 15-20 minutes or until dark golden brown. Cool on a wire rack. Cut into 36 bars. Dust with confectioners' sugar.

FREEZE OPTION: Freeze cooled bars in freezer containers, separating layers with waxed paper. To use, thaw before serving.

1 BAR: *142 cal., 6g fat (2g sat. fat), 18mg chol., 80mg sod., 21g carb. (15g sugars, 1g fiber), 2g pro.*

CHOCOLATE MINCEMEAT BARS

MINIATURE
PEANUT BUTTER TREATS

MINIATURE PEANUT BUTTER TREATS

I have three children and eight grandchildren, and every one of them loves these "peanut butter thingies," as the grandchildren like to call them.
—Jodie McCoy, Tulsa, OK

PREP: 20 MIN. + CHILLING • **BAKE:** 10 MIN./BATCH + COOLING
MAKES: 3½ DOZEN

COOKIE
- ½ cup butter, softened
- ½ cup sugar
- ½ cup packed brown sugar
- 1 large egg, room temperature
- ½ cup creamy peanut butter
- ½ tsp. vanilla extract
- 1¼ cups all-purpose flour
- ¾ tsp. baking soda
- ½ tsp. salt

FILLING
- 42 miniature peanut butter-chocolate cups

1. In a bowl, combine the butter, sugars, egg, peanut butter and vanilla; beat until smooth. Combine the flour, baking soda and salt; gradually add to creamed mixture. Cover and chill for 1 hour or until easy to handle.

2. Roll into 42 walnut-sized balls; place in greased miniature muffin cups. Bake at 375° for 8-9 minutes.

3. Remove from oven; gently press 1 peanut butter cup into each cookie, forming a depression. Cool for 10 minutes before removing to wire racks to cool completely.

1 PIECE: *108 cal., 6g fat (3g sat. fat), 11mg chol., 108mg sod., 12g carb. (9g sugars, 1g fiber), 2g pro.*

BIG & BUTTERY CHOCOLATE CHIP COOKIES

Our version of the classic cookie is based on a recipe from a bakery in California called Hungry Bear. It's big, thick and chewy—perfect for dunking.
—Irene Yeh, Mequon, WI

PREP: 35 MIN. + CHILLING
BAKE: 10 MIN./BATCH
MAKES: ABOUT 2 DOZEN

1 cup butter, softened
1 cup packed brown sugar
¾ cup sugar
2 large eggs, room temperature
1½ tsp. vanilla extract
2⅔ cups all-purpose flour
1¼ tsp. baking soda
1 tsp. salt
1 pkg. (12 oz.) semisweet chocolate chips
2 cups coarsely chopped walnuts, toasted

1. In a large bowl, beat butter and sugars until blended. Beat in eggs and vanilla. In a small bowl, whisk flour, baking soda and salt; gradually beat into butter mixture. Stir in chocolate chips and walnuts.
2. Shape ¼ cupfuls of dough into balls. Flatten each to ¾-in. thickness (2½-in. diameter), smoothing edges as necessary. Place in an airtight container, separating layers with waxed paper or parchment; refrigerate, covered, overnight.
3. To bake, place dough portions 2 in. apart on parchment-lined baking sheets; let stand at room temperature 30 minutes before baking. Preheat oven to 400°.
4. Bake until the edges are golden brown (centers will be light), 10-12 minutes. Cool on pans 2 minutes. Remove to wire racks to cool.
NOTE: To toast nuts, bake in a shallow pan in a 350° oven for 5-10 minutes or cook in a skillet over low heat until lightly browned, stirring occasionally.
1 COOKIE: *311 cal., 19g fat (8g sat. fat), 38mg chol., 229mg sod., 35g carb. (23g sugars, 2g fiber), 4g pro.*

Preserve Freshness with Bread

To keep baked goods soft and moist when storing, add a slice of white bread to the container. It will help preserve moisture in cookies, cakes, muffins and more.

LEMON COCONUT BITES

The tangy lemon flavor of this no-fuss bar dessert is especially delicious on a warm day. It reminds me of selling lemonade on the sidewalk as a little girl.
—Donna Biddle, Elmira, NY

PREP: 25 MIN. • **BAKE:** 20 MIN. + COOLING
MAKES: 4 DOZEN

1½ cups all-purpose flour
½ cup confectioners' sugar
¾ cup cold butter, cubed
4 large eggs, room temperature
1½ cups sugar
½ cup lemon juice
1 tsp. baking powder
¾ cup sweetened shredded coconut

1. In a small bowl, combine the flour and confectioners' sugar; cut in the butter until crumbly. Press into a lightly greased 13x9-in. baking pan. Bake at 350° for 15 minutes.
2. Meanwhile, in another small bowl, beat the eggs, sugar, lemon juice and baking powder until combined. Pour over crust; sprinkle with coconut.
3. Bake at 350° until golden brown, 20-25 minutes. Cool on a wire rack. Cut into 48 bars.
1 BAR: *82 cal., 4g fat (2g sat. fat), 25mg chol., 46mg sod., 11g carb. (8g sugars, 0 fiber), 1g pro.*

BIG & BUTTERY CHOCOLATE CHIP COOKIES

RASPBERRY ALMOND STRIPS

RASPBERRY ALMOND STRIPS

A cup of tea is the perfect complement to these scrumptious cookie strips dressed up with raspberry filling. Chopped almonds make them an extra-special treat.
—Taste of Home *Test Kitchen*

TAKES: 30 MIN. • **MAKES:** 16 COOKIES

- ½ **tube refrigerated sugar cookie dough, softened**
- ⅓ **cup all-purpose flour**
- ¼ **cup finely chopped almonds**
- 3 **Tbsp. raspberry cake and pastry filling**

1. Preheat oven to 350°. In a small bowl, beat cookie dough, flour and almonds until blended. Roll into a 13½x2-in. rectangle on an ungreased baking sheet.
2. Using a wooden spoon handle, make a ¼-in.-deep indentation lengthwise down center of rectangle. Bake 5 minutes.

3. Spoon raspberry filling into indentation. Bake 8-10 minutes longer or until cookie is golden brown. Cool on pan 2 minutes.
4. Remove from pan to a cutting board; cut crosswise into 16 slices. Transfer to a wire rack to cool.
1 COOKIE: *106 cal., 4g fat (1g sat. fat), 2mg chol., 55mg sod., 16g carb. (9g sugars, 1g fiber), 1g pro.*

BENNE CANDY

I love anything that has sesame seeds. This hard candy is a cinch to make with the inexpensive toasted seeds sold at Asian grocery stores. Plus, you'll need only four other ingredients.
—Lily Julow, Lawrenceville, GA

PREP: 10 MIN. • **COOK:** 25 MIN. + COOLING
MAKES: 1¼ LBS. (4 DOZEN PIECES)

- 2 **tsp. plus 2 Tbsp. butter, divided**
- 2⅓ **cups packed brown sugar**
- ½ **cup whole milk**
- 1 **Tbsp. white vinegar**
- 1 **cup sesame seeds, toasted**

1. Grease a baking sheet with 2 tsp. butter; set aside. In a small heavy saucepan, combine brown sugar, milk, vinegar and the remaining butter. Cook and stir over medium heat until a candy thermometer reads 280° (soft-crack stage). Remove from the heat; stir in sesame seeds.
2. Immediately pour onto prepared pan; spread into a 12x9-in. rectangle. Using a sharp knife, score warm candy into 1½-in. squares (do not cut through). Cool completely; break into pieces along scored lines. Store in an airtight container.
NOTE: We recommend that you test your candy thermometer before each use by bringing water to a boil; the thermometer should read 212°. Adjust your recipe temperature up or down based on your test.
1 PIECE: *61 cal., 2g fat (0 sat. fat), 2mg chol., 10mg sod., 11g carb. (10g sugars, 0 fiber), 1g pro.*

STRAWBERRY LEMON CUPCAKES
PAGE 190

Cakes & Pies

Whether you need a showstopper for a special gathering or just want to treat the family to a blissful dessert, you'll find just the thing in this chapter filled with delicious pies, divine cakes and more.

MAKEOVER ITALIAN CREAM CAKE

Toasted pecans and coconut take this cake from good to great, but it's the cream cheese frosting that makes it truly extraordinary— and it has fewer calories than similar cakes!
—Christy White, Oxford, MS

PREP: 40 MIN. • **BAKE:** 20 MIN. + COOLING
MAKES: 16 SERVINGS

- ⅓ cup butter, softened
- 1 cup sugar
- 2 large eggs, room temperature
- ⅓ cup unsweetened applesauce
- ½ tsp. vanilla extract
- 1⅓ cups all-purpose flour
- ¾ tsp. baking soda
- ⅛ tsp. salt
- ⅔ cup buttermilk
- ⅓ cup chopped pecans, toasted
- ¼ cup sweetened shredded coconut, toasted

CREAM CHEESE FROSTING
- 1 pkg. (8 oz.) cream cheese, softened
- 2 Tbsp. butter, softened
- 2 cups confectioners' sugar

- ½ tsp. vanilla extract
- ⅓ cup chopped pecans, toasted

1. Line two 9-in. round baking pans with waxed paper. Coat pans with cooking spray and sprinkle with flour; set aside.
2. In a large bowl, beat butter and sugar until crumbly, about 2 minutes. Add 1 egg at a time, beating well after each addition. Beat in applesauce and vanilla (mixture will appear curdled). Combine the flour, baking soda and salt; add to creamed mixture alternately with buttermilk. Fold in pecans and coconut.
3. Pour into prepared pans. Bake at 350° for 18-22 minutes or until a toothpick inserted in the center comes out clean. Cool for 10 minutes before removing from pans to wire racks to cool completely.
4. For frosting, in a large bowl, beat cream cheese and butter until fluffy. Add the confectioners' sugar and vanilla; beat until smooth. Spread frosting between layers and over top and sides of cake. Sprinkle pecans over cake. Store in the refrigerator.
1 SLICE: *297 cal., 15g fat (7g sat. fat), 56mg chol., 180mg sod., 38g carb. (28g sugars, 1g fiber), 4g pro.*

DOUBLE CHOCOLATE ESPRESSO POUND CAKE

Two of my biggest loves in life—chocolate and coffee—come together in this velvety pound cake. It's one of my favorite desserts to bring to parties. If there's any left over, I love to sneak a slice at breakfast, too.
—Rachel Bernhard Seis, Milwaukee, WI

PREP: 20 MIN. • **BAKE:** 80 MIN. + COOLING
MAKES: 16 SERVINGS

- 5 oz. milk chocolate, chopped
- ¼ cup brewed espresso
- 1 cup butter, softened
- 3 cups sugar
- 5 large eggs, room temperature
- 2 tsp. vanilla extract
- 3 cups all-purpose flour
- 1½ tsp. baking powder
- ½ tsp. salt
- ⅔ cup 2% milk
- 1 cup (6 oz.) dark chocolate chips

FROSTING
- ¼ cup butter, softened
- 3 cups confectioners' sugar
- 3 Tbsp. 2% milk
- 3 tsp. vanilla extract
- ½ tsp. salt

1. In a double boiler or metal bowl over hot water, melt milk chocolate and espresso; stir until smooth. Remove from the heat.
2. In a large bowl, beat butter and sugar until crumbly, about 2 minutes. Add 1 egg at a time, beating well after each addition. Beat in vanilla. Combine the flour, baking powder and salt; add to the creamed mixture alternately with milk, beating well after each addition. Stir in chocolate chips and reserved chocolate mixture.
3. Transfer to a greased and floured 10-in. fluted tube pan. Bake at 325° until a toothpick inserted near the center comes out clean, 80-90 minutes. Cool 10 minutes before removing from pan to a wire rack to cool completely.
4. In a large bowl, beat butter until light and fluffy. Beat in the confectioners' sugar, milk, vanilla and salt; frost cake.
1 SLICE: *573 cal., 22g fat (14g sat. fat), 100mg chol., 344mg sod., 91g carb. (71g sugars, 2g fiber), 6g pro.*

MAKEOVER ITALIAN CREAM CAKE

RAISIN-APPLESAUCE BUNDT CAKE

This cake is one of my grandfather's favorites. He always seems to know when I'm making it—he must have a keen sense of smell! The recipe was passed down from my great-grandmother. Sometimes I can imagine her making it all those years ago.
—Kathie Grenier, Auburn, ME

PREP: 20 MIN. • **BAKE:** 45 MIN. + COOLING
MAKES: 10 SERVINGS

- 1 cup sugar
- ½ cup shortening
- 2 Tbsp. molasses
- 2 cups all-purpose flour
- 1 tsp. baking soda
- 1 tsp. ground cinnamon
- 1 tsp. ground cloves
- ½ tsp. salt
- 1½ cups applesauce
- 1 cup raisins

1. In a bowl, cream sugar and shortening. Beat in molasses until blended; set aside. Sift together flour, baking soda, cinnamon, cloves and salt; add to creamed mixture alternately with applesauce, beating well after each addition. Stir in raisins.

2. Pour into a greased and floured 10-in. tube pan. Bake at 350° until a toothpick comes out clean, about 45 minutes. Cake will not rise to top of pan. After 10 minutes, remove cake from the pan and cool on a wire rack.

1 SLICE: *328 cal., 10g fat (2g sat. fat), 0 chol., 249mg sod., 58g carb. (35g sugars, 2g fiber), 3g pro.*

FIVE-SPICE PUMPKIN PIE

I always make a pumpkin pie for our big pie night party on Thanksgiving Eve. This recipe is an autumn classic with a special spiced-up twist.
—Shawn Barto, Winter Garden, FL

PREP: 30 MIN. + CHILLING
BAKE: 55 MIN. + COOLING
MAKES: 8 SERVINGS

- 1¼ cups all-purpose flour
- ⅛ tsp. salt
- ½ cup shortening
- 1 to 2 Tbsp. ice water
- 1 Tbsp. vodka
- 1 large egg
- 1 Tbsp. water

FIVE-SPICE PUMPKIN PIE

FILLING
- 1 can (15 oz.) pumpkin
- 1 cup evaporated milk
- ¾ cup packed brown sugar
- 2 large eggs
- 1 tsp. ground cinnamon
- 1 tsp. vanilla extract
- ½ tsp. salt
- ½ tsp. Chinese five-spice powder

1. In a small bowl, mix the flour and salt; cut in shortening until crumbly. Gradually add half the ice water and vodka, tossing with a fork until dough holds together when pressed. Add more if needed. Shape into a disk; wrap in plastic. Refrigerate dough for 1 hour or overnight.

2. Preheat oven to 425°. On a lightly floured surface, roll dough to a ⅛-in.-thick circle; transfer to a 9-in. pie plate. Trim pastry to ½ in. beyond rim of plate; flute edge. In a small bowl, whisk egg with water. Brush over pastry; refrigerate until ready to fill.

3. Meanwhile, beat filling ingredients until blended; transfer to crust. Bake on a lower oven rack 15 minutes. Reduce oven setting to 350°; bake until a knife inserted in the center comes out clean, 35-40 minutes longer. (Cover edges with foil during the last 15 minutes to prevent overbrowning if necessary.) Cool completely on a wire rack. Store pie in the refrigerator.

1 SLICE: *345 cal., 16g fat (5g sat. fat), 64mg chol., 244mg sod., 43g carb. (25g sugars, 2g fiber), 6g pro.*

> **TEST KITCHEN TIP**
>
> If decorative cutouts are desired, double pastry amount and divide in two. Roll additional pastry to ⅛-in. thickness; cut out with 1- to 1½-in. leaf-shaped cookie cutters. With a sharp knife, score leaf veins on cutouts. Place on an ungreased baking sheet. Bake at 400° until golden brown, 6-8 minutes. Remove to a wire rack to cool. Arrange around edge of baked pie.

ROCKY ROAD FREEZER PIE

Whip up this simple chocolaty pie the day before and you'll feel like a champ when you serve it on party day.
—Addrenne Roth, Donna, TX

PREP: 15 MIN. + FREEZING • **MAKES:** 8 SERVINGS

- 1½ cups half-and-half cream
- 1 pkg. (3.9 oz.) instant chocolate pudding mix
- 1 carton (8 oz.) frozen whipped topping, thawed
- ⅓ cup semisweet chocolate chips
- ⅓ cup miniature marshmallows
- ⅓ cup chopped pecans
- 1 graham cracker crust (9 in.)
  Miniature marshmallows, chopped pecans and chocolate sauce, optional

In a large bowl, whisk cream and pudding mix for 2 minutes. Fold in whipped topping. Stir in the chocolate chips, marshmallows and pecans. Transfer to pie crust. Freeze until firm, about 6 hours. Remove from the freezer 10 minutes before serving.

1 PIECE: *365 cal., 20g fat (11g sat. fat), 23mg chol., 212mg sod., 41g carb. (29g sugars, 2g fiber), 4g pro.*

RUBY GRAPE PIE

ROCKY ROAD FREEZER PIE

RUBY GRAPE PIE

My wife, Paula, and I grow red and green seedless table grapes on our 75-acre vineyard. Our crop is wonderful eaten out of hand or in salads. Paula also uses them in this unusual and tasty pie.
—Fred Smeds, Reedley, CA

PREP: 20 MIN. • **BAKE:** 50 MIN. + COOLING • **MAKES:** 8 SERVINGS

- 4 cups halved seedless red grapes (about 2 lbs.)
- ⅔ cup sugar
- ½ tsp. ground cinnamon
- 3 Tbsp. cornstarch
- 2 Tbsp. lemon juice
- 1 Tbsp. grated lemon zest
  Pastry for double-crust pie (9 in.)
- 2 Tbsp. butter

1. In a large saucepan, combine grapes, sugar and cinnamon; toss to coat. Let stand for 15 minutes. Combine cornstarch, lemon juice and zest; stir into grape mixture. Bring to a boil; cook and stir for 2 minutes or until thickened.

2. Line a 9-in. pie plate with bottom crust. Pour grape mixture into crust. Dot with butter. Place remaining crust over filling. Trim, seal and flute edges; cut slits in top. Cover edges loosely with foil.

3. Bake at 425° for 20 minutes. Reduce heat to 350° remove foil and bake 30-35 minutes longer or until the crust is golden brown. Cool on a wire rack.

1 SLICE: *400 cal., 17g fat (8g sat. fat), 18mg chol., 231mg sod., 60g carb. (32g sugars, 1g fiber), 3g pro.*

CRANBERRY-ORANGE POUND CAKE

At the summer resort that my husband and I operate in Ontario, we prepare all the meals for our guests, so I'm always trying out new recipes. This lovely, simple cake is in our regular rotation.
—Sheree Swistun, Winnipeg, MB

PREP: 25 MIN. • **BAKE:** 65 MIN. + COOLING
MAKES: 16 SERVINGS (1½ CUPS SAUCE)

- 1½ cups butter, softened
- 2¾ cups sugar
- 6 large eggs, room temperature
- 1 tsp. vanilla extract
- 2½ tsp. grated orange zest
- 3 cups all-purpose flour
- 1 tsp. baking powder
- ½ tsp. salt
- 1 cup sour cream
- 1½ cups chopped fresh or frozen cranberries

VANILLA BUTTER SAUCE

- 1 cup sugar
- 1 Tbsp. all-purpose flour
- ½ cup half-and-half cream
- ½ cup butter, softened
- ½ tsp. vanilla extract

1. In a large bowl, cream butter and sugar until light and fluffy, about 5 minutes. Add 1 egg at a time, beating well after each addition. Stir in vanilla and orange zest. Combine flour, baking powder and salt; add to creamed mixture alternately with sour cream. Fold in cranberries.
2. Pour into a greased and floured 10-in. fluted tube pan. Bake at 350° for 65-70 minutes or until a toothpick inserted in the center comes out clean. Cool 10 minutes before removing from pan to a wire rack to cool completely.
3. In a small saucepan, combine sugar and flour. Stir in cream and butter; bring to a boil over medium heat, stirring constantly. Boil for 2 minutes. Remove from the heat and stir in vanilla. Serve warm over cake.
1 SERVING: *543 cal., 28g fat (17g sat. fat), 155mg chol., 366mg sod., 67g carb. (48g sugars, 1g fiber), 6g pro.*

ROASTED STRAWBERRY SHEET CAKE

My Grandma Gigi loved summer berry cakes. Almost any time I'd call her during the warmer months, she'd invite me over to taste her latest masterpiece. This cake is an ode to her.
—Kristin Bowers, Rancho Palos Verdes, CA

PREP: 1 HOUR • **BAKE:** 30 MIN. + COOLING
MAKES: 24 SERVINGS

- 4 lbs. halved fresh strawberries
- ½ cup sugar

CAKE

- 1 cup butter, softened
- 1½ cups sugar
- 2 large eggs, room temperature
- 2 tsp. almond extract
- 3 cups all-purpose flour
- 3 tsp. baking powder
- 2 tsp. salt
- 1 cup whole milk
- ¼ cup turbinado (washed raw) sugar

1. Preheat oven to 350°. Place strawberries on a parchment-lined rimmed baking sheet. Sprinkle with sugar and toss to coat. Bake until just tender, 35-40 minutes. Cool slightly.
2. Meanwhile, grease a 15x10x1-in. baking pan. In a large bowl, cream butter and sugar until light and fluffy. Add 1 egg at a time, beating well after each addition. Beat in extract. In another bowl, whisk flour, baking powder and salt; add to creamed mixture alternately with milk, beating well after each addition (batter may appear curdled).
3. Transfer to prepared pan. Top with 3 cups roasted strawberries; sprinkle with turbinado sugar. Reserve remaining strawberries for serving. Bake until a toothpick inserted in center comes out clean, 30-35 minutes. Cool completely in pan on a wire rack. Serve with reserved roasted strawberries.
1 PIECE: *235 cal., 9g fat (5g sat. fat), 37mg chol., 329mg sod., 37g carb. (23g sugars, 2g fiber), 3g pro.*

ROASTED STRAWBERRY SHEET CAKE

APPLE PIE CUPCAKES WITH CINNAMON BUTTERCREAM

FLAKY BUMBLEBERRY PIE

When you want to make a lasting impression, make this pie! The crust is one of the flakiest ever, and the filling is so delicious with the different berries and rhubarb.
—Suzanne Alberts, Onalaska, WI

PREP: 20 MIN. + CHILLING
BAKE: 1 HOUR + COOLING
MAKES: 8 SERVINGS

1½ cups all-purpose flour
1 tsp. salt
1 tsp. sugar
1 cup cold butter
¼ cup cold water

FILLING

1 medium tart apple, peeled and diced
1 cup diced fresh or frozen rhubarb, thawed
1 cup fresh or frozen raspberries, thawed and drained
1 cup fresh or frozen blueberries, thawed and drained
1 cup sliced fresh or frozen strawberries, thawed and drained
1 cup sugar
½ cup all-purpose flour
1 Tbsp. lemon juice

1. In a small bowl, combine flour, salt and sugar. Cut in cold butter until mixture resembles coarse crumbs. Gradually add water, tossing with a fork until a ball forms. Cover and refrigerate 1 hour or until easy to handle.
2. Preheat oven to 400°. On a lightly floured surface, roll out half the dough to fit a 9-in. pie plate. Transfer crust to pie plate. Trim to ½ in. beyond edge of plate.
3. In a large bowl, combine the filling ingredients; pour into crust. Roll out the remaining dough; cut decorative shapes with cookie cutters. Place over filling.
4. Bake 20 minutes. Reduce heat to 350°; remove foil. Bake 40-45 minutes or until crust is golden brown and filling is bubbly. Cool on a wire rack.
1 PIECE: *449 cal., 23g fat (14g sat. fat), 61mg chol., 528mg sod., 58g carb. (31g sugars, 3g fiber), 4g pro.*

APPLE PIE CUPCAKES WITH CINNAMON BUTTERCREAM

These apple pie cupcakes are always a hit! They are so easy to make and the flavor just screams fall—but of course they're just as delicious any other time of year, too.
—Jennifer Stowell, Deep River, IA

PREP: 20 MIN. MIN.
BAKE: 20 MIN. + COOLING • **MAKES:** 2 DOZEN

1 pkg. yellow cake mix (regular size)
2 Tbsp. butter
4 medium tart apples, peeled and finely chopped (about 4 cups)
¾ cup packed brown sugar
1 Tbsp. cornstarch
1 Tbsp. water

FROSTING

1 cup butter, softened
3 cups confectioners' sugar
2 Tbsp. heavy whipping cream
1 tsp. vanilla extract
1½ tsp. ground cinnamon
   Thinly sliced apples, optional

1. Prepare and bake cake mix according to package directions for cupcakes.
2. In a large skillet, heat the butter over medium heat. Add chopped apples and brown sugar; cook and stir until apples are tender, 10-12 minutes. In a small bowl, mix cornstarch and water until smooth; stir into pan. Bring to a boil; cook and stir until thickened, 1-2 minutes. Remove from heat; cool completely.
3. Using a paring knife, cut a 1-in.-wide cone-shaped piece from top of each cupcake; discard removed portion. Fill cavity with apple mixture.
4. In a large bowl, combine all frosting ingredients; beat until smooth. Frost cupcakes. If desired, top with apple slices to serve.
1 CUPCAKE: *300 cal., 15g fat (7g sat. fat), 48mg chol., 221mg sod., 41g carb. (32g sugars, 1g fiber), 1g pro.*

FLAKY BUMBLEBERRY PIE

GRANDMA'S STRAWBERRY SHORTCAKE

This recipe is a family-sized version of my grandma's dessert. I can still taste those sweet, juicy berries piled over warm biscuits, with fresh whipped cream on top. My father always made his even more indulgent by buttering his biscuits first.
—Shirley Joan Helfenbein, Lapeer, MI

PREP: 30 MIN. • **BAKE:** 20 MIN. + COOLING
MAKES: 8 SERVINGS

- 2 cups all-purpose flour
- 2 Tbsp. sugar
- 3 tsp. baking powder
- ½ tsp. salt
- ½ cup cold butter, cubed
- 1 large egg, room temperature, beaten
- ⅔ cup half-and-half cream
- 1 cup heavy whipping cream
- 2 Tbsp. confectioners' sugar
- ⅛ tsp. vanilla extract
  Additional butter
- 1½ cups fresh strawberries, sliced

1. Preheat oven to 450°. Combine flour, sugar, baking powder and salt. Cut in butter until mixture resembles coarse crumbs. In another bowl, whisk egg and half-and-half. Add all at once to crumb mixture; stir just until moistened.
2. Spread batter into a greased 8-in. round baking pan, slightly building up the edges. Bake until golden brown, 16-18 minutes. Remove from pan; cool on a wire rack.
3. Beat heavy cream until it begins to thicken. Add confectioners' sugar and vanilla; beat until stiff peaks form. Split cake in half crosswise; butter bottom layer. Spoon half the strawberries over bottom layer. Spread with some whipped cream. Cover with top cake layer. Top with the remaining berries and whipped cream. Cut into wedges.

1 PIECE: *381 cal., 25g fat (16g sat. fat), 98mg chol., 447mg sod., 32g carb. (8g sugars, 1g fiber), 6g pro.*

LEMON POPPY SEED BUNDT CAKE

I complete this luscious cake by brushing on sweetened lemon juice and dusting it with confectioners' sugar.
—Betty Bjarnason, Egbert, ON

PREP: 15 MIN. • **BAKE:** 50 MIN. + COOLING
MAKES: 16 SERVINGS

- 1 pkg. lemon cake mix (regular size)
- 1 pkg. (3.4 oz.) instant lemon pudding mix
- ¾ cup warm water
- ½ cup canola oil
- 4 large eggs, room temperature
- 1 tsp. lemon extract
- 1 tsp. almond extract
- ⅓ cup poppy seeds
- ½ cup confectioners' sugar
  Juice of 1 lemon
  Additional confectioners' sugar, optional

1. In a large bowl, combine cake and pudding mix. Add the water, oil, eggs and extracts. Beat for 30 seconds on low speed. Beat for 2 minutes on medium speed. Stir in poppy seeds. Pour into a greased 12-cup fluted tube pan.
2. Bake at 350° for 50-60 minutes or until a toothpick inserted in the center comes out clean. Cool in pan 10 minutes before inverting onto a serving plate.
3. Combine confectioners' sugar and lemon juice; brush over warm cake. Cool. Dust with additional confectioners' sugar if desired.

1 SLICE: *264 cal., 12g fat (2g sat. fat), 53mg chol., 294mg sod., 37g carb. (23g sugars, 1g fiber), 3g pro.*

GRANDMA'S STRAWBERRY SHORTCAKE

GINGERBREAD CUPCAKES

What a combination! I love how the creamy maple frosting mellows the hearty ginger flavor. If you like gingerbread, these are sure to please!
—Nancy Beckman, Helena, MT

PREP: 25 MIN. • **BAKE:** 20 MIN. + COOLING
MAKES: 1 DOZEN

- ½ cup butter, softened
- ½ cup packed brown sugar
- 1 large egg, room temperature
- ½ cup water
- ½ cup molasses
- 1⅓ cups all-purpose flour
- ¾ tsp. ground cinnamon
- ½ tsp. baking powder
- ½ tsp. baking soda
- ½ tsp. salt
- ½ tsp. ground ginger
- ½ tsp. ground nutmeg
- ¼ tsp. ground allspice

MAPLE FROSTING
- ⅓ cup butter, softened
- 1 oz. cream cheese, softened
- ¼ cup packed brown sugar
- Dash salt
- ¼ cup maple syrup
- ¼ tsp. vanilla extract
- 1 cup confectioners' sugar

1. In a large bowl, cream butter and brown sugar until light and fluffy. Beat in egg. Beat in water and molasses. Combine the flour, cinnamon, baking powder, baking soda, salt, ginger, nutmeg and allspice; add to the creamed mixture. Beat on low speed until combined. Beat on medium for 2 minutes.
2. Fill paper-lined muffin cups two-thirds full. Bake at 350° for 20-25 minutes or until a toothpick inserted in the center comes out clean. Cool for 10 minutes before removing to a wire rack to cool completely.
3. For frosting, in a small bowl, cream the butter, cream cheese, brown sugar and salt until light and fluffy. Beat in maple syrup and vanilla. Gradually beat in confectioners' sugar until smooth. Frost cupcakes. Store in the refrigerator.
1 CUPCAKE: *325 cal., 14g fat (9g sat. fat), 54mg chol., 293mg sod., 49g carb. (34g sugars, 1g fiber), 2g pro.*

LEMON RHUBARB TUBE CAKE

LEMON RHUBARB TUBE CAKE

Nothing says summer like a homey dessert topped with the classic combination of strawberries and rhubarb. It's so refreshing paired with the fresh lemon flavor in the cake.
—Courtney Stultz, Weir, KS

PREP: 35 MIN. • **BAKE:** 50 MIN. + COOLING
MAKES: 12 SERVINGS

- 3 medium lemons
- 1 cup butter, softened
- 2 cups sugar
- 3 large eggs, room temperature
- 3 cups all-purpose flour
- 1 tsp. baking powder
- ½ tsp. baking soda
- ½ tsp. salt
- 1 cup buttermilk

RHUBARB TOPPING
- 1 cup sugar
- 1 cup sliced fresh or frozen rhubarb
- 1 cup halved fresh strawberries
  Confectioners' sugar, optional

1. Preheat oven to 350°. Grease and flour a 10-in. fluted tube pan. Finely grate enough zest from lemons to measure 2 Tbsp. Cut lemons crosswise in half; squeeze juice from lemons.
2. In a large bowl, cream butter and sugar until light and fluffy. Add 1 egg at a time, beating well after each addition. Beat in lemon juice and zest. In another bowl, whisk flour, baking powder, baking soda and salt; add to creamed mixture alternately with buttermilk, beating well after each addition.
3. Transfer batter to prepared pan. Bake until a toothpick inserted in the center comes out clean, 50-60 minutes. Cool in pan 10 minutes before removing to a wire rack to cool.
4. Meanwhile, for topping, combine sugar and rhubarb in a small saucepan. Bring to a boil; reduce heat. Simmer until rhubarb is almost tender, 8-10 minutes. Add halved strawberries; cook until strawberries and rhubarb are softened. Serve with cake. If desired, dust with confectioners' sugar.
1 SLICE WITH ¼ CUP SAUCE: *481 cal., 17g fat (10g sat. fat), 88mg chol., 371mg sod., 78g carb. (53g sugars, 2g fiber), 6g pro.*

SWEET POTATO PIE CAKE ROLL

STRAWBERRY LEMON CUPCAKES

(*SHOWN ON PAGE 180*)

My granddaughter Sydney has acquired a love of baking. While I was visiting her in Tampa, we made these light, fluffy cupcakes. She's a natural—these turned out fantastic!
—Lonnie Hartstack, Clarinda, IA

PREP: 15 MIN. • **BAKE:** 20 MIN. + COOLING
MAKES: 2 DOZEN

- 1 pkg. white cake mix (regular size)
- 3 large eggs, room temperature
- ½ cup 2% milk
- ⅓ cup canola oil
- 2 Tbsp. grated lemon zest
- 3 Tbsp. lemon juice

FROSTING
- 4 cups confectioners' sugar
- 1 cup butter, softened
- ¼ cup crushed fresh strawberries

1. Preheat oven to 350°. Line 24 muffin cups with paper liners.

2. In a large bowl, combine the first 6 ingredients; beat on low speed 30 seconds. Beat on medium 2 minutes. Fill prepared cups half full. Bake until a toothpick inserted in center comes out clean, 18-20 minutes. Cool cupcakes in pans 10 minutes before removing to wire racks to cool completely.

3. For frosting, in a large bowl, combine all ingredients; beat until smooth. Frost cupcakes. Garnish with additional strawberries. Store in the refrigerator.

1 CUPCAKE: *253 cal., 12g fat (6g sat. fat), 44mg chol., 198mg sod., 35g carb. (27g sugars, 1g fiber), 2g pro.*

SWEET POTATO PIE CAKE ROLL

Smooth cream cheese filling is all rolled up in the cinnamony sweet potato flavor of this cake. This change-of-pace dessert tastes just as amazing as it looks.
—Bernice Taylor, Wilson, NC

PREP: 25 MIN. • **BAKE:** 10 MIN. + CHILLING
MAKES: 10 SERVINGS

- 2 large eggs, room temperature
- 1 cup sugar
- ⅔ cup mashed cooked sweet potatoes
- 1 cup self-rising flour
- 1 tsp. ground cinnamon
- 2 Tbsp. confectioners' sugar

CREAM CHEESE FILLING
- 1 pkg. (8 oz.) cream cheese, softened
- 1 cup confectioners' sugar
- 1 Tbsp. butter, melted
- 1 tsp. vanilla extract
- ⅓ cup chopped pecans
  Additional confectioners' sugar, optional

1. Line a greased 15x10x1-in. baking pan with waxed paper and grease the paper; set aside. In a bowl, beat the eggs on high speed for 5 minutes. Gradually beat in sugar until thick and lemon-colored. Add sweet potatoes; mix well. Combine flour and cinnamon; fold into sweet potato mixture. Spread into pan.

2. Bake at 350° for 10-15 minutes or until cake springs back when lightly touched. Cool for 5 minutes; invert cake onto a kitchen towel dusted with confectioners' sugar. Gently peel off waxed paper. Roll up cake in the towel jelly-roll style, starting with a short side. Cool on a wire rack.

3. For filling, in a bowl, beat cream cheese, confectioners' sugar, butter and vanilla until fluffy. Fold in nuts. Unroll cake; spread filling evenly over cake to within ½ in. of edges. Roll up again, without towel. Cover and refrigerate until serving. Dust with confectioners' sugar if desired.

NOTE: As a substitute for 1 cup of self-rising flour, place 1½ tsp. of baking powder and ½ tsp. salt in a measuring cup. Add enough all-purpose flour to measure 1 cup.

1 SLICE: *326 cal., 13g fat (6g sat. fat), 71mg chol., 239mg sod., 49g carb. (35g sugars, 1g fiber), 5g pro.*

DEVIL'S FOOD SNACK CAKE

My husband and his friends request this cake for camping trips because it's easy to transport.
—Julie Danler, Bel Aire, KS

PREP: 30 MIN. • **BAKE:** 35 MIN. + COOLING
MAKES: 24 SERVINGS

- 1 cup quick-cooking oats
- 1¾ cups boiling water
- ¼ cup butter, softened
- ½ cup sugar
- ½ cup packed brown sugar
- 2 large eggs, room temperature
- ⅓ cup buttermilk
- 3 Tbsp. canola oil
- 1 tsp. vanilla extract
- ¾ cup all-purpose flour
- ¾ cup whole wheat flour
- 2 Tbsp. dark baking cocoa
- 1 Tbsp. instant coffee granules
- 1 tsp. baking soda
- ⅛ tsp. salt
- 1 cup (6 oz.) miniature semisweet chocolate chips, divided
- ¾ cup chopped pecans, divided

1. Place oats in a large bowl. Cover with boiling water; let stand for 10 minutes.
2. Meanwhile, in a large bowl, beat butter and sugars until crumbly, about 2 minutes. Add 1 egg at a time, beating well after each addition. Beat in buttermilk, oil and vanilla. Combine the flours, cocoa, coffee granules, baking soda and salt. Gradually add to the creamed mixture. Stir in the oat mixture, ½ cup of chocolate chips and ⅓ cup pecans.
3. Pour into a 13x9-in. baking pan coated with cooking spray. Sprinkle with remaining chips and pecans. Bake at 350° until a toothpick inserted in the center comes out clean, 35-40 minutes. Cool on a wire rack before cutting.
1 PIECE: *174 cal., 9g fat (3g sat. fat), 23mg chol., 91mg sod., 22g carb. (13g sugars, 2g fiber), 3g pro.* **Diabetic exchanges:** *2 fat, 1½ starch.*

GOLDEN PEACH PIE

Many years ago, I entered this pie in the Park County Fair in Livingston. It won a first-place blue ribbon plus a purple ribbon for best all-around! Family and friends agree with the judges—it's a perfectly peachy pie.
—Shirley Olson, Polson, MT

PREP: 20 MIN. • **BAKE:** 50 MIN. + COOLING
MAKES: 8 SERVINGS

- 2 sheets refrigerated pie crust
- 5 cups sliced peeled fresh peaches (about 5 medium)
- 2 tsp. lemon juice
- ½ tsp. grated orange zest
- ⅛ tsp. almond extract
- 1 cup sugar
- ¼ cup cornstarch
- ¼ tsp. ground nutmeg
- ⅛ tsp. salt
- 2 Tbsp. butter

1. Line a 9-in. pie plate with 1 crust; trim, leaving a 1-in. overhang around edge. Set aside. In a large bowl, combine the peaches, lemon juice, orange zest and extract. Combine the sugar, cornstarch, nutmeg and salt. Add to peach mixture; toss gently to coat. Pour into crust; dot with butter.
2. Roll out remaining crust to a ⅛-in.-thick circle; cut into strips. Arrange over filling in a lattice pattern. Trim and seal strips to bottom crust; fold overhang over. Lightly press or flute edge. Cover the edges loosely with foil.
3. Bake at 400° for 40 minutes. Remove foil; bake until crust is golden brown and filling is bubbly, 10-15 minutes longer. Cool on a wire rack. Store in the refrigerator.
1 PIECE: *425 cal., 17g fat (8g sat. fat), 18mg chol., 267mg sod., 67g carb. (36g sugars, 2g fiber), 3g pro.*

GOLDEN PEACH PIE

TOFFEE BROWNIE TRIFLE
PAGE 203

Just Desserts

Bake outside the box! You won't even need to turn on the oven for some of these delectable recipes. Shake things up with homemade ice cream, or add a fruity twist to your favorite classics.

BEST EVER CHEESECAKE

BEST EVER CHEESECAKE

I've passed this recipe along to dozens of folks. My daughter was so fond of it that she wanted to serve it for her wedding instead of a more traditional cake.
—Howard Koch, Lima, OH

PREP: 20 MIN. • **BAKE:** 45 MIN. + CHILLING • **MAKES:** 8 SERVINGS

- 1¼ cups graham cracker crumbs
- ⅓ cup butter, melted
- ¼ cup sugar

FILLING/TOPPING
- 2 pkg. (8 oz. each) cream cheese, softened
- 2 large eggs, room temperature, lightly beaten
- ⅔ cup sugar, divided
- 2 tsp. vanilla extract, divided
  Dash salt
- 1 cup sour cream
  Whipped cream, optional

1. In a bowl, combine the graham cracker crumbs, butter and sugar. Pat into the bottom and 1 in. up the sides of an 8-in. springform pan. Chill.
2. For filling, beat cream cheese and eggs in a bowl on medium speed for 1 minute. Add ⅓ cup sugar, 1 tsp. vanilla and salt. Continue beating until well blended, about 1 minute. Pour the filling into crust.
3. Place pan on a baking sheet. Bake at 350° for 35 minutes. Cool for 10 minutes. For topping, combine the sour cream and remaining sugar and vanilla in a small bowl; spread mixture over cheesecake. Bake 10 minutes longer. Cool completely on a wire rack. Refrigerate cake for 3 hours or overnight. If desired, serve with whipped cream.
1 PIECE: *504 cal., 36g fat (20g sat. fat), 131mg chol., 357mg sod., 40g carb. (30g sugars, 1g fiber), 7g pro.*

MANGO GLACE WITH PINEAPPLE POMEGRANATE SALSA

I'd like to say this dish was a brilliant idea that came from expert planning. But the truth is that between the quickly ripening fruit on my counter and the 100-degree heat, it pretty much invented itself! Very ripe fruit eliminates the need for added sugar.
—Jodi Taffel, Altadena, CA

PREP: 45 MIN. + FREEZING • **MAKES:** 1 DOZEN

- 4 medium ripe mangoes, peeled and chopped
- 1 fresh ripe pineapple, peeled and cut into ½-in. pieces
- 2 Tbsp. lime juice

SALSA
- 4 cups finely chopped fresh pineapple
- ½ cup pomegranate seeds
- ¼ cup minced fresh mint

1. Combine mangoes, pineapple and lime juice in a blender. Cover and process until smooth. Strain through a fine-mesh strainer into a large bowl. Pour into 1¾-in. silicone ice cube trays. Freeze until firm, 8 hours or overnight.
2. Combine salsa ingredients; cover and refrigerate overnight.
3. Remove cubes from freezer 10 minutes before serving. Run a small spatula around edges of each fruit cube to loosen; remove from trays. Serve with salsa.
1 CUBE WITH 4 TSP. SALSA: *137 cal., 1g fat (0 sat. fat), 0 chol., 3mg sod., 35g carb. (29g sugars, 4g fiber), 2g pro.*

MANGO GLACE WITH PINEAPPLE POMEGRANATE SALSA

PUMPKIN PIE ICE CREAM WITH SALTED CARAMEL SAUCE

Truthfully, I want those cozy flavors of Thanksgiving throughout the year. This ice cream has just the right balance of spices, and no matter when you make it, you'll find yourself surrounded in the warmth and love that pumpkin pie has to offer.
—Angie Stewart, Memphis, TN

PREP: 30 MIN. + CHILLING
PROCESS: 20 MIN. + FREEZING
MAKES: 1½ QT. ICE CREAM AND 1¼ CUPS SAUCE

- 3 large egg yolks
- ¾ cup packed brown sugar
- 2 cups heavy whipping cream
- 1½ cups half-and-half cream
- 1 cup canned pumpkin
- 2 tsp. pumpkin pie spice
- 1 tsp. vanilla extract
- ½ tsp. salt

SALTED CARAMEL SAUCE
- 1 cup sugar
- 1 cup heavy whipping cream
- 3 Tbsp. butter, cubed
- 1½ tsp. salt
- 1 tsp. almond extract

1. In a large heavy saucepan, whisk the egg yolks and brown sugar until blended; stir in the heavy cream. Cook over low heat until mixture is just thick enough to coat a metal spoon and a thermometer reads at least 160°, stirring constantly. Do not allow to boil. Remove from heat immediately.
2. Quickly transfer to a large bowl; place bowl in a pan of ice water. Stir gently and occasionally for 2 minutes. Stir in half-and-half, pumpkin, pie spice, vanilla and salt. Press plastic wrap onto surface of custard. Refrigerate several hours or overnight.
3. Fill cylinder of ice cream maker no more than two-thirds full; freeze according to manufacturer's directions. (Refrigerate any remaining mixture until ready to freeze.) Transfer ice cream to freezer containers, allowing headspace for expansion. Freeze until firm, 2-4 hours.
4. For caramel sauce, in a large heavy saucepan, spread sugar; cook, without stirring, over medium-low heat until it begins to melt. Gently drag melted sugar to center of pan so sugar melts evenly. Cook, without stirring, until melted sugar turns a medium-dark amber, 5-10 minutes.

Immediately remove from heat, then slowly stir in the cream, butter, salt and almond extract. Serve caramel sauce with the ice cream. Refrigerate any leftover sauce; keep leftover ice cream frozen.
½ CUP ICE CREAM WITH ABOUT 4 TSP. SAUCE: 410 cal., 29g fat (18g sat. fat), 137mg chol., 455mg sod., 35g carb. (34g sugars, 1g fiber), 4g pro.

LIGHT TOFFEE CRUNCH DESSERT

I cut about 90% of the fat and nearly half the calories from one of my favorite desserts. Try it for yourself. Guests will never suspect the fluffy layered specialty is on the light side.
—Kim Belcher, Kingston Mines, IL

PREP: 20 MIN. + CHILLING
MAKES: 15 SERVINGS

- 1½ cups cold fat-free milk
- 1 pkg. (1 oz.) sugar-free instant vanilla pudding mix
- 2 cartons (8 oz. each) frozen fat-free whipped topping, thawed
- 1 prepared angel food cake (8 to 10 oz.), cut into 1-in. cubes
- 4 Butterfinger candy bars (2.1 oz. each), crushed

1. In a large bowl, whisk milk and pudding mix 2 minutes. Let stand 2 minutes or until soft-set. Stir in 2 cups of whipped topping. Fold in remaining whipped topping.
2. In a 13x9-in. dish coated with cooking spray, layer half of cake cubes, pudding mixture and crushed candy bars. Repeat layers. Cover and refrigerate mixture at least 2 hours before serving.
*¾ CUP: 177 cal., 3g fat (2g sat. fat), 0 chol., 255mg sod., 33g carb. (12g sugars, 1g fiber), 3g pro. **Diabetic exchanges:** 2 starch, ½ fat.*

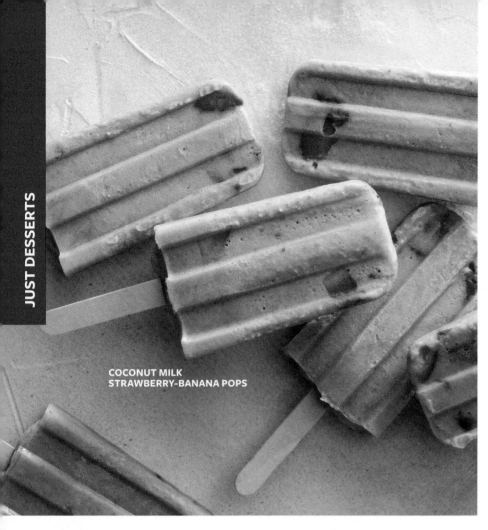

COCONUT MILK
STRAWBERRY-BANANA POPS

½ cup mango nectar
⅓ cup lemon juice
1 Tbsp. cornstarch
2 tsp. grated lemon zest
½ cup butter, cubed
½ cup chopped peeled mango
½ cup mandarin oranges, drained
½ cup seedless red grapes, halved
    Confectioners' sugar

1. Preheat oven to 350°. Place a greased 9-in. springform pan on a double thickness of heavy-duty foil (about 18 in. square). Wrap foil securely around pan. Place on a baking sheet.
2. In a large bowl, whisk the butter, cream, honey, cinnamon and vanilla. Gently pull phyllo apart and add to bowl; toss to coat. Press onto bottom and up the sides of prepared pan. Bake until golden brown, about 40-45 minutes. Cool on a wire rack. Remove foil.
3. Meanwhile, in a small heavy saucepan, whisk egg yolks, sugar, mango nectar, lemon juice, cornstarch and zest until blended. Add butter; cook over medium heat, whisking constantly, until mixture comes just to a boil and is thick enough to coat a metal spoon.
4. Remove from heat immediately. Strain through a fine-mesh strainer into a small bowl. Stir in mango; cool. Press plastic wrap onto surface of custard. Refrigerate until cold.
5. Spoon filling into the crust. Garnish with mandarin oranges and grapes. Remove rim from pan. Dust with confectioners' sugar.
1 SLICE: *424 cal., 27g fat (16g sat. fat), 158mg chol., 360mg sod., 41g carb. (18g sugars, 1g fiber), 6g pro.*

COCONUT MILK STRAWBERRY-BANANA POPS

These four-ingredient freezer pops are a delicious way to use up a pint of fresh strawberries. You'll love the hint of tropical flavor, thanks to the coconut milk.
—Taste of Home *Test Kitchen*

PREP: 10 MIN. + FREEZING
MAKES: 12 SERVINGS

1 can (13.66 oz.) coconut milk
1 pint fresh strawberries, chopped, divided
1 medium banana, sliced
2 Tbsp. pure maple syrup
12 freezer pop molds or 12 paper cups (3 oz. each) and wooden pop sticks

Place coconut milk, 1½ cups strawberries, banana and syrup in a blender; cover and process until smooth. Divide remaining strawberries among 12 molds or paper cups. Pour pureed mixture into molds, filling ¾ full. Top molds with holders. If using cups, top with foil and insert sticks through foil. Freeze until firm, at least 4 hours.
1 POP: *51 cal., 3g fat (3g sat. fat), 0 chol., 5mg sod., 7g carb. (5g sugars, 1g fiber), 1g pro.*

LEMON MANGO KANAFEH

Several years ago I came upon a little neighborhood restaurant making the most incredible Turkish food I'd ever seen or tasted. I was completely blown away by the dessert and had to learn how to make it.
—Jodi Taffel, Altadena, CA

PREP: 35 MIN. + CHILLING
BAKE: 40 MIN. + COOLING
MAKES: 12 SERVINGS

1 cup butter, melted
½ cup half-and-half cream
2 Tbsp. honey
1 tsp. ground cinnamon
1 tsp. vanilla extract
1 pkg. (16 oz.) frozen shredded phyllo dough (kataifi), thawed
FILLING
6 large egg yolks
½ cup sugar

HOT FUDGE PUDDING CAKE

My mom used to make a cake like this when I was younger. Because I'm a dietitian, I love to come up with ways to lighten things up, so I decided to make some healthy changes to Mom's recipe. This version is as good as, if not better than, the original.
—Jackie Termont, Ruther Glen, VA

PREP: 15 MIN. • **BAKE:** 30 MIN.
MAKES: 9 SERVINGS

- 1 cup all-purpose flour
- 1 cup sugar, divided
- 3 Tbsp. plus ¼ cup baking cocoa, divided
- 2 tsp. baking powder
- ¼ tsp. salt
- ½ cup fat-free milk
- ⅓ cup prune baby food
- 1½ tsp. vanilla extract
- ¼ cup plus 2 Tbsp. packed brown sugar
- 1¼ cups boiling water

1. In a large bowl, combine the flour, ¾ cup sugar, 3 Tbsp. cocoa, baking powder and salt. In another bowl, combine the milk, baby food and vanilla. Stir into the dry ingredients just until moistened. Spread into an 8-in. square baking dish coated with cooking spray.
2. Combine brown sugar with remaining sugar and cocoa; sprinkle over the batter. Carefully pour water over the top (do not stir). Bake, uncovered, at 350° until top is set and edges pull away from sides of dish, 28-32 minutes. Serve warm.
1 SERVING: *196 cal., 1g fat (0 sat. fat), 0 chol., 164mg sod., 46g carb. (33g sugars, 1g fiber), 3g pro.*

PEACH PANNA COTTA

This no-bake dessert is guaranteed to cool you off in the summer heat. I really enjoy its texture—the rich and creamy panna cotta balanced by the sweet and pulpy texture of the peach puree.
—Andrea Campbell, Los Angeles, CA

PREP: 30 MIN. + CHILLING • **COOK:** 10 MIN.
MAKES: 8 SERVINGS

- 4 medium peaches, peeled and pitted
- 1 Tbsp. lemon juice
- 1 envelope (¼ oz.) unflavored gelatin
- 1 cup peach nectar, chilled

PANNA COTTA
- 1 envelope (¼ oz.) unflavored gelatin
- 1½ cups cold whole milk
- 1½ cups heavy whipping cream
- ⅓ cup sugar
- 1 tsp. grated lemon zest
- ½ tsp. salt
- ¼ tsp. vanilla extract
  Sliced peeled peaches and fresh mint leaves, optional

1. Place peaches and lemon juice in a blender or food processor. Cover and process until smooth.
2. In a microwave-safe bowl, sprinkle gelatin over the peach nectar; let stand 1 minute. Microwave on high for 30-40 seconds. Stir and let stand 1 minute or until gelatin is completely dissolved. Let stand 5 minutes. Stir in pureed peach mixture. Pour into eight 8-oz. champagne flutes or stemless white wine glasses. Refrigerate until set, at least 3 hours.
3. In a small saucepan, sprinkle gelatin over milk; let stand 1 minute. Heat and stir over low heat until the gelatin is completely dissolved. Stir in cream, sugar, lemon zest, salt and vanilla. Pour over peach gelatin layers. Refrigerate until set, for at least 2 hours. If desired, garnish panna cotta with peach slices and mint leaves.
1 SERVING: *266 cal., 18g fat (11g sat. fat), 55mg chol., 185mg sod., 23g carb. (22g sugars, 1g fiber), 5g pro.*

PEACH PANNA COTTA

NO-BAKE MANGO STRAWBERRY CHEESECAKE

Cheesecake is my mom's favorite dessert. I made this especially for her on Mother's Day to thank her for being such an awesome mom. Decorate to your own taste!
—Elizabeth Ding, El Cerrito, CA

PREP: 45 MIN. + CHILLING
MAKES: 12 SERVINGS

- 2 cups graham cracker crumbs
- ⅔ cup butter, melted
- ⅓ cup sugar

FILLING
- 1 envelope unflavored gelatin
- 3 Tbsp. cold water
- 2 pkg. (8 oz. each) cream cheese, softened
- 1⅓ cups sugar
- 1 cup heavy whipping cream
- 2 tsp. vanilla extract
- ½ large mango, peeled and cubed (about ¾ cup)
- 4 fresh strawberries, chopped

GLAZE
- 1 envelope unflavored gelatin
- 3 Tbsp. plus ½ cup cold water, divided
- ½ large mango, peeled and cubed (about ¾ cup)
  Whipped cream
  Optional: Fresh mango, strawberries

1. In a small bowl, mix crumbs, butter and sugar. Press onto bottom and 1 in. up sides of a greased 8-in. springform pan.
2. For the filling, in a microwave-safe bowl, sprinkle gelatin over cold water; let stand for 1 minute. Microwave on high for 10-20 seconds or just until water is warm but not hot. Stir and let stand until gelatin is completely dissolved, about 1 minute. Cool until partially set.
3. In a large bowl, beat cream cheese and sugar until smooth. Gradually beat in cream, vanilla and gelatin mixture until blended. Fold in mango and strawberries. Pour over crust. Refrigerate filling while preparing glaze.
4. For glaze, in another microwave-safe bowl, sprinkle gelatin over 3 Tbsp. cold water; let stand 1 minute. Microwave on high for 30-40 seconds. Stir and let stand until gelatin is completely dissolved, about 1 minute. Cool gelatin until partially set. Meanwhile, place mango and remaining ½ cup water in a food processor; process until pureed. Stir in gelatin mixture; pour over filling. Refrigerate the cheesecake, loosely covered, overnight.
5. Loosen sides from the pan with a knife. Remove rim from pan. Garnish with the whipped cream and if desired, additional mango and strawberries.

1 SLICE: *495 cal., 32g fat (19g sat. fat), 88mg chol., 285mg sod., 48g carb. (38g sugars, 1g fiber), 5g pro.*

GAM'S HOMEMADE VANILLA ICE CREAM

My grandmother's homemade ice cream is good on its own, but it's also fantastic as a base for fun flavors and toppings.
—Andrea Bolden, Unionville, TN

PREP: 25 MIN. + CHILLING
PROCESS: 20 MIN. + FREEZING
MAKES: 1¾ QT.

- 3 large eggs
- 1 cup sugar
- 5 cups whole milk
- 1 cup half-and-half cream
- ½ cup heavy whipping cream
- 2 tsp. vanilla extract

1. In a large heavy saucepan, whisk eggs and sugar until blended; stir in milk. Cook over low heat until mixture is just thick enough to coat a metal spoon and a thermometer reads at least 160°, stirring constantly. Do not allow mixture to boil. Remove from the heat immediately.
2. Quickly transfer to a large bowl; place bowl in a pan of ice water. Let sit for 2 minutes, occasionally stirring gently. Stir in cream, heavy cream and vanilla. Press plastic wrap onto surface of the custard. Refrigerate several hours or overnight.
3. Fill cylinder of ice cream maker no more than two-thirds full; freeze according to manufacturer's directions. (Refrigerate any remaining mixture until ready to freeze.)
4. Transfer ice cream to freezer containers, allowing headspace for expansion. Freeze until firm, at least 4 hours.

½ CUP: *178 cal., 9g fat (5g sat. fat), 67mg chol., 64mg sod., 20g carb. (19g sugars, 0 fiber), 5g pro.*

NO-BAKE MANGO STRAWBERRY CHEESECAKE

PECAN PIE COBBLER

PECAN PIE COBBLER

I couldn't find a recipe, so I devised this dessert myself. It combines the ease of a cobbler with the rich flavor of pecan pie. It tastes even better with ice cream or whipped topping.
—*Willa Kelley, Edmond, OK*

PREP: 20 MIN. • **BAKE:** 30 MIN. + COOLING • **MAKES:** 12 SERVINGS

- ½ cup butter, cubed
- 1 cup plus 2 Tbsp. all-purpose flour
- ¾ cup sugar
- 3 tsp. baking powder
- ¼ tsp. salt
- ⅔ cup 2% milk
- 1 tsp. vanilla extract
- 1½ cups coarsely chopped pecans
- 1 cup packed brown sugar
- ¾ cup brickle toffee bits
- 1½ cups boiling water
- Vanilla ice cream, optional

1. Preheat oven to 350°. Place butter in a 13x9-in. baking pan; heat pan in oven 3-5 minutes or until butter is melted. Meanwhile, combine the flour, sugar, baking powder and salt. Stir in milk and vanilla until combined.
2. Remove baking pan from oven; add batter. Sprinkle with pecans, brown sugar and toffee bits. Slowly pour boiling water over top (do not stir). Bake, uncovered, until golden brown, 30-35 minutes. Cool on wire rack for 30 minutes (the cobbler will thicken upon cooling). Serve warm, with ice cream if desired.
1 SERVING: *411 cal., 23g fat (8g sat. fat), 26mg chol., 327mg sod., 51g carb. (41g sugars, 2g fiber), 3g pro.*

BLACKBERRY DAIQUIRI SHERBET

The summer I decided to try making sherbet, which is one of my favorites, blackberries were in season in my mom's garden. I love the flavor of daiquiris, and the two blend together beautifully!
—*Shelly Bevington, Hermiston, OR*

PREP: 15 MIN. • **PROCESS:** 30 MIN. + FREEZING • **MAKES:** 1¼ QT.

- 3 cups fresh or frozen blackberries, thawed
- 1 cup sugar
- ¼ tsp. salt
- 1 can (12 oz.) evaporated milk
- 2 Tbsp. lime juice
- 1 tsp. rum extract
- ½ tsp. citric acid

1. Place blackberries, sugar and salt in a food processor; process until smooth. Press through a fine-mesh strainer into a bowl; discard seeds and pulp. Stir remaining ingredients into puree.
2. Fill cylinder of ice cream maker no more than two-thirds full; freeze according to the manufacturer's directions. Transfer sherbet to freezer containers, allowing headspace for expansion. Freeze until firm, 8 hours or overnight.
½ CUP: *147 cal., 3g fat (2g sat. fat), 12mg chol., 96mg sod., 28g carb. (26g sugars, 2g fiber), 3g pro.*

BLACKBERRY DAIQUIRI SHERBET

**NO-CHURN BLUEBERRY
GRAHAM CRACKER ICE CREAM**

BANANA SPLIT CAKE BARS

*Summer isn't summer without a banana split
or two, and these fun bars bring that same
delicious flavor in potluck-perfect bar form.*
—*Jasey McBurnett, Rock Springs, WY*

PREP: 25 MIN. • **BAKE:** 25 MIN. + COOLING
MAKES: 24 SERVINGS

- ½ cup butter, softened
- 1½ cups sugar
- 2 large eggs, room temperature
- 1½ cups mashed ripe bananas (about 3 large)
- 1 cup sour cream
- 2 tsp. vanilla extract
- 2 cups all-purpose flour
- 1 tsp. baking soda
- ¾ tsp. salt
- 2 jars (10 oz. each) maraschino cherries, drained and chopped
- 2 cups (12 oz.) semisweet chocolate chips
- 1 pkg. (10 oz.) miniature marshmallows
  Optional: Chopped salted peanuts, sliced ripe banana or dried banana chips

1. Preheat the oven to 375°. Grease a
15x10x1-in. baking pan.
2. In a large bowl, beat butter and sugar
until crumbly, about 2 minutes. Add eggs;
mix well. Beat in bananas, sour cream and
vanilla. In another bowl, whisk flour, baking
soda and salt; gradually add to the butter
mixture. Transfer to prepared pan.
3. Bake until a toothpick inserted in center
comes out clean, 18-20 minutes. Top the
cake with cherries, chocolate chips,
marshmallows and, if desired, peanuts.
Bake until chips are slightly melted and
marshmallows puff, 3-5 minutes longer.
Cool completely in pan on a wire rack. If
desired, top with sliced ripe bananas or
banana chips before serving.
1 PIECE: *294 cal., 11g fat (6g sat. fat), 28mg
chol., 177mg sod., 52g carb. (38g sugars, 1g
fiber), 3g pro.*

NO-CHURN BLUEBERRY
GRAHAM CRACKER
ICE CREAM

*This sweet and creamy no-churn ice cream
features a fresh blueberry jam swirl and
graham cracker pieces. Use raspberries in
place of blueberries if that's what you have
or like, or just for a different berry flavor.*
—*Heather King, Frostburg, MD*

PREP: 25 MIN. + FREEZING • **MAKES:** 1¾ QT.

- ¾ cup fresh or frozen blueberries
- ¼ cup sugar
- 1 Tbsp. vanilla extract
- 2 cups heavy whipping cream
- 1 cup sweetened condensed milk
- 4 whole graham crackers, coarsely crushed

1. In a small saucepan, combine blueberries,
sugar and vanilla. Bring mixture to a boil;
reduce heat. Simmer until mixture begins
to thicken, for about 5 minutes, stirring
frequently. Cool completely. Refrigerate
until chilled.
2. In a large bowl, beat the cream until soft
peaks form. Add condensed milk; beat until
the mixture thickens. Gently fold graham
crackers into cream mixture. Transfer to
freezer containers, allowing headspace for
expansion. Drop the blueberry mixture by
tablespoonfuls over ice cream. Cut through
ice cream with a knife to swirl. Freeze for
8 hours or overnight before serving.
½ CUP: *226 cal., 15g fat (9g sat. fat), 46mg
chol., 64mg sod., 21g carb. (18g sugars,
0 fiber), 3g pro.*

JASEY MCBURNETT
Rock Springs, WY

BANANA SPLIT CAKE BARS

STRAWBERRY RHUBARB CHEESECAKE BARS

These cheesecake bars layer a buttery pecan shortbread crust with a rich and creamy filling and sweet-tart strawberry-rhubarb jam. We like them so much we cut them into nine bars instead of 16 so we can have more.
—Amanda Scarlati, Sandy, UT

PREP: 30 MIN. + CHILLING
BAKE: 15 MIN. + COOLING
MAKES: 16 SERVINGS

- 1 cup all-purpose flour
- ⅓ cup packed brown sugar
  Dash kosher salt
- ½ cup cold butter, cubed
- ⅓ cup finely chopped pecans

FILLING
- 1 pkg. (8 oz.) cream cheese, softened
- ¼ cup sugar
- 2 Tbsp. 2% milk
- 1 Tbsp. lemon juice
- ½ tsp. vanilla extract
  Dash kosher salt
- 1 large egg, room temperature, lightly beaten

JAM
- ½ cup sugar
- 2 Tbsp. cornstarch
- 1⅓ cups chopped fresh strawberries
- 1⅓ cups sliced fresh or frozen rhubarb
- 1 Tbsp. lemon juice

1. Preheat the oven to 350°. Line an 8-in. square baking pan with parchment, letting ends extend up sides. In a small bowl, mix flour, brown sugar and salt; cut in butter until crumbly. Stir in pecans.

2. Press into bottom of prepared pan. Bake until the edges just begin to brown, 12-15 minutes. Cool completely on a wire rack.

3. In a large bowl, beat cream cheese and sugar until smooth. Beat in milk, lemon juice, vanilla and salt. Add egg; beat on low speed just until blended. Pour over crust.

4. Bake until filling is set, 15-20 minutes. Cool on a wire rack for 1 hour.

5. For jam, in a small saucepan, mix sugar and cornstarch. Add strawberries, rhubarb and lemon juice. Bring to a boil. Reduce heat; simmer, uncovered, until mixture begins to thicken, 6-8 minutes. Cool jam completely. Spread over filling. Refrigerate until set, 8 hours or overnight.

6. Using parchment, carefully remove cheesecake from baking pan. Cut into bars for serving.

NOTE: If using frozen rhubarb, measure rhubarb while still frozen, then thaw completely. Drain in a colander, but do not press liquid out.

1 BAR: *215 cal., 13g fat (7g sat. fat), 41mg chol., 113mg sod., 24g carb. (15g sugars, 1g fiber), 3g pro.*

STRAWBERRY RHUBARB CHEESECAKE BARS

BLUEBERRY ANGEL DESSERT

Make the most of angel food cake, pie filling and whipped topping by creating this light dessert that doesn't keep you in the kitchen for hours. It's the perfect way to end a meal in summer or any time of year.
—Carol Johnson, Tyler, TX

PREP: 10 MIN. + CHILLING
MAKES: 12 SERVINGS

- 1 pkg. (8 oz.) cream cheese, softened
- 1 cup confectioners' sugar
- 1 carton (8 oz.) frozen whipped topping, thawed
- 1 prepared angel food cake (8 to 10 oz.), cut into 1-in. cubes
- 2 cans (21 oz. each) blueberry pie filling

In a large bowl, beat the cream cheese and confectioners' sugar until smooth; fold in whipped topping and cake cubes. Spread evenly into an ungreased 13x9-in. dish; top with the blueberry pie filling. Refrigerate, covered, at least 2 hours before serving.

1 PIECE: *384 cal., 10g fat (7g sat. fat), 21mg chol., 223mg sod., 70g carb. (50g sugars, 3g fiber), 3g pro.*

TOFFEE BROWNIE TRIFLE

(SHOWN ON PAGE 192)
This decadent combination of pantry items is a terrific way to dress up a brownie mix. Try it with other flavors of pudding or substitute your favorite candy bar. It tastes great with low-fat and sugar-free products, too.
—*Wendy Bennett, Sioux Falls, SD*

PREP: 20 MIN. • **BAKE:** 25 MIN. + COOLING
MAKES: 16 SERVINGS

- 1   pkg. fudge brownie mix
      (13x9-in. pan size)
- 2½ cups cold whole milk
- 1   pkg. (3.4 oz.) instant cheesecake
      or vanilla pudding mix
- 1   pkg. (3.3 oz.) instant white
      chocolate pudding mix
- 1   carton (8 oz.) frozen whipped
      topping, thawed
- 2   to 3 Heath candy bars
      (1.4 oz. each), chopped

1. Prepare and bake brownies according to package directions for cakelike brownies, using a greased 13x9-in. baking pan. Cool completely on a wire rack.
2. In a large bowl, beat milk and pudding mixes on low speed for 2 minutes. Let stand until mixture is soft-set, 2 minutes. Fold in whipped topping.
3. Cut the brownies into 1-in. cubes; place half in a 3-qt. glass trifle bowl or serving dish. Cover with half of the pudding. Repeat layers. Sprinkle with chopped candy bars. Refrigerate leftovers.
¾ CUP: *265 cal., 8g fat (4g sat. fat), 7mg chol., 329mg sod., 45g carb. (31g sugars, 1g fiber), 3g pro.*

CARAMEL NUT CRUNCH PIE

This cool and creamy pie has a lot going for it. It's easy to make, it can be assembled well in advance to save time, and it's impressive enough to serve guests. To make this dessert even richer and more delicious, you can chop up some additional peanuts and candy bars and crumble an extra handful or two of Oreo cookies to sprinkle over the top.
—*Andrea Bolden, Unionville, TN*

PREP: 25 MIN. + FREEZING
MAKES: 8 SERVINGS

**CARAMEL NUT
CRUNCH PIE**

- 2   cups Oreo cookie crumbs
- ½   cup honey-roasted peanuts, chopped
- ¼   cup butter, melted
- 6   Snickers candy bars
      (1.86 oz. each), chopped
- 6   cups vanilla ice cream,
      slightly softened
- ¼   cup hot caramel ice cream topping
- ¼   cup hot fudge ice cream topping,
      warmed
      Additional hot caramel and hot fudge
      ice cream topping, optional

1. Preheat oven to 375°. Mix cookie crumbs and peanuts; stir in butter. Press onto the bottom and up sides of a greased 9-in. pie plate. Bake until set, 10-12 minutes. Cool on a wire rack.

2. Fold candy bars into ice cream; spread into prepared crust. Drizzle with caramel and fudge toppings. Loosely cover and freeze until firm, at least 8 hours. If not serving right away, cover the pie securely after it's frozen firm. If desired, drizzle with additional caramel and fudge toppings before serving.
1 PIECE: *733 cal., 39g fat (17g sat. fat), 64mg chol., 487mg sod., 88g carb. (66g sugars, 4g fiber), 11g pro.*

TEST KITCHEN TIP

A store-bought Oreo pie crust makes this treat even easier. Sprinkle the chopped peanuts over the prepared crust, then follow the recipe beginning at the second step.

CREAMY CRANBERRY CHEESECAKE

ORANGE PUMPKIN CHIFFON DESSERT

When pumpkin season rolls around, I like to find new ways to enjoy it in almost all my cooking. This creamy dessert feels so festive this time of year—it gives you classic pumpkin pie flavor with just a kiss of orange.
—Donna Roberts, Manhattan, KS

PREP: 1 HOUR. • **COOK:** 20 MIN. + CHILLING
MAKES: 6 SERVINGS

- 1 Tbsp. unflavored gelatin
- ¼ cup orange juice
- 1¼ cups solid-pack pumpkin
- 1 cup sugar, divided
- ½ cup 2% milk
- 1 tsp. grated orange zest
- ½ tsp. salt
- ½ tsp. ground cinnamon
- ½ tsp. ground nutmeg
- ⅛ tsp. ground ginger
- 3 large eggs, room temperature
- ½ tsp. vanilla extract
  Whipped topping and ground cinnamon, optional

1. In a small saucepan, sprinkle gelatin over orange juice; let stand 1 minute. Add the pumpkin, ½ cup sugar, milk, orange zest, salt, cinnamon, nutmeg and ginger. Heat over low heat, stirring until gelatin and sugar are completely dissolved.
2. In a small bowl, whisk a small amount of hot mixture into egg yolks; return all to pan, whisking constantly. Bring to a gentle boil; cook and stir 2 minutes. Remove from heat; refrigerate 1 hour or until chilled.
3. In a small heavy saucepan, combine egg whites and remaining sugar over low heat. With a portable mixer, beat on low speed over low heat until mixture reaches 160°, about 12-15 minutes. Remove from heat. Add vanilla; beat on high until stiff peaks form. Fold into pumpkin mixture. Spoon into dessert dishes. Refrigerate, covered, 1 hour before serving. If desired, serve with whipped topping and cinnamon.
⅔ CUP: 204 cal., 3g fat (1g sat. fat), 95mg chol., 247mg sod., 40g carb. (37g sugars, 2g fiber), 5g pro.

CREAMY CRANBERRY CHEESECAKE

This creamy cheesecake is perfect for the holidays. And the topping is so good that I prepare it separately and use it as a side dish at Thanksgiving.
—Mary Simonson, Kelso, Washington

PREP: 40 MIN. • **BAKE:** 55 MIN. + CHILLING
MAKES: 16 SERVINGS

- 9 whole cinnamon graham crackers, crushed
- 1 Tbsp. plus 1 cup sugar, divided
- ¼ cup butter, melted
- 2 pkg. (8 oz. each) reduced-fat cream cheese, cubed
- 1 pkg. (8 oz.) fat-free cream cheese, cubed
- ¾ cup fat-free sour cream
- 3 large egg whites, lightly beaten
- 1 Tbsp. lemon juice
- 2 tsp. vanilla extract
- 1 tsp. rum extract

TOPPING:
- ¾ cup sugar
- ¼ cup orange juice
- 2 Tbsp. water
- 1½ tsp. grated orange zest
- ¼ tsp. minced fresh gingerroot
- 2 cups fresh or frozen cranberries
- ¼ cup chopped pecans

1. Combine the cracker crumbs, 1 Tbsp. sugar and butter. Press onto the bottom and 1 in. up the sides of a 9-in. springform pan coated with cooking spray. Place on a baking sheet. Bake at 350° for 10 minutes. Cool on a wire rack.
2. In a large bowl, beat the cream cheeses, sour cream and remaining sugar until smooth. Add egg whites; beat on low just until combined. Beat in lemon juice and extracts. Pour into crust.
3. Place the pan on a double thickness of heavy-duty foil (about 18 in. square). Securely wrap foil around pan. Place in a larger baking pan. Add 1 in. of hot water to larger pan.
4. Bake for 55-60 minutes or until center is just set. Remove pan from water bath. Cool on a wire rack for 10 minutes. Carefully run a knife around edge of pan to loosen; cool 1 hour longer. Remove foil. Chill overnight.
5. In a small saucepan, combine the first 5 topping ingredients; bring to a boil. Add cranberries. Cook over medium heat until the berries pop, about 10 minutes. Stir in pecans; cool. Chill at least 1 hour.
6. Spoon topping over cheesecake to within 1 in. of edges.
1 SLICE: 269 cal., 11g fat (6g sat. fat), 31mg chol., 294mg sod., 35g carb. (27g sugars, 1g fiber), 7g pro.

⏰ 5ⁱ
CARAMELIZED PEARS

After picking an abundant crop of pears, I was looking for new ways to enjoy them. A friend suggested warming them with butter and brown sugar. This tasty recipe was the result! We like the pears with vanilla bean ice cream, but plain vanilla or cinnamon are also quite delicious!
—Sue Gronholz, Beaver Dam, WI

TAKES: 20 MIN. • **MAKES:** 3 CUPS

½ cup packed brown sugar
¼ cup butter, cubed
¼ tsp. ground cinnamon
4 cups chopped peeled ripe pears
   Vanilla ice cream, optional

In a large skillet, combine brown sugar, butter and cinnamon. Cook over medium heat until sugar is dissolved, stirring occasionally, about 4-5 minutes. Add pears; cook and stir until pears are tender, 5-10 minutes longer. Serve over ice cream if desired.

¼ **CUP:** *96 cal., 4g fat (2g sat. fat), 10mg chol., 33mg sod., 16g carb. (13g sugars, 1g fiber), 0 pro.*

TEST KITCHEN TIP

Try swapping fresh apples, peaches, plums or other firm fruit for the pears.

CARAMELIZED PEARS

DIRTY BANANA TRIFLE

What could be better than bananas, cookies and Kahlua? Adjust the Kahlua to make the flavor stronger or weaker.
—Laurie Ann Handlin, Ocean View, DE

PREP: 40 MIN. + CHILLING • **MAKES:** 24 SERVINGS

2 pkg. (8 oz. each) cream cheese, softened
2 cans (14 oz. each) sweetened condensed milk
1½ cups Kahlua (coffee liqueur), chilled
2½ cups cold 2% milk, divided
2 pkg. (3.9 oz. each) instant chocolate pudding mix
3 cartons (8 oz. each) frozen whipped topping, thawed
9 whole chocolate graham crackers, coarsely crushed
2 pkg. (3.4 oz. each) instant banana cream pudding mix
1½ cups coarsely crushed vanilla wafers (about 45 wafers)
5 medium bananas, sliced
   Additional chocolate grahams, wafers and banana slices

1. In a large bowl, beat 1 package cream cheese and 1 can condensed milk until blended. Beat in Kahlua, ½ cup milk and chocolate pudding mixes until thickened, about 2 minutes. Fold in 1 carton whipped topping, then chocolate graham crackers. Set aside.
2. In another large bowl, beat remaining package cream cheese and can of condensed milk until blended. Beat in remaining 2 cups milk and banana pudding mixes until thickened, about 2 minutes. Fold in 1 carton whipped topping, vanilla wafers and bananas.
3. Spread chocolate pudding mixture in the bottom of a 6- or 7-qt. trifle bowl or glass bowl. Layer with 1½ cups whipped topping and the banana pudding mixture; top with remaining 1½ cups whipped topping. Cover and refrigerate overnight.
4. Garnish with additional wafers, crushed chocolate graham crackers and sliced bananas before serving.

1 **CUP:** *381 cal., 16g fat (11g sat. fat), 33mg chol., 326mg sod., 46g carb. (33g sugars, 1g fiber), 5g pro.*

MANGO TIRAMISU

I love tiramisu and I wanted to make one with summer flavors. I swapped Grand Marnier and Malibu rum for the usual coffee liqueur, giving it a tropical twist.
—Carla Mendres, Winnipeg, MB

PREP: 30 MIN. • **COOK:** 5 MIN. + CHILLING
MAKES: 12 SERVINGS

- 2 large egg yolks
- 1 cup confectioners' sugar, divided
- 2 cups heavy whipping cream, divided
- 1 carton (8 oz.) mascarpone cheese
- 2 large navel oranges
- ½ cup coconut rum or orange juice plus ½ tsp. coconut extract
- ½ cup orange liqueur or orange juice
- 1 tsp. vanilla extract
- 1 pkg. (7 oz.) crisp ladyfinger cookies
- 2 medium ripe mangoes, peeled and thinly sliced

1. In top of a double boiler or a metal bowl over simmering water, combine egg yolks, ½ cup confectioners' sugar and ½ cup cream. Whisking constantly, heat mixture until thick and a thermometer reads 160°. Remove from heat; whisk in mascarpone cheese until almost smooth. In another bowl, beat the remaining 1½ cups cream until it begins to thicken. Add the remaining ½ cup confectioners' sugar; beat until soft peaks form. Fold the whipped cream into the mascarpone mixture.

2. Cut oranges crosswise in half; squeeze juice from oranges into a shallow bowl. Stir in rum, orange liqueur and vanilla.

3. Quickly dip half of the ladyfingers into rum mixture and place in the bottom of a 9-in. springform pan. Top with half of the mascarpone mixture and half of the mango slices. Repeat layers. Refrigerate, covered, for at least 8 hours or overnight. To serve, loosen and remove rim.

NOTE: This recipe was prepared with Alessi brand ladyfinger cookies.

1 SLICE: *413 cal., 25g fat (14g sat. fat), 117mg chol., 48mg sod., 38g carb. (31g sugars, 2g fiber), 5g pro.*

NO-BAKE STRAWBERRY DESSERT

Convenience items make the prep work for this refrigerated delight as simple as can be. Serve it in a glass dish for added elegance.
—Sherri Daniels, Clark, SD

PREP: 20 MIN. + CHILLING
MAKES: 20 SERVINGS

- 1 loaf (10½ oz.) angel food cake, cut into 1-in. cubes
- 2 pkg. (.3 oz. each) sugar-free strawberry gelatin
- 2 cups boiling water
- 1 pkg. (20 oz.) frozen unsweetened whole strawberries, thawed
- 2 cups cold 1% milk
- 1 pkg. (1 oz.) sugar-free instant vanilla pudding mix
- 1 carton (8 oz.) frozen reduced-fat whipped topping, thawed Chopped fresh strawberries, optional

1. Arrange cake cubes in a single layer in a 13x9-in. dish. In a bowl, dissolve gelatin in boiling water; stir in the strawberries. Pour over the cake and gently press cake down. Refrigerate until set, about 1 hour.

2. In a large bowl, whisk milk and pudding mix for 2 minutes. Let stand for 2 minutes or until soft-set.

3. Spoon over gelatin layer. Spread with whipped topping. Refrigerate until serving. If desired, garnish dessert with chopped fresh strawberries.

1 PIECE: *92 cal., 2g fat (1g sat. fat), 2mg chol., 172mg sod., 16g carb. (0 sugars, 1g fiber), 2g pro.* **Diabetic exchanges:** *1 starch.*

MANGO TIRAMISU

THOMAS JEFFERSON'S VANILLA ICE CREAM

5i

THOMAS JEFFERSON'S VANILLA ICE CREAM

The third U.S. president is credited with jotting down the first American recipe for this treat. No vanilla bean on hand? Substitute 1 tablespoon vanilla extract for the vanilla bean. Just stir the extract into the cream mixture after the ice-water bath.
—Taste of Home *Test Kitchen*

PREP: 15 MIN. + CHILLING
PROCESS: 20 MIN/BATCH + FREEZING
MAKES: 2¼ QT.

- 2 qt. heavy whipping cream
- 1 cup sugar
- 1 vanilla bean
- 6 large egg yolks

1. In a large heavy saucepan, combine cream and sugar. Split vanilla bean in half lengthwise. With a sharp knife, scrape seeds into pan; add bean. Heat cream mixture over medium heat until bubbles form around sides of pan, stirring to dissolve sugar.

2. In a small bowl, whisk a small amount of the hot mixture into the egg yolks; return all to the pan, whisking constantly.

3. Cook over low heat until mixture is just thick enough to coat a metal spoon and the temperature reaches 160°, stirring mixture constantly. Do not boil. Transfer mixture to a bowl immediately.

4. Place the bowl in a pan of ice water. Stir occasionally, gently, for 2 minutes; discard the vanilla bean. Press waxed paper onto surface of the custard. Refrigerate custard several hours or overnight.

5. Fill cylinder of the ice cream freezer two-thirds full; freeze according to the manufacturer's directions. (Refrigerate remaining mixture until ready to freeze.) Transfer ice cream to a freezer container; freeze for 4-6 hours or until firm. Repeat with remaining mixture.

½ **CUP:** *424 cal., 40g fat (25g sat. fat), 182mg chol., 32mg sod., 14g carb. (14g sugars, 0 fiber), 4g pro.*

5i

CINNAMON APPLE PAN BETTY

I found this recipe soon after I was married 49 years ago. It's quick to put together, and you'll need just a few ingredients that you probably have on hand. It's still a favorite of ours during fall and winter, when apples are at their best.
—Shirley Leister, West Chester, PA

TAKES: 15 MIN. • **MAKES:** 6 SERVINGS

- 3 medium apples, peeled and cubed
- ½ cup butter
- 3 cups cubed bread
- ½ cup sugar
- ¾ tsp. ground cinnamon

In a large skillet, saute apple in butter until tender, 4-5 minutes. Add bread cubes. Stir together sugar and cinnamon; sprinkle over apple mixture and toss to coat. Saute until bread is warmed.

½ **CUP:** *279 cal., 16g fat (10g sat. fat), 41mg chol., 208mg sod., 34g carb. (25g sugars, 2g fiber), 2g pro.*

REINDEER CAKE
PAGE 251

Holiday & Seasonal Celebrations

Festivities and food go hand in hand. Whichever holiday you're preparing for, your family and friends are sure to adore these autumn treats, Christmas specialties and spring refreshments.

Let's Do Brunch

Serve up a sweet and savory feast that proves
leisurely mornings are the best part of the day.

ORANGE-GLAZED HAM

ORANGE-GLAZED HAM

I always thought this delicious ham looked like a sparkling jewel when my mom served it for Easter dinner. The spice rub penetrates every tender slice, and the enticing aroma is only a hint of how good it will taste.
—Ruth Seitz, Columbus Junction, IA

PREP: 10 MIN. • **BAKE:** 2 HOURS
MAKES: 12 SERVINGS

- 1 fully cooked bone-in ham (6 to 8 lbs.)
- 1 Tbsp. ground mustard
- 1 tsp. ground allspice
- ¾ cup orange marmalade

1. Place ham on a rack in a shallow roasting pan. Score the surface of the ham, making diamond shapes ½ in. deep. Combine the mustard and allspice; rub over ham.
2. Bake the ham, uncovered, at 325° until a thermometer reads 140°, 2-2¼ hours. Spread top of ham with marmalade during last hour of baking, basting occasionally.
6 OZ. COOKED HAM: *243 cal., 6g fat (2g sat. fat), 100mg chol., 1203mg sod., 14g carb. (13g sugars, 0 fiber), 34g pro.*

PARMESAN SCONES

The addition of onions gives these scones a nice bite. You can also stir in some basil or oregano if you like. Cream is the secret to really light and tender scones.
—Jolie Stinson, Marion, IN

TAKES: 25 MIN. • **MAKES:** 1 DOZEN

- 2 cups finely chopped onions
- 2 Tbsp. olive oil
- 6 garlic cloves, minced
- 4 cups all-purpose flour
- 2 cups grated Parmesan cheese
- 4 tsp. baking powder
- 1 tsp. salt
- 2 cups heavy whipping cream
   Additional grated Parmesan cheese, optional

1. In a large skillet, saute onions in oil until tender. Add garlic; saute 1 minute longer.
2. In a large bowl, combine flour, cheese, baking powder and salt. Stir in cream just until moistened. Stir in the onion mixture.

PARMESAN SCONES

3. Turn the dough onto a floured surface; knead 10 times. Divide dough in half. Pat each portion into a 6-in. circle. Cut each circle into 6 wedges. Separate wedges and place on a greased baking sheet.
4. Bake at 400° for 12-15 minutes or until light golden brown. If desired, sprinkle with additional cheese in the last 5 minutes of baking. Serve warm.
1 SCONE: *378 cal., 21g fat (12g sat. fat), 66mg chol., 551mg sod., 36g carb. (2g sugars, 2g fiber), 11g pro.*

HEARTY SPINACH SALAD WITH HOT BACON DRESSING

This warm and hearty salad offers old-fashioned flavor. The glossy dressing features a hint of celery seed for a special touch.
—Taste of Home *Test Kitchen*

TAKES: 30 MIN. • **MAKES:** 6 SERVINGS

- 8 cups torn fresh spinach
- 3 bacon strips, diced
- ½ cup chopped red onion
- 2 Tbsp. brown sugar
- 2 Tbsp. cider vinegar
- ¼ tsp. salt
- ¼ tsp. ground mustard
- ⅛ tsp. celery seed
- ⅛ tsp. pepper
- 1 tsp. cornstarch
- ⅓ cup cold water

1. Place the spinach in a large salad bowl; set aside. In a small nonstick skillet, cook bacon over medium heat until crisp. Using a slotted spoon, remove to paper towels to drain.

2. In the drippings, saute onion until tender. Stir in the brown sugar, vinegar, salt, mustard, celery seed and pepper. Combine cornstarch and water until smooth; stir into the skillet. Bring to a boil; cook and stir until thickened, 1-2 minutes.

3. Remove from the heat; pour over spinach and toss to coat. Sprinkle with bacon. Serve salad immediately.

¾ CUP: 97 cal., 7g fat (2g sat. fat), 8mg chol., 215mg sod., 8g carb. (6g sugars, 1g fiber), 2g pro. **Diabetic exchanges:** *1½ fat, 1 vegetable.*

BUFFET SCRAMBLED EGGS

These are my favorite scrambled eggs. The white sauce, flavored with chicken bouillon, keeps the eggs creamy and moist. It's a tasty twist on a morning mainstay.
—Elsie Beachy, Plain City, OH

TAKES: 20 MIN. • **MAKES:** 8 SERVINGS

- 8 Tbsp. butter, divided
- ¼ cup all-purpose flour
- 2 cups whole milk
- 4 tsp. chicken bouillon granules
- 16 large eggs, lightly beaten
  Optional: Minced fresh parsley, tarragon and chives

1. In a small saucepan, melt 2 Tbsp. butter. Stir in flour until smooth. Gradually add milk and bouillon. Bring to a boil; cook and stir for 2 minutes or until thickened. Set sauce aside.

2. In a large skillet, melt remaining butter. Add eggs; cook over medium heat until eggs begin to set, stirring occasionally. Stir in the white sauce. Cook until the eggs are completely set. If desired, sprinkle with parsley, tarragon and chives.

¾ CUP: 304 cal., 24g fat (11g sat. fat), 464mg chol., 692mg sod., 7g carb. (4g sugars, 0 fiber), 15g pro.

HEARTY SPINACH
SALAD WITH HOT
BACON DRESSING

BUFFET SCRAMBLED EGGS

LAVENDER LEMON BARS

LAVENDER LEMON BARS

Hints of lavender and lemon zest in the crust make these treats a favorite.
—*Judith Hilinski, Cuyahoga Falls, OH*

PREP: 20 MIN. • **BAKE:** 25 MIN
MAKES: 2 DOZEN

- ¾ cup butter, softened
- ½ cup confectioners' sugar
- 2 cups all-purpose flour
- ½ cup ground almonds
- 2 tsp. dried lavender flowers
- 2 tsp. grated lemon zest

TOPPING
- 1¾ cups sugar
- ⅓ cup all-purpose flour
- ½ tsp. baking soda
- 4 large eggs
- ⅓ cup lemon juice
  Confectioners' sugar

1. In a small bowl, cream the butter and confectioners' sugar. Add flour, almonds, lavender and lemon zest; beat until crumbly. Pat into an ungreased 13x9-in. baking dish. Bake at 350° for 15 minutes or until edges are golden brown.

2. Meanwhile, in a another small bowl, combine the sugar, flour, baking soda, eggs and lemon juice; beat until frothy. Pour over hot crust. Bake at 350° for 20-25 minutes or until light golden brown. Cool on a wire rack. Dust with confectioners' sugar; cut into bars. Refrigerate leftovers.

NOTE: Look for dried lavender flowers in spice shops. If using lavender from the garden, make sure it hasn't been treated with chemicals.

1 BAR: *185 cal., 8g fat (4g sat. fat), 51mg chol., 95mg sod., 27g carb. (17g sugars, 1g fiber), 3g pro.*

RASPBERRY BELLINI

Loaded with raspberry flavor and fizzy bubbles, this is the perfect brunch drink. Not too tart, not too sweet—just right!
—*Nancy Mueller, Menomonee Falls, WI*

TAKES: 10 MIN. • **MAKES:** 4 SERVINGS

- 1 pkg. (10 oz.) frozen sweetened raspberries, thawed
- 1 Tbsp. lemon juice
- 1 tsp. vanilla extract
- 4 cups chilled prosecco
  Mint leaves and fresh raspberries, optional

1. Place raspberries in a blender; cover and process until pureed. Press through a fine-mesh strainer into a bowl; discard seeds. Stir in lemon juice and vanilla.

2. Fill each champagne flute with 2 Tbsp. raspberry mixture; top with prosecco. If desired, garnish the Bellinis with mint and fresh raspberries.

1 CUP: *270 cal., 0 fat (0 sat. fat), 0 chol., 13mg sod., 25g carb. (18g sugars, 3g fiber), 1g pro.*

> **TEST KITCHEN TIP**
>
> Make it a mocktail. For a drink that's friendly for all, use sparkling apple juice or white grape juice instead of the prosecco.

RASPBERRY BELLINI

Picnic Perfect

Grab a blanket and spread out on the grass.
This summer, the park—or your backyard—
is the coolest dining destination in town.

GRILLED
LEMON
CHICKEN

BLT
MACARONI
SALAD

BLT MACARONI SALAD

A friend served this salad. I had to get the recipe because my husband loves BLT sandwiches, and it's become a favorite of his. It's really nice to serve on the hot and humid days we get so frequently during summer here in Virginia.
—*Mrs. Hamilton Myers Jr., Charlottesville, VA*

TAKES: 30 MIN. • **MAKES:** 6 SERVINGS

- ½ cup mayonnaise
- 3 Tbsp. chili sauce
- 2 Tbsp. lemon juice
- 1 tsp. sugar
- 3 cups cooked elbow macaroni
- ½ cup chopped seeded tomato
- 2 Tbsp. chopped green onions
- 3 cups shredded lettuce
- 4 bacon strips, cooked and crumbled

In a large bowl, combine first 4 ingredients. Add the macaroni, tomatoes and onions; toss to coat. Cover and refrigerate. Just before serving, add lettuce and bacon; toss mixture to coat.

¾ CUP: *259 cal., 17g fat (3g sat. fat), 10mg chol., 287mg sod., 21g carb. (4g sugars, 2g fiber), 5g pro.*

TEST KITCHEN TIP

If you like your pasta salads extra saucy, double the sauce ingredients.

GRILLED LEMON CHICKEN

My chicken gets its subtle bit of pucker from lemonade concentrate. So simple, so sweet!
—*Linda Nilsen, Anoka, MN*

PREP: 5 MIN. • **GRILL:** 40 MIN.
MAKES: 12 SERVINGS

- ¾ cup thawed lemonade concentrate
- ⅓ cup soy sauce
- 1 garlic clove, minced
- 1 tsp. seasoned salt
- ½ tsp. celery salt
- ⅛ tsp. garlic powder
- 2 broiler/fryer chickens (3 to 3½ lbs. each), cut up

1. In a bowl, whisk the first 6 ingredients until combined. Pour half into a shallow glass dish. Cover and refrigerate remaining lemon sauce.

RED-WHITE-AND-BLUE BERRY DELIGHT

2. Dip chicken into sauce, turning to coat; discard sauce. Grill chicken, covered, over medium heat for 30 minutes, turning occasionally. Brush with reserved sauce. Grill about 10-20 minutes longer, brushing frequently with sauce, until a thermometer reads 165°.

5 OZ. COOKED CHICKEN: *320 cal., 17g fat (5g sat. fat), 104mg chol., 504mg sod., 6g carb. (5g sugars, 0 fiber), 34g pro.*

RED-WHITE-AND-BLUE BERRY DELIGHT

Loaded with both fresh strawberries and blueberries, this luscious treat is perfect for any Fourth of July celebration!
—*Constance Fennell, Grand Junction, MI*

PREP: 25 MIN. + CHILLING
MAKES: 8 SERVINGS

- ½ cup sugar
- 2 envelopes unflavored gelatin
- 4 cups white cranberry-peach juice drink, divided
- 1 Tbsp. lemon juice
- 2 cups fresh strawberries, halved
- 2 cups fresh blueberries

CREAM
- ½ cup heavy whipping cream
- 1 Tbsp. sugar
- ¼ tsp. vanilla extract

1. In a large saucepan, combine sugar and gelatin. Add 1 cup cranberry-peach juice; cook and stir over low heat until gelatin is completely dissolved, about 5 minutes. Remove from the heat; stir in lemon juice and remaining cranberry-peach juice.

2. Place strawberries in an 8-cup ring mold coated with cooking spray; add 2 cups of gelatin mixture. Refrigerate until set but not firm, for about 30 minutes. Set aside remaining gelatin mixture.

3. Stir blueberries into remaining gelatin mixture; spoon over strawberry layer. Refrigerate overnight. Unmold onto a serving platter.

4. In a small bowl, beat cream until it begins to thicken. Add sugar and vanilla; beat until stiff peaks form. Serve with gelatin.

1 SERVING WITH 2 TBSP. WHIPPED CREAM: *203 cal., 6g fat (3g sat. fat), 20mg chol., 12mg sod., 38g carb. (35g sugars, 2g fiber), 3g pro.*

CRISP ONION RELISH

DOUBLE HOT HORSERADISH MUSTARD

CHUNKY KETCHUP

CRISP ONION RELISH

I take this relish to picnics for people to use as a condiment on hamburgers and hot dogs. It adds a special zip!
—Marie Patkau, Hanley, SK

PREP: 10 MIN. + CHILLING
MAKES: ABOUT 6 CUPS

- 4 medium sweet onions, halved and thinly sliced
- ½ cup sugar
- ⅓ cup water
- ⅓ cup cider vinegar
- 1 cup mayonnaise
- 1 tsp. celery seed

Place onions in a large bowl. In a small bowl, combine the sugar, water and vinegar; stir until sugar is dissolved. Pour over onions. Cover and refrigerate for at least 3 hours. Drain and discard liquid from the onions. Combine mayonnaise and celery seed; add to the onions and mix well. Store relish in the refrigerator.
2 TBSP.: *47 cal., 3g fat (1g sat. fat), 0 chol., 26mg sod., 4g carb. (3g sugars, 0 fiber), 0 pro.*

DOUBLE HOT HORSERADISH MUSTARD

My family enjoys spicy food so this recipe is wonderful for us. We add it to sandwiches.
—Madeline Cole, Willow, AK

TAKES: 10 MIN. • **MAKES:** ½ CUP

- ¼ cup cider vinegar
- ¼ cup ground mustard
- 3 Tbsp. white wine vinegar
- 2 Tbsp. mustard seed
- 1 Tbsp. prepared horseradish
- 1½ tsp. honey

In a blender, combine all ingredients. Cover and process until smooth. Transfer to a small jar and cover mustard tightly. Store in the refrigerator.
2 TBSP.: *74 cal., 4g fat (0 sat. fat), 0 chol., 18mg sod., 6g carb. (3g sugars, 2g fiber), 3g pro.*

CHUNKY KETCHUP

I came up with chunky homemade ketchup to jazz up chopped steak sandwiches and hot sausage sandwiches for my family. I gave some to our friends, and they enjoyed the fresh-tasting and delicious concoction on hamburgers and stuffed peppers.
—Susan Stahr, Driftwood, PA

PREP: 20 MIN. • **COOK:** 1½ HOURS
MAKES: 3½ CUPS

- 4 cups chopped seeded peeled tomatoes
- 1 medium onion, chopped
- 1 medium green pepper, chopped
- 1 cup sugar
- 1 can (6 oz.) tomato paste
- 1 Tbsp. salt
- ¼ cup white vinegar

1. In a large saucepan, combine the tomatoes, onion, green pepper, sugar, tomato paste and salt; bring to a boil. Reduce heat; simmer, uncovered, until slightly thickened, about 1½ hours.
2. Stir in the vinegar; heat through. Cool to room temperature; store up to 2 weeks in the refrigerator.
2 TBSP.: *40 cal., 0 fat (0 sat. fat), 0 chol., 258mg sod., 10g carb. (9g sugars, 1g fiber), 0 pro.*

Dip those chips!

STRAWBERRY SALSA

In a large bowl, combine 1 pint fresh chopped **strawberries**, 4 seeded and chopped **plum tomatoes**, 1 finely chopped small **red onion** and 1 to 2 minced **jalapeno peppers**. Stir in 2 Tbsp. **lime juice**, 1 Tbsp. **olive oil** and 2 minced **garlic cloves**. Cover and refrigerate 2 hours.

¼ **CUP:** *19 cal., 1g fat (0 sat. fat), 0 chol., 1mg sod., 3g carb. (2g sugars, 1g fiber), 0 pro.* **Diabetic exchanges:** *Free food.* **Makes 4 cups.**

GINGERED MANGO SALSA

Combine 1 cup chopped peeled **mango**, ¼ cup chopped **red onion**, ¼ cup minced fresh **cilantro**, ¼ cup **lime juice**, 2 Tbsp. minced fresh **mint**, 1 Tbsp. minced fresh **gingerroot**, ½ tsp. **olive oil** and ¼ tsp. **salt**. Let stand 30 minutes before serving.

¼ **CUP:** *39 cal., 1g fat (0 sat. fat), 0 chol., 120mg sod., 9g carb. (7g sugars, 1g fiber), 0 pro.* **Diabetic exchanges:** *½ fruit.* **Makes 1¼ cups.**

QUICK PICANTE SAUCE

In a blender, process until smooth a 14½-oz. can drained **diced tomatoes**, ½ cup coarsely chopped **onion**, ½ cup minced **fresh cilantro**, 1 seeded, halved **jalapeno pepper**, 3 Tbsp. **lime juice**, 1 Tbsp. **chili powder**, 1 halved **garlic clove**, ½ tsp. **salt** and ¼ tsp. grated **lime zest**. Serve with chips.

¼ **CUP:** *32 cal., 0 fat (0 sat. fat), 0 chol., 415mg sod., 7g carb. (4g sugars, 2g fiber), 1g pro.* **Diabetic exchanges:** *1 vegetable.* **Makes 1¼ cups.**

SAUCY
BARBECUE
SHRIMP

SOUTHERN
POTATO SALAD

SOUTHERN POTATO SALAD

This potato salad recipe will be perfect for your next church supper or potluck. The sweet pickles add an extra sweetness to this special salad.
—Gene Pitts, Wilsonville, AL

PREP: 30 MIN. + CHILLING
MAKES: 8 SERVINGS

- 5 medium potatoes, peeled and cubed
   Water
- 6 hard-boiled large eggs, chopped
- ½ cup thinly sliced green onions
- ¼ cup chopped sweet pickles
- 1 tsp. prepared mustard
- 1 tsp. celery seed
- 1 cup mayonnaise
   Salt and pepper to taste

Cook potatoes in boiling water until tender. Drain and chill. Add the eggs, onions and pickles; toss well. Stir in mustard, celery seed and mayonnaise. Season with salt and pepper and mix well. Chill potato salad until ready to serve.

¾ **CUP:** *377 cal., 26g fat (4g sat. fat), 169mg chol., 275mg sod., 28g carb. (5g sugars, 2g fiber), 8g pro.*

PULLED BBQ PORK

SAUCY BARBECUE SHRIMP

This rustic Cajun dish is one of our family favorites. Don't remove the shells from the shrimp—the beauty of this dish is in peeling the shrimp and dipping it in the sauce. We have doubled and even tripled the recipe to feed crowds and it's always perfect!
—Debbie Glasscock, Conway, AR

PREP: 20 MIN. • **BAKE:** 20 MIN.
MAKES: 8 SERVINGS

- ½ cup butter, cubed
- 1 medium onion, chopped
- 1 bottle (18 oz.) barbecue sauce
- 1 bottle (12 oz.) pale ale beer or nonalcoholic beer
- 2 lbs. uncooked shell-on shrimp (31-40 per lb.), deveined
   French bread baguette, sliced

1. Preheat oven to 350°. In a large saucepan melt butter over medium-high heat. Add onion; cook and stir until tender, for 8-10 minutes. Stir in barbecue sauce and beer.

2. Place shrimp in a 13x9-in. baking dish. Pour barbecue mixture over top. Bake, uncovered, until shrimp turn pink, about 20-25 minutes, stirring halfway. Serve with baguette slices.

1 **CUP:** *339 cal., 14g fat (8g sat. fat), 168mg chol., 883mg sod., 30g carb. (24g sugars, 1g fiber), 19g pro.*

PULLED BBQ PORK

During years of vacationing on the North Carolina coast, I became hooked on their pork barbecue. The version I developed has become a favorite at potluck dinners.
—Joseph Sarnoski, West Chester, PA

PREP: 15 MIN. • **COOK:** 10 HOURS
MAKES: 8 SERVINGS

- 2 medium onions, finely chopped
- 1 Tbsp. canola oil
- 6 garlic cloves, minced
- 1 tsp. crushed red pepper flakes
- 1 tsp. pepper
- 1 can (14½ oz.) diced tomatoes, undrained
- ¼ cup packed brown sugar
- ¼ cup cider vinegar
- 2 Tbsp. hot pepper sauce
- 1 Tbsp. Worcestershire sauce
- 1 tsp. ground cumin
- 1 boneless pork shoulder butt roast (3 to 4 lbs.)
- 8 kaiser rolls, split

1. In a large skillet, saute onions in oil until tender. Add the garlic, pepper flakes and pepper; cook 1 minute longer. Stir in the tomatoes, brown sugar, vinegar, hot pepper sauce, Worcestershire and cumin. Cook over medium heat until heated through and sugar is dissolved.

2. Cut roast in half. Place in a 5-qt. slow cooker; pour sauce over the top. Cover and cook on low for 10-12 hours or until meat is tender. Remove roast; cool slightly. Skim fat from cooking juices. Shred the meat with 2 forks and return to the slow cooker. Heat through. With a slotted spoon, place ¾ cup meat mixture on each roll.

1 **SANDWICH:** *518 cal., 21g fat (7g sat. fat), 101mg chol., 528mg sod., 44g carb. (12g sugars, 3g fiber), 36g pro.*

OVERNIGHT SLAW

1. In a large bowl, combine the first 7 ingredients. Stir in half of the onions and bacon. Transfer the mixture to a greased 13x9-in. baking dish.
2. Cover and bake at 350° for 45 minutes. Sprinkle with remaining onions and bacon. Bake, uncovered, 5-10 minutes longer or until bubbly.

¾ CUP: *285 cal., 9 g fat (3 g sat. fat), 10 mg chol., 860 mg sod., 46 g carb., 7 g fiber, 7 g pro.*

KEY WEST FLANK STEAK

My husband, Jason, is the cook in our family. This is his recipe, inspired by his Colombian roots and our visits to Key West. Sometimes we grill extra lime and onion slices alongside. Serve with sides of rice and fried plantains.
—Gretchen Ospina, Columbia Heights, MN

PREP: 20 MIN. + MARINATING
GRILL: 15 MIN. + STANDING
MAKES: 4 SERVINGS

- 1   large red onion, sliced
- 1   cup minced fresh cilantro
- ¼   cup white wine vinegar
- ¼   cup Key lime juice
- 3   Tbsp. extra virgin olive oil, divided
- 6   Key limes, halved
- 1   beef flank steak (1 lb.)
- 1   tsp. kosher salt
- ⅛   tsp. pepper

1. In a small bowl, combine onion, cilantro, vinegar, lime juice and 2 Tbsp. oil until blended. Pour 1 cup marinade into a large bowl or shallow dish. Add lime halves. Rub steak with remaining oil; sprinkle with salt and pepper. Add to the bowl; turn to coat. Refrigerate 8 hours or overnight. Cover and refrigerate remaining marinade.
2. Drain steak, discarding marinade and limes in bowl. Place reserved marinade in a food processor; process until chopped.
3. Grill steak, covered, over medium heat or broil 4 in. from heat until the meat reaches desired doneness (for medium-rare, a thermometer should read 135°; medium, 140°), about 6-8 minutes per side. Baste occasionally with reserved marinade. Let stand 10 minutes before thinly slicing steak across the grain.

3 OZ. COOKED STEAK: *271 cal., 16g fat (5g sat. fat), 54mg chol., 431mg sod., 12g carb. (3g sugars, 3g fiber), 23g pro.* **Diabetic exchanges:** *3 lean meat, 1½ fat.*

OVERNIGHT SLAW

I love to make this recipe. It's so easy to prepare using my food processor. And you can make it fresh in fall and winter months when salad ingredients are less abundant.
—Nancy Brown, Janesville, WI

PREP: 15 MIN. + CHILLING
MAKES: 8 SERVINGS

- 1   medium head cabbage, shredded
- 4   mild white onions, thinly sliced
- 2   large carrots, shredded
- ½   cup vinegar
- ½   cup sugar
- 1   tsp. ground mustard
- 1   tsp. celery seed
- 1   tsp. salt
- ⅛   tsp. pepper
- ½   cup vegetable oil

In a large bowl, combine cabbage, onions and carrots; set aside. In a saucepan, combine vinegar, sugar, mustard, celery seed, salt and pepper; bring to a boil, stirring until sugar is dissolved. Remove from the heat and stir in oil. Pour over cabbage mixture. Cool mixture to room temperature. Cover and refrigerate overnight; stir several times.

¾ CUP: *238 cal., 14g fat (2g sat. fat), 0 chol., 325mg sod., 28g carb. (21g sugars, 5g fiber), 3g pro.*

SWEET & SPICY BAKED BEANS

This dish is a hit with guests and family, and people often ask for the recipe. It's simple and it's delicious.
—Elliot Wesen, Arlington, TX

PREP: 15 MIN. ● **BAKE:** 50 MIN.
MAKES: 14 SERVINGS

- 2   cans (28 oz. each) baked beans
- 1   can (20 oz.) unsweetened crushed pineapple, drained
- 1   cup spicy barbecue sauce
- ½   cup molasses
- 2   Tbsp. prepared mustard
- ½   tsp. pepper
- ¼   tsp. salt
- 1   can (6 oz.) french-fried onions, crushed, divided
- 5   bacon strips, cooked and crumbled, divided

SWEET CORN-TOMATO SALAD

KEY WEST FLANK STEAK

SWEET CORN-TOMATO SALAD

Whenever I make this for family events and parties, it reminds me of our fun barbecues and picnics through the years. Using fresh summer sweet corn and basil makes a huge difference in this recipe.
—Jessica Kleinbaum, Plant City, FL

PREP: 15 MIN. • **COOK:** 10 MIN. + CHILLING
MAKES: 10 SERVINGS

8 medium ears sweet corn, husks removed
1 large sweet red pepper, chopped
2 cups cherry tomatoes, halved
1 small red onion, finely chopped
¼ cup coarsely chopped fresh basil

DRESSING
½ cup canola oil
¼ cup rice vinegar
2 Tbsp. lime juice
1¼ tsp. salt
½ to 1 tsp. hot pepper sauce
½ tsp. garlic powder
½ tsp. grated lime zest
¼ tsp. pepper

1. Place corn in a large stockpot; add water to cover. Bring to a boil. Cook, covered, until crisp-tender, 6-8 minutes; drain. Cool slightly. Cut corn from cobs and place in a large bowl. Stir in the red pepper, tomatoes and onion.

2. In a small bowl, whisk the dressing ingredients until blended. Pour over corn mixture; toss to coat. Refrigerate, covered, at least 1 hour.

¾ **CUP:** *192 cal., 12g fat (1g sat. fat), 0 chol., 407mg sod., 21g carb. (9g sugars, 3g fiber), 3g pro.* **Diabetic exchanges:** *2 fat, 1 starch, 1 vegetable.*

Thanksgiving, Your Style

Celebrate the big feast your own way. From timeless classics to tweaks on tradition, no matter what's on the menu this year, everyone has a place at the table.

HERB-GLAZED TURKEY

APRICOT-APPLE CIDER

Country Fresh

You're a lover of breezy chats, open windows and pure, homespun charm. Spread your table with the simple family favorites that feel like coming home.

EASY BATTER
ROLLS

SWEET POTATOES
AU GRATIN

MAPLE-GLAZED
GREEN BEANS

APRICOT-APPLE CIDER

Dried apricots give this comforting cider a delicious twist. Add cranberries, cinnamon, allspice and cloves, and you have made the perfect hot drink to sip on cool nights.
—Ginnie Busam, Pewee Valley, KY

PREP: 20 MIN. • **COOK:** 3 HOURS
MAKES: 13 SERVINGS (2½ QT.)

- 8   cups unsweetened apple juice
- 1   can (12 oz.) ginger ale
- ½   cup dried apricots, halved
- ½   cup dried cranberries
- 2   cinnamon sticks (3 in.)
- 1   Tbsp. whole allspice
- 1   Tbsp. whole cloves

1. In a 5-qt. slow cooker, combine apple juice and ginger ale. Place the apricots, cranberries, cinnamon sticks, allspice and the cloves on a double thickness of cheesecloth; bring up corners of cloth and tie with string to form a bag. Place in slow cooker; cover.
2. Cook cider on high until heated through, 3-4 hours. Discard spice bag.
¾ CUP: *79 cal., 0 fat (0 sat. fat), 0 chol., 8mg sod., 20g carb. (17g sugars, 0 fiber), 0 pro.* **Diabetic exchanges:** *2 fruit.*

HERB-GLAZED TURKEY

Honey and corn syrup blend with savory herbs and seasonings to give this turkey a slightly sweet flavor. This tried-and-true recipe never fails to win me compliments.
—Charlene Melenka, Vegreville, AB

PREP: 10 MIN.
BAKE: 3½ HOURS + STANDING
MAKES: 18 SERVINGS

- 1   turkey (14 to 16 lbs.)
- ¼   cup olive oil
- 2   tsp. dried thyme
- 1½ tsp. salt, divided
- 1¼ tsp. pepper, divided
- 1   cup honey
- 1   cup corn syrup
- ¼   cup butter, melted
- 2   tsp. dried rosemary, crushed
- 1   tsp. rubbed sage
- 1   tsp. dried basil

1. Brush turkey with oil; tie the drumsticks together. Place turkey breast side up on a rack in a roasting pan. Combine the thyme, 1 tsp. salt and 1 tsp. pepper; sprinkle evenly over turkey. Bake, uncovered, at 325° for 2 hours.
2. In a small bowl, combine honey, corn syrup, butter, rosemary, sage, basil, and remaining salt and pepper. Brush over the turkey. Bake until a thermometer inserted in thickest part of thigh reads 170°-175°, about 90 minutes longer, basting frequently with pan drippings. Cover loosely with foil if turkey browns too quickly. Remove from oven. Cover and let stand for 15 minutes before carving.
7 OZ. COOKED TURKEY: *570 cal., 25g fat (8g sat. fat), 197mg chol., 380mg sod., 30g carb. (24g sugars, 0 fiber), 56g pro.*

SWEET POTATOES AU GRATIN

This rich sweet potato casserole couldn't be any easier to make—or more delicious to eat!
—Patti Kirchhoff, Lake Geneva, WI

PREP: 10 MIN. • **BAKE:** 40 MIN.
MAKES: 6 SERVINGS

- 2   large uncooked sweet potatoes, peeled and sliced ¼ in. thick
- 1   large egg
- 2   cups heavy whipping cream
- ¾   tsp. salt
- ⅛   tsp. ground nutmeg
       Pinch pepper
- 3   Tbsp. grated Parmesan cheese
       Minced fresh thyme, optional

Place potatoes in a greased 8-in. square baking dish. In a bowl, beat egg. Add cream, salt, nutmeg and pepper; mix well. Pour over potatoes; sprinkle with cheese. Bake, uncovered, at 375° until the potatoes are tender, 40-45 minutes. If desired, top with fresh thyme to serve.
1 SERVING: *412 cal., 31g fat (19g sat. fat), 124mg chol., 385mg sod., 30g carb. (14g sugars, 3g fiber), 6g pro.*

APRICOT-APPLE CIDER

MAPLE-GLAZED GREEN BEANS

After I picked my first green beans one year, I wanted to make a savory dish that was unique, quick, and packed with flavor. I loved this so much I couldn't stop eating it, so the next day I picked more beans and made this delicious side dish again.
—Merry Graham, Newhall, CA

TAKES: 25 MIN. • **MAKES:** 4 SERVINGS

- 3   cups cut fresh green beans
- 1   large onion, chopped
- 4   bacon strips, cut into 1-in. pieces
- ½   cup dried cranberries
- ¼   cup maple syrup
- ¼   tsp. salt
- ¼   tsp. pepper
- 1   Tbsp. bourbon, optional

1. In a large saucepan, place steamer basket over 1 in. of water. Place beans in basket. Bring water to a boil. Reduce the heat to maintain a low boil; steam, covered, until crisp-tender, 4-5 minutes.
2. Meanwhile, in a large skillet, cook onion and bacon over medium heat until bacon is crisp; drain. Stir cranberries, syrup, salt, pepper and, if desired, bourbon into onion mixture. Add beans; heat through, tossing to combine.
¾ **CUP:** *173 cal., 3g fat (1g sat. fat), 7mg chol., 302mg sod., 35g carb. (24g sugars, 4g fiber), 4g pro.*

EASY BATTER ROLLS

EASY BATTER ROLLS

The first thing my guests ask when they come for dinner is if I'm serving these dinner rolls. The buns are so light, airy and delicious that I'm constantly asked for the recipe.
—Thomasina Brunner, Gloversville, NY

PREP: 30 MIN. + RISING • **BAKE:** 15 MIN.
MAKES: 1 DOZEN

- 3   cups all-purpose flour
- 2   Tbsp. sugar
- 1   pkg. (¼ oz.) active dry yeast
- 1   tsp. salt
- 1   cup water
- 2   Tbsp. butter
- 1   large egg, room temperature
     Melted butter

1. In a large bowl, combine 2 cups flour, sugar, yeast and salt. In a saucepan, heat water and butter to 120°-130°. Add to dry ingredients; beat until blended. Add egg; beat on low speed for 30 seconds, then on high for 3 minutes. Stir in remaining flour (batter will be stiff). Do not knead. Cover and let rise in a warm place until doubled, about 30 minutes.
2. Stir dough down. Fill 12 greased muffin cups half full. Cover and let rolls rise until doubled, about 15 minutes.
3. Bake at 350° until golden brown, for 15-20 minutes. Cool for 1 minute before removing from pan to a wire rack. Brush tops with melted butter.
FREEZE OPTION: Freeze the cooled rolls in airtight containers. To use, microwave each roll on high until warmed, 30-45 seconds.
1 ROLL: *147 cal., 3g fat (1g sat. fat), 21mg chol., 219mg sod., 26g carb. (2g sugars, 1g fiber), 4g pro.*

Casually Chic

You're a firm believer that friends are family, too. Call 'em all over for a laid-back, come-as-you-are gathering filled with new traditions and an extra shot of fun.

SLOW-COOKER TURKEY BREAST WITH CRANBERRY GRAVY

EASY PEASY BISCUITS

BUTTERNUT SQUASH
MAC & CHEESE

CRUNCHY BACON
BLUE CHEESE RED PEPPER
BRUSSEL SPROUTS

SPICED APPLE CIDER
JELLY SHOTS

SPICED APPLE CIDER JELLY SHOTS

These spiced, spiked gelatin squares are sure to get the party started at fall get-togethers. But if you're going for the more traditional shot-style look, pour the tasty mixture into 2-ounce plastic cups and refrigerate until set.
—Rachel Bernhard Seis, Milwaukee, WI

PREP: 10 MIN. • **COOK:** 5 MIN. + CHILLING
MAKES: 64 SQUARES

- 1½ cups cold apple cider or juice
- 4 envelopes unflavored gelatin
- 1 cup sugar
- 1½ cups ginger-flavored vodka
- 2 tsp. Angostura bitters
- 2 Tbsp. cinnamon sugar
  Thinly sliced apple, optional

1. Pour apple cider into a large saucepan and sprinkle gelatin over top; let stand, without stirring, until gelatin softens, about 5 minutes. Whisk in sugar. Heat and stir over low heat until sugar and gelatin are completely dissolved, 8-10 minutes (do not boil); remove from heat. Stir in vodka; pour the mixture into a 9-in. square baking pan coated with cooking spray. Refrigerate, uncovered, until the gelatin mixture is firm, about 2 hours.

2. To unmold, run a sharp knife along edges of gelatin; invert onto a cutting board and lift off pan. Cut into 64 squares; brush tops with bitters and sprinkle with cinnamon sugar. If desired, garnish with apple slices.

1 SQUARE: *28 cal., 0 fat (0 sat. fat), 0 chol., 1mg sod., 4g carb. (4g sugars, 0 fiber), 0 pro.*

SLOW-COOKER TURKEY BREAST WITH CRANBERRY GRAVY

I created this dish one day when I was craving Thanksgiving dinner, and it was still over a month away. You get all the bells and whistles of Thanksgiving dinner with such little effort. Add a vegetable, some mashed potatoes and you're ready to eat.
—Cyndy Gerken, Naples, FL

PREP: 25 MIN. • **COOK:** 3 HOURS
MAKES: 12 SERVINGS

- 2 boneless skinless turkey breast halves (2 to 3 lbs. each)
- ½ tsp. salt
- ½ tsp. pepper
- 3 fresh thyme sprigs
- 2 Tbsp. butter
- 1 cup whole-berry cranberry sauce
- 1 cup apple cider or juice
- ½ cup chicken stock
- 1 envelope onion soup mix
- 2 Tbsp. maple syrup
- 1 Tbsp. Worcestershire sauce
- ¼ cup all-purpose flour
- ¼ cup water

1. Place turkey in a 5- or 6-qt. slow cooker; sprinkle with salt and pepper. Add thyme and dot with butter. Combine cranberry sauce, cider, stock, soup mix, syrup and Worcestershire; pour over turkey. Cook, covered, on low for 3-4 hours or until a thermometer inserted in turkey reads at least 165°. Remove turkey and keep warm.

2. Transfer the cooking juices to a large saucepan; discard thyme sprigs. Combine the flour and water until smooth. Bring the cranberry mixture to a boil; gradually stir in flour mixture until smooth. Cook and stir until thickened, about 2 minutes. Slice turkey; serve with cranberry sauce.

5 OZ. COOKED TURKEY WITH ⅓ CUP GRAVY: *259 cal., 4g fat (2g sat. fat), 91mg chol., 537mg sod., 17g carb. (10g sugars, 1g fiber), 36g pro.*

SPICED APPLE CIDER JELLY SHOTS

CRUNCHY BACON-BLUE CHEESE BRUSSELS SPROUTS

This is my family's absolute favorite dish on the holiday table. What's not to love with the mixed aroma of garlic, onions, bacon, and blue cheese floating through your home?
—Rozanne Gooding, Carlsbad, CA

PREP: 15 MIN. • **COOK:** 20 MIN.
MAKES: 6 SERVINGS

- ¼ cup avocado oil
- 3 cups halved fresh Brussels sprouts
- ½ cup sliced red onions
- ½ cup sliced sweet red pepper
- 2 cups fresh or frozen cranberries
- 2 Tbsp. balsamic vinegar
- 1 garlic clove, minced
- ½ cup crumbled blue cheese
- ½ cup crumbled cooked bacon
- ¾ tsp. salt
- ½ tsp. pepper
- ½ cup chopped cashews or pecans

In a large skillet, heat oil over medium heat. Add Brussels sprouts, onions and red pepper; cook and stir until crisp-tender, 8-10 minutes. Add cranberries, vinegar and garlic. Cook just until berries are tender, about 10 minutes. Remove from the heat. Stir in the cheese, bacon, salt and pepper. Sprinkle with cashews. Serve warm.

⅔ **CUP:** *268 cal., 20g fat (5g sat. fat), 11mg chol., 736mg sod., 15g carb. (5g sugars, 4g fiber), 10g pro.*

EASY PEASY BISCUITS

I love that I can make these biscuits and have enough left over to freeze for another meal. They are wonderful with homemade peach preserves.
—Amanda West, Shelbyville, TN

PREP: 25 MIN. • **BAKE:** 10 MIN.
MAKES: 2 DOZEN

- 4 cups all-purpose flour
- 4 Tbsp. baking powder
- 1 Tbsp. sugar
- 1 Tbsp. ground flaxseed
- 1 tsp. sea salt
- 1 cup coconut oil, solid
- 1½ cups 2% milk

EASY PEASY BISCUITS

1. Preheat oven to 450°. In a large bowl, whisk flour, baking powder, sugar, flaxseed and salt. Add coconut oil and cut in with a pastry blender until mixture resembles coarse crumbs. Add the milk; stir just until mixture is moistened.

2. Turn onto a lightly floured surface; knead gently 8-10 times. Pat or roll the dough to a rectangle ½ in. thick; fold dough into thirds (as you would a letter). Pat or roll dough again into a rectangle ½ in. thick; cut with a pizza cutter or knife into 24 biscuits, each about 2½ in. square. Place 1½ in. apart on an ungreased baking sheet. Bake until light brown, 8-10 minutes. Serve warm.

FREEZE OPTION: Freeze the cooled baked biscuits in airtight containers. To use, heat in a preheated 350° oven 15-20 minutes.

1 BISCUIT: *167 cal., 10g fat (8g sat. fat), 1mg chol., 328mg sod., 17g carb. (1g sugars, 1g fiber), 3g pro.*

BUTTERNUT SQUASH MAC & CHEESE

I created this dish after my father had triple bypass surgery. He loves comfort food, and I wanted him to be able to enjoy a rich and tasty dish like mac & cheese without all the fat and butter. It's also a great way to sneak in some veggies for children.
—Megan Schwartz, New York, NY

PREP: 35 MIN. • **BAKE:** 15 MIN.
MAKES: 6 SERVINGS

- 8 oz. uncooked whole wheat elbow macaroni
- 1 medium butternut squash (about 3 lbs.), seeded and cubed
- ¼ cup plain Greek yogurt
- 1 cup fat-free milk
- 1 tsp. salt
- ¼ tsp. pepper
  Dash ground nutmeg
- 1½ cups (6 oz.) shredded sharp cheddar cheese
- ½ cup shredded Parmesan cheese
- ½ cup soft whole wheat bread crumbs

1. Preheat oven to 400°. Cook pasta according to package directions for al dente. Place squash in a large saucepan; add water to cover. Bring to a boil. Cook, covered, 8-10 minutes or until tender.

2. Meanwhile, place yogurt, milk, salt, pepper and nutmeg in a blender. Drain squash and transfer to blender; cover and process until pureed. Return mixture to saucepan; heat through. Stir in cheeses until melted.

3. Drain pasta; add to squash mixture. Toss to coat. Transfer to a greased 8-in. square baking dish. Sprinkle with bread crumbs.

4. Bake, uncovered, until golden brown, 15-20 minutes.

1¼ **CUPS:** *422 cal., 13g fat (7g sat. fat), 36mg chol., 750mg sod., 60g carb. (10g sugars, 12g fiber), 20g pro.*

Adventurous

You're bold, daring and not afraid to shake things up—including the menu.
Make the meal as vibrant as you are and give this Turkey Day a twist.

**GRILLED HULI HULI
TURKEY DRUMSTICKS**

**BUTTERNUT SQUASH
PANZANELLA SALAD**

**SPARKLING
APPLE PIE
ON THE ROCKS**

BOHEMIAN COLLARDS

OLIVE OIL MASHED POTATOES WITH PANCETTA

BOHEMIAN COLLARDS

2. Meanwhile, in a large skillet, cook the pancetta in 1 Tbsp. oil over medium heat until crisp. Add garlic; cook for 1 minutes longer. Remove from the heat.

3. Drain potatoes; transfer to a large bowl. Mash potatoes with remaining oil. Stir in parsley, pancetta mixture, salt and pepper.

⅔ CUP: 206 cal., 11g fat (2g sat. fat), 7mg chol., 313mg sod., 23g carb. (2g sugars, 2g fiber), 4g pro. **Diabetic exchanges:** *2 fat, 1½ starch.*

GRILLED HULI HULI TURKEY DRUMSTICKS

I'm never one to do things traditionally, so when it came time to host Thanksgiving, I went in a completely tropical direction.
—*Jacyn Siebert, San Francisco, CA*

PREP: 15 MIN. + MARINATING
GRILL: 40 MIN. + STANDING
MAKES: 12 SERVINGS

- 1 cup packed brown sugar
- ¾ cup ketchup
- ¾ cup reduced-sodium soy sauce
- ⅓ cup sherry or chicken broth
- 1 Tbsp. minced fresh gingerroot
- 1 Tbsp. minced garlic
- 6 turkey drumsticks (1½ lbs. each)
- 1 bunch green onions, chopped

1. Mix the first 6 ingredients. Reserve 1⅓ cups for basting; cover and refrigerate. Add drumsticks to the remaining mixture. Refrigerate 8 hours or overnight.

2. Drain turkey, discarding marinade. Place turkey on greased grill rack. Grill, covered, over indirect medium heat, 40-45 minutes or until a thermometer reads 175°. Turn the drumsticks occasionally throughout cooking; during the last 10 minutes baste often with reserved marinade. Let stand 15 minutes; garnish with green onions.

8 OZ. COOKED TURKEY: 486 cal., 20g fat (6g sat. fat), 171mg chol., 671mg sod., 16g carb. (15g sugars, 0 fiber), 57g pro.

BOHEMIAN COLLARDS

I've added unconventional ingredients to these collards that make them exquisite on the palate and on the plate.
—*Ally Phillips, Murrells Inlet, SC*

PREP: 20 MIN. • **COOK:** 35 MIN.
MAKES: 8 SERVINGS

- 1 large bunch collard greens (about 2 lbs.)
- 6 bacon strips, chopped
- 1 Tbsp. olive oil
- ½ cup chicken broth
- 1½ cups frozen corn (about 7½ oz.)
- 1 cup chopped sweet red pepper
- ½ tsp. salt
- ¼ tsp. crushed red pepper flakes
- ¼ tsp. pepper

1. Trim thick stems from collard greens; coarsely chop leaves. In a Dutch oven, cook bacon over medium heat until crisp, stirring occasionally. Remove with a slotted spoon; drain on paper towels. Cook and stir collard greens in bacon drippings and oil just until coated. Add broth; bring to a boil. Reduce heat; simmer, covered, until greens are very tender, 25-30 minutes.

2. Add corn, red pepper, salt, pepper flakes and pepper. Cook and stir until heated through. Sprinkle with bacon.

½ CUP: 168 cal., 11g fat (3g sat. fat), 14mg chol., 369mg sod., 13g carb. (2g sugars, 5g fiber), 7g pro. **Diabetic exchanges:** *2 fat, 1 starch.*

OLIVE OIL MASHED POTATOES WITH PANCETTA

Classic American mashed potatoes take a trip to Italy with olive oil, garlic and pancetta.
—*Bryan Kennedy, Kaneohe, HI*

TAKES: 20 MIN. • **COOK:** 20 MIN.
MAKES: 8 SERVINGS

- 3 lbs. Yukon Gold potatoes, peeled and cubed
- 3 slices pancetta or bacon, chopped
- 1 Tbsp. plus ¼ cup olive oil, divided
- 4 garlic cloves, minced
- ⅓ cup minced fresh parsley
- ½ tsp. salt
- ½ tsp. pepper

1. Place potatoes in a large saucepan and cover with water. Bring to a boil. Reduce the heat; cover and simmer until tender, 15-20 minutes.

HOW-TO

Easy Artistry

Cutting green onions thinly on the diagonal is an easy way to give them a delicate look, especially attractive in Asian dishes.

BUTTERNUT SQUASH PANZANELLA SALAD

This colorful salad is easy to make—and it's even easier if you use precut chunks of butternut squash. You can use pecans in place of the almonds or watercress instead of the arugula or spinach.
—Nancy Buchanan, Costa Mesa, CA

PREP: 25 MIN. • **BAKE:** 20 MIN.
MAKES: 8 SERVINGS

- 6 cups cubed day-old French bread (bite-sized cubes)
- 3 Tbsp. olive oil
- ½ tsp. chili powder
- ¼ tsp. salt

SALAD

- 4 cups cubed peeled butternut squash (1½-in. cubes)
- 1½ cups sliced fresh mushrooms
- ½ cup olive oil, divided
- ½ tsp. salt, divided
- ½ tsp. pepper, divided
- 6 cups fresh arugula or fresh baby spinach
- 6 Tbsp. sherry vinegar
- 3 shallots, thinly sliced
- ½ cup salted roasted almonds
- 6 Tbsp. crumbled goat cheese

1. Preheat oven to 400°. Toss bread cubes with oil, chili powder and salt. Spread evenly in an ungreased 15x10x1-in. baking pan. Bake until golden brown, about 5 minutes. Transfer to a large bowl; cool. In another large bowl, combine squash and mushrooms. Add 2 Tbsp. oil, ¼ tsp. salt and ¼ tsp. pepper; toss to coat. Transfer to a greased 15x10x1-in. baking pan. Roast until tender, 20-25 minutes, stirring occasionally.
2. Add the arugula and squash mixture to the toasted bread. In a small bowl, whisk together vinegar, shallots and remaining oil, salt and pepper. Drizzle over salad; toss gently to combine. Top with almonds and goat cheese. Serve immediately.
¾ **CUP:** 361 cal., 26g fat (4g sat. fat), 7mg chol., 435mg sod., 29g carb. (5g sugars, 4g fiber), 7g pro.

SPARKLING APPLE PIE ON THE ROCKS

Here is the perfect fall cocktail. Apple cider mixed with a cinnamon caramel apple syrup and topped with bubbly—it's the best holiday drink ever!
—Becky Hardin, St. Peters, MO

PREP: 30 MIN. + COOLING
MAKES: 8 SERVINGS

- 3 cups apple cider or juice, chilled, divided
- 1 cup caramel ice cream topping, plus additional for dipping
- 2 cinnamon sticks (3 in.)
- 1 tsp. ground cinnamon
  Gold sprinkles
  Ice cubes
- 1 bottle (750 milliliters) brut champagne, chilled

Apple slices and additional cinnamon sticks, optional

1. In a small saucepan, bring 1 cup cider, 1 cup caramel topping, cinnamon sticks and cinnamon to a boil. Reduce heat; simmer until the liquid is reduced to 1 cup, about 15 minutes. Cool mixture slightly; discard the cinnamon sticks.
2. Place sprinkles and additional caramel topping in separate shallow bowls. Hold each glass upside down and dip rim in caramel topping, then dip in sprinkles.
3. To serve, fill glasses with ice. Add 2 Tbsp. cooled cinnamon syrup to each; top with remaining cider and champagne. If desired, garnish with apple slices and additional cinnamon sticks.
⅔ **CUP:** 198 cal., 0 fat (0 sat. fat), 0 chol., 149mg sod., 36g carb. (33g sugars, 0 fiber), 1g pro.

SPARKLING APPLE
PIE ON THE ROCKS

Christmas Morning Magic

A leisurely brunch is the best present. Check it off your list ahead of time.

FESTIVE CRANBERRY
FRUIT SALAD

THREE-CHEESE QUICHE

**CHRISTMAS MORNING
SWEET ROLLS**

**CHRISTMAS MORNING
SWEET ROLLS**

CHRISTMAS MORNING
SWEET ROLLS

*These make-ahead rolls have been a holiday
tradition for years. Eggnog in the frosting
makes them an extra special treat to serve
on Christmas morning.*
—Kimberly Williams, Brownsburg, IN

PREP: 45 MIN. + CHILLING • **BAKE:** 20 MIN.
MAKES: 1 DOZEN

1   pkg. (¼ oz.) active dry yeast
1   cup warm water (110° to 115°)
½   cup sugar
1   tsp. salt
4   to 4½ cups all-purpose flour
¼   cup canola oil
1   large egg, room temperature

FILLING
⅓   cup sugar
1½ tsp. ground cinnamon
¼   tsp. ground nutmeg
3   Tbsp. butter, softened

FROSTING
2½ cups confectioners' sugar
5   Tbsp. butter, softened
½   tsp. ground cinnamon
½   tsp. vanilla extract
2   to 3 Tbsp. eggnog

1. In a small bowl, dissolve yeast in warm
water. In a large bowl, combine sugar, salt,
1 cup flour, oil, egg and the yeast mixture;
beat on medium speed until smooth. Stir in
enough remaining flour to form a soft
dough (dough will be sticky).
2. Do not knead. Place in a greased bowl,
turning once to grease the top. Cover with
plastic wrap and refrigerate overnight.
3. For filling, in a small bowl, mix sugar,
cinnamon and nutmeg. Punch down dough;
turn onto a lightly floured surface. Roll into
a 18x8-in. rectangle. Spread with butter to
within ½ in. of edges; sprinkle with sugar
mixture. Roll up jelly-roll style, starting with
a long side; pinch seam to seal. Cut into
12 slices.

4. Place in a greased 13x9-in. baking pan,
cut side down. Cover with a kitchen towel;
let rise in a warm place until doubled, about
45 minutes.
5. Preheat oven to 350°. Bake until golden
brown, 20-25 minutes. Place on a wire rack
to cool slightly. Beat confectioners' sugar,
butter, cinnamon, vanilla and enough of the
eggnog to reach the desired spreading
consistency; spread over warm rolls.
1 ROLL: *424 cal., 13g fat (5g sat. fat), 37mg
chol., 267mg sod., 72g carb. (39g sugars, 2g
fiber), 5g pro.*

TEST KITCHEN TIP

Give the frosting a little holiday
cheer by adding ½ tsp. rum extract.

THREE-CHEESE QUICHE

Try eggs and cheese at their best. Guests often remark about how tall, light and fluffy this crustless entree is. I think you'll love it.
—Judy Reagan, Hannibal, MO

PREP: 15 MIN. • **BAKE:** 45 MIN. + STANDING
MAKES: 6 SERVINGS

- 7 large eggs
- 5 large egg yolks
- 1 cup heavy whipping cream
- 1 cup half-and-half cream
- 1 cup shredded part-skim mozzarella cheese
- ¾ cup shredded sharp cheddar cheese, divided
- ½ cup shredded Swiss cheese
- 2 Tbsp. finely chopped oil-packed sun-dried tomatoes
- 1½ tsp. salt-free seasoning blend
- ¼ tsp. dried basil

1. Preheat oven to 350°. In a large bowl, combine eggs, egg yolks, whipping cream, half-and-half, mozzarella cheese, ½ cup cheddar cheese, Swiss cheese, tomatoes, seasoning blend and basil; pour into a greased 9-in. deep-dish pie plate. Sprinkle with remaining cheddar cheese.

2. Bake until a knife inserted in the center comes out clean, 45-50 minutes. Let stand 10 minutes before cutting.

FREEZE OPTION: Securely wrap individual portions of cooled quiche in plastic and foil; freeze. To use, partially thaw in refrigerator overnight. Remove from the refrigerator 30 minutes before baking. Preheat oven to 350°. Unwrap quiche; reheat in oven until heated through and a thermometer inserted in center reads 165°.

1 PIECE: *449 cal., 37g fat (21g sat. fat), 524mg chol., 316mg sod., 5g carb. (3g sugars, 0 fiber), 22g pro.*

FESTIVE CRANBERRY FRUIT SALAD

This fruit salad goes together quickly and is a tradition on my Christmas table.
—Rousheen Arel Wolf, Delta Junction, AK

TAKES: 25 MIN. • **MAKES:** 14 SERVINGS

- 1 pkg. (12 oz.) fresh or frozen cranberries
- ¾ cup water
- ½ cup sugar
- 5 medium apples, diced
- 2 medium firm bananas, sliced
- 1½ cups fresh or frozen blueberries, thawed
- 1 can (11 oz.) mandarin oranges, undrained
- 1 cup fresh or frozen raspberries, thawed
- ¾ cup fresh strawberries, halved

1. In a large saucepan, combine the cranberries, water and sugar. Cook and stir over medium heat until berries pop, about 15 minutes. Remove from the heat; cool slightly.

2. In a large bowl, combine the remaining ingredients. Add cranberry mixture; stir gently. Refrigerate until serving.

¾ CUP: *105 cal., 0 fat (0 sat. fat), 0 chol., 2mg sod., 27g carb. (21g sugars, 4g fiber), 1g pro.*

FESTIVE CRANBERRY FRUIT SALAD

MAKE-AHEAD EGGS
BENEDICT TOAST CUPS

**MONTE CRISTO
CASSEROLE WITH
RASPBERRY SAUCE**

❄ MAKE-AHEAD EGGS BENEDICT TOAST CUPS

When I was growing up, we had a family tradition of having eggs Benedict with champagne and orange juice for our Christmas breakfast. But now that I'm cooking, a fussy breakfast isn't my style. So I came up with a dish with the flavors of traditional eggs Benedict I could make ahead of time that also freezes well.
—Lyndsay Wells, Ladysmith, BC

PREP: 30 MIN. • **BAKE:** 10 MIN.
MAKES: 1 DOZEN

- 6   English muffins, split
- 1   envelope hollandaise sauce mix
- 12 slices Canadian bacon, quartered
- 1   tsp. pepper
- 1   Tbsp. olive oil
- 6   large eggs
- 1   Tbsp. butter

1. Preheat oven to 375°. Flatten muffin halves with a rolling pin; press into greased muffin cups. Bake until lightly browned, about 10 minutes.
2. Meanwhile, prepare hollandaise sauce according to package directions; cool slightly. Sprinkle bacon with pepper. In a large skillet, cook bacon in oil over medium heat until partially cooked but not crisp. Remove to paper towels to drain. Divide bacon among the muffin cups. Wipe the skillet clean.
3. Whisk the eggs and ½ cup of cooled hollandaise sauce until blended. In the same skillet, heat butter over medium heat. Pour in egg mixture; cook and stir until eggs are thickened and no liquid egg remains. Divide egg mixture among muffin cups; top with the remaining hollandaise sauce. Bake until heated through, 8-10 minutes.
OVERNIGHT OPTION: Refrigerate unbaked cups, covered, overnight. Bake until golden brown, 10-12 minutes.
FREEZE OPTION: Cover and freeze unbaked cups in muffin cups until firm. Transfer to an airtight container; return to freezer. To use, bake the cups in a muffin tin as directed; increase the time to 25-30 minutes. Cover the toast cups loosely with foil if needed to prevent overbrowning.
1 TOAST CUP: 199 cal., 11g fat (5g sat. fat), 114mg chol., 495mg sod., 15g carb. (2g sugars, 1g fiber), 9g pro.

MONTE CRISTO CASSEROLE WITH RASPBERRY SAUCE

My husband is a fan of the ham and cheese sandwich known as the Monte Cristo, so I came up with a baked casserole based on the classic recipe. It makes a terrific brunch dish.
—Mary Steiner, Parkville, MD

PREP: 20 MIN. + CHILLING
BAKE: 30 MIN. + STANDING
MAKES: 10 SERVINGS (1¾ CUPS SAUCE)

- 1   loaf (1 lb.) French bread, cut into 20 slices
- 2   Tbsp. Dijon mustard
- ½   lb. sliced deli ham
- ½   lb. sliced Swiss cheese
- ½   lb. sliced deli turkey
- 6   large eggs
- 1½   cups whole milk
- 2   tsp. sugar
- 2   tsp. vanilla extract

TOPPING
- ½   cup packed brown sugar
- ¼   cup butter, softened
- ½   tsp. ground cinnamon

RASPBERRY SAUCE
- ⅓   cup sugar
- 1   Tbsp. cornstarch
- ¼   cup cold water
- ¼   cup lemon juice
- ¼   cup maple syrup
- 2   cups fresh or frozen raspberries

1. Line a greased 13x9-in. baking dish with half of the bread. Spread mustard over bread. Layer with ham, cheese, turkey and remaining bread (dish will be full).
2. In a large bowl, whisk eggs, milk, sugar and vanilla; pour over top. Refrigerate, covered, overnight.
3. Preheat oven to 375°. Remove casserole from refrigerator while oven heats. In a small bowl, mix the topping ingredients; sprinkle over casserole. Bake, uncovered, 30-40 minutes or until golden brown.
4. Meanwhile, in a small saucepan, combine sugar and cornstarch. Stir in water, lemon juice and maple syrup until smooth. Add the raspberries. Bring to a boil; cook and stir sauce until thickened, about 2 minutes. Cool slightly.
5. Let casserole stand 10 minutes before cutting. Serve with sauce.
1 SERVING WITH ABOUT 3 TBSP. SAUCE: 476 cal., 17g fat (8g sat. fat), 167mg chol., 906mg sod., 55g carb. (29g sugars, 3g fiber), 25g pro.

Sweets for Santa

Fill your cookie tray with sugar and spice and everything nice.

CRYSTALLIZED GINGERBREAD CHOCOLATE CHIP COOKIES

CRYSTALLIZED GINGERBREAD CHOCOLATE CHIP COOKIES

This recipe is the best of two worlds—gingerbread and chocolate chip cookies. Since they're combined you don't have to choose between them.
—Colleen Delawder, Herndon, VA

PREP: 30 MIN. + CHILLING
BAKE: 10 MIN./BATCH • **MAKES:** 9 DOZEN

- 1½ cups unsalted butter, softened
- 1 cup packed brown sugar
- ½ cup sugar
- 2 large eggs, room temperature
- ½ cup molasses
- 3 tsp. vanilla extract
- 4 cups all-purpose flour
- 4 tsp. baking soda
- 2 tsp. ground ginger
- 2 tsp. ground cinnamon
- ¾ tsp. salt
- ½ tsp. pepper
- 1 pkg. (10 oz.) miniature semisweet chocolate chips
- ⅓ cup finely chopped crystallized ginger
  Additional sugar

1. In a large bowl, cream butter and sugars until light and fluffy. Beat in eggs, molasses and vanilla. In another bowl, whisk flour, baking soda, ground ginger, cinnamon, salt and pepper; gradually beat into creamed mixture. Stir in the chocolate chips and crystallized ginger. Refrigerate, covered, until firm enough to shape, at least 2 hours.
2. Preheat the oven to 350°. Shape level tablespoonfuls of dough into balls; roll in additional sugar. Place balls 2 in. apart on parchment-lined baking sheets. Bake until until set and edges begin to brown, about 8-10 minutes. Cool cookies on the pans 2 minutes. Remove to wire racks to cool. Store in airtight containers.
1 COOKIE: *69 cal., 3g fat (2g sat. fat), 10mg chol., 64mg sod., 10g carb. (6g sugars, 0 fiber), 1g pro.*

> **TEST KITCHEN TIP**
> These cookies will spread some, but not too much. You can easily fit 12 cookies on each baking sheet.

PINEAPPLE COCONUT TASSIES

PINEAPPLE COCONUT TASSIES

These cookies may sound and look fancy, but they're rather easy to make Their simplicity makes them an ideal choice for baking with children. My granddaughter enjoys helping me measure the ingredients. Children also can help shape the dough into balls, and then you can finish them together.
—Connie Shuff, York, PA

PREP: 40 MIN.
BAKE: 20 MIN./BATCH + COOLING
MAKES: 40 COOKIES

- 1 cup unsalted butter, softened
- ½ cup confectioners' sugar
- 1 tsp. vanilla extract
- 2 cups cake flour
- 2 Tbsp. cornstarch
- ½ tsp. salt

FILLING
- 1½ cups sweetened shredded coconut
- 1 cup pineapple ice cream topping
- ½ cup sugar
- ¼ cup chopped macadamia nuts
- 1 large egg, room temperature
- 2 tsp. cornstarch

ICING
- ½ cup confectioners' sugar
- 1 Tbsp. 2% milk
- ½ tsp. coconut extract

1. Preheat oven to 350°. Cream butter and confectioners' sugar until light and fluffy. Beat in vanilla. In another bowl, whisk flour, cornstarch and salt; gradually beat into creamed mixture. Shape dough into 1-in. balls; press evenly onto bottom and up the sides of 40 greased and floured mini muffin cups.
2. In a small bowl, mix coconut, ice cream topping, sugar, macadamia nuts, egg and cornstarch. Place 1 Tbsp. in each cup. Bake until edges are golden and filling is puffed, 20-25 minutes. Cool in pans 5-10 minutes. Carefully remove to wire racks to cool.
3. In a small bowl, combine confectioners' sugar, milk and coconut extract. Drizzle over cookies; let dry completely.
1 COOKIE: *136 cal., 7g fat (4g sat. fat), 17mg chol., 48mg sod., 19g carb. (9g sugars, 0 fiber), 1g pro.*

SEA SALT MINT WHITE MOCHA COOKIES

This recipe came from my mom's Grandma Alice, who taught her how to bake. Our Grandma Alice always had a fresh plate of warm cookies on her counter. I learned some of her recipes by heart as a child, and I've been making this one in particular since high school. It tastes like Christmas.

—Kristin Bowers, Rancho Palos Verdes, CA

PREP: 20 MIN. • **BAKE:** 15 MIN./BATCH
MAKES: 26 COOKIES

1 cup butter-flavored shortening
¾ cup sugar
¾ cup packed brown sugar
2 large eggs, room temperature
1 tsp. mint extract
1½ cups all-purpose flour
1 Tbsp. instant espresso powder
1 tsp. sea salt
1 tsp. baking soda
2 cups old-fashioned oats
1 pkg. (10 to 12 oz.) white baking chips

1. Preheat oven to 350°. In a large bowl, cream shortening and sugars until light and fluffy. Beat in eggs and extract. In another bowl, whisk flour, espresso powder, salt and baking soda; gradually beat into creamed mixture. Stir in oats and white chips.

2. Drop dough by scant ¼ cupfuls 2 in. apart onto parchment-lined baking sheets. Bake until edges begin to brown, 12-15 minutes. Cool on pans 5 minutes. Remove to wire racks to cool. Store in an airtight container.

1 COOKIE: *229 cal., 12g fat (4g sat. fat), 17mg chol., 140mg sod., 28g carb. (19g sugars, 1g fiber), 3g pro.*

SEA SALT MINT WHITE MOCHA COOKIES

CINNAMON ROLL MACARONS

These macarons are a winter/fall staple for me. Inspired by the classic cinnamon roll, they are a delicious treat for a cold or snowy day. They pair well with a mug of tea and can be eaten as a dessert or just a snack. Other fillings would taste great, too—custard, mousse, ganache, or a different buttercream.
—Elizabeth Ding, El Cerrito, CA

PREP: 45 MIN • **BAKE:** 10 MIN./BATCH
MAKES: 5 DOZEN

- 4 large egg whites
- 1½ cups almond flour
- 1¼ cups confectioners' sugar
- ½ tsp. ground cinnamon
- ¾ cup sugar

FILLING
- 4 oz. cream cheese, softened
- 3 Tbsp. butter, softened
- 1 tsp. vanilla extract
- 1½ cups confectioners' sugar
  Additional ground cinnamon

1. Place the egg whites in a small bowl; let stand at room temperature for 30 minutes. Sift almond flour, confectioners' sugar and cinnamon together twice.
2. Preheat oven to 325°. Beat the egg whites on medium speed until soft peaks form. Gradually add the sugar, 1 Tbsp. at a time, beating on high until stiff peaks form. Fold in almond flour mixture.
3. Cut a small hole in a corner of a food-safe plastic bag. Pipe 1-in.-diameter cookies 2 in. apart onto parchment-lined baking sheets. Bake until lightly browned and firm to the touch, 9-12 minutes. Transfer cookies on the parchment paper to wire racks; cool cookies completely.
4. For filling, in a small bowl, beat cream cheese and butter until creamy. Beat in vanilla. Gradually beat in confectioners' sugar until fluffy. Refrigerate until mixture firms to desired spreading consistency, about 10 minutes.
5. Spread about ¼ tsp. filling onto the bottom of each of half of the cookies; top with the remaining cookies. Sprinkle with additional cinnamon. Store macarons in airtight containers in the refrigerator.
1 SANDWICH COOKIE: *60 cal., 3g fat (1g sat. fat), 3mg chol., 15mg sod., 9g carb. (8g sugars, 0 fiber), 1g pro.*

CINNAMON ROLL MACARONS

JAMAICAN CHOCOLATE COOKIES WITH CARAMEL CREME

I made these for an office party cookie contest—and not a crumb was left on the platter. Sweet potatoes are the secret ingredient. Canned sweet potatoes work, too, if you're short on time.
—Noelle Myers, Grand Forks, ND

PREP: 45 MIN. + STANDING
BAKE: 10 MIN./BATCH + COOLING
MAKES: ABOUT 2½ DOZEN

- 1 pkg. (11½ oz.) semisweet chocolate chunks, divided
- ½ cup butter, softened
- ½ cup confectioners' sugar
- ½ cup mashed sweet potatoes
- 1 tsp. minced fresh gingerroot
- ½ tsp. vanilla extract
- 1¼ cups all-purpose flour
- ¼ cup cornstarch
- 2 Tbsp. baking cocoa
- 1½ tsp. baking powder
- ¼ tsp. baking soda
- ¼ tsp. plus ⅛ tsp. salt, divided
- ⅔ cup whipped cream cheese
- ⅓ cup dulce de leche
- 2 Tbsp. sweetened condensed milk
- ⅛ tsp. ground cinnamon
- ⅛ tsp. ground allspice

1. Preheat oven to 375°. In a microwave, melt ⅔ cup chocolate chunks; stir until smooth. Cool slightly. In a large bowl, cream butter and confectioners' sugar until light and fluffy. Beat in sweet potatoes, cooled chocolate, ginger and vanilla. In another bowl, whisk flour, cornstarch, baking cocoa, baking powder, baking soda and ¼ tsp. salt; gradually beat into creamed mixture.
2. Shape dough into ¾-in. balls; place 2½ in. apart on parchment-lined baking sheets. Flatten slightly with bottom of a glass dipped in confectioners' sugar. Bake until edges are firm, 8-10 minutes. Remove from pans to wire racks to cool completely.
3. Meanwhile, whisk the cream cheese, dulce de leche, sweetened condensed milk, cinnamon, allspice and remaining salt until smooth. Spread filling on bottoms of half of the cookies; cover with remaining cookies.
4. For the chocolate coating, microwave remaining chocolate chunks; stir until smooth. Dip cookies halfway into melted chocolate; let stand until set. Store between pieces of waxed paper in an airtight container in the refrigerator.
1 SANDWICH COOKIE: *134 cal., 7g fat (5g sat. fat), 12mg chol., 103mg sod., 17g carb. (10g sugars, 1g fiber), 2g pro.*

BAKLAVA THUMBPRINT COOKIES

SPICED EGGNOG RUM COOKIES

I created a new holiday cookie recipe the time I had a lot of eggnog on hand. Its flavor is subtle, but it transforms the usual sugar cookies into something special.
—Mark Banick, Salem, OR

PREP: 25 MIN. + CHILLING
BAKE: 10 MIN./BATCH + COOLING
MAKES: 4 DOZEN

- ¾ cup butter, softened
- 1¼ cups sugar
- 1 large egg, room temperature
- 1 cup eggnog, divided
- 1¾ tsp. rum extract, divided
- 3½ cups all-purpose flour
- 1 tsp. baking powder
- ½ tsp. ground cinnamon
- ½ tsp. ground nutmeg
- ¼ tsp. salt
- ¼ tsp. ground ginger
- ¼ tsp. ground allspice
- 3 cups confectioners' sugar
  Colored sugar or sprinkles

1. In a large bowl, cream butter and sugar until light and fluffy. Beat in egg, ⅓ cup eggnog and 1 tsp. extract. In another bowl, whisk flour, baking powder, cinnamon, nutmeg, salt, ginger and allspice; gradually beat into creamed mixture.
2. Divide dough in half and shape each portion into a disk; cover and refrigerate until firm enough to roll, about 30 minutes.
3. Preheat oven to 375°. On a lightly floured surface, roll each portion of the dough to ¼-in. thickness. Cut with a floured 3¼-in. star-shaped cookie cutter. Place 1 in. apart on parchment paper-lined baking sheets.
4. Bake until cookie edges begin to brown, 8-10 minutes. Cool on pans 1 minute. Remove to wire racks to cool completely. For glaze, mix the confectioners' sugar, remaining extract and enough remaining eggnog to reach a drizzling consistency; drizzle over cookies. Decorate as desired.
1 COOKIE: *114 cal., 3g fat (2g sat. fat), 14mg chol., 50mg sod., 20g carb. (13g sugars, 0 fiber), 1g pro.*

BAKLAVA THUMBPRINT COOKIES

The topping on my sister-in-law's peach cobbler was so delicious that I asked for the recipe, then decided to use that to top a cookie I developed with the flavors of baklava. My adult son tried one and immediately ate two more—and that's unusual for him! It's a good recipe to mix up the night before and bake fresh the next day for company.
—Sharon Eshelman, Harrington, DE

PREP: 30 MIN. + CHILLING
BAKE: 15 MIN./BATCH • **MAKES:** 2 DOZEN

- 1 cup sugar
- ½ cup butter, softened
- 2 large eggs, room temperature
- 1 tsp. almond extract
- 1 tsp. vanilla extract
- 2¼ cups all-purpose flour
- 1 tsp. baking powder
- ½ tsp. salt

TOPPING
- 3 Tbsp. sugar
- 2 tsp. ground cinnamon
- ½ cup honey
- ¾ cup chopped walnuts

1. In a large bowl, cream sugar and butter until blended. Beat in eggs, one at a time, and extracts. In another bowl, whisk flour, baking powder and salt; gradually beat into creamed mixture. Wrap dough in plastic; refrigerate until firm enough to form into balls, about 30 minutes.
2. Preheat oven to 375°. For topping, combine sugar and cinnamon; set aside. Shape dough into 1-in. balls; refrigerate again if dough becomes too warm. Place 2½ in. apart on parchment-lined baking sheets. Bake 8 minutes. Press a deep indentation in center of each cookie with the back of a rounded teaspoon. Fill each with honey and walnuts; sprinkle with cinnamon sugar. Return to oven and bake until edges begin to brown, 7-9 minutes longer. Cool on pans 1 minute. Remove cookies to wire racks to cool. Store in an airtight container.
1 COOKIE: *168 cal., 7g fat (3g sat. fat), 26mg chol., 106mg sod., 25g carb. (16g sugars, 1g fiber), 2g pro.*

CHOCOLATE LEBKUCHEN CHERRY BALLS

Here's my twist on the traditional German holiday lebkuchen—with a surprise inside. Maraschino cherries add a sweet and unexpected punch to the holiday spice of gingersnaps.
—Arlene Erlbach, Morton Grove, IL

PREP: 45 MIN. + CHILLING • **MAKES:** 5 DOZEN

- 40 gingersnap cookies
- 1 pkg. (8 oz.) cream cheese, softened
- 1½ cups semisweet chocolate chips, divided
- 1¼ cups sliced almonds, divided
- 2 Tbsp. chopped candied orange zest
- 1 tsp. almond extract
- 60 maraschino cherries, stems removed

1. Place gingersnaps, cream cheese, ½ cup chocolate chips, ½ cup almonds, orange zest and extract in a food processor; process until combined. Refrigerate until firm enough to form into balls. Pat cherries dry with paper towels. Wrap each cherry with a rounded tablespoonful of cream cheese mixture; shape into a ball. Freeze until firm, about 20 minutes.

2. Chop remaining sliced almonds; set aside. In a double boiler, melt remaining chocolate chips; stir until smooth. Dip cherry balls in chocolate; allow excess to drip off. Sprinkle the balls with almonds. Place on waxed paper. Refrigerate until set, about 1 hour.

1 BALL: *76 cal., 4g fat (2g sat. fat), 4mg chol., 37mg sod., 10g carb. (7g sugars, 1g fiber), 1g pro.*

GINGER S'MORES

I've spent a few years now perfecting this recipe to get a soft, flavorful cookie while balancing the marshmallow and chocolate so they don't overpower the cookie. I think I finally got it! Recently I added orange zest—it really complements the other flavors.
—Lynsay Benson, Minnetonka, MN

PREP: 30 MIN. + CHILLING
BAKE: 10 MIN./BATCH + COOLING
MAKES: 2 DOZEN

- 1 cup butter, softened
- ¼ cup shortening
- 1 cup packed brown sugar
- ½ cup sugar
- 2 large eggs, room temperature
- 2 Tbsp. molasses
- 3 cups all-purpose flour
- 3 Tbsp. instant vanilla pudding mix
- 1 tsp. baking soda
- ¾ tsp. ground ginger
- ¾ tsp. ground cinnamon
- ½ tsp. salt
- ½ tsp. ground allspice
- ¼ tsp. pepper
- 1 cup milk chocolate chips

FILLING
- 1 cup confectioners' sugar
- 2 cups frozen whipped topping, thawed
- ⅔ cup marshmallow creme
- ½ Tbsp. 2% milk

1. In a large bowl, cream butter, shortening and sugars until light and fluffy. Beat in the eggs and molasses. In another bowl, whisk the flour, pudding mix, baking soda, ginger, cinnamon, salt, allspice and pepper; add gradually and beat into creamed mixture. Divide dough in half and shape each portion into a disk; wrap in plastic wrap. Refrigerate 30 minutes or until firm enough to roll.

2. Preheat oven to 350°. On a lightly floured surface, roll each portion of the dough to ⅛-in. thickness. Cut with a floured 1¾-in. square-shaped cookie cutter. Place the cookies 1 in. apart on parchment-lined baking sheets.

3. Bake until set, 12-14 minutes. Cool on pans 2 minutes. Remove to wire racks to cool completely. In a microwave, melt chocolate chips; stir until smooth. Spread 1 tsp. melted chocolate on the bottom of half of the cookies. Let stand until set.

4. Meanwhile, beat filling ingredients until blended. Spread 1 Tbsp. over chocolate; cover with remaining cookies. Store in the refrigerator in airtight container.

1 SANDWICH COOKIE: *294 cal., 13g fat (8g sat. fat), 37mg chol., 187mg sod., 40g carb. (27g sugars, 1g fiber), 3g pro.*

CHOCOLATE LEBKUCHEN CHERRY BALLS

CARROT SPICE THUMBPRINT COOKIES

Carrot cake is a family favorite, and these delicious cookies taste just like it, with all the ingredients you'd expect—grated carrots, toasted walnuts, cinnamon and cloves—plus dried cranberries. And they're topped off with a rich cream cheese frosting. Who could resist? It's like eating a piece of carrot cake without a fork!
—Susan Bickta, Kutztown, PA

PREP: 30 MIN.
BAKE: 10 MIN./BATCH + COOLING
MAKES: 5 DOZEN

- 1 cup margarine, softened
- 1 cup sugar
- ½ cup packed brown sugar
- 2 large eggs, room temperature
- 2 tsp. vanilla extract
- 3 cups all-purpose flour
- 1½ tsp. ground cinnamon
- 1 tsp. baking powder
- ¾ tsp. salt
- ½ tsp. baking soda
- ⅛ tsp. ground cloves
- 1½ cups shredded carrots
- ⅔ cup chopped walnuts, toasted
- ½ cup dried cranberries

FROSTING
- ½ cup butter, softened
- 4 oz. cream cheese, softened
- 2 cups confectioners' sugar
- 1 tsp. vanilla extract
  Additional confectioners' sugar

1. Preheat oven to 375°. In a large bowl, cream margarine and sugars until light and fluffy. Beat in eggs and vanilla. In another bowl, whisk the flour, cinnamon, baking powder, salt, baking soda and cloves; gradually beat into creamed mixture. Stir in carrots, walnuts and cranberries.
2. Drop dough by rounded tablespoonfuls 2 in. apart onto parchment-lined baking sheets. Press a deep indentation in center of each with the back of a ½-tsp. measure.
3. Bake until cookie edges begin brown, 10-12 minutes. Reshape indentations as needed. Cool on pans 5 minutes. Remove to wire racks to cool completely.
4. For frosting, beat butter, cream cheese, confectioners' sugar and vanilla until blended. To serve, fill each cookie with about 1½ tsp. frosting; sprinkle with additional confectioners' sugar. Store leftover filled cookies in refrigerator.

**CARROT SPICE
THUMBPRINT COOKIES**

1 COOKIE: *167 cal., 9g fat (3g sat. fat), 17mg chol., 146mg sod., 21g carb. (14g sugars, 1g fiber), 2g pro.*

COCONUT, LIME & PISTACHIO COOKIES

These delightful cookies look like Christmas but taste like summer.
—Barbara Crusan, Pass Christian, MS

PREP: 30 MIN. • **BAKE:** 10 MIN./BATCH
MAKES: ABOUT 5½ DOZEN

- 1 cup shortening
- 1½ cups sugar
- 2 large eggs, room temperature
- 4 tsp. lime juice
- 1¼ cups all-purpose flour
- 1 pkg. (3.4 oz.) instant coconut cream pudding mix
- 1½ tsp. baking soda
- ½ tsp. baking powder
- 1 cup pistachios, chopped
- 1 cup dried cranberries
- 1 large egg white, room temperature
- 1 cup sweetened shredded coconut
- 1½ tsp. grated lime zest

1. Preheat oven to 375°. In a large bowl, cream shortening and sugar until light and fluffy. Beat in the eggs and lime juice. In another bowl, whisk flour, pudding mix, baking soda and baking powder; gradually beat into creamed mixture. Stir in the pistachios and dried cranberries. With clean beaters, beat egg white on medium speed until thick and foamy; stir in coconut.
2. Drop dough by rounded tablespoonfuls 2 in. apart onto ungreased baking sheets. Flatten slightly with bottom of a glass dipped in sugar. Top with coconut mixture. Bake until until the edges begin to brown, 10-12 minutes. Remove from pans to wire racks to cool. Sprinkle with lime zest. Store in airtight containers.

1 COOKIE: *82 cal., 4g fat (1g sat. fat), 5mg chol., 59mg sod., 10g carb. (8g sugars, 0 fiber), 1g pro.*

Merry & Bright

Deck your holiday cakes with a little glisten and glamour to let the dessert table shine.

REINDEER CAKE

REINDEER CAKE

Whether you turn this cake into a reindeer or decorate it with your own creative vision, the three-layer stunner will command center stage at your next holiday get-together. So go ahead and embrace your baking prowess!
—Lauren Knoelke, Des Moines, IA

PREP: 1 HOUR • **BAKE:** 25 MIN. + COOLING
MAKES: 20 SERVINGS

- 2¼ cups cake flour
- 1½ cups sugar
- 3½ tsp. baking powder
- ½ tsp. salt
- ½ cup unsalted butter, cubed
- 4 large egg whites, room temperature
- ¾ cup 2% milk, divided
- 1 tsp. clear vanilla extract
- ½ tsp. almond extract
- ⅓ cup red and green jimmies

BUTTERCREAM
- 6 oz. dark chocolate, chopped
- ¼ cup heavy whipping cream
- 6 large egg whites
- 1½ cups sugar
- ½ tsp. cream of tartar
- ½ tsp. salt
- 2 cups unsalted butter, cubed
- 1½ tsp. vanilla extract
- ½ cup baking cocoa
  Optional edible decorations: Cookies, gold mist, melted chocolate, candy coating, gold pearl sprinkles

1. Preheat oven to 350°. Line the bottoms of three 6-in. round baking pans with parchment; grease and flour parchment and sides of pans.

2. In a large bowl, whisk flour, sugar, baking powder and salt. Beat in the butter until crumbly. Add egg whites, one at a time, beating well after each addition. Gradually beat in ¼ cup milk and extracts; beat on medium until light and fluffy, for about 2 minutes. Gradually beat in the remaining milk. Gently fold in jimmies.

3. Transfer batter to prepared pans. Bake until a toothpick inserted in center comes out clean, 25-30 minutes. Cool cake in pans 10 minutes before removing to wire racks; remove paper. Cool completely.

4. For buttercream, in a microwave, melt chocolate with cream until smooth, stirring every 30 seconds. Set aside to cool slightly. In a heatproof bowl of a stand mixer, whisk egg whites, sugar, cream of tartar and salt until blended. Place over simmering water in a large saucepan over medium heat. Whisking constantly, heat mixture until a thermometer reads 160°, 8-10 minutes.

5. Remove from the heat. With whisk attachment of stand mixer, beat on high speed until cooled to 90°, about 7 minutes. Gradually beat in butter, a few tablespoons at a time, on medium speed until smooth; beat in vanilla extract and the melted chocolate mixture. Gradually beat in cocoa through a sifter.

6. Spread frosting between layers and over top and sides of cake. Reserve remaining buttercream to decorate. Decorate as desired or follow directions below. Store cake in refrigerator.

1 SLICE: *463 cal., 28g fat (17g sat. fat), 65mg chol., 242mg sod., 52g carb. (37g sugars, 1g fiber), 5g pro.*

TO CREATE ANTLERS, using your favorite cutout cookie dough, cut two shapes with a gingerbread boy cookie cutter. Stretch into antler shapes and bake. Pipe melted chocolate over cooled cookies for texture. Once set, spray with edible gold mist; dry.

TO CREATE EARS, cut two 2-in. hearts from dough and bake. While still warm, mold each cookie onto the back of a large metal spoon; let stand until cool. Spray with edible gold mist; let dry. Dip edges in melted chocolate. Let set.

TO CREATE MANE, place ears and antlers on top of cake. Using decorator tips of your choice, pipe designs on top of the cake between the two antlers and the two ears. Add store-bought meringues and any other desired decorations.

TO CREATE EYES, pipe melted chocolate onto parchment and refrigerate until set. Once set, attach to front of cake.

TO CREATE NOSE, dip a vanilla wafer into melted red candy coating disks; let dry completely. Place nose on front of cake.

ADD EDIBLE GOLD PEARL SPRINKLES around base of cake.

HOLIDAY
SNOWFLAKE CAKE
PAGE 254

CHOCOLATE
COMFORT CAKE

CHOCOLATE COMFORT CAKE

This moist and delicious chocolate cake is usually the first dessert to go. People even eat the crumbs. It's always my top choice for holiday dinners.
—Ellen Riley, Murfreesboro, TN

PREP: 15 MIN. • **BAKE:** 50 MIN. + COOLING
MAKES: 12 SERVINGS

- 1 pkg. dark chocolate cake mix (regular size)
- 1 pkg. (3.9 oz.) instant chocolate pudding mix
- 4 large eggs, room temperature
- 1 cup sour cream
- ¾ cup canola oil
- ¾ cup brewed coffee
- ½ cup sugar
- 6 Tbsp. unsalted butter
- 4 oz. semisweet chocolate, chopped
- 2 oz. unsweetened chocolate, chopped

1. In a large bowl, combine the first 7 ingredients; beat on low speed for 30 seconds. Beat on medium for 2 minutes.
2. Pour into a well-greased 10-in. fluted tube pan. Bake at 350° until a toothpick inserted near the center comes out clean, 50-55 minutes. Cool cake for 10 minutes before removing from pan to a wire rack to cool completely.
3. In top of double boiler, melt butter and chocolate. Stir occasionally until mixture is glossy and smooth. Drizzle over cake.
1 SLICE: *541 cal., 32g fat (12g sat. fat), 82mg chol., 459mg sod., 61g carb. (36g sugars, 3g fiber), 6g pro.*

UPSIDE-DOWN FRUITCAKE

I get tired of people bad-mouthing holiday fruitcakes. It's one of my favorite holiday flavors and I look forward to it every year. This year, I decided to combine it with everyone's favorite, upside-down cake. Try to say no to this fruitcake; I dare you!
—James Schend, Pleasant Prairie, WI

PREP: 25 MIN. • **BAKE:** 30 MIN.
MAKES: 9 SERVINGS

- ⅓ cup butter
- ½ cup packed brown sugar
- 1 Tbsp. light corn syrup
- 2 Tbsp. bourbon
- 1½ cups chopped mixed candied fruit

UPSIDE-DOWN FRUITCAKE

CAKE
- ½ cup butter, softened
- ⅓ cup sugar
- 1 large egg, room temperature
- ⅓ cup molasses
- 1½ cups all-purpose flour
- ½ tsp. ground ginger
- ½ tsp. ground cinnamon
- ½ tsp. salt
- ½ tsp. baking powder
- ¼ tsp. baking soda
- ¼ cup warm water
- ½ cup chopped pecans

1. Preheat oven to 350°. Line the bottom and sides of an 8-in. square baking pan with heavy-duty foil; grease the foil. In a small saucepan, combine butter, brown sugar and corn syrup. Cook and stir over low heat until sugar is melted, about 5 minutes. Remove from heat; stir in bourbon. Pour into prepared pan. Sprinkle syrup mixture with candied fruit.
2. In a large bowl, cream softened butter and sugar until light and fluffy. Beat in egg and molasses. Combine the flour, ginger, cinnamon, salt, baking powder and baking soda; add to creamed mixture alternately with water, beating well after each addition. Stir in pecans.
3. Drop batter by spoonfuls over fruit; spread carefully. Bake until a toothpick inserted in the center comes out clean, 30-35 minutes. Cool for 5 minutes before inverting onto a serving plate; remove foil. Serve warm.
1 PIECE: *521 cal., 22g fat (11g sat. fat), 66mg chol., 386mg sod., 81g carb. (57g sugars, 4g fiber), 4g pro.*

MAMA'S SPICE CAKE

Whenever I get a craving for a really tasty old-fashioned treat, I make this cake. For generations, great cooks in my family have been baking it, and their families have been enjoying its wonderful spice flavor, nutty crunch and rich frosting.
—Nancy Duty, Jacksonville, FL

PREP: 30 MIN. • **BAKE:** 35 MIN. + COOLING
MAKES: 16 SERVINGS

- 1½ cups sugar
- 1 cup raisins, chopped
- 1 cup water
- ¾ cup butter, cubed
- 1 tsp. ground cinnamon
- ½ tsp. ground allspice
- ¼ tsp. ground cloves
- ¼ tsp. ground nutmeg
- 4 large eggs, separated, room temperature
- 2 cups all-purpose flour
- 3 tsp. baking powder
- ½ tsp. salt
- ¼ tsp. baking soda
- ¾ cup chopped pecans

CREAM CHEESE FROSTING
- 1 pkg. (8 oz.) cream cheese, softened
- ¼ cup butter, softened
- 1 tsp. vanilla extract
  Pinch salt
- 4 cups confectioners' sugar
  Optional: Additional chopped pecans, cinnamon sticks, fresh bay leaves, fresh rosemary sprigs, confectioners' sugar

1. In a large saucepan, combine the first 8 ingredients; cook and stir over medium-low heat until sugar is dissolved. Remove from the heat; cool.
2. In a large bowl, beat egg yolks; gradually stir in spice mixture. Combine the flour, baking powder, salt and baking soda; add gradually to spice mixture until blended. Stir in pecans. In a small bowl, beat the egg whites until soft peaks form; fold into the batter.
3. Pour into 2 greased and floured 9-in. round baking pans. Bake at 325° until a toothpick inserted in the center comes out clean, 35-40 minutes. Cool for 10 minutes before removing from pans to wire racks to cool completely.

4. For frosting, in a large bowl, beat cream cheese and butter until fluffy. Add vanilla and salt. Gradually beat in confectioners' sugar until smooth. To decorate, spread frosting between layers and over top and sides of cake, leaving cake slightly exposed on the sides. If desired, top with pecans, cinnamon sticks, fresh bay leaves, fresh rosemary sprigs and confectioners' sugar. Store in the refrigerator.
1 PIECE: 482 cal., 22g fat (11g sat. fat), 99mg chol., 353mg sod., 69g carb. (53g sugars, 1g fiber), 5g pro.

HOLIDAY SNOWFLAKE CAKE

(*SHOWN ON PAGE 252*)
The coconut sprinkled on this old-fashioned fluffy white cake gives the impression of snow inside the house—without the cold. It's such a beautiful dessert and a very fitting end to a delicious winter meal.
—Lynne Peterson, Salt Lake City, UT

PREP: 40 MIN. • **BAKE:** 15 MIN. + COOLING
MAKES: 12 SERVINGS

- 2 large eggs plus 4 large egg yolks, room temperature
- 1½ cups sugar
- 1 cup whole milk
- ½ cup butter, cubed
- 2½ cups all-purpose flour
- 1 Tbsp. baking powder
- 1 tsp. vanilla extract
- ½ cup chopped nuts, optional

FROSTING
- 1¾ cups sugar
- ½ cup water
- 4 large egg whites
- ½ tsp. cream of tartar
- 1 tsp. vanilla extract
- 2 cups sweetened shredded coconut

1. In a large bowl, beat the eggs, egg yolks and sugar until light and fluffy, for about 5 minutes. In a small saucepan, heat milk and butter until butter melts. Combine flour and baking powder; add to the egg mixture alternately with milk mixture. Beat until well mixed. Add vanilla. Fold in the chopped nuts if desired.

2. Pour into 3 greased 9-in. round baking pans. Bake at 350° until a toothpick inserted in the center comes out clean, 15-18 minutes. Cool in pans 10 minutes before removing the cake to wire racks to cool completely.
3. For frosting, in a saucepan, combine sugar and water. Bring to a boil; cook over medium-high heat until a thermometer reads 244° (firm-ball stage).
4. Meanwhile, beat egg whites and cream of tartar in a bowl on high speed until foamy. Slowly pour the hot sugar syrup over the egg whites while beating continuously. Continue beating on high until stiff glossy peaks form, about 7 minutes. Add vanilla; beat until the frosting cools slightly and reaches desired consistency.
5. Place 1 cake layer on a serving plate; spread with ¾ cup frosting. Sprinkle with ¼ cup coconut. Repeat layers. Top with the remaining cake layer. Frost top and sides of cakes with remaining frosting; sprinkle with remaining coconut..
1 PIECE: 376 cal., 12g fat (8g sat. fat), 97mg chol., 195mg sod., 62g carb. (45g sugars, 1g fiber), 5g pro.

READER REVIEW

"Excellent. This cake was fun to make, and the icing is so pretty. Had my granddaughter decorate with mini jelly beans. We had it for Easter dinner dessert. It sure made a lot of servings and kept well."
—DUBLINLAB, TASTEOFHOME.COM

MAMA'S SPICE CAKE

CREAMY ARTICHOKE DIP
PAGE 263

Potluck Pleasers

Discover a dish that is sure to be a hit at your next gathering! Just flip through the following pasta salads, sandwiches, dips, mains and sweet finger foods. You'll find something sure to delight everyone.

**BACON-WRAPPED
SPAM BITES**

GRILLED PINEAPPLE WITH LIME DIP

*Serve this dish as an appetizer or dessert—
the choice is yours! If desired, roll the
pineapple spears in flaked coconut
before grilling.*
—Taste of Home *Test Kitchen*

PREP: 20 MIN. + MARINATING • **GRILL:** 10 MIN.
MAKES: 8 SERVINGS

- 1 fresh pineapple
- ¼ cup packed brown sugar
- 3 Tbsp. honey
- 2 Tbsp. lime juice

LIME DIP
- 3 oz. cream cheese, softened
- ¼ cup plain yogurt
- 2 Tbsp. honey
- 1 Tbsp. brown sugar
- 1 Tbsp. lime juice
- 1 tsp. grated lime zest

1. Peel and core pineapple; cut vertically
into 8 wedges. Cut each wedge horizontally
into 2 spears. In a bowl or shallow dish,
combine the brown sugar, honey and lime
juice; add pineapple and turn to coat. Cover
and refrigerate for 1 hour.
2. In a small bowl, beat cream cheese until
smooth. Beat in the yogurt, honey, brown
sugar, lime juice and zest. Cover and
refrigerate until serving.
3. Coat the grill rack with cooking spray
before starting the grill. Drain pineapple,
discarding marinade. Grill pineapple spears,
covered, over medium heat for 3-4 minutes
on each side or until golden brown. Serve
with lime dip.
2 SPEARS WITH 2 TBSP. DIP: *160 cal., 4g fat
(2g sat. fat), 12mg chol., 41mg sod., 32g
carb. (28g sugars, 2g fiber), 2g pro.*

BACON-WRAPPED SPAM BITES

*These sweet and savory bites use Spam—
a favorite ingredient in Hawaii—in a fun
new way. Bet you can't stop at just one!*
—Taste of Home *Test Kitchen*

PREP: 20 MIN. • **BAKE:** 15 MIN.
MAKES: 32 PIECES

- 16 bacon strips
- 1 can (12 oz.) reduced-sodium
  SPAM, cut into 32 cubes
- 32 wooden toothpicks
- ⅓ cup yellow mustard
- ¼ cup maple syrup
- 1 garlic clove, minced

1. Preheat oven to 400°. Cut bacon strips
crosswise in half. In a large skillet, cook
bacon over medium heat until partially
cooked but not crisp. Remove to paper
towels to drain; keep warm.
2. Wrap a bacon piece around each Spam
cube; secure with a toothpick. Place in a
15x10x1-in. ungreased baking pan. Bake for
10 minutes. In a bowl, combine mustard,
syrup and garlic; drizzle over the bacon-
wrapped Spam. Bake until bacon is crisp,
5-10 minutes longer.
1 APPETIZER: *60 cal., 4g fat (1g sat. fat),
12mg chol., 211mg sod., 2g carb. (2g sugars,
0 fiber), 3g pro.*

TEST KITCHEN TIP

To make ahead, wrap the Spam with
bacon and secure with a toothpick.
Store bites, covered, in the
refrigerator for up to 2 days.

MARINATED SHRIMP

My husband's aunt shared this recipe with me ages ago. Not only is it a Christmas Eve tradition in my home, but in the homes of our grown children as well.
—Delores Hill, Helena, MT

PREP: 5 MIN. + MARINATING • **COOK:** 10 MIN.
MAKES: ABOUT 3 DOZEN

- 2 lbs. uncooked jumbo shrimp, peeled and deveined
- 1 cup olive oil
- 2 garlic cloves, minced
- 4 tsp. dried rosemary, crushed
- 2 tsp. dried oregano
- 2 bay leaves
- 1 cup dry white wine or chicken broth
- ¾ tsp. salt
- ⅛ tsp. pepper

1. In a bowl, combine the shrimp, oil, garlic, rosemary, oregano and bay leaves. Cover and refrigerate for 2-4 hours.
2. Pour shrimp and marinade into a large deep skillet. Add wine, salt and pepper. Cover and cook over medium-low heat for 10-15 minutes or until shrimp turn pink, stirring occasionally. Discard bay leaves. Transfer with a slotted spoon to a serving dish.
1 PIECE: *40 cal., 2g fat (0 sat. fat), 31mg chol., 42mg sod., 0 carb. (0 sugars, 0 fiber), 4g pro.*

MARINATED SHRIMP

PIXIE DUST COOKIES

PIXIE DUST COOKIES

These crisp and buttery cookies are based on a favorite Scottish shortbread recipe. They're just the right amount of sweet—and fun to decorate!
—Peggy Goodrich, Enid, OK

PREP: 20 MIN. • **BAKE:** 10 MIN./BATCH • **MAKES:** ABOUT 3½ DOZEN

- ¾ cup plus 2 Tbsp. butter, softened
- ¼ cup sugar
- 2 cups all-purpose flour
   Pearl dust

1. Preheat oven to 350°. In a large bowl, cream butter and sugar. Gradually beat in flour (dough will be crumbly). Shape into a ball.
2. On a lightly floured surface, press dough to ½-in. thickness. Cut with a floured 1-in. diamond-shaped cookie cutter. Place 1 in. apart on ungreased baking sheets. Sprinkle with pearl dust. Bake 12-15 minutes or until firm. Cool on pans 2 minutes. Remove to wire racks to cool.
1 COOKIE: *55 cal., 3g fat (2g sat. fat), 9mg chol., 26mg sod., 6g carb. (1g sugars, 0 fiber), 1g pro.*

SANTORINI LAMB SLIDERS

I love lamb burgers, so I created a crowd-friendly slider version. The tzatziki sauce is best made a day or two in advance to allow the flavors to mingle.

—Cristina Certano, Colorado Springs, CO

PREP: 30 MIN. + CHILLING • **GRILL:** 10 MIN.
MAKES: 10 SERVINGS

- 1   cup plain Greek yogurt
- ½   cup shredded peeled cucumber
- 1¼ tsp. salt, divided
- 1   lb. ground lamb
- 1   Tbsp. grated lemon zest
- 4   garlic cloves, minced, divided
- 2   tsp. dried oregano
- ¼   tsp. plus ⅛ tsp. pepper, divided
- 1   tsp. lemon juice
- 1   tsp. dill weed
- 10 mini buns or mini ciabatta buns
- 10 Bibb lettuce leaves or Boston lettuce leaves
- 1   medium red onion, thinly sliced
- 1   cup crumbled feta cheese

1. Line a strainer or colander with 4 layers of cheesecloth or 1 coffee filter; place over a bowl. Place yogurt in prepared strainer; cover yogurt with sides of cheesecloth. Refrigerate 2-4 hours. Meanwhile, place cucumber in a colander over a plate; sprinkle with ¼ tsp. salt and toss. Let stand 30 minutes.

2. For burgers, in a large bowl, combine lamb, lemon zest, 2 garlic cloves, oregano, ¾ tsp. salt and ¼ tsp. pepper, mixing lightly but thoroughly. Shape into ten ½-in.-thick patties. Refrigerate 30 minutes.

3. For sauce, remove yogurt from cheesecloth to a bowl; discard strained liquid. Squeeze cucumber and blot dry with paper towels. Add cucumber, lemon juice, dill, remaining 2 garlic cloves, remaining ¼ tsp. salt and remaining ⅛ tsp. pepper to yogurt, stirring until combined.

4. Grill burgers, covered, over medium heat until a thermometer reads 160°, 3-4 minutes on each side. Grill buns over medium heat, cut sides down, for 30-60 seconds or until toasted. Serve burgers on buns with lettuce, red onion, feta and sauce.

1 SLIDER: *228 cal., 12g fat (5g sat. fat), 43mg chol., 531mg sod., 16g carb. (3g sugars, 1g fiber), 14g pro.*

SANTORINI LAMB SLIDERS

THE BEST EVER LASAGNA

My brother, Joe, created this lasagna based on our mom's recipe. It's a family favorite at Christmas, thanks to the special ingredients that make it magnifico.
—Stephanie Marchese, Whitefish Bay, WI

PREP: 2¾ HOURS
BAKE: 1 HOUR + STANDING
MAKES: 15 SERVINGS

- 1 medium onion, chopped
- 2 Tbsp. olive oil
- 4 garlic cloves, minced
- 1 can (6 oz.) tomato paste
- 2 cans (28 oz. each) crushed tomatoes in puree
- 6 cups water
- 1 cup chopped fresh basil
- 2¼ tsp. sugar, divided
- 1 tsp. salt
- 1 lb. bulk Italian sausage
- 4 Italian sausage links
- 1 carton (16 oz.) whole milk ricotta cheese
- 8 cups shredded mozzarella cheese, divided
- 1 large egg, beaten
- ¼ tsp. dried basil
- 12 sheets no-cook lasagna noodles
- 21 slices provolone cheese
- ⅓ cup grated Parmesan cheese

THE BEST EVER LASAGNA

1. In a Dutch oven, cook onion in olive oil over medium heat until tender, 4-5 minutes. Add garlic; cook 1 minute. Stir in tomato paste and cook, stirring constantly, until fragrant, 3-4 minutes. Add crushed tomatoes, water, fresh basil, 2 tsp. sugar and salt. Bring to a boil; reduce heat. Simmer 1 hour, stirring occasionally.
2. Meanwhile, cook bulk sausage in a skillet over medium heat until no longer pink, breaking into crumbles, 8-10 minutes; drain. Add to sauce; simmer until mixture is thickened, about 1 hour longer.
3. While sauce simmers, preheat the oven to 350°. Place sausage links on a rimmed baking sheet; roast until cooked through, 35-40 minutes. Remove and let cool slightly; slice into ¼-in.-thick pieces.
4. In a small bowl, mix ricotta cheese, 1 cup mozzarella cheese, egg, dried basil and the remaining sugar.
5. In a greased 13x9-in. baking dish, spread 2 cups sauce. Arrange 4 noodles over sauce; spread with a third of the ricotta mixture. Add 7 provolone slices, a third of the sliced sausage and 1½ cups mozzarella cheese. Repeat layers 2 more times, using only 1 cup sauce per layer. Spread with 2 cups sauce (reserve remaining sauce for serving on the side), remaining 2½ cups mozzarella cheese and the Parmesan cheese (dish will be full).
6. Place dish on a rimmed baking sheet and bake, uncovered, until bubbly and deep golden brown, 60-65 minutes. Let stand 15 minutes before serving. Serve with the remaining meat sauce.
1 PIECE: *509 cal., 33g fat (15g sat. fat), 106mg chol., 1185mg sod., 27g carb. (9g sugars, 3g fiber), 29g pro.*

SUNFLOWER POPCORN BARS

Kansas is called the Sunflower State because of the wild sunflowers that grow here abundantly. Cultivated sunflowers are an important crop for many Kansas farmers, too.
—Karen Ann Bland, Gove City, KS

TAKES: 25 MIN. • **MAKES:** 4 DOZEN

- 1 cup sugar
- ½ cup light corn syrup
- ½ cup honey
- ½ cup peanut butter
- ¼ cup butter, softened
- 1 tsp. vanilla extract
- 1 cup salted sunflower kernels
- 4 qt. popped popcorn

1. In a large saucepan over medium heat, bring the sugar, corn syrup and honey to a boil, stirring often. Boil for 2 minutes. Remove from the heat; stir in the peanut butter, butter and vanilla until smooth. Add sunflower kernels.
2. Place popcorn in a large bowl. Add the syrup and stir to coat. Press into 2 greased 13x9-in. pans. Cut into 48 bars. Store in an airtight container.
NOTE: Reduced-fat peanut butter is not recommended for this recipe.
1 BAR: *96 cal., 5g fat (1g sat. fat), 3mg chol., 76mg sod., 13g carb. (9g sugars, 1g fiber), 2g pro.*

❄ CRANBERRY BRIE PINWHEELS

People may wonder when you found the time to make these crisp, flaky pinwheels—but they're really quite easy to do. And the filling is bursting with savory goodness and a touch of sweetness.
—Marcia Kintz, South Bend, IN

PREP: 20 MIN. • **BAKE:** 15 MIN. • **MAKES:** 1 DOZEN

- 1 sheet frozen puff pastry, thawed
- 2 Tbsp. Dijon mustard
- 2 Tbsp. honey
- 1 cup finely chopped fresh spinach
- ½ cup finely chopped Brie cheese
- ½ cup finely chopped walnuts
- ¼ cup dried cranberries, finely chopped

1. Unfold pastry. Combine mustard and honey; spread over pastry. Layer with spinach, cheese, walnuts and cranberries. Roll up jelly-roll style; cut into 12 slices. Place cut side down on an ungreased baking sheet.
2. Bake at 400° until golden brown, 15-20 minutes.
FREEZE OPTION: Freeze cooled appetizers in a freezer container. To use, reheat appetizers on a parchment-lined baking sheet in a preheated 400° oven until crisp and heated through.
1 SERVING: *173 cal., 10g fat (3g sat. fat), 6mg chol., 167mg sod., 18g carb. (5g sugars, 2g fiber), 4g pro.*

SLOW-COOKED CARNITAS

CRANBERRY BRIE PINWHEELS

SLOW-COOKED CARNITAS

This hearty entree is delicious and easy to simmer in a slow cooker all day long. Sometimes, instead of using tortillas, I place the pork on top of shredded lettuce for a tasty salad.
—Lisa Glogow, Aliso Viejo, CA

PREP: 20 MIN. • **COOK:** 6 HOURS • **MAKES:** 12 SERVINGS

- 1 boneless pork shoulder butt roast (3 to 4 lbs.)
- 3 garlic cloves, thinly sliced
- 2 tsp. olive oil
- ½ tsp. salt
- ½ tsp. pepper
- 1 bunch green onions, chopped
- 1½ cups minced fresh cilantro
- 1 cup salsa
- ½ cup chicken broth
- ½ cup tequila or additional chicken broth
- 2 cans (4 oz. each) chopped green chiles
- 12 flour tortillas (8 in.) or corn tortillas (6 in.), warmed
  Fresh cilantro leaves, sliced red onion and chopped tomatoes, optional

1. Cut roast in half; place in a 5-qt. slow cooker. Sprinkle with the garlic, oil, salt and pepper. Add the onions, cilantro, salsa, broth, tequila and chiles. Cover and cook on low for 6-8 hours or until meat is tender.
2. Remove meat; cool slightly. Shred with 2 forks and return to the slow cooker; heat through. Spoon about ⅔ cup meat mixture onto each tortilla; serve with toppings of your choice.
1 TACO: *363 cal., 15g fat (5g sat. fat), 67mg chol., 615mg sod., 28g carb. (1g sugars, 1g fiber), 24g pro.*

CREAMY ARTICHOKE DIP

(SHOWN ON PAGE 256)

This creamy dip is a family favorite. My sister Teresa got the recipe from a friend and passed it along to me. It's loaded with four types of cheese, artichoke hearts and just the right amount of spice.
—Mary Spencer, Greendale, WI

PREP: 20 MIN. • **COOK:** 1 HOUR
MAKES: 5 CUPS

- 2   cans (14 oz. each) water-packed artichoke hearts, rinsed, drained and coarsely chopped
- 2   cups shredded part-skim mozzarella cheese
- 1   pkg. (8 oz.) cream cheese, cubed
- 1   cup shredded Parmesan cheese
- ½   cup mayonnaise
- ½   cup shredded Swiss cheese
- 2   Tbsp. lemon juice
- 2   Tbsp. plain yogurt
- 1   Tbsp. seasoned salt
- 1   Tbsp. chopped seeded jalapeno pepper
- 1   tsp. garlic powder
     Tortilla chips

In a 3-qt. slow cooker, combine the first 11 ingredients. Cover and cook on low for 1 hour or until heated through. Serve with tortilla chips.

NOTE: Wear disposable gloves when cutting hot peppers; the oils can burn skin. Avoid touching your face.

¼ **CUP:** *152 cal., 12g fat (5g sat. fat), 27mg chol., 519mg sod., 4g carb. (1g sugars, 0 fiber), 7g pro.*

BRATWURST SUPPER

This simple dinner grills to perfection in heavy-duty foil packets. Loaded with chunks of bratwurst, red potatoes, mushrooms and carrots, it's easy to season with onion soup mix and a little soy sauce.
—Janice Meyer, Medford, WI

PREP: 10 MIN. • **GRILL:** 45 MIN.
MAKES: 12 SERVINGS

- 3   lbs. uncooked bratwurst links
- 3   lbs. small red potatoes, cut into wedges
- 1   lb. baby carrots
- 1   large red onion, sliced and separated into rings
- 2   jars (4½ oz. each) whole mushrooms, drained
- ¼   cup butter, cubed
- 1   envelope onion soup mix
- 2   Tbsp. soy sauce
- ½   tsp. pepper

1. For each of 2 foil packets, arrange a double thickness of heavy-duty foil (about 17x15 in.) on a flat surface.
2. Cut brats into thirds. Divide the brats, potatoes, carrots, onion and mushrooms evenly between the 2 double-layer foil pieces. Dot with butter. Sprinkle with soup mix, soy sauce and pepper. Bring edges of foil together; crimp to seal, forming 2 large packets. Seal tightly; turn to coat.
3. Grill, covered, over medium heat for 23-28 minutes on each side or until vegetables are tender and sausage is no longer pink. Open foil carefully to allow steam to escape.

1 SERVING: *524 cal., 37g fat (14g sat. fat), 94mg chol., 1445mg sod., 28g carb. (4g sugars, 3g fiber), 19g pro.*

BRATWURST SUPPER

RORO'S PINEAPPLE COOKIES

FIVE CHEESE ZITI AL FORNO

After having the Five Cheese Ziti at the Olive Garden, I wanted to make my own version, and I think I got pretty close. I always double this when I'm making it and freeze the second one for another meal.
—Keri Whitney, Castro Valley, CA

PREP: 20 MIN. • **BAKE:** 50 MIN. + STANDING
MAKES: 12 SERVINGS

- 1½ lbs. (about 7½ cups) ziti or small tube pasta
- 2 jars (24 oz. each) marinara sauce
- 1 jar (15 oz.) Alfredo sauce
- 2 cups shredded part-skim mozzarella cheese, divided
- ½ cup reduced-fat ricotta cheese
- ½ cup shredded provolone cheese
- ½ cup grated Romano cheese

TOPPING
- ½ cup grated Parmesan cheese
- ½ cup panko (Japanese) bread crumbs
- 3 garlic cloves, minced
- 2 Tbsp. olive oil
  Minced fresh parsley or basil, optional

1. Preheat oven to 350°. Cook pasta according to package directions for al dente; drain.
2. In a large saucepan, combine marinara sauce, Alfredo sauce, 1 cup mozzarella, ricotta, provolone, and Romano. Heat over medium heat until cheeses are melted. Stir in cooked pasta; pour mixture into a greased 13x9-in. baking dish. Top with remaining 1 cup mozzarella cheese.
3. Combine Parmesan, bread crumbs, garlic and olive oil; sprinkle over pasta.
4. Bake, uncovered, until mixture is bubbly and topping is golden brown, 30-40 minutes. Let stand 10 minutes before serving. Garnish with fresh parsley or basil if desired.
FREEZE OPTION: Cool unbaked casserole; cover and freeze. To use, partially thaw in refrigerator overnight. Remove from refrigerator 30 minutes before baking. Preheat oven to 350°. Cover casserole with foil; bake 50 minutes. Uncover; bake 15-20 minutes longer or until heated through and a thermometer inserted in center reads 165°.
1 CUP: *449 cal., 15g fat (8g sat. fat), 32mg chol., 960mg sod., 59g carb. (11g sugars, 4g fiber), 21g pro.*

RORO'S PINEAPPLE COOKIES

My memories of Christmas always include my mom's pineapple cookies. The kids called her Roro, and we still make them every year to keep her memory alive. You can substitute your favorite flavor of preserves for the pineapple.
—Donna Scarano, East Hanover, NJ

PREP: 20 MIN.
BAKE: 20 MIN./BATCH + COOLING
MAKES: ABOUT 2 DOZEN

- 2 cups all-purpose flour
- 2 Tbsp. sugar
- 3 tsp. baking powder
- ½ tsp. salt
- ¼ cup butter, softened
- 1 large egg, room temperature
- ⅓ cup water
- ½ cup pineapple preserves
- ½ cup confectioners' sugar

1. Preheat oven to 375°. Combine flour, sugar, baking powder and salt; cut in butter until well blended. In a small bowl, whisk egg with water. Gradually add to flour mixture; stir to form a soft dough.
2. Turn onto a lightly floured surface; divide into 2 portions. Roll each half into a 12x6-in. rectangle. Spread ¼ cup preserves down the center of each. Starting at a long side, fold dough over filling; fold other side over top. Pinch to seal seams and edges. Place seam side down on parchment-lined baking sheets.
3. Bake until lightly browned, 20-25 minutes. Cut each rectangle diagonally into 1-in. strips. Remove to wire racks to cool completely. Dust with confectioners' sugar.
1 COOKIE: *88 cal., 2g fat (1g sat. fat), 13mg chol., 128mg sod., 16g carb. (8g sugars, 0 fiber), 1g pro.*

FIVE CHEESE ZITI
AL FORNO

SEASONED TURKEY SANDWICHES

This recipe steals the show at any potluck or family reunion, and it's been a huge hit at graduation parties, football dinners and more.
—LaVonne Hegland, St. Michael, MN

PREP: 45 MIN. + RISING
GRILL: 2½ HOURS + STANDING
MAKES: 24 SANDWICHES

HOMEMADE SANDWICH BUNS
2   pkg. (¼ oz. each) active dry yeast
2   cups warm water (110° to 115°), divided
½   cup sugar
1   large egg, room temperature
3   Tbsp. shortening
1   tsp. salt
6½ to 7 cups all-purpose flour
3   Tbsp. butter, softened

GRILLED TURKEY
2   tsp. salt
2   tsp. garlic powder
2   tsp. pepper
1   turkey (14 to 16 lbs.)
½   cup butter, cubed
    Optional toppings: Lettuce leaves, tomato slices, red onion slices, mayonnaise

1. In a large bowl, dissolve yeast in ½ cup warm water. Add sugar, egg, shortening, salt, remaining 1½ cups water and 2 cups flour. Beat until smooth. Stir in enough remaining flour to form a soft dough (dough will be sticky).

2. Turn onto a floured surface; knead until smooth and elastic, about 6-8 minutes. Place in a greased bowl, turning once to grease top. Cover and let rise in a warm place until doubled, about 1 hour.

3. Punch dough down. Turn onto a lightly floured surface; divide in half. Divide each portion into 12 pieces. Shape each into a ball. Place 3 in. apart on greased baking sheets. Brush with butter. Cover and let rise until doubled, about 30 minutes.

4. Bake at 400° for 8-10 minutes or until golden brown. Remove to wire racks to cool.

5. Meanwhile, combine the salt, garlic powder and pepper; rub over turkey. Place butter inside turkey cavity; tie drumsticks together. Prepare grill for indirect medium heat. Tuck wings under turkey and place with breast side up in a disposable roasting pan; place on grill rack.

6. Grill, covered, for 1 hour. If using a charcoal grill, add 10 briquettes to coals. Baste with pan drippings. Cover and grill 1½-2 hours longer or until a thermometer reads 180°, adding 10 briquettes to maintain heat and brushing with pan drippings every 30 minutes. (Cover loosely with foil if turkey browns too quickly.)

7. Cover and let stand 20 minutes before carving. Split buns in half; fill with sliced turkey. If desired, serve with toppings.

6 OZ. COOKED TURKEY WITH BUN: *513 cal., 21g fat (8g sat. fat), 166mg chol., 452mg sod., 31g carb. (5g sugars, 1g fiber), 46g pro.*

FRESH CUCUMBER SALAD

Crisp, garden-fresh cukes are always in season when we hold our family reunion, and they really shine in this simple cucumber salad. The recipe can easily be expanded to make large quantities, too.
—Betsy Carlson, Rockford, IL

PREP: 10 MIN. + CHILLING
MAKES: 10 SERVINGS

3   medium cucumbers, sliced
1   cup sugar
¾   cup water
½   cup white vinegar
3   Tbsp. minced fresh dill or parsley

Place cucumbers in a 1½- to 2-qt. glass container. In a jar with a tight-fitting lid, shake the remaining ingredients until combined. Pour over cucumbers. Cover and refrigerate overnight. Serve with a slotted spoon.

½ CUP: *87 cal., 0 fat (0 sat. fat), 0 chol., 0 sod., 22g carb. (21g sugars, 1g fiber), 1g pro.*

SEASONED TURKEY SANDWICHES

CASHEW-CHICKEN ROTINI SALAD

I've tried many chicken salad recipes over the years, but this is my very favorite. It's fresh, fruity and refreshing, and the cashews add wonderful crunch. Every time I serve it at a potluck or picnic, I get rave reviews—and I always come home with an empty bowl!
—Kara Cook, Elk Ridge, UT

PREP: 30 MIN. + CHILLING
MAKES: 12 SERVINGS

- 1 pkg. (16 oz.) spiral or rotini pasta
- 4 cups cubed cooked chicken
- 1 can (20 oz.) pineapple tidbits, drained
- 1½ cups sliced celery
- ¾ cup thinly sliced green onions
- 1 cup seedless red grapes
- 1 cup seedless green grapes
- 1 pkg. (5 oz.) dried cranberries
- 1 cup ranch salad dressing
- ¾ cup mayonnaise
- 2 cups salted cashews

1. Cook pasta according to package directions. Meanwhile, in a large bowl, combine the chicken, pineapple, celery, onions, grapes and cranberries. Drain pasta and rinse in cold water; stir into chicken mixture.

2. In a small bowl, whisk the ranch dressing and mayonnaise. Pour over salad and toss to coat. Cover and refrigerate for at least 1 hour. Just before serving, stir in cashews.

1⅓ CUPS: 661 cal., 37g fat (6g sat. fat), 44mg chol., 451mg sod., 59g carb. (24g sugars, 4g fiber), 23g pro.

LAYERED CHRISTMAS GELATIN

My jewel-toned gelatin always makes an appearance at our Christmas feast. Filled with cranberries and pineapple, the sweet-tart salad could even serve as a light dessert.
—Diane Schefelker, Ireton, IA

PREP: 30 MIN. + CHILLING
MAKES: 10 SERVINGS

- 1 pkg. (3 oz.) lime gelatin
- 1 cup boiling water
- ⅓ cup unsweetened pineapple juice
- 1 cup crushed pineapple, drained

LAYERED CHRISTMAS GELATIN

CREAM CHEESE LAYER
- 1 tsp. unflavored gelatin
- 2 Tbsp. cold water
- 1 pkg. (8 oz.) cream cheese, softened
- ⅓ cup whole milk

BERRY LAYER
- 2 pkg. (3 oz. each) strawberry gelatin
- 2 cups boiling water
- 1 can (14 oz.) whole-berry cranberry sauce
  Optional ingredients: thawed whipped topping, lime wedges and fresh strawberries

1. Dissolve lime gelatin in boiling water; stir in pineapple juice. Stir in pineapple. Pour into an 11x7-in. dish; refrigerate until set.

2. In a small saucepan, sprinkle unflavored gelatin over cold water; let stand 1 minute. Heat over low heat, stirring until gelatin is completely dissolved. Transfer to a small bowl. Beat in cream cheese and milk until smooth. Spread over lime layer; refrigerate until set.

3. Dissolve strawberry gelatin in boiling water; stir in cranberry sauce. Cool for 10 minutes. Carefully spoon over cream cheese layer. Refrigerate until set.

4. Cut into squares. If desired, serve with whipped topping, lime wedges and fresh strawberries.

1 PIECE: 267 cal., 8g fat (5g sat. fat), 26mg chol., 139mg sod., 46g carb. (39g sugars, 1g fiber), 5g pro.

> **TEST KITCHEN TIP**
>
> Homemade whipped cream topping truly tastes best. Beat 1 cup heavy whipping cream on high until slightly thickened, then add 3 Tbsp. confectioners' sugar and ½ tsp. vanilla extract and beat until soft peaks form.

SOUTHWESTERN BEAN DIP

GRILLED FIRECRACKER POTATO SALAD

I can eat potato salad all the time. A little spice is nice, so I use cayenne and paprika in this grilled salad that comes with its own fireworks.
—Ashley Armstrong, Kingsland, GA

PREP: 20 MIN. • **GRILL:** 20 MIN. + CHILLING
MAKES: 16 SERVINGS (1 CUP EACH)

  3 lbs. small red potatoes (about 30), quartered
  2 Tbsp. olive oil
  1 tsp. salt
  ½ tsp. pepper
DRESSING
  1½ cups mayonnaise
  ½ cup finely chopped onion
  ¼ cup Dijon mustard
  2 Tbsp. sweet pickle relish
  ½ tsp. paprika
  ¼ tsp. cayenne pepper
SALAD
  6 hard-boiled large eggs, chopped
  2 celery ribs, finely chopped
    Minced fresh chives, optional

1. Toss potatoes with oil, salt and pepper; place in a grill wok or basket. Grill, covered, over medium heat 20-25 minutes or until potatoes are tender, stirring occasionally. Transfer the potatoes to a large bowl; cool slightly.
2. In a small bowl, mix dressing ingredients. Add dressing, eggs and celery to potatoes; toss to combine. Refrigerate, covered, 1-2 hours or until cold. If desired, sprinkle with chives.
NOTE: If you do not have a grill wok or basket, use a large disposable foil pan and poke holes in the bottom of the pan.
1 CUP: *265 cal., 20g fat (3g sat. fat), 77mg chol., 398mg sod., 16g carb. (2g sugars, 2g fiber), 4g pro.*

SOUTHWESTERN BEAN DIP

Just by using different brands of chili beans, you can make this dip as spicy as you like it. My family could eat this as a complete meal.
—Jeanne Shear, Sabetha, KS

PREP: 20 MIN. • **BAKE:** 30 MIN.
MAKES: ABOUT 9 CUPS

  2 lbs. ground beef
  1 Tbsp. dried minced onion
  1 can (8 oz.) tomato sauce
  1 can (16 oz.) kidney beans, rinsed and drained
  1 can (16 oz.) chili beans, undrained
  4 cups shredded cheddar cheese
    Sliced jalapeno pepper
    Tortilla chips

1. Preheat oven to 350°. In a large skillet, cook beef over medium heat until no longer pink; drain. Transfer to a bowl; add the onion. Mash with a fork until crumbly; set aside.
2. In a blender, process tomato sauce and beans until chunky. Add to beef mixture and mix well. Spoon half into a greased 13x9-in. baking dish; top with half of the cheese. Repeat layers.
3. Bake, uncovered until cheese is melted, about 30 minutes. Top with sliced jalapeno. Serve warm with chips.
2 TBSP.: *53 cal., 3g fat (2g sat. fat), 13mg chol., 88mg sod., 3g carb. (0 sugars, 1g fiber), 4g pro.*

HERBED BREAD TWISTS

A blend of herbs and a special shape dress up ordinary frozen bread dough in my unbelievably easy recipe.
—Deb Stapert, Comstock Park, MI

PREP: 30 MIN. + RISING • **BAKE:** 10 MIN. • **MAKES:** 2 DOZEN

- ¼ cup butter, softened
- ¼ tsp. garlic powder
- ¼ tsp. each dried basil, marjoram and oregano
- 1 loaf (1 lb.) frozen bread dough, thawed
- ¾ cup shredded part-skim mozzarella cheese
- 1 large egg
- 1 Tbsp. water
- 4 tsp. sesame seeds

1. In a small bowl, combine butter and seasonings. On a lightly floured surface, roll dough into a 12-in. square. Spread with butter mixture to within ½ in. of edges; sprinkle with cheese.
2. Fold dough into thirds. Cut widthwise into 24 strips. Twist each strip twice; pinch ends to seal. Place 2 in. apart on greased baking sheets. Cover and let rise in a warm place until doubled, about 40 minutes.
3. Beat egg and water; brush over dough. Sprinkle with sesame seeds. Bake at 375° until light golden brown, 10-12 minutes. Remove from pans to wire racks.
1 TWIST: *84 cal., 4g fat (2g sat. fat), 17mg chol., 140mg sod., 10g carb. (1g sugars, 1g fiber), 3g pro.*

HERBED BREAD TWISTS

HOT COCOA WITH ALMOND MILK

HOT COCOA WITH ALMOND MILK

Change up ordinary hot cocoa by stirring some dark baking cocoa into vanilla almond milk. Top it off with berry marshmallow creme or a plain large marshmallow, if you like, and add your favorite pretty sprinkles.
—Cindy Reams, Philipsburg, PA

TAKES: 15 MIN. • **MAKES:** 8 SERVINGS (1 CUP EACH)

- ½ cup sugar
- ½ cup dark baking cocoa or baking cocoa
- 2 cartons (32 oz. each) vanilla almond milk
- 1 tsp. vanilla extract
  Large marshmallows or strawberry marshmallow creme, optional
  Assorted sprinkles, optional

In a large saucepan, combine sugar and dark baking cocoa; gradually whisk in almond milk. Heat until bubbles form around sides of pan, whisking occasionally. Remove from heat; stir in vanilla. If desired, serve with large marshmallows and sprinkles.
1 CUP: *155 cal., 3g fat (0 sat. fat), 0 chol., 150mg sod., 32g carb. (28g sugars, 2g fiber), 2g pro.*

ITALIAN ORANGE-FIG COOKIES

ITALIAN ORANGE-FIG COOKIES

This is one of the first holiday cookies I made when I found out I could no longer eat gluten. In those eight years, six of my family members and friends have also had to give up gluten, so these delicious Italian cookies have now become a treasured holiday tradition for all of us. By the way, no one will know they're gluten-free unless you tell them! The cookies last for weeks if stored in a dry place.
—*Suzanne Banfield, Basking Ridge, NJ*

PREP: 20 MIN. • **BAKE:** 25 MIN./BATCH • **MAKES:** ABOUT 3 DOZEN

- 2 pkg. (8 oz. each) almond paste
- 1 cup sugar, divided
- 1 cup confectioners' sugar, divided
- 2 Tbsp. apricot preserves
- 3 large egg whites, room temperature
- ½ cup dried figs, finely chopped
- 1 Tbsp. grated orange peel

1. Preheat oven to 325°. Place almond paste, ½ cup sugar and ½ cup confectioners' sugar in a food processor; pulse until fine crumbs form. Add preserves and 1 egg white at a time, pulsing after each addition to combine. Transfer almond mixture to a large bowl; fold in figs and orange peel (dough will be sticky).
2. Place remaining sugars in separate shallow bowls. Drop tablespoonfuls of dough into sugar. Gently coat and shape into 1¼-in. balls. Repeat in confectioners' sugar. Place 1 in. apart on parchment-lined baking sheets. Bake 24-28 minutes or until tops are cracked and bottoms are golden brown. Remove to wire racks to cool.
1 COOKIE: 96 cal., 3g fat (0 sat. fat), 0 chol., 6mg sod., 16g carb. (14g sugars, 1g fiber), 1g pro.

ARTICHOKE CRESCENT APPETIZERS

This colorful appetizer is sure to please guests at any affair. My family loves it both warm and cold.
—*Mary Ann Dell, Phoenixville, PA*

PREP: 20 MIN. • **BAKE:** 15 MIN. • **MAKES:** 2 DOZEN

- 1 tube (8 oz.) refrigerated crescent rolls
- 2 Tbsp. grated Parmesan cheese
- 6 oz. cream cheese, softened
- ½ cup sour cream
- 1 large egg
- ½ tsp. dill weed
- ¼ tsp. seasoned salt
- 1 can (14 oz.) water-packed artichoke hearts, rinsed, drained and chopped
- ⅓ cup thinly chopped green onions
- 1 jar (2 oz.) diced pimientos, drained

1. Unroll crescent dough and press onto the bottom and ½ in. up the sides of an ungreased 13x9-in. baking dish; seal seams and perforations. Sprinkle with Parmesan cheese. Bake at 375° until lightly browned, 8-10 minutes.
2. Meanwhile, in a small bowl, beat the cream cheese, sour cream and egg until smooth. Stir in dill and seasoned salt. Spread over crust. Sprinkle with artichokes, green onions and pimientos.
3. Bake until edges are golden brown, 15-20 minutes. Cut into 24 pieces.
1 PIECE: 81 cal., 5g fat (2g sat. fat), 16mg chol., 163mg sod., 6g carb. (2g sugars, 0 fiber), 2g pro.

ARTICHOKE CRESCENT APPETIZERS

DUTCH APPLE PIE TARTLETS

These adorable mini apple pies make a delightful addition to a dessert buffet or snack tray. The recipe calls for convenient frozen phyllo shells, so they're surprisingly easy to prepare. The lemon curd filling adds a unique flavor twist.
—Mary Ann Lee, Clifton Park, NY

PREP: 15 MIN.
BAKE: 20 MIN.
MAKES: 2½ DOZEN

- 1 cup finely chopped peeled apple
- ¼ cup lemon curd
- 2 pkg. (1.9 oz. each) frozen miniature phyllo tart shells

TOPPING
- ½ cup all-purpose flour
- 3 Tbsp. sugar
- ½ tsp. ground cinnamon
- ¼ cup cold butter
  Confectioners' sugar

1. In a small bowl, combine apples and lemon curd. Spoon into tart shells.
2. In another bowl, combine the flour, sugar and cinnamon; cut in butter until mixture resembles fine crumbs. Spoon over the apple mixture. Place on an ungreased baking sheet.
3. Bake at 350° for 18-20 minutes or until golden brown. Cool on wire racks for 5 minutes. Dust with confectioners' sugar. Serve warm or at room temperature. Refrigerate leftovers.
1 TARTLET: *57 cal., 3g fat (1g sat. fat), 6mg chol., 22mg sod., 7g carb. (3g sugars, 0 fiber), 1g pro.* **Diabetic exchanges:** *½ starch, ½ fat.*

WILD RICE-STUFFED PORK LOIN

This recipe features wild rice and apricot stuffing tucked inside a tender pork roast.
—Kim Rubner, Worthington, IA

PREP: 20 MIN.
BAKE: 1½ HOURS + STANDING
MAKES: 10 SERVINGS

- 1 whole boneless pork loin roast (4 lbs.), trimmed
- 1 tsp. salt
- ½ tsp. garlic powder
- ¼ tsp. pepper
- 2 cups wild rice, cooked and drained

WILD RICE-STUFFED PORK LOIN

- 1½ cups coarsely chopped dried apricots
- 1 cup chopped onion
- ¾ cup finely chopped celery
- ¾ cup minced fresh parsley
- ½ tsp. rubbed sage
- ½ tsp. dried thyme
- ½ cup chicken broth
- 10 bacon strips
  Apricot preserves, optional

1. To butterfly pork roast, cut a lengthwise slit down the center of the pork loin to within ½ in. of bottom. Open loin so it lies flat. On each half, make another lengthwise slit down the center to within ½ in. of bottom. Cover and flatten to ¼-in. thickness. Uncover; sprinkle with salt, garlic powder and pepper.
2. In a large bowl, combine the rice, apricots, onion, celery, parsley, sage, thyme and broth. Spread stuffing evenly over pork, ¼ -½ in. thick. Roll up jelly-roll style, starting with a long side. Tie the roast at 1½- to 2-in. intervals with kitchen string. Place the remaining stuffing in a greased shallow 2-qt. baking dish; set aside.
3. Bake roast, uncovered, at 350° 1 hour. Remove roast from oven; carefully remove string. Place bacon strips over top of roast, overlapping slightly. Bake until bacon is browned and crisp and a thermometer reads 160°, 30-45 minutes longer. If needed, broil 4 in. from heat until bacon reaches desired crispness. Meanwhile, cover and bake remaining stuffing until heated through, about 30 minutes.
4. Let roast stand for 10 minutes before slicing. If desired, brush with apricot preserves before slicing.
1 SERVING: *436 cal., 20g fat (7g sat. fat), 109mg chol., 547mg sod., 23g carb. (10g sugars, 3g fiber), 41g pro.*

READ 'EM & EAT
PAGE 278

Pop-Up Party

You always have a reason to celebrate when family and friends are near. Show your appreciation of one another with a laid-back party at home.

ALT-
EGGSTRAVAGANZA

Whether you feel artsy or just feel like having snacks, call your crew for a creative day of dipping, dyeing and decorating by the dozen.

Aunt
Frances'
Lemonade
with
Candied
Citrus

Hard-boiled eggs
can be left out at
room temperature
for up to two hours.

A metal whisk allows you to dye the eggs and not your fingers.

Strawberry Ricotta Bruschetta

Edamame Hummus

lias

EASTER EGGS ARE BLANK CANVASES READY FOR YOUR IMAGINATION.

For a marbled effect, add a few drops of food coloring to a bowl of whipped cream, and swirl using a toothpick. Roll eggs in the rainbow mixture and let sit for 45 minutes to an hour before rinsing in water.

To add a message, dip eggs in your choice of homemade or store-bought egg dyes. Let dry, then write words, draw a picture or add a pattern on the egg using an opaque white food-safe marker.

To stamp a pattern, use mini rubber stamps—like the flower ones shown here—dipped in food dye poured onto a paper towel or napkin. Make sure you choose tiny stamps so you can see the entire shape.

TWO WAYS TO HARD-BOIL EGGS

Instant Pot: Insert steam rack at bottom of Instant Pot; add 1 cup water. Place eggs on rack and lock lid; cook on low pressure 5 minutes. Let pressure naturally release 5 minutes. Immediately transfer eggs to ice water to cool for 5 minutes.

Stovetop: Place eggs in a saucepan; cover by 1 inch with cold water. Bring to a boil; remove from heat, cover and let stand for 12 minutes. Drain eggs and immediately transfer to ice water to cool.

DIY EASTER EGG DYE

In a glass cup, mix ½ cup boiling **water,** 1 tsp. **white vinegar** and drops of **food coloring** to reach desired color.

STRAWBERRY RICOTTA BRUSCHETTA
(SHOWN ON PAGE 275)

Here's an interesting spin on bruschetta. A creamy ricotta cheese spread is the ideal complement to the sweet and minty strawberry topping.
—Laura Stricklin, Jackson, MS

TAKES: 25 MIN. • **MAKES:** 2 DOZEN

24 slices French bread
   baguette (½ in. thick)
3 Tbsp. butter, melted
3 cups fresh strawberries, chopped
3 Tbsp. minced fresh mint
3 Tbsp. honey
½ cup ricotta cheese
2 Tbsp. seedless strawberry jam
1½ tsp. grated lemon zest

1. Brush bread slices with butter; place on an ungreased baking sheet. Bake at 375° for 8-10 minutes or until lightly browned.
2. Meanwhile, in a small bowl, combine the strawberries, mint and honey; set aside. In another bowl, combine the ricotta, jam and lemon zest. Spread ricotta mixture over toast; top with strawberry mixture.
1 PIECE: *89 cal., 3g fat (1g sat. fat), 6mg chol., 88mg sod., 14g carb. (4g sugars, 1g fiber), 2g pro.* **Diabetic exchanges:** *1 starch, ½ fat.*

AUNT FRANCES' LEMONADE
(SHOWN ON PAGE 274)

My sister and I spent a week each summer with our Aunt Frances, who always had this thirst-quenching lemonade in a stoneware crock in the refrigerator. It makes a refreshing drink after a hot day of running around.
—Debbie Reinhart, New Cumberland, PA

TAKES: 15 MIN.
MAKES: 16 SERVINGS (1 GALLON)

5 lemons
5 limes
5 oranges
3 qt. water
1½ to 2 cups sugar

1. Squeeze the juice from 4 each of the lemons, limes and oranges; pour into a gallon container.

2. Thinly slice the remaining fruit and set aside for garnish. Add the water and sugar to the juices; mix well. Store in the refrigerator. Serve over ice with fruit slices.
1 CUP: *92 cal., 0 fat (0 sat. fat), 0 chol., 1mg sod., 24g carb. (21g sugars, 1g fiber), 0 pro.*

CANDIED CITRUS
This tart and sweet candied citrus is so easy to make, and it adds a zippy pop to drinks, desserts and more.
—Taste of Home *Test Kitchen*

PREP: 5 MIN. • **COOK:** 30 MIN. + STANDING
MAKES: ABOUT 1 DOZEN CITRUS SLICES

2¼ cups sugar
2 cups water
10 to 12 large tangerine or
   medium orange slices

1. In a Dutch oven, combine sugar and water; bring to a boil. Add citrus slices; reduce heat to medium. Cook until slices are translucent, about 20 minutes, turning occasionally. Reduce heat; simmer until slices are tender but still intact, about 10 minutes, turning occasionally.
2. Using a slotted spoon or tongs, remove slices to a wire rack or a parchment-lined pan. Let stand at room temperature overnight to dry. (Save syrup for another use.) If desired, cut slices in half; use to garnish drinks or decorate a cake, pie or other dessert.

EDAMAME HUMMUS
(SHOWN ON PAGE 275)
We love hummus at our house. This recipe is a scrumptious and refreshing twist on an old favorite, and it's a wonderful way to incorporate healthy soy into our diets.
—Marla Clark, Albuquerque, NM

TAKES: 15 MIN. • **MAKES:** 3 CUPS

1 pkg. (16 oz.) frozen shelled
   edamame, thawed
½ cup tahini
½ cup water
⅓ to ½ cup lemon juice
2 garlic cloves, minced
1 tsp. sea salt
¼ cup olive oil
¼ cup minced fresh mint
2 jalapeno peppers, seeded
   and chopped
   Assorted fresh vegetables
   Rice crackers

Microwave edamame, covered, on high until tender, 2-3 minutes. Transfer to a food processor; add remaining ingredients. Process until smooth, 1-2 minutes. Serve with vegetables and crackers.
¼ CUP: *167 cal., 13g fat (2g sat. fat), 0 chol., 167mg sod., 7g carb. (1g sugars, 2g fiber), 7g pro.*

Candied Citrus

Read 'em & Eat!

Host a book club for your friends and grace your table with these sweet delights.

CHOCOLATE-CARAMEL
RUM COFFEE

JAM-TOPPED
MINI CHEESECAKES

RUSTIC CHOCOLATE
RASPBERRY TART

CHOCOLATE-CARAMEL
RUM COFFEE

CHOCOLATE-CARAMEL RUM COFFEE

This decadent coffee drink can stand alone as a final course or as a delightful complement to any chocolate or caramel dessert. Our family loves it after a special dinner or just for sipping in front of the fireplace.
—*Joyce Conway, Westerville, OH*

TAKES: 25 MIN. • **MAKES:** 8 SERVINGS

- 2 cans (12 oz. each) evaporated milk
- ¾ cup rum
- ½ cup chocolate syrup
- ½ cup caramel sundae syrup
- ¼ cup packed brown sugar
- 4 cups hot brewed coffee
- 2 Tbsp. coffee liqueur

COFFEE WHIPPED CREAM
- 1 cup heavy whipping cream
- 6 Tbsp. confectioners' sugar
- 2 Tbsp. coffee liqueur
  Instant espresso powder, optional

1. In a large saucepan, combine the milk, rum, syrups and brown sugar. Cook over medium heat until hot (do not boil). Stir in coffee and liqueur.

2. Meanwhile, in a small bowl, beat the cream until it begins to thicken. Add the confectioners' sugar; beat until stiff peaks form. Fold in liqueur until combined.

3. Pour coffee mixture into mugs. Garnish with a dollop of coffee whipped cream and, if desired, espresso powder.

1 CUP COFFEE WITH ¼ CUP COFFEE WHIPPED CREAM: *437 cal., 16g fat (11g sat. fat), 68mg chol., 166mg sod., 50g carb. (43g sugars, 0 fiber), 7g pro.*

STRAWBERRY CHOCOLATE TRUFFLES

Decadent truffles showcase an amazing combination of strawberries and chocolate. I often double the recipe so I can give some to the neighbors.
—*Pat Habiger, Spearville, KS*

PREP: 45 MIN. + CHILLING
MAKES: 3½ DOZEN

- 4 milk chocolate candy bars (7 oz. each), halved
- 1 cup heavy whipping cream
- ¼ cup strawberry spreadable fruit
- 1½ tsp. vanilla extract
- 1¼ cups chopped almonds, toasted

1. Place chocolate in a food processor; cover and process until chopped. In a small saucepan, bring cream just to a boil. Pour over chocolate; cover and process until smooth. Stir in spreadable fruit and vanilla until combined. Transfer to a small bowl; cool to room temperature, stirring occasionally. Refrigerate until firm, about 3 hours.

2. Shape into 1-in. balls. Roll in almonds.

1 TRUFFLE: *147 cal., 10g fat (4g sat. fat), 12mg chol., 17mg sod., 13g carb. (11g sugars, 1g fiber), 2g pro.*

STRAWBERRY
CHOCOLATE TRUFFLES

RUSTIC CHOCOLATE RASPBERRY TART

Here's a delectable dessert that all ages will enjoy. With its raspberries and its Nutella-covered pastry crust, you won't be able to get enough of this.
—Christina Seremetis, Rockland, MA

PREP: 20 MIN. + CHILLING
BAKE: 45 MIN. + COOLING
MAKES: 8 SERVINGS

- 5 oz. cream cheese, softened
- 6 Tbsp. butter, softened
- 1½ cups all-purpose flour

FILLING
- 2 cups fresh raspberries
- 2 Tbsp. sugar
- 1 tsp. cornstarch
- ⅓ cup Nutella

1. Process cream cheese and butter in a food processor until blended. Add flour; process just until a dough forms. Shape into a disk; wrap in plastic. Refrigerate 1 hour or overnight.
2. Preheat oven to 350°. In a small bowl, toss raspberries, sugar and cornstarch with a fork, mashing some of the berries slightly.
3. On a lightly floured surface, roll dough into a 14x8-in. rectangle. Transfer to a parchment-lined baking sheet. Spread with Nutella to within 1 in. of edges. Top with raspberry mixture. Fold pastry edge toward center of tart, pleating and pinching as needed.
4. Bake until the crust is golden brown, 45-50 minutes. Transfer tart to a wire rack to cool.

1 PIECE: 315 cal., 19g fat (10g sat. fat), 41mg chol., 130mg sod., 34g carb. (12g sugars, 3g fiber), 5g pro.

JAM-TOPPED MINI CHEESECAKES

JAM-TOPPED MINI CHEESECAKES

Presto! We turned cheesecake into irresistible bite-sized snacks with these cute little treats. Feel free to swap in your favorite flavor of jam.
—Taste of Home *Test Kitchen*

PREP: 20 MIN. • **BAKE:** 15 MIN. + CHILLING
MAKES: 9 SERVINGS

- ⅔ cup graham cracker crumbs
- 2 Tbsp. butter, melted
- 1 pkg. (8 oz.) cream cheese, softened
- ⅓ cup sugar
- 1 tsp. vanilla extract
- 1 large egg, room temperature
- 3 Tbsp. assorted jams, warmed

1. In a small bowl, combine graham cracker crumbs and butter. Press gently onto the bottom of 9 paper-lined muffin cups. In another small bowl, beat the cream cheese, sugar and vanilla until smooth. Add egg; beat on low speed just until combined. Spoon over crusts.

2. Bake at 350° for 15-16 minutes or until centers are set. Cool for 10 minutes before removing from pan to a wire rack to cool completely. Refrigerate for at least 1 hour.
3. Remove paper liners, and top each cheesecake with 1 tsp. jam.

1 MINI CHEESECAKE: 198 cal., 13g fat (7g sat. fat), 53mg chol., 141mg sod., 19g carb. (14g sugars, 0 fiber), 3g pro.

HOW-TO

Warm Eggs for Better Baking

Many recipes benefit from room-temperature eggs, and it's an easy thing to do. Just place the eggs in hot water while you prep your recipe. They'll be ready when it's time to get cracking.

RUSTIC CHOCOLATE RASPBERRY TART

SNOW CONE SOCIAL

WITH GROWN-UP TWISTS
ON A CHILDHOOD CLASSIC,
IT DOESN'T GET ANY COOLER
THAN THIS BACKYARD BASH.

Create shaved ice using a blender with a "crush" setting. Slowly add water for a slushy effect; add more ice as needed.

Avoid sticky hands by setting prepared snow cones in highball glasses. A bonus: They'll keep your hands from getting chilly.

Slurp every bit of flavor using straws made with small scoops at the end. They let you spoon up the slush and sip the syrup.

PINA COLADA SYRUP

Combine 1 cup **cream of coconut**, ¾ cup **rum** and ¾ cup **unsweetened pineapple juice**.
—*Lauren Ebeling, Downers Grove, IL*

BLUE RASPBERRY SYRUP

Simmer 1 cup **sugar** and ¾ cup **water** until sugar is dissolved; remove from heat. Add 1 envelope **unsweetened blue raspberry Kool-Aid** and 1 tsp. **lemon juice**; cool.
—*Amanda Kippert, Tucson, AZ*

FUZZY NAVEL SYRUP

Simmer 1 cup **sugar** and ½ cup **water** until sugar is dissolved; remove from heat. Stir in 1 envelope **unsweetened orange Kool-Aid mix** and 1 tsp. **lemon juice**. Cool completely; stir in ½ cup **peach schnapps liqueur**.
—*Matthew Cross, Downers Grove, IL*

SHIRLEY TEMPLE SYRUP

Simmer 1 cup **sugar** and 1 cup **pomegranate juice** until sugar is dissolved; remove from heat. If desired, stir in 1 tsp. fresh **lemon juice**; cool.
—*Taste of Home Test Kitchen*

MARGARITA SYRUP

Simmer 1 cup **sugar**, ½ cup **water** and 2 tsp. **grated lime zest** until sugar is dissolved; remove from heat. Cool completely. Strain through a fine-mesh strainer into a bowl; discard lime zest. Stir in ¼ cup **tequila**, 2 Tbsp. **fresh lime juice** and 2 Tbsp. **Triple Sec**.
—*Monique Perez, Chicago, IL*

- - - - - - - - - - - - - - - - - - -

All syrups may be kept in the refrigerator up to 4 days.

5i

COOKIES & CREAM TRUFFLE BALLS

For easy truffles, I roll crushed Oreos and cream cheese into balls and dunk them in white chocolate. They're so simple.
—*Carla Giorgio, New York, NY*

PREP: 30 MIN. + FREEZING
MAKES: ABOUT 3 DOZEN

- 1 pkg. (14.3 oz.) Oreo cookies
- 1 pkg. (8 oz.) cream cheese, softened
- 1 pkg. (10 to 12 oz.) white baking chips, melted
  Jimmies and sprinkles, optional

1. Pulse cookies in a food processor until fine crumbs form. Add cream cheese; pulse just until blended. Refrigerate, covered, until firm enough to shape.
2. Shape mixture into 1-in. balls; place on waxed paper-lined baking sheets. Freeze, covered, several hours or overnight.
3. Dip balls in melted chips; allow excess to drip off. Return to pans. If desired, sprinkle immediately with jimmies and sprinkles. Let stand until set. Store in covered containers in the refrigerator.
1 TRUFFLE: 117 cal., 7g fat (3g sat. fat), 8mg chol., 73mg sod., 13g carb. (10g sugars, 0 fiber), 1g pro.

TOTABLE TAILGATE

Load the car with the cooler and chairs. With these make-ahead ideas, you'll score the first parking space.

Tailgate Timeline
Cornhole Tourney @ 11:00
Lunch starts @ 1:00
Kick off @ 3:00

It's a snap to set up the party with easy-prep dishes and fun store-bought snacks.

BIG-BATCH BLOODY MARYS

Tailgates, game-day parties and big brunches call for a Bloody Mary recipe that caters to a bunch.
—Taste of Home *Test Kitchen*

TAKES: 20 MIN. • **MAKES:** 8 SERVINGS

- 8 cups tomato juice
- ½ cup lemon juice
- ¼ cup lime juice
- 2 Tbsp. Worcestershire sauce
- 4 tsp. prepared horseradish, optional
- 1 tsp. celery salt
- 1 tsp. pepper
- 1 tsp. hot pepper sauce
- 2 cups vodka

OPTIONAL GARNISHES
   Celery ribs, pickle spears, green and ripe olives, cucumber slices, pickled mushrooms, cubed cheese, beef sticks, cherry tomatoes and/or cocktail shrimp

In a pitcher, stir together first 8 ingredients. For each serving, pour about 1 cup over ice with ¼ cup vodka; add optional garnishes as desired.
1¼ CUPS: *180 cal., 1g fat (0 sat. fat), 0 chol., 817mg sod., 12g carb. (7g sugars, 1g fiber), 2g pro.*

DIJON-BACON DIP FOR PRETZELS

With just four ingredients that you probably already have in your pantry or fridge, this appetizer comes together in a snap. Start with a teaspoon or two of horseradish and add more to taste.
—Isabelle Rooney, Summerville, SC

TAKES: 5 MIN. • **MAKES:** 1½ CUPS

- 1 cup mayonnaise
- ½ cup Dijon mustard
- ¼ cup bacon bits or crumbled cooked bacon
- 1 to 3 tsp. prepared horseradish
   Pretzels

Combine the first 4 ingredients. Chill until serving. Serve with pretzels.
2 TBSP.: *154 cal., 16g fat (2g sat. fat), 8mg chol., 428mg sod., 1g carb. (0 sugars, 0 fiber), 2g pro.*

TAILGATE SAUSAGES

You'll need just a handful of ingredients to fix these tasty sandwiches. Fully cooked sausages are stuffed with cheese and a homemade relish, then wrapped in foil so they're easy to transport and a breeze to grill.
—Matthew Hass, Ellison Bay, WI

TAKES: 20 MIN. • **MAKES:** 4 SERVINGS

- ½ cup giardiniera, drained
- ½ tsp. sugar
- 4 cooked Italian sausage links
- 4 slices provolone cheese
- 4 brat buns or hot dog buns, split
   Additional giardiniera, optional

1. In a bowl, combine giardiniera and sugar; set aside.
2. Place cheese in buns; top with sausages and giardiniera mixture. Wrap individually in a double thickness of heavy-duty foil (about 12x10 in.). Grill, uncovered, over medium-hot heat for 8-10 minutes or until heated through and cheese is melted. Open foil carefully to allow steam to escape. If desired, serve with additional giardiniera.
NOTE: Giardiniera, a pickled vegetable mixture, is available in mild and hot varieties and can be found in the Italian or pickle section of your grocery store.
1 SERVING: *584 cal., 33g fat (15g sat. fat), 84mg chol., 1401mg sod., 39g carb. (9g sugars, 2g fiber), 31g pro.*

Make garnish skewers ahead of time using a variety of classic Bloody Mary fixings, such as cheese cubes, beef sticks, olives, pickled mushrooms and tiny tomatoes. Then guests can pick a favorite combo and plunk it into their cups.

Keep a stash of pony-size beer bottles nearby to serve as a chaser alongside Bloody Marys—the way it's done in many bars across the Upper Midwest, especially in Bloody Mary-loving Wisconsin.

Extra fixings help guests gussy up the drinks to suit their own tastes. Lemon wedges, hot sauce, steak sauce and horseradish are popular add-ins.

BUILDING MEMORIES

Invite your favorite amateur architects over
to design customized gingerbread cabins
with creative candy decor.

GARLIC-PARMESAN
CHEESE BALL

WARM
SPICED
NUTS

MULLED
GRAPE
CIDER

THE BLUEPRINT FOR SWEET SUCCESS

Baking your own
gingerbread base
is the classic way
to begin, but it can
be time-consuming.
Make it easier by
starting with a kit,
like the A-frame
version we used here.

Let it snow! Blanket
the surface around
your gingerbread
house with shredded
coconut. Add a sweet
snowman outside
using marshmallows
decorated with
tinted royal icing.

Search your pantry
for building material
inspiration. Grab a
bag of pretzels or a
box of cereal, or raid
your secret candy
stash. Get creative
adding fun details to
your edible edifice.

Use graham crackers to create custom additions, like a dormer, an entryway or a towering chimney.

A sisal tree set near a gingerbread cabin creates an extra-woodsy scene.

ITALIAN PASTA SAUCE

When my daughter Kris got married, her new husband made something special for their wedding buffet—a big batch of this flavorful pasta sauce. His grandmother brought the recipe from Italy nearly 100 years ago.
—Judy Braun, Juneau, WI

PREP: 25 MIN. • **COOK:** 2½ HOURS
MAKES: 20 SERVINGS

- 4 lbs. ground beef
- 1 lb. bulk Italian sausage
- 1 large onion, finely chopped
- 3 celery ribs, finely chopped
- 4 garlic cloves, minced
- 2 Tbsp. olive oil
- 3 cans (28 oz. each) crushed tomatoes in puree
- 3 cans (6 oz. each) tomato paste
- 3 cups chicken or beef broth
- 1 lb. fresh mushrooms, sliced
- ¾ cup minced fresh parsley
- 1 Tbsp. sugar
- 2 to 3 tsp. salt
- ½ tsp. pepper
- ½ tsp. ground allspice, optional
  Hot cooked pasta

1. In a Dutch oven or soup kettle, cook beef in 2 batches over medium heat until no longer pink; drain and set aside. Cook sausage over medium heat until no longer pink; drain and set aside. In the same pan, saute onion, celery and garlic in oil until vegetables are tender.
2. Return the beef and sausage to the pan. Add the next 9 ingredients, including allspice if desired, and bring to a boil. Reduce heat; cover and simmer until sauce reaches desired thickness, stirring occasionally, 2-3 hours. Serve over pasta.
FREEZE OPTION: Freeze cooled sauce in freezer containers. To use, partially thaw in refrigerator overnight. Heat through in a saucepan, stirring occasionally. Add a little broth or water if necessary.
1 CUP: *284 cal., 15g fat (5g sat. fat), 57mg chol., 821mg sod., 16g carb. (9g sugars, 3g fiber), 23g pro.*

HOMEMADE ALFREDO SAUCE

When I found out I had celiac disease and couldn't have fettuccine Alfredo, I was determined to figure out a way to re-create it. This has now become one of my most requested dishes. I use gluten-free multigrain pasta, but you can use any style of pasta.
—Jackie Charlesworth Stiff, Frederick, CO

PREP: 20 MIN. • **COOK:** 20 MIN.
MAKES: 6 SERVINGS

- 3 Tbsp. butter
- ½ cup finely chopped shallots
- 5 garlic cloves, minced
- 2 cups heavy whipping cream
- 1¼ cups shredded Asiago cheese
- 1 cup grated Parmesan cheese, divided
- ¾ cup grated Romano cheese
- ¼ tsp. salt
- ¼ tsp. pepper
- 1 pkg. (12 oz.) uncooked gluten-free pasta

1. In a large saucepan, heat butter over medium heat. Add shallots; cook and stir until tender, 2-3 minutes. Add garlic; cook 1 minute longer. Add cream; cook and stir until heated through. Stir in Asiago, ½ cup Parmesan, Romano cheese, salt and pepper; bring to a boil, stirring constantly. Reduce heat; simmer, uncovered, until thickened, about 10 minutes, whisking occasionally.
2. Meanwhile, cook pasta according to package directions. Drain, reserving 1 cup pasta water; place pasta in a large bowl. Add sauce; toss to coat. Thin as desired with reserved pasta water. Serve with the remaining ½ cup Parmesan cheese.
1 CUP: *740 cal., 51g fat (31g sat. fat), 141mg chol., 692mg sod., 52g carb. (4g sugars, 3g fiber), 23g pro.*

ITALIAN PASTA SAUCE

MULLED GRAPE CIDER

(SHOWN ON PAGE 286)

I came up with this recipe one year when I tried to make grape jelly and ended up with 30 jars of delicious grape syrup instead. I simmered the syrup with spices to make a pretty autumn drink.
—Sharon Harmon, Orange, MA

PREP: 20 MIN. • **COOK:** 3 HOURS
MAKES: 12 SERVINGS (3 QT.)

5 lbs. Concord grapes
8 cups water, divided
1½ cups sugar
8 whole cloves
4 cinnamon sticks (4 in.)
   Dash ground nutmeg

1. In a large saucepan, combine grapes and 2 cups water; bring to a boil, stirring constantly. Press through a strainer; reserve juice and discard skins and seeds.
2. Pour juice through a double layer of cheesecloth into a 5-qt. slow cooker. Add the sugar, cloves, cinnamon sticks, nutmeg and remaining water. Cover and cook on low for 3 hours. Discard cloves and cinnamon sticks.
1 CUP: *231 cal., 1g fat (0 sat. fat), 0 chol., 4mg sod., 59g carb. (56g sugars, 0 fiber), 1g pro.*

GARLIC-PARMESAN CHEESE BALL

(SHOWN ON PAGE 286)

This garlic cheese ball is one of our entertaining mainstays. It complements most meals and is so easy to prepare and dress up with a variety of garnishes.
—Susan Seymour, Valatie, NY

PREP: 10 MIN. + CHILLING
MAKES: ABOUT 2 CUPS

11 oz. cream cheese, softened
⅓ cup grated Parmesan cheese
¼ cup mayonnaise
½ tsp. dried oregano
¼ tsp. garlic powder or
   ½ to 1 tsp. minced garlic
¾ cup chopped walnuts, optional
   Assorted fresh vegetables and/or crackers

In a large bowl, combine first 5 ingredients. Shape into a ball. Roll in walnuts if desired. Wrap tightly; chill 2 hours. Serve with fresh vegetables and/or crackers.
2 TBSP.: *98 cal., 10g fat (5g sat. fat), 21mg chol., 109mg sod., 1g carb. (1g sugars, 0 fiber), 2g pro.*

WARM SPICED NUTS

I like to set out bowls of spiced nuts when hosting holiday parties. Sometimes I stir in M&M's for a sweet and salty snack.
—Jill Matson, Zimmerman, MN

PREP: 5 MIN. • **BAKE:** 30 MIN. • **MAKES:** 3 CUPS

1 cup pecan halves
1 cup unblanched almonds
1 cup unsalted dry roasted peanuts
3 Tbsp. butter, melted
4½ tsp. Worcestershire sauce
1 tsp. chili powder
½ tsp. garlic salt
¼ tsp. cayenne pepper

1. In a large bowl, combine the pecans, almonds and peanuts. Combine butter and Worcestershire sauce; pour over nuts and toss to coat.
2. Spread in a single layer in an ungreased 15x10x1-in. baking pan. Bake at 300° until browned, about 30 minutes, stirring occasionally.
3. Transfer warm nuts to a bowl. Combine the chili powder, garlic salt and cayenne; sprinkle over nuts and stir to coat. Serve warm, or allow to cool before storing in an airtight container.
¼ CUP: *231 cal., 22g fat (4g sat. fat), 8mg chol., 123mg sod., 7g carb. (2g sugars, 3g fiber), 6g pro.*

WARM SPICED NUTS

**NATURAL ROOM SCENTS
PAGE 299**

Spa Day at Home

Kick back and relax—you deserve it! With these recipes for refreshing drinks, beauty masks and more, you'll bring the restful atmosphere of a spa right into your home as you pamper yourself and friends.

Pretty Delicious

Infuse your daily dose of H2O with refreshing fruit, herbs and spices.

It's simple!
Just combine all ingredients with 2 quarts of cold water. Refrigerate for 12 to 24 hours. Strain before serving.

Pomegranate & Pear Infused Water
½ small pear, sliced
¼ cup pomegranate seeds
1 cinnamon stick (3 in.)

Grapefruit & Coriander Infused Water
½ small grapefruit, peeled and sliced
1 tsp. coriander seeds

Rosemary & Ginger Infused Water
3 fresh rosemary sprigs
1 Tbsp. minced fresh gingerroot

Pineapple & Mint Infused Water
¼ fresh pineapple, sliced
3 fresh mint sprigs

Raspberry & Lemon Infused Water
1 cup fresh raspberries
3 lemon slices

A taste-great tip:
Gently crush fresh herbs, toast dry spices or lightly muddle fresh fruit to get the most flavor in your water.

Apple, Ginger & Vanilla Infused Water
1 medium tart apple, sliced
1 Tbsp. sliced fresh gingerroot
½ tsp. vanilla extract

Grape & Mint Infused Water
1 cup seedless red grapes, halved
3 fresh mint sprigs

Tangerine & Thyme Infused Water
2 tangerines, sliced
3 fresh thyme sprigs

Cranberry, Orange & Cardamom Infused Water
1 cup fresh cranberries
½ small navel orange, sliced
4 cardamom pods

Blackberry & Sage Infused Water
1 cup fresh blackberries
3 fresh sage sprigs

ALMOND-PECAN
DATE TRUFFLES

ALMOND-PECAN DATE TRUFFLES

My daughter and I came across a date candy recipe when she was learning about ancient Egypt. We changed some of the spices and nuts to suit our tastes. These sweet, simple truffles are ideal for when you want something quick yet festive.
—Lori Daniels, Beverly, WV

PREP: 20 MIN. + CHILLING
MAKES: ABOUT 1½ DOZEN

- ⅓ cup apple juice
- 1 pkg. (8 oz.) chopped dates
- 1 cup finely chopped pecans, toasted
- 1¼ tsp. ground cinnamon
- ¼ tsp. ground nutmeg
- 1 cup ground almonds, toasted

1. In a microwave, warm apple juice. Stir in dates; let stand 5 minutes to soften, stirring occasionally. Remove dates from apple juice; discard liquid. Transfer dates to the bowl of a food processor fitted with the blade attachment; process until smooth. Add pecans and spices; pulse just until combined (mixture will be thick).
2. Shape mixture into 1-in. balls; place on a waxed paper-lined baking sheet. Refrigerate, covered, 30-60 minutes.
3. Roll date balls in almonds.
1 **DATE BALL:** *109 cal., 7g fat (1g sat. fat), 0 chol., 0 sod., 12g carb. (9g sugars, 2g fiber), 2g pro.*

CANNELLINI BEAN HUMMUS

My version of hummus features a delightful nuttiness from tahini, a peanut butter-like paste made from ground sesame seeds. The beans pack a lot of protein so it's a healthy snack.
—Marina Castle Kelley, Canyon Country, CA

TAKES: 5 MIN. • **MAKES:** 1¼ CUPS

- 2 garlic cloves, peeled
- 1 can (15 oz.) cannellini beans, rinsed and drained
- ¼ cup tahini
- 3 Tbsp. lemon juice
- 1½ tsp. ground cumin
- ¼ tsp. salt
- ¼ tsp. crushed red pepper flakes
- 2 Tbsp. minced fresh parsley
  Pita breads, cut into wedges
  Assorted fresh vegetables

1. Place garlic in a food processor; cover and process until minced. Add the beans, tahini, lemon juice, cumin, salt and pepper flakes; cover and process until smooth.
2. Transfer to a small bowl; stir in parsley. Refrigerate until serving. Serve with pita wedges and assorted fresh vegetables.
2 **TBSP.:** *78 cal., 4g fat (1g sat. fat), 0 chol., 114mg sod., 8g carb. (0 sugars, 2g fiber), 3g pro.* **Diabetic exchanges:** *1 fat, ½ starch.*

You can grind rolled oats in a blender, in a food processor, or by hand with a mortar and pestle.

Made by Hand

For silky, supple skin, look no further than a few simple pantry ingredients.

Hand Scrub

Mix 1 Tbsp. each **raw honey, ground rolled oats, fresh lemon juice** and **fine brown sugar** until well blended. Over the sink, apply half the mixture to hands and massage it in for 1 minute; leave on for 10 minutes. Wash off with warm water; rinse with cool water. Store remaining mixture in an airtight container in the refrigerator for up to 4 days. Apply twice weekly. *Makes 2 applications.*

IF THE ELEMENTS HAVE BEEN HARSH ON YOUR HANDS, NEVER FEAR. A SWEET MIXTURE OF KITCHEN STAPLES WILL LEAVE YOUR SKIN FEELING AS SMOOTH AS SILK. HERE'S WHY:

Rolled Oats
Ground rolled oats act as a gentle exfoliant. They're also calming, anti-inflammatory and nonirritating to most skin types.

Raw Honey
Raw honey is packed with antioxidants that can slow the signs of aging. Plus, it's moisturizing and soothing, creating a healthy glow and making hands feel smoother.

Lemon Juice
The citric acid in lemon juice can help lighten discoloration and fade dark spots. When used regularly, it can help make your skin look brighter and younger.

Brown Sugar
The glycolic acid in sugar acts as a natural skin peel, sloughing off dead cells and accelerating skin cell turnover. Brown sugar is finer than white sugar and easier on sensitive skin, such as hands and face.

Beauty Buzz

Make this invigorating body scrub from simple pantry ingredients in mere minutes.

If you're a coffee lover, the idea of using precious coffee beans in a body scrub might shock you, but give this DIY product a shot—you'll be glad you did! Coffee scrubs aren't just for exfoliation and boosting circulation. The caffeine in the beans can also plump and tighten your skin, helping reduce the appearance of cellulite. Plus, the coconut oil will leave your skin silky smooth.

Coffee Body Scrub

Mix together ½ cup finely ground **coffee** and ½ cup **brown sugar.** Pour ½ cup melted **coconut oil** into the coffee mixture, then add 1 tsp. **vanilla extract.** Mix until well combined. *Makes 4 applications.*

To use, gently rub the mixture over your body. Leave it on for a few minutes, then rinse thoroughly. (Be careful if using the scrub in the shower, as the oil can make the floor a bit slippery.)

MINTY PINEAPPLE RUM

This delicious drink is a fabulous way to use fresh mint and celebrate summer. If the pineapple isn't as ripe as you'd like, add a bit more sugar. Save any leftover pineapple-mint syrup in an airtight glass container, or freeze the mixture in ice cube trays to use later.
—Colleen Delawder, Herndon, VA

TAKES: 10 MIN. • **MAKES:** 14 SERVINGS (¾ CUP EACH)

- 6 Tbsp. fresh lime juice (about 3 limes)
- 4 cups cubed fresh pineapple (1 in.)
- 40 fresh mint leaves
- ⅔ cup superfine sugar
- ⅛ tsp. kosher salt
- 1½ cups light rum
  Ice cubes
- 7 cups club soda, chilled
  GARNISH
  Fresh pineapple slices and additional fresh mint leaves

Place the first 5 ingredients in a blender; cover and process until pureed. Transfer to a 1½-qt. pitcher; stir in rum. Pour ⅓ cup into each glass. Add ice; pour ½ cup soda over ice. Garnish with a pineapple slice and additional mint leaves.
¾ CUP: *118 cal., 0 fat (0 sat. fat), 0 chol., 44mg sod., 17g carb. (14g sugars, 1g fiber), 0 pro.*

MINTY PINEAPPLE RUM

Happy Feet

The winter months can be tough on your feet. Before it's time to break out your strappy sandals, why not give your feet a little TLC?

This DIY milk bath is a quick, easy way to pamper your feet with common pantry ingredients. The lactic acid in milk is great for your skin, helping to heal and hydrate dry patches. Plus, this recipe includes honey to soothe and moisturize the skin, as well as vanilla, which has anti-inflammatory properties to calm irritated patches.

The finishing touch is baking soda, which serves as a gentle exfoliant to slough off dead skin. The end result? Sandal-ready feet, just in time for warmer weather!

Soothing Milk Bath

Pour 3-4 cups **milk** into a microwave-safe container. (Use as much milk as will be needed to cover your feet.) Heat in a microwave until the milk is slightly warmed but is still comfortable to the touch, for 1½-2 minutes. Add 2 Tbsp. **honey** and 1 tsp. **vanilla extract;** gently whisk until combined. Pour warm milk into a container large enough for both feet. Submerge feet in milk; let soak 5 minutes. Sprinkle 2 Tbsp. **baking soda** over feet, gently scrubbing rough patches of skin. Let feet soak for an additional 5-10 minutes, then rinse thoroughly. If desired, use a pumice stone to buff away dead skin. Apply moisturizing lotion to feet. *Makes 1 foot bath.*

Line up several filled jars on the table and float a candle in each for a pretty spring centerpiece.

Fresh Air

Set the mood. Relax your senses with these natural homemade fragrances.

Spring Lemon
- 1 lemon, sliced and seeded
- 2 to 3 stems dried lavender
- 2 to 3 stems fresh rosemary

Dreamsicle
- 1 blood orange, halved, seeded and sliced
- 1 vanilla bean, split, or 1 tsp. pure vanilla extract
- 5 to 6 leaves fresh mint

Fresh Cucumber
- ½ medium cucumber, sliced
- 1½-in. piece fresh ginger, peeled and thinly sliced
- 5 leaves fresh basil

How to Make Natural Room Scents

WELCOME VISITORS TO YOUR HOME WITH SIMMERING HERBAL AROMAS, OR BOTTLE THEM UP AS A NICE HOSTESS GIFT AND BE THE GUEST THAT GETS INVITED BACK.

What you'll do:

AS A ROOM SCENT:
1. Place citrus or cucumber slices in a small saucepan.
2. Add the remaining ingredients and enough water to cover the contents by 1 in.
3. Heat to boiling; reduce heat to low and simmer, adding more water as needed, for 1-2 hours.

AS A GIFT:
1. Place citrus or cucumber slices in a wide-mouth glass jar. Add remaining ingredients.
2. Add enough cold water to cover the contents.
3. Seal, decorate and add a tag with heating instructions. Keep chilled until simmering time.

More Scent Ideas:
GRAPEFRUIT, LIME, LEMONGRASS, SAGE, CLOVES, CINNAMON, NUTMEG, THYME

STRAWBERRY-CARROT SMOOTHIES

My children resist veggies, but they love smoothies. This one packs in lots of good-for-you fruits and veggies—but to my kids, it's just a fun and delicious sipper.
—*Elisabeth Larsen, Pleasant Grove, UT*

TAKES: 5 MIN. • **MAKES:** 5 SERVINGS

- 2 **cups (16 oz.) reduced-fat plain Greek yogurt**
- 1 **cup carrot juice**
- 1 **cup orange juice**
- 1 **cup frozen pineapple chunks**
- 1 **cup frozen unsweetened sliced strawberries**

Place all ingredients in a blender; cover and process until smooth.
1 CUP: *141 cal., 2g fat (1g sat. fat), 5mg chol., 79mg sod., 20g carb. (15g sugars, 1g fiber), 10g pro. Diabetic exchanges: 1 fruit, ½ reduced-fat milk.*

STRAWBERRY-CARROT SMOOTHIES

Lip Smackers

Use leftover peppermint candy to make a festive smile smoother.

Even if you're diligent about applying lip balm in the winter, you still might end up with dry, flaky lips. Luckily, it couldn't be easier to make a DIY lip scrub. (And don't forget to make enough to gift friends or stuff in stockings!)

This peppermint lip scrub uses just three ingredients—including candy canes! The end result? A refreshing seasonal scrub that will leave your lips plump and smooth...just in case you encounter any mistletoe.

Peppermint Lip Scrub

Place several **peppermint candies** or **candy canes** in a food processor, then pulse until finely ground. The candies should be roughly the consistency of sugar. In a bowl, mix 1 Tbsp. **white sugar** and 1 Tbsp. **coconut oil.** Mix in 2 Tbsp. finely ground peppermint candy until well combined. Store in a small airtight jar. *Makes 6 applications.*

To use, scoop out a small amount with your finger, then gently rub the mixture over your lips, focusing on dry areas. If there's extra scrub left on your lips, you can rinse them—but we won't tell if you lick the sweet mixture off instead.

Cool as a Cucumber

Keep your facial skin hydrated and healthy on the hottest days with this natural DIY toner made from garden ingredients.

A toner's main purpose is to protect and restore your skin's pH balance, which keeps it healthy and glowing. Luckily, cucumbers naturally have the same pH as skin, making them the perfect ingredient for a natural DIY face toner. Nutrient-rich cucumbers can also help reduce inflammation, restore moisture and prevent wrinkles, so pull one out of your crisper drawer and make it part of your beauty routine.

This recipe packs a one-two punch with the help of aloe vera. A little bit of aloe will soothe sunburns, minimize acne and leave skin refreshed and hydrated. Whip up the recipe in just a few minutes, then head outside to enjoy the sunny days of summer.

Cucumber Aloe Face Toner

Peel and slice ½ **cucumber.** In a food processor, place slices and a 1-in. cutting from an **aloe vera plant.** (You can substitute 1 tsp. 100% aloe vera gel.) Process the ingredients until pulpy. Strain the mixture through a sieve or cheesecloth twice to remove the solids. Stir in 2 Tbsp. **water.** Store toner in a small container or spray bottle. Store leftover toner in the fridge for up to 1 week. *Makes about ¼ cup.*

To use, after cleansing your face, soak a cotton pad with toner and gently wipe it on your face and neck: Or, use a spray bottle to spritz toner on face. Follow with moisturizer.

Substitutions & Equivalents

EQUIVALENT MEASURES

3 TEASPOONS	= 1 tablespoon	**16 TABLESPOONS**	= 1 cup
4 TABLESPOONS	= ¼ cup	**2 CUPS**	= 1 pint
5⅓ TABLESPOONS	= ⅓ cup	**4 CUPS**	= 1 quart
8 TABLESPOONS	= ½ cup	**4 QUARTS**	= 1 gallon

FOOD EQUIVALENTS

MACARONI	1 cup (3½ ounces) uncooked	= 2½ cups cooked
NOODLES, MEDIUM	3 cups (4 ounces) uncooked	= 4 cups cooked
POPCORN	3 cups (4 ounces) uncooked	= 8 cups popped
RICE, LONG GRAIN	1 cup uncooked	= 3 cups cooked
RICE, QUICK-COOKING	1 cup uncooked	= 2 cups cooked
SPAGHETTI	1 cup uncooked	= 4 cups cooked
BREAD	1 slice	= ¾ cup soft crumbs, ¼ cup fine dry crumbs
GRAHAM CRACKERS	7 squares	= ½ cup finely crushed
BUTTERY ROUND CRACKERS	12 crackers	= ½ cup finely crushed
SALTINE CRACKERS	14 crackers	= ½ cup finely crushed
BANANAS	1 medium	= ⅓ cup mashed
LEMONS	1 medium	= 3 tablespoons juice, 2 teaspoons grated zest
LIMES	1 medium	= 2 tablespoons juice, 1½ teaspoons grated zest
ORANGES	1 medium	= ¼-⅓ cup juice, 4 teaspoons grated zest

CABBAGE	1 head = 5 cups shredded	**GREEN PEPPER**	1 large = 1 cup chopped
CARROTS	1 pound = 3 cups shredded	**MUSHROOMS**	½ pound = 3 cups sliced
CELERY	1 rib = ½ cup chopped	**ONIONS**	1 medium = ½ cup chopped
CORN	1 ear fresh = ⅔ cup kernels	**POTATOES**	3 medium = 2 cups cubed
ALMONDS	1 pound = 3 cups chopped	**PECAN HALVES**	1 pound = 4½ cups chopped
GROUND NUTS	3¾ ounces = 1 cup	**WALNUTS**	1 pound = 3¾ cups chopped

EASY SUBSTITUTIONS

WHEN YOU NEED...		USE...
BAKING POWDER	1 teaspoon	½ teaspoon cream of tartar + ¼ teaspoon baking soda
BUTTERMILK	1 cup	1 tablespoon lemon juice or vinegar + enough milk to measure 1 cup (let stand 5 minutes before using)
CORNSTARCH	1 tablespoon	2 tablespoons all-purpose flour
HONEY	1 cup	1¼ cups sugar + ¼ cup water
HALF-AND-HALF CREAM	1 cup	1 tablespoon melted butter + enough whole milk to measure 1 cup
ONION	1 small, chopped (⅓ cup)	1 teaspoon onion powder or 1 tablespoon dried minced onion
TOMATO JUICE	1 cup	½ cup tomato sauce + ½ cup water
TOMATO SAUCE	2 cups	¾ cup tomato paste + 1 cup water
UNSWEETENED CHOCOLATE	1 square (1 ounce)	3 tablespoons baking cocoa + 1 tablespoon shortening or oil
WHOLE MILK	1 cup	½ cup evaporated milk + ½ cup water

Cooking Terms

AL DENTE An Italian term meaning "to the tooth." Used to describe pasta that is cooked but still firm.

BASTE To moisten food with melted butter, pan drippings, marinade or other liquid to add flavor and juiciness.

BEAT To mix rapidly with a spoon, fork, wire whisk or electric mixer.

BLEND To combine ingredients until just mixed.

BOIL To heat liquids until bubbles that cannot be stirred down are formed. In the case of water, the temperature will reach 212 degrees at sea level.

BONE To remove all bones from meat, poultry or fish.

BROIL To cook food 4 to 6 inches from a direct, radiant heat source.

CREAM To blend ingredients to a smooth consistency by beating; frequently done with butter and sugar for baking.

CUT IN To break down and distribute cold butter, margarine or shortening into a flour mixture with a pastry blender or two knives.

DASH A measurement less than ⅛ teaspoon that is used for herbs, spices and hot pepper sauce. This is not a precise measurement.

DREDGE To coat foods with flour or other dry ingredients. Most often done with pot roasts and stew meat before browning.

FLUTE To make a "V" shape or scalloped edge on pie crust with your thumb and fingers.

FOLD To blend dissimilar ingredients by careful and gentle turning with a spatula. Used most commonly to incorporate whipped cream, beaten egg whites, fruit, candy or nuts into a thick, heavy batter.

JULIENNE To cut foods into long thin strips much like matchsticks. Used often for salads and stir-fries.

KNEAD To work dough by using a pressing and folding action to make it smooth and elastic.

MARINATE To tenderize and/or flavor foods, usually vegetables or uncooked meat, by placing them in a mixture that may contain oil, vinegar, wine, lime or lemon juice, and herbs and spices.

MINCE To cut into very fine pieces. Often used for garlic, hot peppers and fresh herbs.

PARBOIL To boil foods, usually vegetables, until partially cooked. Most often used when vegetables are to be finished using another cooking method or chilled for marinated salads or dips.

PINCH A measurement less than ⅛ teaspoon that is easily held between the thumb and index finger. This is not a precise measurement.

PULSE To process foods in a food processor or blender with short bursts of power.

PUREE To mash solid foods into a smooth mixture with a food processor, mill, blender or sieve.

SAUTE To fry quickly in a small amount of fat, stirring almost constantly. Most often done with onions, mushrooms and other chopped vegetables.

SCORE To cut slits partway through the outer surface of foods. Often required for ham or flank steak.

SIMMER To cook liquids, or a combination of ingredients with liquid, at just under the boiling point (180-200°). The surface of the liquid will have some movement and there may be small bubbles around the sides of the pan.

STEAM To cook foods covered on a rack or in a steamer basket over a small amount of boiling water. Most often used for vegetables.

STIR-FRY To cook meats, grains and/or vegetables with a constant stirring motion, in a small amount of oil, in a wok or skillet over high heat.

General Index

This handy index lists every recipe by food category, major ingredient and/or cooking method, so you can easily locate recipes that suit your needs.

✓ Indicates an Eat Smart recipe

APPETIZERS
(*also see Salsas*)
Cold Appetizers
Garlic-Parmesan Cheese Ball, 289
Pomegranate Pistachio Crostini, 8
Salted Caramel & Dark
  Chocolate Figs, 6
✓Strawberry Ricotta
  Bruschetta, 277
Taco Pinwheels, 103
Dips & Spreads
Baked Onion Dip, 12
✓Cannellini Bean Hummus, 294
Creamy Artichoke Dip, 263
Dijon-Bacon Dip for Pretzels, 285
✓Edamame Hummus, 277
Fruity Horseradish Cream Cheese, 9
Smoky Chicken Spread, 14
Southwestern Bean Dip, 268
Zippy Curry Dip, 7
Hot Appetizers
Artichoke Crescent Appetizers, 270
Bacon-Wrapped Spam Bites, 258
Bang Bang Shrimp Cake Sliders, 6
Barbecued Meatballs, 8
Beef Wellington Fried Wontons, 10
✓Chicken Skewers with Cool
  Avocado Sauce, 9
Cranberry Brie Pinwheels, 262
✓Grilled Bruschetta, 10
✓Grilled Pineapple with
  Lime Dip, 258
Honey-Barbecue Chicken Wings, 12
Italian Sausage Mushrooms, 14
✓Marinated Shrimp, 259
Mushroom & Smoked
  Gouda Puff, 13
Pumpkin Pinwheels, 15
Santorini Lamb Sliders, 260
✓Stuffed Asiago-Basil
  Mushrooms, 14
Snacks
✓Warm Spiced Nuts, 289

APPLES & APPLESAUCE
Apple Kuchen Bars, 176
Apple Pie Cupcakes with Cinnamon
  Buttercream, 186
Apple Pie Ricotta Waffles, 149
✓Applesauce-Glazed Pork Chops, 53

Cinnamon Apple Pan Betty, 207
✓Dutch Apple Pie Tartlets, 271
✓Festive Cranberry Fruit Salad, 239
Peanut Butter, Apple &
  Raisin Sandwich, 40
✓Pressure-Cooker Cinnamon
  Applesauce, 121
Raisin-Applesauce Bundt Cake, 183
Upside-Down Apple
  Bacon Pancake, 160
Zucchini Apple Bread, 136

ARTICHOKES
Artichoke Crescent Appetizers, 270
Chicken & Artichoke Lasagna, 71
Creamy Artichoke Dip, 263

ARUGULA
✓Butternut Squash Panzanella
  Salad, 235
Turkey & Apple Arugula Salad
  in a Jar, 107
✓ Warm Roasted Beet Salad, 22

ASPARAGUS
Asparagus with Tarragon
  Lemon Sauce, 111
✓Balsamic Asparagus Salad, 26
Crab & Asparagus Soup, 39
✓Lemon-Parmesan Broiled
  Asparagus, 116

AVOCADO
Avocado & Grapefruit Salad, 28
✓California Avocado Salad, 23
California Chicken Club Pizza, 87
✓Chicken Skewers with Cool
  Avocado Sauce, 9
Chicken, Nectarine &
  Avocado Salad, 99
Dressed-Up Steak Salad, 21
Strawberry-Avocado
  Tossed Salad, 25

BACON
Bacon & Date Goat Cheese
  Burgers, 39
Bacon Cheeseburgers with
  Fry Sauce, 37
Bacon-Chicken Club Pizza, 61

Bacon-Wrapped Spam Bites, 258
Badger State Stuffing, 119
BLT Salad, 29
✓Bohemian Collards, 234
Brussels Sprouts Brown Betty, 125
California Chicken Club Pizza, 87
Chicken Cordon Bleu, 81
Cinnamon Whiskey BBQ
  Chicken Wraps, 34
Cobb Salad Club Sandwich, 34
Crunchy Bacon Blue Cheese Red
  Pepper Brussel Sprouts, 231
Dijon-Bacon Dip for Pretzels, 285
✓Easy Beans & Potatoes
  with Bacon, 123
Fiesta Scrambled Eggs, 157
Lemony Tortellini Bacon Salad, 19
Pressure-Cooker Cuban
  Ropa Vieja, 81
Roasted Red Potato Salad, 18
Southern Shrimp & Grits, 84
Spanish Hominy, 112
Spinach Quiche with Potato
  Crust, 149
Sweet & Spicy Peanut
  Butter-Bacon Sandwiches, 46
The Elvis Sandwich, 40
Upside-Down Apple Bacon
  Pancake, 160
Vegetable Frittata, 154
Walnut Glazed Bacon, 165
Wild Rice-Stuffed Pork Loin, 271

BANANAS
Banana Split Cake Bars, 200
✓Coconut Milk
  Strawberry-Banana Pops, 196
Dirty Banana Trifle, 205
Gluten-Free Banana Bread, 135
Raspberry-Banana Breakfast
  Tacos, 166
The Elvis Sandwich, 40

BARS & BROWNIES
Apple Kuchen Bars, 176
Banana Split Cake Bars, 200
Chocolate Mincemeat Bars, 177
Lavender Lemon Bars, 215
Lemon Coconut Bites, 178
Peanut Butter Pretzel Bars, 174

Skillet Chocolate Chunk
  Walnut Blondies, 173
Sunflower Popcorn Bars, 261

BEANS
✓Cannellini Bean Hummus, 294
✓Hearty Pita Tacos, 52
One-Pot Dinner, 55
Senate Bean Potpie, 89
Simple Chicken Enchiladas, 83
✓Slow-Cooked Stuffed Peppers, 83
Southwestern Bean Dip, 268
Sweet & Spicy Baked Beans, 222

BEEF & CORNED BEEF
(also see Ground Beef)
Basil-Butter Steaks with
  Roasted Potatoes, 62
Beef Broccoli Stir-Fry, 66
Cast-Iron Skillet Steak, 148
Chinese Scallion Pancake
  Beef Rolls, 44
Dressed-Up Steak Salad, 21
Grilled Beef & Blue Cheese
  Tacos, 73
✓Key West Flank Steak, 222
Pressure-Cooker Cuban
  Ropa Vieja, 81
✓Pressure-Cooker Sauerbraten, 93
Reuben Salad in a Jar, 22
Sesame Ginger Beef Skewers, 85
Slow-Cooker Pot Roast, 90
Spicy Corned Beef Tacos, 66
Steak Sandwiches with
  Quick-Pickled Vegetables, 47
Thai-Inspired Roast Beef
  Sandwich, 40
The Best Ever Chili, 42

BEVERAGES
✓Apple & Ginger Infused Water, 293
✓Apricot-Apple Cider, 226
Aunt Frances' Lemonade, 277
Big-Batch Bloody Marys, 285
✓Blackberry & Sage Infused
  Water, 293
Blue Raspberry Syrup, 283
Chocolate-Caramel Rum
  Coffee, 280
✓Cranberry, Orange & Cardamom
  Infused Water, 293
Frozen Cherry Margaritas, 13
Fuzzy Navel Syrup, 283
✓Grape & Mint Infused Water, 293
✓Grapefruit & Coriander Infused
  Water, 292
Hot Cocoa with Almond Milk, 269
✓Hot Ginger Coffee, 14

✓Iced Honeydew Mint Tea, 15
Margarita Syrup, 283
Minty Pineapple Rum, 296
Mulled Grape Cider, 289
Pina Colada Syrup, 283
✓Pineapple & Mint Infused
  Water, 292
✓Pomegranate & Pear Infused
  Water, 292
✓Raspberry & Lemon Infused
  Water, 292
Raspberry Bellini, 215
✓Rosemary & Ginger Infused
  Water, 292
Salty Dog Sangria, 7
Shirley Temple Syrup, 283
So-Healthy Smoothies, 148
Sparkling Apple Pie on
  the Rocks, 235
Spiced Apple Cider Jelly Shots, 230
✓Strawberry-Carrot Smoothies, 300
✓Tangerine & Thyme Infused
  Water, 293

BISCUITS & BISCUIT MIX
Chicken Biscuit Potpie, 96
Chicken Biscuit Skillet, 67
Easy Peasy Biscuits, 231
Extra Quick Yeast Rolls, 144
French Onion Drop Biscuits, 139
✓Makeover Cheddar Biscuits, 142

BLACKBERRIES
✓Blackberry Daiquiri Sherbet, 199
Lemon Blackberry Tortilla
  French Toast, 156
Three-Berry Freezer Jam, 130

BLUEBERRIES
Aunt Betty's Blueberry Muffins, 143
Blueberry Chops with Cinnamon
  Sweet Potatoes, 78
Ginger Blueberry Jam, 129
Lemon Blueberry Whoopie
  Pies, 170
No-Churn Blueberry Graham
  Cracker Ice Cream, 200
Red-White-and-Blue Berry
  Delight, 217

BREADS, ROLLS & MUFFINS
(also see Breakfast & Brunch)
Aunt Betty's Blueberry Muffins, 143
Berry Cream Muffins, 137
Butter Dips, 142
✓Candy Cane Chocolate
  Mini Loaves, 135

Cheesy Garlic Herb Quick
  Bread, 137
✓Cranberry Orange Almond
  Quick Bread, 143
Easy Batter Rolls, 227
✓English Muffin Bread, 140
Extra Quick Yeast Rolls, 144
Focaccia Barese, 140
French Onion Drop Biscuits, 139
Garlic Herb Bubble Loaf, 136
German Chocolate Ring, 138
Gluten-Free Banana Bread, 135
Hazelnut Date Pumpkin Bread, 144
✓Herb Quick Bread, 145
Herbed Bread Twists, 269
✓Makeover Cheddar Biscuits, 142
Parmesan Scones, 211
✓Popovers for 2, 138
✓Pumpkin Pan Rolls, 145
✓Rolled Buttermilk Biscuits, 134
Stollen Butter Rolls, 139
Swiss Cheese Bread, 134
Zucchini Apple Bread, 136

BREAKFAST & BRUNCH
Breads
Christmas Morning Sweet Rolls, 238
Maple-Walnut Sticky Buns, 156
Orange Cheesecake Breakfast
  Rolls, 165
Rhubarb Fritters, 151
Egg Dishes
Buffet Scrambled Eggs, 212
Cheddar-Butternut Squash
  Clafoutis, 150
Fiesta Scrambled Eggs, 157
Ham & Cheddar Brunch Ring, 166
Make-Ahead Eggs Benedict
  Toast Cups, 241
Meat-and-Potato Quiche, 100
Mustard Ham Strata, 155
Open-Faced Frico
  Egg Sandwich, 162
Pepperoni & Sausage Deep-Dish
  Pizza Quiche, 160
Slow-Cooker Breakfast Burritos, 154
Spicy Egg Bake, 102
Spinach Quiche with Potato
  Crust, 149
Three-Cheese Quiche, 239
Vegetable Frittata, 154

French Toast, Pancakes
  & Waffles
Apple Pie Ricotta Waffles, 149
Chocolate Chip Pancakes, 157
Lemon Blackberry Tortilla
  French Toast, 156

BREAKFAST & BRUNCH
French Toast, Pancakes & Waffles (*continued*)
Puff Pancake with Bourbon Peaches, 162
Savory Mustard Chicken & Stuffing Waffles, 163
Sweet Potato Dutch Baby with Praline Syrup, 163
Upside-Down Apple Bacon Pancake, 160
Grains
✓Almond-Chai Granola, 164
✓Autumn Power Porridge, 158
Pumpkin Cream of Wheat, 151
Other
Cast-Iron Skillet Steak, 148
Crescent Zucchini Pie, 159
Monte Cristo Casserole with Raspberry Sauce, 241
Orange-Glazed Ham, 211
Petite Sausage Quiches, 167
Raspberry-Banana Breakfast Tacos, 166
Shakshuka Breakfast Pizza, 164
Sausage & Eggs Over Cheddar-Parmesan Grits, 167
Southern Hash Browns & Ham Sheet-Pan Bake, 159
Walnut Glazed Bacon, 165
Smoothies & Yogurt Bowls
✓Power Berry Smoothie Bowl, 155
✓Rhubarb Compote with Yogurt & Almonds, 158
So-Healthy Smoothies, 148

BROCCOLI
Beef Broccoli Stir-Fry, 66
Broccoli Shrimp Alfredo, 63
Cheesy Broccoli Soup in a Bread Bowl, 47
✓Corn & Broccoli in Cheese Sauce, 110
Lemony Tortellini Bacon Salad, 19

BRUSSELS SPROUTS
✓Air-Fryer Garlic-Rosemary Brussels Sprouts, 128
Brussels Sprouts Brown Betty, 125
Brussels Sprouts with Pecans & Honey, 120
Crunchy Bacon Blue Cheese Red Pepper Brussel Sprouts, 231

BURGERS
Bacon & Date Goat Cheese Burgers, 39
Bacon Cheeseburgers with Fry Sauce, 37
Chicken Parmesan Burgers, 44

CABBAGE & COLESLAW MIX
(*also see Sauerkraut*)
Bang Bang Shrimp Cake Sliders, 6
Cilantro Blue Cheese Slaw, 20
✓Egg Roll Noodle Bowl, 53
Holiday Slaw with Apple Cider Dressing, 27
✓Italian Cabbage Soup, 35
Overnight Slaw, 222
Shrimp Pad Thai, 64
Spicy Corned Beef Tacos, 66
Vietnamese Crunchy Chicken Salad, 25

CAKE MIX
Apple Pie Cupcakes with Cinnamon Buttercream, 186
Chocolate Comfort Cake, 253
Lemon Poppy Seed Bundt Cake, 188
Strawberry Lemon Cupcakes, 190

CAKES & CUPCAKES
Apple Pie Cupcakes with Cinnamon Buttercream, 186
Chocolate Comfort Cake, 253
Cranberry-Orange Pound Cake, 185
✓Devil's Food Snack Cake, 191
Double Chocolate Espresso Pound Cake, 182
Gingerbread Cupcakes, 189
Grandma's Strawberry Shortcake, 188
Holiday Snowflake Cake, 254
✓Hot Fudge Pudding Cake, 197
Lemon Poppy Seed Bundt Cake, 188
Lemon Rhubarb Tube Cake, 189
Makeover Italian Cream Cake, 182
Mama's Spice Cake, 254
Raisin-Applesauce Bundt Cake, 183
Reindeer Cake, 251
Roasted Strawberry Sheet Cake, 185
Strawberry Lemon Cupcakes, 190
Sweet Potato Pie Cake Roll, 190
Upside-Down Fruitcake, 253

CANDIES
✓ Almond-Pecan Date Truffles, 294
Benne Candy, 179
Ben's English Toffee, 173
Chocolate Billionaires, 171
Chocolate Lebkuchen Cherry Balls, 248
Cookies & Cream Truffle Balls, 283
Gumdrop Fudge, 171

Nut Fruit Bark, 172
Strawberry Chocolate Truffles, 280
Sundae Funday Bark, 176

CARAMEL
Caramel Nut Crunch Pie, 203
Caramelized Pears, 205
Chocolate Billionaires, 171
Chocolate-Caramel Rum Coffee, 280
Jamaican Chocolate Cookies with Caramel Creme, 245
Pumpkin Pie Ice Cream with Salted Caramel Sauce, 195
Salted Caramel & Dark Chocolate Figs, 6

CARROTS
✓Carrot, Parsnip & Potato Gratin, 124
Carrot Spice Thumbprint Cookies, 249
✓Cilantro Ginger Carrots, 116
✓Sesame, Sunflower & Carrot Salad, 30
Teriyaki Glazed Chicken, 63

CAULIFLOWER
Cauliflower Dill Kugel, 117
Chicken Cordon Bleu Soup, 45
✓Sneaky Turkey Meatballs, 75

CHEESE
(*also see Cream Cheese; Goat Cheese*)
Appetizers
Baked Onion Dip, 12
Cranberry Brie Pinwheels, 262
Creamy Artichoke Dip, 263
Garlic-Parmesan Cheese Ball, 289
Mushroom & Smoked Gouda Puff, 13
Santorini Lamb Sliders, 260
Southwestern Bean Dip, 268
✓Stuffed Asiago-Basil Mushrooms, 14
Breads
Cheesy Garlic Herb Quick Bread, 137
✓Makeover Cheddar Biscuits, 142
Parmesan Scones, 211
Swiss Cheese Bread, 134
Breakfast & Brunch
Apple Pie Ricotta Waffles, 149
Cheddar-Butternut Squash Clafoutis, 150
Crescent Zucchini Pie, 159
Ham & Cheddar Brunch Ring, 166

Open-Faced Frico Egg
   Sandwich, 162
Pepperoni & Sausage Deep-Dish
   Pizza Quiche, 160
Sausage & Eggs Over
   Cheddar-Parmesan Grits, 167
Shakshuka Breakfast Pizza, 164
Three-Cheese Quiche, 239

Main Dishes
Bacon-Chicken Club Pizza, 61
Broccoli Shrimp Alfredo, 63
✓ Butternut Squash Mac
   & Cheese, 231
Caesar Chicken with Feta, 60
Cheddar Beef Enchiladas, 92
Chicken & Artichoke Lasagna, 71
Chicken Cordon Bleu, 81
Contest-Winning Eggplant
   Parmesan, 87
Crunchy Baked Chicken, 72
Five Cheese Ziti al Forno, 264
Grilled Beef & Blue Cheese
   Tacos, 73
Homemade Alfredo Sauce, 288
Lasagna Toss, 91
✓Mediterranean Pork & Orzo, 56
✓Mexi-Mac Skillet, 51
Parmesan Pork Roast, 70
Pesto-Chicken Penne Casseroles, 85
Saucy Mac & Cheese, 65
Skillet Ham & Rice, 62
✓Spinach, Shrimp & Ricotta
   Tacos, 58
The Best Ever Lasagna, 261
✓Vegetarian Linguine, 58

Salads
Cilantro Blue Cheese Slaw, 20
✓Warm Roasted Beet Salad, 22

Sandwiches
Chicken Parmesan Burgers, 44
Cuban Roasted Pork Sandwiches, 37
Fig, Caramelized Onion & Goat
   Cheese Panini, 43
Salmon Sliders with Sun-Dried
   Tomato Spread, 38
Santorini Lamb Sliders, 260

Side Dishes
Cheddar Spirals, 131
✓Corn & Broccoli in Cheese
   Sauce, 110
Crunchy Bacon Blue Cheese Red
   Pepper Brussel Sprouts, 231
✓Lemon-Parmesan Broiled
   Asparagus, 116
Root Vegetable Pavé, 131

Soups
Cheesy Broccoli Soup in a
   Bread Bowl, 47

**FIG, CARAMELIZED ONION &
GOAT CHEESE PANINI, PAGE 43**

Chicken Cordon Bleu
   Soup, 45

CHERRIES
Banana Split Cake Bars, 200
Chocolate Lebkuchen
   Cherry Balls, 248
Frozen Cherry Margaritas, 13
✓Grilled Pork Tenderloin with
   Cherry Salsa Molé, 72
Nut Fruit Bark, 172
Spiced Cherry Chutney, 127

CHICKEN
Appetizers
✓Chicken Skewers with Cool
   Avocado Sauce, 9
Honey-Barbecue Chicken Wings, 12
Smoky Chicken Spread, 14
Breakfast
Savory Mustard Chicken &
   Stuffing Waffles, 163
Main Dishes
Bacon-Chicken Club Pizza, 61
Caesar Chicken with Feta, 60
California Chicken Club Pizza, 87
Chicken & Artichoke Lasagna, 71
Chicken Biscuit Potpie, 96
Chicken Biscuit Skillet, 67
Chicken Cordon Bleu, 81

Chicken with Pineapple, 50
Creamy Curried Chicken, 55
Crunchy Baked Chicken, 72
Flaky Chicken Wellington, 99
✓Ginger-Curry Chicken Tacos, 78
✓Grilled Buttermilk Chicken, 96
Grilled Lemon Chicken, 217
Herbed Chicken with Wild Rice, 92
Mongolian Chicken, 74
Pesto-Chicken Penne
   Casseroles, 85
Pressure-Cooker Chicken
   Cacciatore, 88
Pressure-Cooker Mediterranean
   Chicken Orzo, 90
Quick Chicken Piccata, 56
Roasted Honey Mustard
   Chicken, 80
Savory Mustard Chicken & Stuffing
   Waffles, 163
Simple Chicken Enchiladas, 83
Teriyaki Glazed Chicken, 63
Salads
Cashew-Chicken Rotini Salad, 267
✓Chicken & Apple Salad
   with Greens, 31
Chicken, Nectarine & Avocado
   Salad, 99
Vietnamese Crunchy Chicken
   Salad, 25

CHICKEN (*continued*)
Sandwiches
Chicken Parmesan Burgers, 44
Cinnamon Whiskey BBQ
   Chicken Wraps, 34
Cobb Salad Club Sandwich, 34
Cranberry-Walnut Chicken
   Salad Sandwiches, 43
Peanut Butter, Chicken
   & Basil Sandwich, 40
Soups
Chicken Cordon Bleu Soup, 45
Creamy Chicken Soup, 35

CHOCOLATE
(*also see White Chocolate*)
Banana Split Cake Bars, 200
Ben's English Toffee, 173
Big & Buttery Chocolate
   Chip Cookies, 178
✓Candy Cane Chocolate
   Mini Loaves, 135
Caramel Nut Crunch Pie, 203
Chocolate Billionaires, 171
Chocolate-Caramel Rum
   Coffee, 280
Chocolate Chip Pancakes, 157
Chocolate Mincemeat Bars, 177
✓Devil's Food Snack Cake, 191
Double Chocolate Espresso
   Pound Cake, 182
German Chocolate Ring, 138
✓Hot Fudge Pudding Cake, 197
Jamaican Chocolate Cookies with
   Caramel Creme, 245
Nut Fruit Bark, 172
Peanut Butter, Krispies &
   Chocolate Sandwich, 41
Peanut Butter Pretzel Bars, 174
Peanut Butter S'mores Sandwich, 41
Rocky Road Freezer Pie, 184
Rustic Chocolate Raspberry
   Tart, 281
Salted Caramel & Dark
   Chocolate Figs, 6
Skillet Chocolate Chunk
   Walnut Blondies, 173
Strawberry Chocolate Truffles, 280

COCONUT & COCONUT MILK
✓Coconut Milk
   Strawberry-Banana Pops, 196
Creamy Curried Chicken, 55
German Chocolate Ring, 138
Holiday Snowflake Cake, 254
Lemon Coconut Bites, 178
Pineapple Coconut Tassies, 243
Quick Ambrosia Fruit Salad, 28

COFFEE
✓Candy Cane Chocolate
   Mini Loaves, 135
Chocolate-Caramel Rum
   Coffee, 280
Double Chocolate Espresso
   Pound Cake, 182
✓Hot Ginger Coffee, 14

CONDIMENTS & PICKLES
(*also see Jam, Jelly, Marmalade &*
   Preserves; Marinades; Salsa)
Basil Salt, 127
Best Ever Sweet Pickles, 114
Candied Citrus, 277
Chunky Ketchup, 218
Cinnamon-Orange
   Honey Butter, 123
Crisp Onion Relish, 218
Double Hot Horseradish
   Mustard, 218
Homemade Pear Honey, 111
Homemade Steak Seasoning, 123
Honey-Thyme Butter, 129
Lime Salt, 124
✓Pressure-Cooker Cinnamon
   Applesauce, 121
Spiced Cherry Chutney, 127
Sriracha Salt, 130
Steak Sandwiches with
   Quick-Pickled Vegetables, 47

COOKIES
Baklava Thumbprint cookies, 246
Big & Buttery Chocolate
   Chip Cookies, 178
Carrot Spice Thumbprint
   Cookies, 249
Chewy German Chocolate
   Cookies, 172
✓Cinnamon Roll Macarons, 245
Coconut, Lime & Pistachio
   Cookies, 249
Crystallized Gingerbread Chocolate
   Chip Cookies, 243
Ginger S'mores, 248
Italian Orange-Fig Cookies, 270
Jamaican Chocolate Cookies with
   Caramel Creme, 245
Lemon Blueberry Whoopie
   Pies, 170
Miniature Peanut Butter Treats, 177
Pineapple Coconut Tassies, 243
Pixie Dust Cookies, 259
Raspberry Almond Strips, 179
Roro's Pineapple Cookies, 264
Sea Salt Mint White Mocha
   Cookies, 244

Spiced Eggnog Rum Cookies, 246
Vanilla-Butter Sugar Cookies, 174

CORN
✓Corn & Broccoli in Cheese
   Sauce, 110
✓Miso-Buttered Succotash, 113
✓Sweet Corn-Tomato Salad, 223
✓Turkey-Sweet Potato Stew, 104

CRANBERRIES
✓Autumn Power Porridge, 158
Coconut, Lime & Pistachio
   Cookies, 249
Cranberry Brie Pinwheels, 262
✓Cranberry Orange Almond
   Quick Bread, 143
Cranberry-Orange Pound Cake, 185
Cranberry Waldorf Gelatin, 20
Cranberry-Walnut Chicken
   Salad Sandwiches, 43
Creamy Cranberry Cheesecake, 204
Crunchy Bacon Blue Cheese Red
   Pepper Brussel Sprouts, 231
✓Festive Cranberry Fruit Salad, 239
Layered Christmas Gelatin, 267
Maple-Glazed Green Beans, 227
Pressure-Cooker Cranberry Mustard
   Pork Loin, 82
Quinoa Wilted Spinach Salad, 21
✓Slow-Cooker Turkey Breast with
   Cranberry Gravy, 230

CREAM CHEESE
Artichoke Crescent Appetizers, 270
Best Ever Cheesecake, 194
Blueberry Angel Dessert, 202
Broccoli Shrimp Alfredo, 63
Chocolate Lebkuchen Cherry
   Balls, 248
Cookies & Cream Truffle Balls, 283
Creamy Cranberry Cheesecake, 204
Dirty Banana Trifle, 205
Fruity Horseradish Cream
   Cheese, 9
Garlic-Parmesan Cheese Ball, 289
Hasselback Sweet Potatoes, 118
Italian Sausage Mushrooms, 14
Jam-Topped Mini Cheesecakes, 281
Lemon Blackberry Tortilla
   French Toast, 156
Makeover Italian Cream Cake, 182
Mama's Spice Cake, 254
No-Bake Mango Strawberry
   Cheesecake, 198
Orange Cheesecake Breakfast
   Rolls, 165
Pumpkin Pinwheels, 15

Rustic Chocolate Raspberry
   Tart, 281
Strawberry Rhubarb Cheesecake
   Bars, 202
Sweet Potato Pie Cake Roll, 190
Taco Pinwheels, 103

CUCUMBERS
Best Ever Sweet Pickles, 114
✓Cucumber Melon Salad, 26
Fresh Cucumber Salad, 266

DATES
✓Almond-Pecan Date Truffles, 294
Bacon & Date Goat Cheese
   Burgers, 39
Hazelnut Date Pumpkin Bread, 144

DESSERTS
(also see Bars & Brownies; Cakes &
   Cupcakes; Candies; Cookies;
   Pies & Tarts)
Cheesecakes
Best Ever Cheesecake, 194
Creamy Cranberry Cheesecake, 204
Jam-Topped Mini Cheesecakes, 281
No-Bake Mango Strawberry
   Cheesecake, 198
Strawberry Rhubarb
   Cheesecake Bars, 202
Cobblers
Cinnamon Apple Pan Betty, 207
Pecan Pie Cobbler, 199
Ice Cream & Frozen Desserts
✓Blackberry Daiquiri Sherbet, 199
Caramel Nut Crunch Pie, 203
✓Coconut Milk
   Strawberry-Banana Pops, 196
Gam's Homemade Vanilla
   Ice Cream, 198
✓Mango Glace with Pineapple
   Pomegranate Salsa, 194
No-Churn Blueberry Graham
   Cracker Ice Cream, 200
Pumpkin Pie Ice Cream with Salted
   Caramel Sauce, 195
Thomas Jefferson's Vanilla
   Ice Cream, 207
Other
Banana Split Cake Bars, 200
Blueberry Angel Dessert, 202
Candied Citrus, 277
Caramelized Pears, 205
Dirty Banana Trifle, 205
✓Hot Fudge Pudding Cake, 197
Layered Christmas Gelatin, 267
Lemon Mango Kanafeh, 196
✓Light Toffee Crunch Dessert, 195

Mango Tiramisu, 206
✓No-Bake Strawberry Dessert, 206
✓Orange Pumpkin Chiffon
   Dessert, 204
Peach Panna Cotta, 197
Red-White-and-Blue Berry
   Delight, 217
Toffee Brownie Trifle, 203

EGGS
Buffet Scrambled Eggs, 212
Cheddar-Butternut Squash
   Clafoutis, 150
Fiesta Scrambled Eggs, 157
Grilled Firecracker Potato Salad, 268
Make-Ahead Eggs Benedict
   Toast Cups, 241
Meat-and-Potato Quiche, 100
Monte Cristo Casserole with
   Raspberry Sauce, 241
Mustard Ham Strata, 155
Open-Faced Frico Egg
   Sandwich, 162
Pepperoni & Sausage Deep-Dish
   Pizza Quiche, 160
Roasted Red Potato Salad, 18
Sausage & Eggs Over
   Cheddar-Parmesan Grits, 167
Shakshuka Breakfast Pizza, 164
Slow-Cooker Breakfast Burritos, 154
Southern Potato Salad, 221
Spicy Egg Bake, 102
Spinach Quiche with Potato
   Crust, 149
Thomas Jefferson's Vanilla
   Ice Cream, 207
Three-Cheese Quiche, 239
Vegetable Frittata, 154

FIGS
Fig, Caramelized Onion & Goat
   Cheese Panini, 43
Italian Orange-Fig Cookies, 270
Salted Caramel & Dark
   Chocolate Figs, 6

FISH
Baked Salmon Cakes, 57
✓Baked Tilapia, 60
Haddock en Papillote, 50
✓Lemon-Parsley Baked Cod, 54
Salmon Sliders with Sun-Dried
   Tomato Spread, 38
✓Salmon Supreme with Ginger
   Soy Sauce, 67
Tuna & Pea Casserole, 74
Tuna Zucchini Cakes, 62

FRUIT
(also see specific kinds)
Apricot-Apple Cider, 226
Avocado & Grapefruit Salad, 28
Cashew-Chicken Rotini Salad, 267
Chicken, Nectarine & Avocado
   Salad, 99
✓Cucumber Melon Salad, 26
✓Festive Cranberry Fruit Salad, 239
Flaky Bumbleberry Pie, 186
✓Iced Honeydew Mint Tea, 15
✓Mango Glace with Pineapple
   Pomegranate Salsa, 194
Mulled Grape Cider, 289
Pineapple Kiwi Jam, 125
Pomegranate Pistachio Crostini, 8
✓Power Berry Smoothie Bowl, 155
Quick Ambrosia Fruit Salad, 28
Ruby Grape Pie, 184
Salty Dog Sangria, 7
So-Healthy Smoothies, 148
Stollen Butter Rolls, 139
✓Strawberry-Carrot Smoothies, 300
Sundae Funday Bark, 176
Turkey & Apple Arugula Salad
   in a Jar, 107
Upside-Down Fruitcake, 253
Wild Rice-Stuffed Pork Loin, 271

GELATIN
Cranberry Waldorf Gelatin, 20
Layered Christmas Gelatin, 267
No-Bake Mango Strawberry
   Cheesecake, 198
✓No-Bake Strawberry Dessert, 206
✓Orange Pumpkin Chiffon
   Dessert, 204
Peach Panna Cotta, 197
Pina Colada Jam, 120
Red-White-and-Blue Berry
   Delight, 217
Spiced Apple Cider Jelly Shots, 230

GOAT CHEESE
Fig, Caramelized Onion & Goat
   Cheese Panini, 43
Salted Caramel & Dark
   Chocolate Figs, 6
✓Wilted Spinach Salad with
   Butternut Squash, 29

GRILLED RECIPES
Bacon & Date Goat Cheese
   Burgers, 39
Bacon Cheeseburgers with
   Fry Sauce, 37
Blueberry Chops with Cinnamon
   Sweet Potatoes, 78

GRILLED RECIPES (continued)

Bratwurst Supper, 263
✓Chicken Skewers with Cool
   Avocado Sauce, 9
Cinnamon Whiskey BBQ
   Chicken Wraps, 34
Clambake Packets, 80
Grilled Beef & Blue
   Cheese Tacos, 73
✓Grilled Bruschetta, 10
✓Grilled Buttermilk Chicken, 96
Grilled Firecracker Potato Salad, 268
Grilled Huli Huli Turkey
   Drumsticks, 234
Grilled Lemon Chicken, 217
✓Grilled Pineapple with
   Lime Dip, 258
✓Grilled Pork Tenderloin with
   Cherry Salsa Molé, 72
✓Key West Flank Steak, 222
Peach-Glazed Ribs, 75
Santorini Lamb Sliders, 260
Seasoned Turkey Sandwiches, 266
Sesame Ginger Beef Skewers, 85
Tailgate Sausages, 285

GRITS & HOMINY

Sausage & Eggs Over
   Cheddar-Parmesan Grits, 167
Southern Shrimp & Grits, 84
Spanish Hominy, 112

GROUND BEEF

Bacon & Date Goat Cheese
   Burgers, 39
Bacon Cheeseburgers with
   Fry Sauce, 37
Barbecued Meatballs, 8
Beef Wellington Fried Wontons, 10
Cheddar Beef Enchiladas, 92
Enchilada Casser-Olé!, 76
Ground Beef Taco Salad, 19
✓Hearty Pita Tacos, 52
Italian Pasta Sauce, 288
Lasagna Toss, 91
Macaroni Taco Bake, 93
Meat-and-Potato Quiche, 100
✓Mexi-Mac Skillet, 51
Mom's Meat Loaf for 2, 71
One-Pot Dinner, 55
One-Pot Spaghetti Dinner, 73
✓Potato-Topped Ground
   Beef Skillet, 77
Seasoned Taco Meat, 100
Skillet Beef & Macaroni, 57
Southwestern Bean Dip, 268
Spicy Egg Bake, 102
Taco Pizza Squares, 102

Tacos in a Bowl, 61
The Best Ever Chili, 42

HAM

Antipasto Salad Platter, 31
Chicken Cordon Bleu, 81
Chicken Cordon Bleu Soup, 45
Cobb Salad Club Sandwich, 34
Cuban Roasted Pork Sandwiches, 37
Curried Ham & Split Pea Soup, 46
Ham & Cheddar Brunch Ring, 166
Mustard Ham Strata, 155
Orange-Glazed Ham, 211
Pea Soup with Ham, 46
Senate Bean Potpie, 89
Skillet Ham & Rice, 62
Southern Hash Browns & Ham
   Sheet-Pan Bake, 159

HONEY

✓Almond-Chai Granola, 164
Almond Pork Chops with
   Honey Mustard, 91
Baklava Thumbprint Cookies, 246
Brussels Sprouts with Pecans
   & Honey, 120
Cinnamon-Orange Honey
   Butter, 123
Fig, Caramelized Onion & Goat
   Cheese Panini, 43
Herb-Glazed Turkey, 226
Honey-Thyme Butter, 129
Orange-Spice Marinade, 115
Parmesan Pork Roast, 70
✓Peanut Butter, Honey & Pear
   Open-Faced Sandwiches, 38
Peanut Butter, Strawberry &
   Honey Sandwich, 41
✓Rhubarb Compote with Yogurt
   & Almonds, 158
Roasted Honey Mustard Chicken, 80

HOT PEPPERS

Slow-Cooked Carnitas, 262
Spicy Peanut Butter & Pork
   Sandwich, 41
✓Spinach, Shrimp & Ricotta
   Tacos, 58
The Best Ever Chili, 42

JAM, JELLY, MARMALADE
   & PRESERVES

Barbecued Meatballs, 8
Bourbon Peach Jam, 118
Fruity Horseradish Cream Cheese, 9
Ginger Blueberry Jam, 129
Ginger-Peach Marinade, 115
Italian Orange-Fig Cookies, 270

Jam-Topped Mini Cheesecakes, 281
Lemon Blackberry Tortilla
   French Toast, 156
Orange-Glazed Ham, 211
Pina Colada Jam, 120
Pineapple Kiwi Jam, 125
Roro's Pineapple Cookies, 264
Southern Hash Browns & Ham
   Sheet-Pan Bake, 159
Strawberry Chocolate Truffles, 280
Three-Berry Freezer Jam, 130
Vanilla Pear Berry Jam, 110

LAMB

Santorini Lamb Sliders, 260

LASAGNA

Chicken & Artichoke Lasagna, 71
Lasagna Toss, 91
The Best Ever Lasagna, 261

LEMONS & LEMONADE

Aunt Frances' Lemonade, 277
Grilled Lemon Chicken, 217
Heavenly Greek Marinade, 115
Lavender Lemon Bars, 215
Lemon Blueberry Whoopie
   Pies, 170
Lemon Coconut Bites, 178
Lemon Mango Kanafeh, 196
✓Lemon-Parmesan Broiled
   Asparagus, 116
✓Lemon-Parsley Baked Cod, 54
Lemon Poppy Seed Bundt Cake, 188
Lemon Rhubarb Tube Cake, 189
Rosemary-Lemon Butter, 123
Strawberry Lemon Cupcakes, 190

LETTUCE
(also see Arugula)

Antipasto Salad Platter, 31
BLT Salad, 29
✓Chicken & Apple Salad
   with Greens, 31
Dressed-Up Steak Salad, 21
Lemony Tortellini Bacon Salad, 19
Reuben Salad in a Jar, 22
Strawberry-Avocado
   Tossed Salad, 25

LIMES

Coconut, Lime & Pistachio
   Cookies, 249
✓Grilled Pineapple with
   Lime Dip, 258
✓Key West Flank Steak, 222
Lime Salt, 124
✓Quick Picante Sauce, 219

Thai-Inspired Roast Beef
   Sandwich, 40
Aunt Frances' Lemonade, 277
Pineapple Kiwi Jam, 125

MANGOES & MANGO NECTAR
✓Gingered Mango Salsa, 219
Lemon Mango Kanafeh, 196
✓Mango Glace with Pineapple
   Pomegranate Salsa, 194
Mango Tiramisu, 206
No-Bake Mango Strawberry
   Cheesecake, 198

MAPLE SYRUP
Gingerbread Cupcakes, 189
Maple Butter, 123
Maple-Glazed Green Beans, 227
Maple-Walnut Sticky Buns, 156
Northwoods Marinade, 115
Sweet Potato Dutch Baby with
   Praline Syrup, 163

MARINADES
Balsamic Mustard Marinade, 115
Ginger-Peach Marinade, 115
Heavenly Greek Marinade, 115
Honey-Garlic Marinade, 115
Huli Huli Marinade, 115
Northwoods Marinade, 115
Orange-Spice Marinade, 115
Ranch Marinade, 115
Southwest Chili Marinade, 115
Tangy Barbecue Marinade, 115

**MARSHMALLOWS &
   MARSHMALLOW CREME**
Banana Split Cake Bars, 200
Ginger S'mores, 248
Peanut Butter S'mores Sandwich, 41
Rocky Road Freezer Pie, 184

MEATBALLS & MEAT LOAVES
Barbecued Meatballs, 8
Mom's Meat Loaf for 2, 71
✓Sneaky Turkey Meatballs, 75

MOLASSES
Crystallized Gingerbread Chocolate
   Chip Cookies, 243
Gingerbread Cupcakes, 189
Sweet & Spicy Baked Beans, 222

MUSHROOMS
Badger State Stuffing, 119
Beef Wellington Fried Wontons, 10
Creamy Shrimp Pasta, 54
Italian Sausage Mushrooms, 14

Mushroom & Smoked Gouda
   Puff, 13
Skillet Ham & Rice, 62
✓Stuffed Asiago-Basil
   Mushrooms, 14

NOODLES
✓Egg Roll Noodle Bowl, 53
One-Pot Dinner, 55
✓Pressure-Cooker Sauerbraten, 93
Shrimp Pad Thai, 64
Tacos in a Bowl, 61
Tuna & Pea Casserole, 74

NUTS
(*also see Peanuts & Peanut Butter*)
Appetizers
Cranberry Brie Pinwheels, 262
Pomegranate Pistachio Crostini, 8
Warm Spiced Nuts, 289
Breads
✓Cranberry Orange Almond
   Quick Bread, 143
German Chocolate Ring, 138
Hazelnut Date Pumpkin Bread, 144
Zucchini Apple Bread, 136
Breakfast & Brunch
✓Almond-Chai Granola, 164
✓Autumn Power Porridge, 158
Maple-Walnut Sticky Buns, 156
✓Rhubarb Compote with Yogurt &
   Almonds, 158
Sweet Potato Dutch Baby with
   Praline Syrup, 163
Walnut Glazed Bacon, 165
Desserts
✓Almond-Pecan Date Truffles, 294
Baklava Thumbprint Cookies, 246
Ben's English Toffee, 173
Big & Buttery Chocolate
   Chip Cookies, 178
Chocolate Billionaires, 171
Coconut, Lime & Pistachio
   Cookies, 249
Nut Fruit Bark, 172
Pecan Pie Cobbler, 199
Raspberry Almond Strips, 179
Rocky Road Freezer Pie, 184
Skillet Chocolate Chunk
   Walnut Blondies, 173
Strawberry Chocolate Truffles, 280
Upside-Down Fruitcake, 253
Main Dish
Haddock en Papillote, 50
Salads
Cashew-Chicken Rotini Salad, 267
✓Chicken & Apple Salad
   with Greens, 31

✓Chinese Spinach-Almond Salad, 18
Cranberry Waldorf Gelatin, 20
✓Wilted Spinach Salad with
   Butternut Squash, 29
Sandwiches
Cranberry-Walnut Chicken
   Salad Sandwiches, 43
Side Dishes
Brussels Sprouts with Pecans
   & Honey, 120
Butternut-Pineapple Crumble, 126

OATS
✓Almond-Chai Granola, 164
✓Autumn Power Porridge, 158
Sea Salt Mint White Mocha
   Cookies, 244

OLIVES
Antipasto Salad Platter, 31
Focaccia Barese, 140
Pressure-Cooker Mediterranean
   Chicken Orzo, 90

ONIONS
Baked Onion Dip, 12
Cauliflower Dill Kugel, 117
Chinese Scallion Pancake
   Beef Rolls, 44
Crisp Onion Relish, 218
Crunchy Baked Chicken, 72
Overnight Slaw, 222
Parmesan Scones, 211

ORANGES
Aunt Frances' Lemonade, 277
✓California Avocado Salad, 23
Candied Citrus, 277
Cranberry-Orange Pound Cake, 185
Hasselback Sweet Potatoes, 118
Mango Tiramisu, 206
Orange Cheesecake Breakfast
   Rolls, 165
✓Orange Pumpkin Chiffon
   Dessert, 204
Orange-Spice Marinade, 115
✓Orange Yogurt Dressing, 23

PASTA
(*also see Noodles*)
BLT Macaroni Salad, 217
✓Butternut Squash Mac
   & Cheese, 231
Cashew-Chicken Rotini Salad, 267
Cheddar Spirals, 131
Chicken & Artichoke Lasagna, 71
Creamy Shrimp Pasta, 54
Five Cheese Ziti al Forno, 264

PASTA (continued)

Homemade Alfredo Sauce, 288
Italian Pasta Sauce, 288
Lasagna Toss, 91
Lemony Tortellini Bacon Salad, 19
Linguine with Herbed
  Clam Sauce, 76
Macaroni Taco Bake, 93
✓Mediterranean Pork & Orzo, 56
✓Mexi-Mac Skillet, 51
One-Pot Spaghetti Dinner, 73
Pea & Crab Pasta Salad, 18
Pesto-Chicken Penne Casseroles, 85
Pressure-Cooker Chicken
  Cacciatore, 88
Pressure-Cooker Mediterranean
  Chicken Orzo, 90
Saucy Mac & Cheese, 65
Sausage & Squash Penne, 82
Skillet Beef & Macaroni, 57
The Best Ever Lasagna, 261
✓The Best Marinara Sauce, 121
✓Vegetarian Linguine, 58

PEACHES

Bourbon Peach Jam, 118
Golden Peach Pie, 191
Peach-Glazed Ribs, 75
Peach Panna Cotta, 197
Puff Pancake with Bourbon
  Peaches, 162

PEANUTS & PEANUT BUTTER

Caramel Nut Crunch Pie, 203
Miniature Peanut Butter Treats, 177
Peanut Butter, Apple &
  Raisin Sandwich, 40
Peanut Butter, Chicken &
  Basil Sandwich, 40
✓Peanut Butter, Honey & Pear
  Open-Faced Sandwiches, 38
Peanut Butter, Krispies &
  Chocolate Sandwich, 41
Peanut Butter Pretzel Bars, 174
Peanut Butter S'mores
  Sandwich, 41
Southern Peanut Butter
  Mayo Sandwich, 40
Spicy Peanut Butter &
  Pork Sandwich, 41
Sundae Funday Bark, 176
Sweet & Spicy Peanut
  Butter-Bacon Sandwiches, 46
Thai-Inspired Roast Beef
  Sandwich, 40
The Elvis Sandwich, 40
Vietnamese Crunchy
  Chicken Salad, 25

PEARS

Caramelized Pears, 205
Homemade Pear Honey, 111
✓Peanut Butter, Honey & Pear
  Open-Faced Sandwiches, 38
Vanilla Pear Berry Jam, 110

PEAS

Curried Ham & Split Pea Soup, 46
✓Hearty Vegetable Split
  Pea Soup, 46
✓Minty Sugar Snap Peas, 114
Mongolian Chicken, 74
Pea Soup with Ham, 46
Tuna & Pea Casserole, 74

PIES & TARTS

Caramel Nut Crunch Pie, 203
✓Dutch Apple Pie Tartlets, 271
Five-Spice Pumpkin Pie, 183
Flaky Bumbleberry Pie, 186
Golden Peach Pie, 191
Rocky Road Freezer Pie, 184
Ruby Grape Pie, 184
Rustic Chocolate Raspberry
  Tart, 281

PINEAPPLE

Butternut-Pineapple Crumble, 126
Chicken with Pineapple, 50
✓Grilled Pineapple with
  Lime Dip, 258
Homemade Pear Honey, 111
✓Mango Glace with Pineapple
  Pomegranate Salsa, 194
Minty Pineapple Rum, 296
Pina Colada Jam, 120
Pineapple Coconut Tassies, 243
Pineapple Kiwi Jam, 125

PIZZAS

Bacon-Chicken Club Pizza, 61
California Chicken Club Pizza, 87
Shakshuka Breakfast Pizza, 164
Taco Pizza Squares, 102

PORK

(also see Bacon; Ham; Sausage)
Almond Pork Chops with
  Honey Mustard, 91
✓Applesauce-Glazed Pork Chops, 53
Blueberry Chops with Cinnamon
  Sweet Potatoes, 78
✓Braised Pork Loin Chops, 51
Breaded Pork Chops, 53
✓Chinese Spinach-Almond Salad, 18
Cuban Roasted Pork Sandwiches, 37
✓Egg Roll Noodle Bowl, 53

✓Grilled Pork Tenderloin with
  Cherry Salsa Molé, 72
✓Mediterranean Pork & Orzo, 56
Parmesan Pork Roast, 70
Peach-Glazed Ribs, 75
Pork Chops with Chili Sauce, 53
Pressure-Cooker Cranberry Mustard
  Pork Loin, 82
Pulled BBQ Pork, 221
Slow-Cooked Carnitas, 262
Spicy Peanut Butter & Pork
  Sandwich, 41
✓Tender Sweet & Sour
  Pork Chops, 64
Wild Rice-Stuffed Pork Loin, 271

POTATOES

Basil-Butter Steaks with Roasted
  Potatoes, 62
Bratwurst Supper, 263
✓Carrot, Parsnip & Potato
  Gratin, 124
✓Easy Beans & Potatoes
  with Bacon, 123
Grilled Firecracker Potato Salad, 268
✓Olive Oil Mashed Potatoes
  with Pancetta, 234
✓Potato-Topped Ground Beef
  Skillet, 77
Ranch Potato Salad, 28
Roasted Honey Mustard Chicken, 80
Roasted Red Potato Salad, 18
Root Vegetable Pavé, 131
Slow-Cooker Breakfast Burritos, 154
Southern Hash Browns & Ham
  Sheet-Pan Bake, 159
Southern Potato Salad, 221
Spinach Quiche with Potato
  Crust, 149

PRESSURE-COOKER RECIPES

Pressure-Cooker Chicken
  Cacciatore, 88
✓Pressure-Cooker Cinnamon
  Applesauce, 121
Pressure-Cooker Cranberry
  Mustard Pork Loin, 82
Pressure-Cooker Cuban
  Ropa Vieja, 81
Pressure-Cooker Mediterranean
  Chicken Orzo, 90
✓Pressure-Cooker Sauerbraten, 93

PUMPKIN

Five-Spice Pumpkin Pie, 183
Hazelnut Date Pumpkin Bread, 144
✓Orange Pumpkin Chiffon
  Dessert, 204

Pumpkin Cream of Wheat, 151
✓Pumpkin Pan Rolls, 145
Pumpkin Pie Ice Cream with Salted
 Caramel Sauce, 195

QUINOA
✓Autumn Power Porridge, 158
Quinoa Wilted Spinach Salad, 21

RAISINS
Peanut Butter, Apple &
 Raisin Sandwich, 40
Raisin-Applesauce Bundt
 Cake, 183
✓Sesame, Sunflower &
 Carrot Salad, 30

RASPBERRIES
Berry Cream Muffins, 137
Monte Cristo Casserole with
 Raspberry Sauce, 241
Raspberry-Banana Breakfast
 Tacos, 166
Raspberry Bellini, 215
Rustic Chocolate Raspberry
 Tart, 281
Three-Berry Freezer Jam, 130

RHUBARB
Lemon Rhubarb Tube Cake, 189
✓Rhubarb Compote with Yogurt
 & Almonds, 158
Rhubarb Fritters, 151
Strawberry Rhubarb Cheesecake
 Bars, 202

RICE
Beef Broccoli Stir-Fry, 66
Chicken with Pineapple, 50
Creamy Curried Chicken, 55
Herbed Chicken with
 Wild Rice, 92
Mongolian Chicken, 74
Pressure-Cooker Cuban
 Ropa Vieja, 81
Skillet Ham & Rice, 62
Teriyaki Glazed Chicken, 63
Texas-Style Spanish Rice, 112
Wild Rice-Stuffed Pork Loin, 271

SALADS & DRESSINGS
Coleslaw
Cilantro Blue Cheese Slaw, 20
Holiday Slaw with Apple
 Cider Dressing, 27
Overnight Slaw, 222
Dressing
✓Orange Yogurt Dressing, 23

Fruit & Gelatin Salads
Cranberry Waldorf Gelatin, 20
✓Festive Cranberry Fruit Salad, 239
Quick Ambrosia Fruit Salad, 28
Green Salads
✓Butternut Squash Panzanella
 Salad, 235
✓Hearty Spinach Salad with
 Hot Bacon Dressing, 212
Quinoa Wilted Spinach Salad, 21
Strawberry-Avocado Tossed
 Salad, 25
✓Wilted Spinach Salad with
 Butternut Squash, 29
Main-Dish Salads
Antipasto Salad Platter, 31
BLT Salad, 29
Cashew-Chicken Rotini Salad, 267
✓Chicken & Apple Salad
 with Greens, 31
Chicken, Nectarine &
 Avocado Salad, 99
✓Chinese Spinach-Almond Salad, 18
Dressed-Up Steak Salad, 21
Ground Beef Taco Salad, 19
Lemony Tortellini Bacon Salad, 19
Pea & Crab Pasta Salad, 18
Reuben Salad in a Jar, 22
Turkey & Apple Arugula Salad
 in a Jar, 107
Vietnamese Crunchy Chicken
 Salad, 25
Other Salads
Avocado & Grapefruit Salad, 28
BLT Macaroni Salad, 217
✓California Avocado Salad, 23
✓Cucumber Melon Salad, 26
Potato Salads
Grilled Firecracker Potato
 Salad, 268
Ranch Potato Salad, 28
Roasted Red Potato Salad, 18
Southern Potato Salad, 221
Vegetable Salads
✓Balsamic Asparagus Salad, 26
Fresh Cucumber Salad, 266
✓Israeli Pepper Tomato Salad, 27
✓Sesame, Sunflower & Carrot
 Salad, 30
✓Sweet Corn-Tomato Salad, 223
✓Tangy Cilantro Lime
 Confetti Salad, 30
✓Warm Roasted Beet Salad, 22

SALSA
✓Gingered Mango Salsa, 219
✓Grilled Pork Tenderloin with
 Cherry Salsa Molé, 72

✓Quick Picante Sauce, 219
✓Strawberry Salsa, 219

SANDWICHES
(*also see Burgers*)
Bang Bang Shrimp Cake Sliders, 6
Chinese Scallion Pancake
 Beef Rolls, 44
Cinnamon Whiskey BBQ
 Chicken Wraps, 34
Cobb Salad Club Sandwich, 34
Cranberry-Walnut Chicken Salad
 Sandwiches, 43
Cuban Roasted Pork Sandwiches, 37
Fig, Caramelized Onion & Goat
 Cheese Panini, 43
Lobster Rolls, 45
Open-Faced Frico Egg
 Sandwich, 162
Peanut Butter, Apple & Raisin
 Sandwich, 40
Peanut Butter, Chicken &
 Basil Sandwich, 40
✓Peanut Butter, Honey & Pear
 Open-Faced Sandwiches, 38
Peanut Butter, Krispies & Chocolate
 Sandwich, 41
Peanut Butter, Pickle & Potato
 Chip Sandwich, 41
Peanut Butter S'mores Sandwich, 41
Peanut Butter, Strawberry &
 Honey Sandwich, 41
Pulled BBQ Pork, 221
Salmon Sliders with Sun-Dried
 Tomato Spread, 38
Santorini Lamb Sliders, 260
Seasoned Turkey Sandwiches, 266
Southern Peanut Butter
 Mayo Sandwich, 40
Spicy Peanut Butter &
 Pork Sandwich, 41
Steak Sandwiches with
 Quick-Pickled Vegetables, 47
Sweet & Spicy Peanut
 Butter-Bacon Sandwiches, 46
Thai-Inspired Roast Beef
 Sandwich, 40
The Elvis Sandwich, 40

SAUERKRAUT
Badger State Stuffing, 119
Reuben Salad in a Jar, 22

SAUSAGE
Antipasto Salad Platter, 31
Bratwurst Supper, 263
Clambake Packets, 80
Italian Pasta Sauce, 288

SAUSAGE (continued)

Italian Sausage Mushrooms, 14
Pepperoni & Sausage Deep-Dish
   Pizza Quiche, 160
Petite Sausage Quiches, 167
Sausage & Eggs Over
   Cheddar-Parmesan Grits, 167
Sausage & Squash Penne, 82
Slow-Cooker Breakfast Burritos, 154
Tailgate Sausages, 285
The Best Ever Lasagna, 261

SEAFOOD

Bang Bang Shrimp Cake Sliders, 6
Broccoli Shrimp Alfredo, 63
Clambake Packets, 80
Crab & Asparagus Soup, 39
Crab Egg Foo Yong, 65
✓Creamy Scallop Crepes, 88
Creamy Shrimp Pasta, 54
Linguine with Herbed
   Clam Sauce, 76
Lobster Rolls, 45
✓Marinated Shrimp, 259
Over-the-Border Shrimp
   Enchiladas, 70
Pea & Crab Pasta Salad, 18
Saucy Barbecue Shrimp, 221
Shrimp Chowder, 36
Shrimp Pad Thai, 64
Southern Shrimp & Grits, 84
✓Spinach, Shrimp & Ricotta
   Tacos, 58

SIDE DISHES

✓Air-Fryer Garlic-Rosemary
   Brussels Sprouts, 128
Asparagus with Tarragon
   Lemon Sauce, 111
Badger State Stuffing, 119
✓Bohemian Collards, 234
Brussels Sprouts Brown
   Betty, 125
Brussels Sprouts with Pecans
   & Honey, 120
Butternut-Pineapple Crumble, 126
✓Carrot, Parsnip & Potato
   Gratin, 124
Cauliflower Dill Kugel, 117
Cheddar Spirals, 131
✓Cilantro Ginger Carrots, 116
✓Corn & Broccoli in Cheese
   Sauce, 110
Crunchy Bacon Blue Cheese Red
   Pepper Brussels Sprouts, 231
✓Easy Beans & Potatoes with
   Bacon, 123
Hasselback Sweet Potatoes, 118

✓Lemon-Parmesan Broiled
   Asparagus, 116
Maple-Glazed Green Beans, 227
✓Minty Sugar Snap Peas, 114
✓Miso-Buttered Succotash, 113
✓Olive Oil Mashed Potatoes
   with Pancetta, 234
Root Vegetable Pavé, 131
Spanish Hominy, 112
Sweet & Spicy Baked Beans, 222
Sweet Potatoes au Gratin, 226
Texas-Style Spanish Rice, 112

SLOW-COOKER RECIPES

Apricot-Apple Cider, 226
Cheddar Spirals, 131
Chicken & Artichoke Lasagna, 71
Corn & Broccoli in Cheese
   Sauce, 110
Creamy Artichoke Dip, 263
✓Easy Beans & Potatoes
   with Bacon, 123
✓Hearty Vegetable Split
   Pea Soup, 46
Herbed Chicken with Wild Rice, 92
✓Italian Cabbage Soup, 35
Mulled Grape Cider, 289
Parmesan Pork Roast, 70
Pulled BBQ Pork, 221
Shrimp Chowder, 36
Slow-Cooked Carnitas, 262
✓Slow-Cooked Stuffed Peppers, 83
Slow-Cooker Breakfast Burritos, 154
Slow-Cooker Pot Roast, 90
✓Slow-Cooker Turkey Breast, 89
✓Slow-Cooker Turkey Breast with
   Cranberry Gravy, 230
Spanish Hominy, 112

SOUPS

Cheesy Broccoli Soup in a
   Bread Bowl, 47
Chicken Cordon Bleu Soup, 45
Crab & Asparagus Soup, 39
Creamy Chicken Soup, 35
Curried Ham & Split Pea Soup, 46
✓Hearty Vegetable Split
   Pea Soup, 46
✓Italian Cabbage Soup, 35
Pea Soup with Ham, 46
Shrimp Chowder, 36
The Best Ever Chili, 42

SPA & BEAUTY RECIPES

Coffee Body Scrub, 296
Cucumber Aloe Face Toner, 301
Dreamsicle Room Scent, 299
Fresh Cucumber Room Scent, 299

Hand Scrub, 295
Peppermint Lip Scrub, 300
Soothing Milk Bath, 297
Spring Lemon Room Scent, 299

SPINACH

Chicken, Nectarine & Avocado
   Salad, 99
✓Chinese Spinach-Almond Salad, 18
Creamy Curried Chicken, 55
Creamy Shrimp Pasta, 54
✓Hearty Spinach Salad with Hot
   Bacon Dressing, 212
✓Mediterranean Pork & Orzo, 56
Quinoa Wilted Spinach Salad, 21
✓Spinach, Shrimp & Ricotta
   Tacos, 58
✓Wilted Spinach Salad with
   Butternut Squash, 29

STRAWBERRIES

✓Coconut Milk
   Strawberry-Banana Pops, 196
Grandma's Strawberry
   Shortcake, 188
Lemon Rhubarb Tube Cake, 189
No-Bake Mango Strawberry
   Cheesecake, 198
✓No-Bake Strawberry Dessert, 206
Peanut Butter, Strawberry &
   Honey Sandwich, 41
Red-White-and-Blue Berry
   Delight, 217
Roasted Strawberry Sheet Cake, 185
Strawberry-Avocado Tossed
   Salad, 25
Strawberry Lemon Cupcakes, 190
Strawberry Rhubarb Cheesecake
   Bars, 202
✓Strawberry Ricotta
   Bruschetta, 277
✓Strawberry Salsa, 219
Three-Berry Freezer Jam, 130
Vanilla Pear Berry Jam, 110

SWEET POTATOES

Blueberry Chops with Cinnamon
   Sweet Potatoes, 78
Hasselback Sweet Potatoes, 118
Sweet Potato Dutch Baby with
   Praline Syrup, 163
Sweet Potato Pie Cake Roll, 190
Sweet Potatoes au Gratin, 226
✓Turkey-Sweet Potato Stew, 104

TOMATOES

Basil-Butter Steaks with
   Roasted Potatoes, 62

BLT Salad, 29
Chunky Ketchup, 218
Dressed-Up Steak Salad, 21
Focaccia Barese, 140
✓Grilled Bruschetta, 10
Ground Beef Taco Salad, 19
✓Israeli Pepper Tomato Salad, 27
Italian Pasta Sauce, 288
✓Mexi-Mac Skillet, 51
Mongolian Chicken, 74
One-Pot Dinner, 55
One-Pot Spaghetti Dinner, 73
Pressure-Cooker Chicken
   Cacciatore, 88
✓Quick Picante Sauce, 219
Salmon Sliders with Sun-Dried
   Tomato Spread, 38
Shakshuka Breakfast Pizza, 164
Spanish Hominy, 112
✓Strawberry Salsa, 219
✓Sweet Corn-Tomato Salad, 223
The Best Ever Chili, 42
The Best Ever Lasagna, 261
✓The Best Marinara Sauce, 121

TORTILLAS
Cheddar Beef Enchiladas, 92
Cinnamon Whiskey BBQ
   Chicken Wraps, 34
Enchilada Casser-Olé!, 76
Grilled Beef & Blue Cheese
   Tacos, 73
Lemon Blackberry Tortilla
   French Toast, 156
Over-the-Border Shrimp
   Enchiladas, 70
Simple Chicken Enchiladas, 83
Slow-Cooked Carnitas, 262
Slow-Cooker Breakfast Burritos, 154
Spicy Corned Beef Tacos, 66
✓Spinach, Shrimp & Ricotta
   Tacos, 58
Taco Pinwheels, 103

TURKEY
Cobb Salad Club Sandwich, 34
Grilled Huli Huli Turkey
   Drumsticks, 234
Herb-Glazed Turkey, 226
Lemon-Garlic Turkey Breast, 89
✓Rosemary Turkey Breast, 104
Seasoned Turkey Sandwiches, 266
✓Slow-Cooker Turkey Breast, 89
✓Slow-Cooker Turkey Breast with
   Cranberry Gravy, 230
✓Sneaky Turkey Meatballs, 75
Turkey & Apple Arugula Salad
   in a Jar, 107

Turkey Lattice Pie, 107
✓Turkey-Sweet Potato Stew, 104

VEGETABLES
(*also see specific kinds*)
✓Bohemian Collards, 234
Contest-Winning Eggplant
   Parmesan, 87
Crab Egg Foo Yong, 65
✓Easy Beans & Potatoes
   with Bacon, 123
✓Israeli Pepper Tomato Salad, 27
✓Italian Cabbage Soup, 35
Maple-Glazed Green Beans, 227
Pea & Crab Pasta Salad, 18
✓Pressure-Cooker Sauerbraten, 93
Root Vegetable Pavé, 131
✓Slow-Cooked Stuffed Peppers, 83
Spinach Quiche with Potato
   Crust, 149
Steak Sandwiches with
   Quick-Pickled Vegetables, 47
✓Tangy Cilantro Lime Confetti
   Salad, 30
Vegetable Frittata, 154
✓Vegetarian Linguine, 58
✓Warm Roasted Beet Salad, 22

VEGETARIAN RECIPES
Appetizers
Artichoke Crescent Appetizers, 270
Baked Onion Dip, 12
Cranberry Brie Pinwheels, 262
Creamy Artichoke Dip, 263
✓Edamame Hummus, 277
Fruity Horseradish Cream
   Cheese, 9
✓Gingered Mango Salsa, 219
✓Grilled Bruschetta, 10
✓Grilled Pineapple with Lime
   Dip, 258
Pomegranate Pistachio Crostini, 8
Pumpkin Pinwheels, 15
✓Quick Picante Sauce, 219
Salted Caramel & Dark
   Chocolate Figs, 6
✓Stuffed Asiago-Basil
   Mushrooms, 14
Zippy Curry Dip, 7
Breakfast & Brunch
Chocolate Chip Pancakes, 157
Festive Cranberry Fruit Salad, 239
Puff Pancake with Bourbon
   Peaches, 162
Pumpkin Cream of Wheat, 151
✓Rhubarb Compote with Yogurt
   & Almonds, 158
Three-Cheese Quiche, 239

Main Dishes
✓Butternut Squash Mac
   & Cheese, 231
Contest-Winning Eggplant
   Parmesan, 87
Five Cheese Ziti al Forno, 264
Homemade Alfredo Sauce, 288
Saucy Mac & Cheese, 65
✓Slow-Cooked Stuffed Peppers, 83
✓Vegetarian Linguine, 58
Sandwiches
Open-Faced Frico Egg
   Sandwich, 162
✓Peanut Butter, Honey & Pear
   Open-Faced Sandwiches, 38
Soup
✓Hearty Vegetable Split
   Pea Soup, 46

WHITE CHOCOLATE
Cookies & Cream Truffle Balls, 283
Gumdrop Fudge, 171
Sea Salt Mint White Mocha
   Cookies, 244
Sundae Funday Bark, 176

WINTER SQUASH
Butternut-Pineapple Crumble, 126
✓Butternut Squash Mac
   & Cheese, 231
✓Butternut Squash Panzanella
   Salad, 235
Cheddar-Butternut Squash
   Clafoutis, 150
Sausage & Squash Penne, 82
✓Wilted Spinach Salad with
   Butternut Squash, 29

ZUCCHINI & SUMMER SQUASH
Crescent Zucchini Pie, 159
Pina Colada Jam, 120
Zucchini Apple Bread, 136

Alphabetical Index

This convenient index lists every recipe in alphabetical order, so you can easily find your favorite dishes.

✓ Indicates an Eat Smart recipe

A

✓Air-Fryer Garlic-Rosemary
  Brussels Sprouts, 128
✓Almond-Chai Granola, 164
✓Almond-Pecan Date Truffles, 294
Almond Pork Chops with
  Honey Mustard, 91
Antipasto Salad Platter, 31
✓Apple & Ginger Infused Water, 293
Apple Kuchen Bars, 176
Apple Pie Cupcakes with Cinnamon
  Buttercream, 186
Apple Pie Ricotta Waffles, 149
✓Applesauce-Glazed Pork Chops, 53
✓Apricot-Apple Cider, 226
Artichoke Crescent Appetizers, 270
Asparagus with Tarragon Lemon
  Sauce, 111
Aunt Betty's Blueberry Muffins, 143
Aunt Frances' Lemonade, 277
✓Autumn Power Porridge, 158
Avocado & Grapefruit Salad, 28

B

Bacon & Date Goat Cheese
  Burgers, 39
Bacon Cheeseburgers with
  Fry Sauce, 37
Bacon-Chicken Club Pizza, 61
Bacon-Wrapped Spam Bites, 258
Badger State Stuffing, 119
Baked Onion Dip, 12
Baked Salmon Cakes, 57
✓Baked Tilapia, 60
Baklava Thumbprint Cookies, 246
✓Balsamic Asparagus Salad, 26
Balsamic Mustard Marinade, 115
Banana Split Cake Bars, 200
Bang Bang Shrimp Cake Sliders, 6
Barbecued Meatballs, 8
Basil-Butter Steaks with Roasted
  Potatoes, 62
Basil Salt, 127
Beef Broccoli Stir-Fry, 66
Beef Wellington Fried Wontons, 10
Benne Candy, 179
Ben's English Toffee, 173
Berry Cream Muffins, 137
Best Ever Cheesecake, 194

Best Ever Sweet Pickles, 114
Big & Buttery Chocolate
  Chip Cookies, 178
Big-Batch Bloody Marys, 285
✓Blackberry & Sage Infused
  Water, 293
✓Blackberry Daiquiri Sherbet, 199
BLT Macaroni Salad, 217
BLT Salad, 29
Blue Raspberry Syrup, 283
Blueberry Angel Dessert, 202
Blueberry Chops with Cinnamon
  Sweet Potatoes, 78
✓Bohemian Collards, 234
Bourbon Peach Jam, 118
✓Braised Pork Loin Chops, 51
Bratwurst Supper, 263
Breaded Pork Chops, 53
Broccoli Shrimp Alfredo, 63
Brussels Sprouts Brown
  Betty, 125
Brussels Sprouts with Pecans
  & Honey, 120
Buffet Scrambled Eggs, 212
Butter Dips, 142
Butternut-Pineapple Crumble, 126
✓Butternut Squash Mac
  & Cheese, 231
✓Butternut Squash Panzanella
  Salad, 235

C

Caesar Chicken with Feta, 60
✓California Avocado Salad, 23
California Chicken Club Pizza, 87
Candied Citrus, 277
✓Candy Cane Chocolate
  Mini Loaves, 135
✓Cannellini Bean Hummus, 294
Caramel Nut Crunch Pie, 203
Caramelized Pears, 205
✓Carrot, Parsnip & Potato
  Gratin, 124
Carrot Spice Thumbprint
  Cookies, 249
Cashew-Chicken Rotini Salad, 267
Cast-Iron Skillet Steak, 148
Cauliflower Dill Kugel, 117
Cheddar Beef Enchiladas, 92

Cheddar-Butternut Squash
  Clafoutis, 150
Cheddar Spirals, 131
Cheesy Broccoli Soup in a
  Bread Bowl, 47
Cheesy Garlic Herb Quick
  Bread, 137
Chewy German Chocolate
  Cookies, 172
✓Chicken & Apple Salad
  with Greens, 31
Chicken & Artichoke Lasagna, 71
Chicken Biscuit Potpie, 96
Chicken Biscuit Skillet, 67
Chicken Cordon Bleu, 81
Chicken Cordon Bleu Soup, 45
Chicken, Nectarine & Avocado
  Salad, 99
Chicken Parmesan Burgers, 44
✓Chicken Skewers with Cool
  Avocado Sauce, 9
Chicken with Pineapple, 50
Chinese Scallion Pancake
  Beef Rolls, 44
✓Chinese Spinach-Almond Salad, 18
Chocolate Billionaires, 171
Chocolate-Caramel Rum
  Coffee, 280
Chocolate Chip Pancakes, 157
Chocolate Comfort Cake, 253
Chocolate Lebkuchen
  Cherry Balls, 248
Chocolate Mincemeat Bars, 177
Christmas Morning Sweet Rolls, 238
Chunky Ketchup, 218
Cilantro Blue Cheese Slaw, 20
✓Cilantro Ginger Carrots, 116
Cinnamon Apple Pan Betty, 207
Cinnamon-Orange Honey
  Butter, 123
✓Cinnamon Roll Macarons, 245
Cinnamon Whiskey BBQ
  Chicken Wraps, 34
Clambake Packets, 80
Cobb Salad Club Sandwich, 34
Coconut, Lime & Pistachio
  Cookies, 249
✓Coconut Milk
  Strawberry-Banana Pops, 196

Coffee Body Scrub, 296
Contest-Winning Eggplant
    Parmesan, 87
Cookies & Cream Truffle Balls, 283
✓Corn & Broccoli in Cheese
    Sauce, 110
Crab & Asparagus Soup, 39
Crab Egg Foo Yong, 65
Cranberry Brie Pinwheels, 262
✓Cranberry Orange Almond
    Quick Bread, 143
✓Cranberry, Orange & Cardamom
    Infused Water, 293
Cranberry-Orange Pound Cake, 185
Cranberry Waldorf Gelatin, 20
Cranberry-Walnut Chicken Salad
    Sandwiches, 43
Creamy Artichoke Dip, 263
Creamy Chicken Soup, 35
Creamy Cranberry Cheesecake, 204
Creamy Curried Chicken, 55
✓Creamy Scallop Crepes, 88
Creamy Shrimp Pasta, 54
Crescent Zucchini Pie, 159
Crisp Onion Relish, 218
Crunchy Bacon Blue Cheese Red
    Pepper Brussel Sprouts, 231
Crunchy Baked Chicken, 72
Crystallized Gingerbread Chocolate
    Chip Cookies, 243
Cuban Roasted Pork Sandwiches, 37
Cucumber Aloe Face Toner, 301
✓Cucumber Melon Salad, 26
Curried Ham & Split Pea Soup, 46
Curry Butter, 123

D

✓Devil's Food Snack Cake, 191
Dijon-Bacon Dip for Pretzels, 285
Dirty Banana Trifle, 205
Double Chocolate Espresso
    Pound Cake, 182
Double Hot Horseradish
    Mustard, 218
Dreamsicle Room Scent, 299
Dressed-Up Steak Salad, 21
✓Dutch Apple Pie Tartlets, 271

E

Easy Batter Rolls, 227
✓Easy Beans & Potatoes
    with Bacon, 123
Easy Peasy Biscuits, 231
✓Edamame Hummus, 277
✓Egg Roll Noodle Bowl, 53
Enchilada Casser-Olé!, 76
✓English Muffin Bread, 140
Extra Quick Yeast Rolls, 144

F

✓Festive Cranberry Fruit Salad, 239
Fiesta Scrambled Eggs, 157
Fig, Caramelized Onion & Goat
    Cheese Panini, 43
Five Cheese Ziti al Forno, 264
Five-Spice Pumpkin Pie, 183
Flaky Bumbleberry Pie, 186
Flaky Chicken Wellington, 99
Focaccia Barese, 140
French Onion Drop Biscuits, 139
Fresh Cucumber Room Scent, 299
Fresh Cucumber Salad, 266
Frozen Cherry Margaritas, 13
Fruity Horseradish Cream Cheese, 9
Fuzzy Navel Syrup, 283

G

Gam's Homemade Vanilla
    Ice Cream, 198
Garlic Herb Bubble Loaf, 136
Garlic-Parmesan Cheese Ball, 289
German Chocolate Ring, 138
Ginger Blueberry Jam, 129
✓Ginger-Curry Chicken Tacos, 78

Ginger-Peach Marinade, 115
Ginger S'mores, 248
Gingerbread Cupcakes, 189
✓Gingered Mango Salsa, 219
Gluten-Free Banana Bread, 135
Golden Peach Pie, 191
Grandma's Strawberry
    Shortcake, 188
✓Grape & Mint Infused Water, 293
✓Grapefruit & Coriander Infused
    Water, 292
Grilled Beef & Blue Cheese
    Tacos, 73
✓Grilled Bruschetta, 10
✓Grilled Buttermilk Chicken, 96
Grilled Firecracker Potato Salad, 268
Grilled Huli Huli Turkey
    Drumsticks, 234
Grilled Lemon Chicken, 217
✓Grilled Pineapple with
    Lime Dip, 258
✓Grilled Pork Tenderloin with
    Cherry Salsa Molé, 72
Ground Beef Taco Salad, 19
Gumdrop Fudge, 171

ENCHILADA CASSER-OLÉ!, PAGE 76

MINTY PINEAPPLE RUM, PAGE 296

Lemon Rhubarb Tube Cake, 189
Lemony Tortellini Bacon Salad, 19
✓Light Toffee Crunch Dessert, 195
Lime Salt, 124
Linguine with Herbed Clam
    Sauce, 76
Lobster Rolls, 45

M

Macaroni Taco Bake, 93
Make-Ahead Eggs Benedict
    Toast Cups, 241
✓Makeover Cheddar Biscuits, 142
Makeover Italian Cream Cake, 182
Mama's Spice Cake, 254
✓Mango Glace with Pineapple
    Pomegranate Salsa, 194
Mango Tiramisu, 206
Maple Butter, 123
Maple-Glazed Green Beans, 227
Maple-Walnut Sticky Buns, 156
Margarita Syrup, 283
✓Marinated Shrimp, 259
Meat-and-Potato Quiche, 100
✓Mediterranean Pork & Orzo, 56
✓Mexi-Mac Skillet, 51
Miniature Peanut Butter Treats, 177
Minty Pineapple Rum, 296
✓Minty Sugar Snap Peas, 114
✓Miso-Buttered Succotash, 113
Mom's Meat Loaf for 2, 71
Mongolian Chicken, 74
Monte Cristo Casserole with
    Raspberry Sauce, 241
Mulled Grape Cider, 289
Mushroom & Smoked
    Gouda Puff, 13
Mustard Ham Strata, 155

N

No-Bake Mango Strawberry
    Cheesecake, 198
✓No-Bake Strawberry Dessert, 206
No-Churn Blueberry Graham
    Cracker Ice Cream, 200
Northwoods Marinade, 115
Nut Fruit Bark, 172

O

✓Olive Oil Mashed Potatoes
    with Pancetta, 234
One-Pot Dinner, 55
One-Pot Spaghetti Dinner, 73
Open-Faced Frico Egg
    Sandwich, 162
Orange Cheesecake Breakfast
    Rolls, 165
Orange-Glazed Ham, 211

H

Haddock en Papillote, 50
Ham & Cheddar Brunch Ring, 166
Hand Scrub, 295
Hasselback Sweet Potatoes, 118
Hazelnut Date Pumpkin Bread, 144
✓Hearty Pita Tacos, 52
✓Hearty Spinach Salad with Hot
    Bacon Dressing, 212
✓Hearty Vegetable Split
    Pea Soup, 46
Heavenly Greek Marinade, 115
Herb Butter, 123
Herb-Glazed Turkey, 226
✓Herb Quick Bread, 145
Herbed Bread Twists, 269
Herbed Chicken with Wild Rice, 92
Holiday Slaw with Apple
    Cider Dressing, 27
Holiday Snowflake Cake, 254
Homemade Alfredo Sauce, 288
Homemade Pear Honey, 111
Homemade Steak Seasoning, 123
Honey-Barbecue Chicken
    Wings, 12
Honey-Garlic Marinade, 115
Honey-Thyme Butter, 129
Hot Cocoa with Almond Milk, 269
✓Hot Fudge Pudding Cake, 197
✓Hot Ginger Coffee, 14
Huli Huli Marinade, 115

I

✓Iced Honeydew Mint Tea, 15
✓Israeli Pepper Tomato Salad, 27
✓Italian Cabbage Soup, 35
Italian Orange-Fig Cookies, 270
Italian Pasta Sauce, 288
Italian Sausage Mushrooms, 14

J

Jam-Topped Mini Cheesecakes, 281
Jamaican Chocolate Cookies with
    Caramel Creme, 245

K

✓Key West Flank Steak, 222

L

Lasagna Toss, 91
Lavender Lemon Bars, 215
Layered Christmas Gelatin, 267
Lemon Blackberry Tortilla
    French Toast, 156
Lemon Blueberry Whoopie
    Pies, 170
Lemon Coconut Bites, 178
Lemon-Garlic Turkey Breast, 89
Lemon Mango Kanafeh, 196
✓Lemon-Parmesan Broiled
    Asparagus, 116
✓Lemon-Parsley Baked Cod, 54
Lemon Poppy Seed Bundt Cake, 188

✓Orange Pumpkin Chiffon
   Dessert, 204
Orange-Spice Marinade, 115
✓Orange Yogurt Dressing, 23
Over-the-Border Shrimp
   Enchiladas, 70
Overnight Slaw, 222

P
Parmesan Pork Roast, 70
Parmesan Scones, 211
Pea & Crab Pasta Salad, 18
Pea Soup with Ham, 46
Peach-Glazed Ribs, 75
Peach Panna Cotta, 197
Peanut Butter, Apple &
   Raisin Sandwich, 40
Peanut Butter, Chicken &
   Basil Sandwich, 40
✓Peanut Butter, Honey & Pear
   Open-Faced Sandwiches, 38
Peanut Butter, Krispies & Chocolate
   Sandwich, 41
Peanut Butter, Pickle & Potato
   Chip Sandwich, 41
Peanut Butter Pretzel Bars, 174
Peanut Butter S'mores Sandwich, 41
Peanut Butter, Strawberry &
   Honey Sandwich, 41
Pecan Pie Cobbler, 199
Peppermint Lip Scrub, 300
Pepperoni & Sausage Deep-Dish
   Pizza Quiche, 160
Pesto-Chicken Penne Casseroles, 85
Petite Sausage Quiches, 167
Pina Colada Jam, 120
Pina Colada Syrup, 283
✓Pineapple & Mint Infused
   Water, 292
Pineapple Coconut Tassies, 243
Pineapple Kiwi Jam, 125
Pixie Dust Cookies, 259
✓Pomegranate & Pear Infused
   Water, 292
Pomegranate Pistachio Crostini, 8
✓Popovers for 2, 138
Pork Chops with Chili Sauce, 53
✓Potato-Topped Ground
   Beef Skillet, 77
✓Power Berry Smoothie Bowl, 155
Pressure-Cooker Chicken
   Cacciatore, 88
✓Pressure-Cooker Cinnamon
   Applesauce, 121
Pressure-Cooker Cranberry Mustard
   Pork Loin, 82
Pressure-Cooker Cuban

Ropa Vieja, 81
Pressure-Cooker Mediterranean
   Chicken Orzo, 90
✓Pressure-Cooker Sauerbraten, 93
Puff Pancake with Bourbon
   Peaches, 162
Pulled BBQ Pork, 221
Pumpkin Cream of Wheat, 151
✓Pumpkin Pan Rolls, 145
Pumpkin Pie Ice Cream with Salted
   Caramel Sauce, 195
Pumpkin Pinwheels, 15

Q
Quick Ambrosia Fruit Salad, 28
Quick Chicken Piccata, 56
✓Quick Picante Sauce, 219
Quinoa Wilted Spinach Salad, 21

R
Raisin-Applesauce Bundt Cake, 183
Ranch Marinade, 115
Ranch Potato Salad, 28
Raspberry Almond Strips, 179
✓Raspberry & Lemon Infused
   Water, 292
Raspberry-Banana Breakfast
   Tacos, 166
Raspberry Bellini, 215
Red-White-and-Blue Berry
   Delight, 217
Reindeer Cake, 251
Reuben Salad in a Jar, 22
✓Rhubarb Compote with Yogurt
   & Almonds, 158
Rhubarb Fritters, 151
Roasted Honey Mustard Chicken, 80
Roasted Red Potato Salad, 18
Roasted Strawberry Sheet Cake, 185
Rocky Road Freezer Pie, 184
✓Rolled Buttermilk Biscuits, 134
Root Vegetable Pavé, 131
Roro's Pineapple Cookies, 264
✓Rosemary & Ginger Infused
   Water, 292
Rosemary-Lemon Butter, 123
✓Rosemary Turkey Breast, 104
Ruby Grape Pie, 184
Rustic Chocolate Raspberry
   Tart, 281

S
Salmon Sliders with Sun-Dried
   Tomato Spread, 38
✓Salmon Supreme with Ginger
   Soy Sauce, 67
Salted Caramel & Dark
   Chocolate Figs, 6

Salty Dog Sangria, 7
Santorini Lamb Sliders, 260
Saucy Barbecue Shrimp, 221
Saucy Mac & Cheese, 65
Sausage & Eggs Over
   Cheddar-Parmesan Grits, 167
Sausage & Squash Penne, 82
Savory Mustard Chicken &
   Stuffing Waffles, 163
Sea Salt Mint White Mocha
   Cookies, 244
Seasoned Taco Meat, 100
Seasoned Turkey Sandwiches, 266
Senate Bean Potpie, 89
Sesame Ginger Beef Skewers, 85
✓Sesame, Sunflower &
   Carrot Salad, 30
Shakshuka Breakfast Pizza, 164
Shirley Temple Syrup, 283
Shrimp Chowder, 36
Shrimp Pad Thai, 64
Simple Chicken Enchiladas, 83
Skillet Beef & Macaroni, 57
Skillet Chocolate Chunk Walnut
   Blondies, 173
Skillet Ham & Rice, 62
Slow-Cooked Carnitas, 262
✓Slow-Cooked Stuffed Peppers, 83
Slow-Cooker Breakfast Burritos, 154
Slow-Cooker Pot Roast, 90
✓Slow-Cooker Turkey Breast, 89
✓Slow-Cooker Turkey Breast with
   Cranberry Gravy, 230
Smoky Chicken Spread, 14
✓Sneaky Turkey Meatballs, 75
So-Healthy Smoothies, 148
Soothing Milk Bath, 297
Southern Hash Browns & Ham
   Sheet-Pan Bake, 159
Southern Peanut Butter
   Mayo Sandwich, 40
Southern Potato Salad, 221
Southern Shrimp & Grits, 84
Southwest Chili Marinade, 115
Southwestern Bean Dip, 268
Spanish Hominy, 112
Sparkling Apple Pie on
   the Rocks, 235
Spiced Apple Cider Jelly Shots, 230
Spiced Cherry Chutney, 127
Spiced Eggnog Rum Cookies, 246
Spicy Corned Beef Tacos, 66
Spicy Egg Bake, 102
Spicy Peanut Butter & Pork
   Sandwich, 41
Spinach Quiche with Potato
   Crust, 149
✓Spinach, Shrimp & Ricotta

Tacos, 58

S
(continued)
Spring Lemon Room Scent, 299
Sriracha Salt, 130
Steak Sandwiches with
  Quick-Pickled Vegetables, 47
Stollen Butter Rolls, 139
Strawberry-Avocado
  Tossed Salad, 25
✓Strawberry-Carrot
  Smoothies, 300
Strawberry Chocolate Truffles, 280
Strawberry Lemon Cupcakes, 190
Strawberry Rhubarb Cheesecake
  Bars, 202
✓Strawberry Ricotta
  Bruschetta, 277
✓Strawberry Salsa, 219
✓Stuffed Asiago-Basil
  Mushrooms, 14
Sundae Funday Bark, 176
Sunflower Popcorn Bars, 261
Sweet & Spicy Baked Beans, 222
Sweet & Spicy Peanut Butter-Bacon
  Sandwiches, 46
✓Sweet Corn-Tomato Salad, 223
Sweet Potato Dutch Baby with
  Praline Syrup, 163
Sweet Potato Pie Cake Roll, 190
Sweet Potatoes au Gratin, 226

Swiss Cheese Bread, 134

T
Taco Pinwheels, 103
Taco Pizza Squares, 102
Tacos in a Bowl, 61
Tailgate Sausages, 285
✓Tangerine & Thyme Infused
  Water, 293
Tangy Barbecue Marinade, 115
✓Tangy Cilantro Lime Confetti
  Salad, 30
✓Tender Sweet & Sour
  Pork Chops, 64
Teriyaki Glazed Chicken, 63
Texas-Style Spanish Rice, 112
Thai-Inspired Roast Beef
  Sandwich, 40
The Best Ever Chili, 42
The Best Ever Lasagna, 261
✓The Best Marinara Sauce, 121
The Elvis Sandwich, 40
Thomas Jefferson's Vanilla
  Ice Cream, 207
Three-Berry Freezer Jam, 130
Three-Cheese Quiche, 239
Toffee Brownie Trifle, 203
Tuna & Pea Casserole, 74
Tuna Zucchini Cakes, 62
Turkey & Apple Arugula Salad
  in a Jar, 107

Turkey Lattice Pie, 107
✓Turkey-Sweet Potato Stew, 104

U
Upside-Down Apple Bacon
  Pancake, 160
Upside-Down Fruitcake, 253

V
Vanilla-Butter Sugar Cookies, 174
Vanilla Pear Berry Jam, 110
Vegetable Frittata, 154
✓Vegetarian Linguine, 58
Vietnamese Crunchy Chicken
  Salad, 25

W
Walnut Glazed Bacon, 165
✓Warm Roasted Beet Salad, 22
✓Warm Spiced Nuts, 289
Wild Rice-Stuffed Pork Loin, 271
✓Wilted Spinach Salad with
  Butternut Squash, 29

Z
Zippy Curry Dip, 7
Zucchini Apple Bread, 136

**VANILLA-BUTTER
SUGAR COOKIES, 174**